OP
Vol I + II 50.00 set

EARLY ENGLISH STAGES

1300 to 1660

Volume Three: Plays and their Makers to 1576

EARLY

ENGLISH

STAGES

1300 to 1660

Volume Three: Plays and their Makers
to 1576

by
GLYNNE WICKHAM
Head of the Department of Drama, University of Bristol

LONDON AND HENLEY: Routledge & Kegan Paul
NEW YORK: Columbia University Press
1981

First published in 1981
by Routledge & Kegan Paul Ltd
39 Store Street, London WC1E 7DD,
Broadway House, Newtown Road,
Henley-on-Thames, Oxon RG9 1EN

and Columbia University Press
Columbia University, New York

Filmset in Monophoto Baskerville 169 by
Thomson Press (India) Limited, New Delhi
and printed in Great Britain by
Thomson Litho Ltd

British Library Cataloguing in Publication Data
Wickham, Glynne
  Early English stages, 1300–1660.
  Vol. 3: Plays and their makers to 1576
  1. Theater—England—History
  792'.0942   PN2585

ISBN 0 7100 0218 1

Library of Congress Cataloging in Publication Data (Revised)
Wickham, Glynne William Gladstone.
  Early English stages, 1300 to 1660.
  Includes bibliographies.
  CONTENTS: v. 1. 1300 to 1576.—v. 2. 1576 to 1660.—
v. 3.   Plays and their makers to 1576.
  1.   Theater—England—History. 2. Theaters—Stage-
setting and scenery. 3. English drama—History and
criticism. I. Title.
PN2587.W53   792'.094   59–2245

ISBN 0 231 08938 4 (vol. 3)

To
GR, GB and JL

ACKNOWLEDGMENTS

To Dalhousie University I owe the Senior Killam Research Professorship that gave me the time away from normal administrative, teaching and production duties without which I could not have assembled this book; and to Dean James Gray and Professor Allan Bevan in that doyen of Canadian universities I owe as great a debt for friendly help and encouragement throughout my year of residence in its hospitable English Department.

Among the many individuals to whom I am indebted for the time and courtesy accorded to me in reading early drafts of one chapter or another, for drawing my attention to evidence that I had overlooked, and for making suggestions that resulted in the removal of ambiguities or errors that might otherwise still have been present in the text, Dr. Ron Huebert and Professor Ernest Sprott in the English Department at Dalhousie, George Hibbard, Professor of English at the University of Waterloo, Ontario, Dr. David Staines, Research Fellow in English at Harvard University, and Professors W. D. Howarth and John Burrow of Bristol University merit my especial thanks. For help in reading and correcting proofs my thanks are due to Michael and Estelle Morgan and to Oliver Neville.

A similar debt is due to my colleagues John Northam and Michael Anderson in the Drama Department and to Jim Tester and Brian Warmington in the Department of Classics at Bristol University for advice and assistance with the translations from the Greek and Latin texts quoted in this book. To Dr. Irena Janiska Swederska I owe the copy of the painting of 'The Three Maries' (Plate III, No. 4) which I noticed in the Museum of Medieval Art in Cracow, but of which no photograph or postcard was then available.

For permission to reproduce other pictorial material I have to thank the Victoria and Albert Museum, London; the Musée Rollin at Autun, France; the Caisse Nationale des Monuments Historiques et des Sites, Paris; the Rev. W. H. Bates of Pickering; Giraudon, Paris; Oxford University Press; and Blackwell, Oxford.

Much of the first two sections of the chapter on English comedy was originally prepared as a contribution to a volume of essays, *Comedy: The European Heritage*, edited by W. D. Howarth and published by Eyre Methuen (1978), and I am grateful for permission to reprint it here in an expanded form and within a broader context.

ACKNOWLEDGMENTS

Finally I would like to thank the Directors of Routledge & Kegan Paul for allowing me completely to rewrite Chapter IV of Volume One, 'Miracle Plays', prior to the issue of a second edition, and thus to bring it into line with the steady flow of scholarly work that has overtaken it during the past two decades.

CONTENTS

ILLUSTRATIONS

(Between pages 166 and 167)

x

ABBREVIATIONS, CUE-TITLES, SYMBOLS, ETC.

DMC   Karl Young, *The Drama of the Mediaeval Church*, 2 vols, 1933.

CFMA   Les Classiques Français du Moyen Age.

EES   Glynne Wickham, *Early English Stages:* Vol. I, 1959 (reprinted 1963); Vol. II (Pt 1), 1963; Vol. II (Pt 2), 1972.

EETS   Editions of the Early English Text Society.

EMP   *English Morality Plays and Moral Interludes*, ed. Edgar T. Schell and J. D. Shuchter, New York, 1969.

ER   A. G. Dickens, *The English Reformation*, 1964.

ES   Sir Edmund Chambers, *The Elizabethan Stage*, 4 vols, 1923.

H-D   W. C. Hazlitt's edition of Robert Dodsley's *Collection of Old Plays*, 15 vols, 1874–6.

LPME   G. R. Owst, *Literature and Pulpit in Mediaeval England*, 1933.

Med. Stage   Sir Edmund Chambers, *The Mediaeval Stage*, 2 vols, 1903.

MFD   Grace Frank, *The Medieval French Drama*, 1954.

MSC   *Malone Society Collections.*

MSR   *Malone Society Reprints.*

PQE   J. Nichols, *The Progresses and Public Processions of Queen Elizabeth*, 3 vols, 2nd ed., 1823.

RO (E&M) A. Feuillerat, 'Documents relating to the Revels at Court in the Time of King Edward VI and Queen Mary' (the Loseley MSS.) in *Materialien zur Kunde des älteren englischen Dramas*, ed. W. Bang, Vol. XLIV, Louvain, 1914.

RO (Eliz)   A. Feuillerat, 'Documents relating to the Office of the Revels in the Time of Queen Elizabeth' in *Materialien zur Kunde des älteren englischen Dramas*, ed. W. Bang, Vol. XXI, Louvain, 1908.

A NOTE ON PLAY TEXTS AND EDITIONS

The present situation respecting editions of Tudor interludes is so chaotic—and responsibility for this must rest as squarely with departments of English and Drama the world over as with publishers—that it is still not possible to refer students to a reliable, uniform edition of them all.

The Malone Society has been endeavouring for some seventy years to set this position to rights, but its series of reprints is still flawed by serious, if understandable, gaps. Among the earlier plays, both Henry Medwall's I and II *Nature* and I and II *Fulgens and Lucres* are missing; and so is John Skelton's *Magnyficence*. Among the later plays Thomas Lupton's *All for Money* is missing and so is George Walpull's *The Tyde Taryeth no Man*; for both these plays students have thus to turn to the *Shakespeare Jahrbuch* editions of 1904 and 1907. They are similarly dependent, as things stand now, on early foreign editions for access to Medwall's *Nature* (Brandl's and Bang's) and the anonymous *Godly Queen Hester* (Bang's).

J. M. Manly's two volumes of *Specimens of the Pre-Shakespearean Drama* of 1897 still offer the best reprints of *Mundus et Infans*, *Hick-Scorner* and *Nice Wanton*; a no less authoritative text of *Thersytes* is to be found in A. W. Pollard's *English Miracle Plays Moralities and Interludes* of even earlier date (1st ed. 1890; latest reprint 1965). Lewis Wager's *The Life and Repentaunce of Marie Magdalene* was respectably edited and reprinted by F. I. Carpenter, Chicago, 1904; a scholarly text of and introduction to the anonymous *Misogonus* was provided in 1911 by R. W. Bond in *Early Plays from the Italian*, and F. S. Boas and A. W. Reed followed suit with Medwall's *Fulgens and Lucres* in 1926; but it has taken another half century for the plays of William Wager to be similarly treated and made generally available by R. M. Benbow (Lincoln, Nebr., 1967).

However, this still leaves John Rastell's *The Four Elements*, Thomas Ingelend's *The Disobedient Child*, Ulpian Fulwell's *Like Will to Like* and at least three anonymous plays of consequence—*New Custom*, *Trial of Treasure* and *Youth* for editions of which until recently students had still to rely either on J. O. Halliwell's editions for the Percy Society (1842–9), or on W. C. Hazlitt's edition of Dodsley's *A Select Collection of Old*

Plays (4th ed., 15 vols, 1874–6), or do without. Nor is there yet a reliable, uniform edition of all John Heywood's plays. Only in 1972 were Heywood's *Play of the Weather*, Fulwell's *Like Will to Like* and the anonymous *Youth* rescued by the Penguin English Library in *Tudor Interludes* (ed. Peter Happé), while Heywood's *The Play of Love* had to wait until 1978 to find a place among the Malone Society's Reprints (ed. G. R. Proudfoot). Students can, of course, fall back on the 143 volumes of *Tudor Facsimile Texts* issued by J. S. Farmer between 1907 and 1914 (always supposing that they have access to a library that possesses the texts they want, which many university libraries do not) or, failing that, on Farmer's own, modernized editions of '*Lost*' *Tudor Plays* and '*Anonymous*' *Tudor Plays* printed between 1905 and 1907. Yet if students rely on the latter they will find that in the course of up-dating the spelling and punctuation Farmer has not only altered the true sense of the dialogue in many places, as well as the rhyme-schemes, but has frequently eliminated the stanzaic forms of the verse and invariably dispensed with line numeration. The texts themselves are therefore anything but reliable, and any referencing of quotations from them is made extremely difficult.

Confronted with this jungle, I proposed at first to offer a straight-forward list of cue-titles for reference purposes within this list of abbreviations; but, as confusion became the worse confounded as work on this volume proceeded, I decided to abandon this approach to the problem. Instead, therefore, I have provided in the Notes a full list of editions from first printing to the present day against each play whenever it is first cited in the text; thereafter I have referred the reader back to that note; and finally I have provided a composite list of plays and editions (after my 'List of Books') pp. 323–35 below.

If this solution to the problem strikes readers as clumsy, I can only offer my apologies and solicit their support in persuading the Council of the Malone Society to make a priority of completing the reprinting of all plays of the Tudor era not yet included in this Society's current list of reprints. In selecting texts for quotation I have tried consistently to combine strict adherence to the original (MS or 1st printed edition) with ready intelligibility for the modern reader. This objective has led me at times to prefer the original; at others to modernize spelling, or punctuation, or both, but whenever I have chosen one of these options I have alerted the reader to this action in an accompanying note. At other times again it seemed better to quote direct from a reliable modern edition and refer the reader back to the original either in the text immediately above or below, or in an accompanying note. This method serves at least to supply the reader with a choice that matches his personal preference with local availability of texts.

INTRODUCTION TO
VOLUMES THREE AND FOUR

D RAMA or theatre—call it which you will—is a social art, and
condemned on that account to keep in touch with its audience or
wither: its language must be comprehensible, its images recognizable,
and the actions that it imitates must be relevant to the community at
the time of performance. This is not to say that it cannot be recondite,
even esoteric, given a coterie audience whose own sense of identity and
security rests on its very separation, or apartness, from the public at
large: 'caviare to the general' as Hamlet so succinctly describes this
situation. Similarly, at the other margin of this broad spectrum, and
reduced to what Hamlet no less graphically described as 'inexplicable
dumb-shows and noise', it has the capacity to appeal to the lowest
common denominator of public taste. The point at issue is that by
operating within a social context drama more often appears to be a
crude and vulgar than a pure and refined art form.

Accordingly, historians and critics of this art are constantly having
to deflect their attention away from particular texts (and the stages for
which they were designed) towards the auditorium and the spectators
for whom they were devised. What did audiences *want* to hear and see?
What did their governments *permit* them to hear and see? Who was the
piper who called the tune? The playwright or the actors? The priest,
the schoolmaster, the poet, or the journalist? Or was the public the true
piper? Was it the princes who commissioned plays, or the people who,
if pleased, applauded and, if not, registered their displeasure with
empty seats?

Questions of this sort create large digressions in any adequate
historical account of the development of a particular dramatic form:
the answers, equally, often cause such developments to differ widely
in different countries even within a narrow chronological period. Thus,
for example, the Reformation and the Counter-Reformation served
between them to create vastly different climates of opinion for both the
presentation of drama and its criticism in, say, England and Italy, or
Spain and Germany, during the sixteenth century. Depending on the
historical period in question, these digressions force historians and
critics into areas of social anthropology or moral philosophy; into
foreign and domestic politics, theological debates, literary and

aesthetic concepts; or into several of them at once. In consequence it becomes difficult for either writer or reader to retain any sharply focused image of what lay at the heart of dramatic art and dramatic experience in a particular country and at a particular point in time. Why, for instance, should the lengthy English cycles of miracle plays have succeeded in holding the stage for 200 years? Did the astonishing longevity of their appeal repose in the satisfaction that audiences derived from the explanations of God's ways to Man provided by the anonymous script-writers? Or in the spirit of competition that urged the merchants and artisans of the trade guilds to pay taxes and fines in order to outpace one another in the excellence of their respective tableaux? Or in the general sense of relaxation and revelry which the obligatory Corpus Christi holiday engendered among spectators and participants alike? Clearly, no answer can be given without at least exploring all three avenues of possible explanation. Thus the digressions multiply; and, as they do so, so the heart of the mystery drifts further away from view.

The decision which I took some twenty years ago to examine English drama and theatre of the Middle Ages and Renaissance, 1300–1660, as a single entity embracing profound and often rapid changes of direction (like those translating a Roman Catholic into a Protestant-orientated audience, or that transforming a wholly amateur into a predominantly professional system of theatrical management) invited just such digressions on a very wide front with corresponding loss of focus.

As a protection against this danger, I chose the words *Early English Stages* to describe the contents of these volumes because I have always regarded the stage, or acting-area, as being the focal point of all dramatic and theatrical endeavour; only when the play is in performance can it be experienced as dramatic art, for ultimately it is the relationship between the acting-area and the auditorium that determines the nature and quality of the relationship between actor and spectator, between spectator and play-maker, and thus, at two removes, between actor and society. I use the word play-maker here, rather than playwright, not only because a play is so much more than just a text, however remarkable from a literary standpoint that text may be, but because in any case the earliest ideas of the play in England embraced both a visual and a physical dimension in its creation—display, exhibition and spectacle on the one hand, and movement and activity on the other. The play, moreover, served either to expound or to emphasize the abiding significance of the event dramatized or else to figure in concrete images the abstract issue that had occasioned its creation. This is as true of early dramatic activity in a religious context as in a secular one: in the latter, games provided the nucleus, while in the former music and ceremonial played as large a part as words, if not larger. What both have in common is a self-evident sense of occasion. It is the occasion in every instance that is being celebrated; and what was done mimetically existed, or was brought into being, because it had some bearing upon the occasion, reflecting it, commenting on it, explaining it.

We are talking here of an epoch where a holy day in the Christian calendar sense of the word was also a holiday in the recreational sense, and where the one was virtually inseparable from the other in the life of society; we are also talking about societies in which the ability to read and write was still restricted to a small fraction of the population, and where any *idea* was more readily communicated to the majority in terms of sharply contrasted actions, signs and pictures than in those of verbal debate. Thus the idea of the onward thrust of winter, darkness and cold being defeated by the recurrence of spring, as observed annually following the winter solstice (and again following the vernal equinox), was more easily translated into a mimetic dance that exemplified this principle through rivalry, combat, death and resuscitation than into a treatise on the sequence of the seasons. It is this idea, albeit assimilated into a Christian context, that informs the reflective utterance of the character, Perseverance, in *Hick-Scorner* (*c.* 1510):

> 'Whan I go by my-selfe, ofte I do remembre
> The grete kyndnes that God shewed unto man,
> For to be borne in the moneth of Decembre,
> Whan the daye waxeth shorte and the nyght longe:'
> (ed. Manly, ll. 86–9)

Similarly, the significance of a marriage, a birth, or the smooth transfer of authority within society from one ruler dead to a living successor is more swiftly and forcefully demonstrated (and to a wider audience) in animated pictures that relate these events emblematically both to nature and to the future of the society in question, than in any written statement. Funeral and coronation pageantry, and the annual Lord Mayor's Shows in London's streets in the sixteenth and seventeenth centuries provide obvious examples of this principle in action.

In medieval and Tudor England the ideas implicit both in the intellectual concept of calendar feasts and in the experience of physical respite from daily labour became subsumed and were made explicit within the word 'festival'. Festivals existed to commemorate occasions: that is, those aspects of life that provoked 'a sense of occasion' making one day in the year—or group of days—more special, more significant than the others which surrounded it. This pattern of thinking came to be expressed in ever more elaborate games, some athletic, others mimetic, some a conjunction of the two; games which some people were better qualified to play than others, but which nevertheless invited as vigorous a response from spectators as from participants. Most of these games acquired a natural, tripartite structure: a relatively long gestative, preparatory period, followed by the strictly regulated and formally ordered game itself, leading into a terminal period of more spontaneous release and reaction. Medieval tournaments, with their allegorical and heraldic proclamations, the theatricality of the ceremony and physical combats in the lists, and festive, evening celebrations surrounding the award of prizes in the banquet hall offer vivid illustrations.* In general, the longer the preparatory period and the slower the build-up to the playing of the game itself, the more enjoyable and satisfying was the ultimate release of tension and communal revelry likely to be. Every athlete who subjects himself to the strain of training for a race or game recognizes the truth of this today: so does every actor and theatrical technician in terms of the rehearsal period and first night; it is not so obvious to those of us who, whether it is to watch sport or to see a play, now have only to sit at home and switch on the television set. By becoming itself a domestic commonplace, television has stripped all vestigial sense of occasion away from such games, athletic or mimetic, leaving only the image of the game or play, followed by the mildest possible emotional reactions to its outcome.† We thus need to reawaken that sense of excitement, even awe, that formerly surrounded these exhibitions—as much because, to our medieval ancestors, they were occasional and rare events as because of any special virtue latent in the performances themselves— if we are to recognize the relationships that originally linked drama to occasion.

Volume Three

Having examined in the preceding volumes the rich variety of dramatic and theatrical forms within which this sense of occasion was expressed and celebrated during the three centuries separating Chaucer's England from Dryden's—tournaments, civic pageants, *tableaux vivants*, mummings, disguisings, masques and plays religious, polemical, and social—it is now time to return to the beginning, to examine the nature of the occasions that were thus exhibited to public scrutiny

*See *EES*.i.13–50.

†The saturation coverage lavished on early space launchings or, more recently, on World Cup football matches, provides examples of exceptions which, by their rarity, serve to reinforce the point.

in dramatic form, and to try to trace as closely as the surviving evidence will permit both the precise relationship between the drama and the festivals it served to celebrate, and those major shifts of emphasis in public thinking that caused old forms to decay and new ones to take their place. These, therefore, are the primary objectives encompassed within the bounds of this volume and its sequel.

Throughout the earlier volumes, I have asked readers to regard the year 1576 as a watershed in the affairs of the English theatre, partly because that year marks the start of permanently established play-houses for the *regular* presentation of plays to a paying public (at least in London); partly because that year marks a determination on the part of the central government finally to suppress performance and publication of all drama of an overtly religious character; and partly because that year and its immediate successors mark the emergence of a style of play recognizably different from surviving antecedents, even if many particular features are clearly retained from earlier models. In switching attention in this volume and its sequel from the theatre to plays, it will be my case that my earlier insistence upon the need to recognize the 1570s as a watershed in the annals of English drama, far from being contradicted or even challenged by an examination of the theatre's relationships with festivals and a sense of occasion, is strongly reinforced and corroborated by the sharp change of direction implicit in the substitution of regular weekday performances by actors who commissioned and presented plays in order to earn their daily bread, for those former, occasional and infrequent performances, production of which had been governed by holidays and the opportunity created by obligatory leisure for audiences to attend performances. In short, what study of the evidence clearly reveals is that the advent of regular, professional play-production was accompanied by a corresponding emphasis upon a play's ability to attract and entertain audiences and a steady decline in its dependence upon celebration, still less upon commemoration, of event and occasion: and it is precisely at this point in Elizabethan and Jacobean England that masques, entertainments, and civic pageantry on the one hand, and plays on the other, part company. The former survive in those sections of society where a sense of hierarchy remained at its zenith to reassert the old, time-honoured dispensations; the latter emerge at self-assertively bourgeois and popular levels in society as pleasures that can be bought and thus proclaim a new order of things that was to engender as much hostility as approval.

The old order, in the course of its development over more than five centuries, had come to narrow its focus both in terms of its central concerns and in its related time scale. A drama initially devoted to assisting to establish faith in the divinity of Christ *sub specie aeternitatis* had narrowed, first to a primary preoccupation with the fate of the individual soul on Judgment Day, and then to a principal concern with the health of the Commonwealth or nation both in the present and in the immediate future. And even this degree of preoccupation with private and political morality was beginning to be eroded as actors' concern for their own income and status in society became an increasingly important factor in theatrical politics during the sixteenth century.

As this occurred, so the audience itself came to split into two distinct and largely separate entities, the one exemplified by those patrons who, in order to be numbered among the élite, preferred to pay the higher prices demanded for admission to private playhouses; the other by those whose incomes would not stretch beyond the admission prices charged by the public playhouses. The former are typified from the painter's standpoint as early as 1598 by John Lyly in his *Entertainment at Mitcham* (ed. Leslie Hotson, p. 27).

> *Paynter* And I [will keep] this board* for a country mistress, who cares not how she be painted, so she be painted. Our art grows stale; for where in elder ages, none were coloured but memorable for their vertues to paint out imitation to posterity, now every Citizen's wife that wears a taffeta kirtle and a velvet hat ... must have her picture in the parlour. And if one hereafter ask, 'who was this?' 'It was one of the companies of such a trade, or a Justice of Peace his wife, of such a shire.'
>
> (11.231–42: spelling and punctuation modernized)

The change which he thus laments he attributes to the purchasing power of money.

> 'But it is not in us only, but in mocking of ancient monuments; for now, if anyone die rich, he must have a tombe and an epitaph, when nothing remaineth for memory, but that he died so much worth; so that heretofore vertue was intered in tombs of gold; now gold is buried with vertue's ensigns.'
>
> (ll. 242–9)

Play-makers, actors and company managers quickly noted these shifts of purchasing power linked with fashionable behaviour and started to offer playbills specifically designed to cater for these two audiences, each being regarded as complementary to but independent of the other, instead of striving to satisfy both audiences simultaneously.

board: i.e. canvas.

Thus commercial advantage, fashion and aesthetic modes came to replace the common bond of occasion that had formerly kept courtier and artisan in touch with each other as neighbours within a single society physically mustered around common stages, and spiritually united in a mutual concern for the welfare of the Commonwealth and humanity as a whole. In short, the homogeneity that is so marked a characteristic of medieval and Tudor audiences, finally crumbled in the period 1576–1642 to be replaced by new structures closely allied to social self-consciousness and the growing educational and economic divisions in English society.

Book Two of this volume is devoted to plays, and to the considerations that affected play-makers in constructing them as they did; to a dawning consciousness of dramatic genre; to the implications of state censorship; to 'device'—that remarkable juxtaposition of visual and verbal figures as the nucleus around which the scenario was built and upon which the text was imposed; and finally to that dichotomy between moral values ('earnest' in medieval parlance, embracing religious, political and social concerns) and entertainment ('play' or 'game' in medieval vocabulary) that emerged in the sixteenth and seventeenth centuries under the influence first of Lutheran and then of Calvinist theology, reinforced by professionalism and which, in doing so, served also to translate the medieval and Tudor play-maker, or maker of interludes, into a man of letters, and thus into the modern playwright or dramatist who hopes to earn his living from writing.

Book Three of this volume is devoted to a closer study of dramatic genre; in other words to the disentanglement of classical, medieval, and Renaissance concepts of comedy, tragedy and tragi-comedy. For so long as drama served to celebrate occasion in Christian Europe, the commentary on, or exposition of, the nature and significance of that occasion inevitably took precedence in play-makers' minds over any consideration of dramatic genre of the kind that preoccupied Aristotle or Horace in earlier times; and since most of the occasions celebrated were firmly geared to significant points of Christian doctrine, doctrine itself served to give the drama its particular shapes and forms. There was little reason for this to change while the Church was itself of one mind in matters of dogma, although the changing shape of society, brought about by the growth of towns and material wealth, affected the composition of audiences and with it their likes and dislikes. Nevertheless, entertainments of a predominantly secular character undoubtedly coexisted with those presented for overtly devotional or didactic purposes; and in these, ebulliently comic and realistic elements came to take precedence over more serious ideological ones. Once established, they proved too popular to ignore and opened the way before the close of the fifteenth century to the exploitation of dramatic art for predominantly commercial ends.

With the Reformation, new doctrines replaced those of the old faith, translating the drama into a battleground for political polemic which, in the event, served in England paradoxically to retard humanist interest in genre still further and to preserve the addiction to 'mongrel tragi-comedy' for much longer than was the case in either Italy or France.

Volume Four

It remains in the final volume of *Early English Stages* to disentangle what, in 1601, Polonius was still able to describe as 'pastoral-comical, historical-pastoral, tragical-historical, tragical-comical-historical-pastoral, scene individable or poem unlimited'—a process that occurred in the thirty-year period between Henslowe's building of 'The Rose' in 1587, and the death of Shakespeare and the publication of Ben Jonson's *Works* in 1616.

In one sense the traditional links between drama and occasion became, during these decades, more sharply defined and more firmly entrenched in civic pageants and court masques; yet just as self-evidently those links that had formerly existed between occasion and stage-plays, whether intended for public or private playhouses, gave way to debates about genre and to attempts to distinguish between the relative authority of actors and authors in the theatre. The difficulties and problems inherent in these debates are as readily discernible in the difference between Sir Philip Sidney's contemptuous dismissal of 'mongrel tragi-comedy' in his *Defence of Poesie* (published in 1595) and John Fletcher's championship of it a mere ten years later in his Preface to *The Faithful Shepherdess* (published 1609), as they are in Hemings's and Condell's doubts about where to place *Troilus and Cressida* and *Pericles* in the Shakespeare First Folio, or in determining the frontier between tragedy and melodrama in the plays of Tourneur, Webster and Heywood. No less puzzling, at least to the modern critic, is the rapidity of both the rise and fall in popularity of the chronicle play. None of these matters can be fully understood, however, without taking notice of the shift in ultimate control of the theatre at James I's accession into the hands of the Court.

Discussion of these issues will then be followed by an account of entertainments, masques and civic pageants in the seventeenth century where occasion continues to supply the *raison d'être* of the performance, and thus to keep traditional concepts of device alive in all men's minds as a factor in dramatic composition overriding all others.

As rehearsed in Volume Two (Pt I, pp. 121–49), the point in time when these controversies begin to reveal a genuine change of attitude and approach both to the dramatist's task and to his status among men of letters coincides with Shakespeare's death and Ben Jonson's publication of his own *Works* in 1616. These twin events, followed by the award of the laureateship to Jonson by James I in 1617, mark a shift of balance and direction in all English playhouses with the actors beginning to surrender their previous hegemony over the writers to their erstwhile employees.

It is my personal belief that Jonson, after seeing his own plays and masques through the press, and as laureate to the King following Shakespeare's death, was the natural choice for the new leaders of the King's Men to make when seeking a reader to help them publish all of Shakespeare's plays as a single folio volume, and that it was on this account that Jonson was asked by Hemings and Condell to provide the commendatory encomium. Thereafter, any play-maker had to ask himself whether he wished to be regarded as a journalist, ready to collaborate with others on putting a play together as quickly as possible for ready cash, or whether he intended to present *the text* of his play to the critical scrutiny of a discriminating and opinionated readership as the sole begetter of his own work, and as a candidate for the reversion of the laureate's crown. Both alternatives remained open to individual choice until the closing of the playhouses in 1642; but for those who opted to write plays with only one eye focused on the playhouse audience and the other turned towards likely readers of the published text, drama had to all intents and purposes ceased to exist as a commemorative and celebratory art, and had become an extension of literary and philosophical endeavour instead. When an author views drama in this light, he is apt to forget that the actors and the natural laws of the theatre stand between him and the public; and having once forgotten that, he rapidly starts writing dialogue that is as unspeakable as it is remote from any form of utterance normal to mankind: although this does not excuse the banalities of heroic tragedy in Restoration England, it does in part explain it.

It is my intention to conclude Volume Four by returning to the stage and to take up those most elusive of topics, acting and play-production. In doing so I am well aware that no critic or historian can hope to discuss any medieval, Tudor, or Stuart production with the same authenticity, or even within the same terms of reference, as the reviewer of a play in any theatre today: the actors are dead and so are the audiences who applauded, booed or walked out on the

original 'first nights' and subsequent revivals, and their testimony
has passed largely beyond recall. All that today's historian and critic
can do is to piece together those fragments of testimony that some
enthusiasts and rather more opponents of the theatre of those times
happened to record in sermons, letters, journals, account books,
prologues and epilogues and other written documents—a process that
excludes automatically all actors and spectators who could not or did
not leave written records behind them. To these fragments he may
however add the information which is released from within the shorthand of the play-makers' texts as soon as their plays are put into rehearsal. This information is more substantial than anybody who chooses
only to read plays can easily comprehend.

A convenient example is supplied by Shakespeare in *Love's Labour's
Lost* during the Pageant of the Nine Worthies when Berowne unkindly
snatches the club wielded by Don Armado in the role of Hercules.
The text runs as follows:

Armado	'The armipotent Mars, of lances the almighty,
	Gave Hector a gift,'—
Dumain	A gilt nutmeg.
Berowne	A lemon.
Longaville	Stuck with cloves.
Dumain	No, cloven.
Armado	Peace!
	'The armipotent Mars, etc. . . . '

(V.ii. 633–40)*

There are no accompanying stage-directions and the dialogue reads
like nonsense; at best it would seem that the three lordlings are supplying gratuitous suggestions to define the nature of Mars' gift to Hector.
In rehearsal actors find this notion difficult to translate into action and
feel embarrassed. Yet *as shorthand for action* the dialogue is quite explicit.
Armado is referring to Hector's mace. Dumain grabs it: the head
comes away from the pole to which it was attached, leaving Armado
looking ridiculous. Dumain describes literally what he is now holding
in his hand: a gilt nutmeg! Berowne snatches it from Dumain: he
thinks it is a lemon and says so. Longaville then takes it from Berowne
and, pulls some of the gilded cloves out of the surface. He then returns
it to Dumain who restores it to the head of the bare pole in Armado's
hand from which it has been parted—'cloven'. It becomes Hector's
mace again, but it has been deflated in the course of these four short
interjections from an heroic accoutrement into the ludicrous stage

*This and all subsequent quotations from Shakespeare's plays is from *The London
Shakespeare*, ed. J. Munro, unless otherwise stated.

property that it actually is. This action is as hurtful as it is funny, and is very easy for all the actors concerned to handle: all embarrassment disappears. A mirror is held up to nature: visual and verbal images correspond: together they inform and entertain.*

A no less cogent example is offered in the opening scene of *As You Like It*: again there are no stage-directions.

Orlando	The courtesy of nations allows you my better, in that you are the first born; but the same tradition takes not away my blood, were there twenty brothers betwixt us. I have as much of my father in me as you, albeit, I confess, your coming before me is nearer to his reverence.
Oliver	What, boy!
Orlando	Come, come, elder brother, you are too young in this.
Oliver	Wilt thou lay hands on me, villain?
Orlando	I am no villain. I am the youngest son of Sir Rowland de Boys: he was my father, and he is thrice a villain that says such a father begot villains. Wert thou not my brother, I would not take this hand from thy throat till this other had pulled out thy tongue for saying so. Thou has railed on thyself.
Adam	Sweet masters, be patient. For your father's remembrance, be at accord.
Oliver	Let me go, I say.
Orlando	I will not, till I please: you shall hear me.

(I.i. 38–54)

Orlando starts speaking under stress but retains his self-control until his brother uses the offensive word 'boy'. (Aufidius is later to use the same tactic with Coriolanus and gets the same response.) Orlando reacts by laying one hand on Oliver's arm and the other on his throat. Oliver, frightened by the 'boy's' strength, protests. Adam intervenes ineffectually. Only when Orlando is assured that Oliver lacks strength to fight back and will listen does he relax his hold. No stage-directions are necessary when the action has been as clearly visualized by the dramatist and incorporated so accurately within the dialogue.

Even a particular vocal inflection of a word or group of words can illuminate a whole scene or a character, like the thrice-repeated 'mildly' given to Caius Marcius just before he quits his mother's home to present himself to the people in the gown of humility at the Forum.

Careful scrutiny of arrangements for the doubling of roles, costume changes, and specific scenic items in many Tudor plays can also yield up

---

*I first saw this treatment accorded to this scene in a production by the Bristol Old Vic Theatre School directed by the Principal, Mr Brenner, in 1969; having used it myself in a subsequent production, I am now fully convinced of its correctness.

valuable information about stage-conventions and production techniques,* more especially if it is collated with that yielded by the texts
of the many quasi-dramatic activities—entertainments, masques
and civic pageants—to which the leading professional actors and
play-makers of the period chose to contribute their talents.

Even so, when all possible sources of information contemporary
with the event are compounded, today's historian and critic has to
admit that only tentative statements relating to the principles of
acting and production can emerge, and these must not be pushed to
the point where they are translated into dogmatic assertions of fact.

By the same token, the idea, so current today, that any actor or
director is enabled to make definitive pronouncements on Elizabethan
and Jacobean acting styles, stage conventions and production methods
when fortified with nothing more substantial than the predilections
of his own ego, mingled with the jargon of the fashionable *avant-garde*,
must be just as ruthlessly resisted.

The truth is, as men and women of the Middle Ages and the Elizabethan era recognized better than we do, that the theatre is at best
but a metaphor, 'game' not 'earnest'. Neoplatonist distinctions between
the City of God (the New Jerusalem) and the corrupted world of man,
between signs, emblems, or devices on the one hand and the idea itself,
the thing signified, or the shape of ultimate reality on the other,
came to be expressed figuratively in terms of the similarities and
differences between the universe and theatrical images of it—*Theatrum
Orbis Terrarum*, the Great Globe itself; and if we wish to know what
actors thought was required of them by their audiences, what actors
expected of their play-makers, and what monks, preachers, burghers
and schoolmasters alike, between the tenth century and the seventeenth, came to regard as normal production techniques, it is imperative to learn first to understand the special quality of the mirror
that they held up to nature, and the uses to which they put it. With
that accomplished it becomes possible to discuss theatrical representation in terms that would at least have been understood in England
between Chaucer's day and Dryden's, a view which I hope to sub-
stantiate in this volume and its sequel.

*See the discussion of *Mundus et Infans* in Ch. VII, pp. 163–5 below.

BOOK ONE

Drama and Occasion

I

DRAMA AND FESTIVAL

---

1 A sense of occasion

I N the latter half of the twentieth century when drama, in the form of films and television plays, can be summoned into one's home at almost any hour of day or night throughout the year by the mere turning of a knob or pressing of a switch, and when this well-nigh magical phenomenon is taken for granted, no one should be surprised that students now find it hard to realize that in every other century this was not so; that to see a play was a rare social event, surrounded by an aura of eager anticipation and excitement. Its very rarity highlighted the break with normal routine that a visit to the theatre represented. For many adults this was associated only with Christmas, an anniversary, a special celebration; and for children it possessed the additional attraction of being admitted, at least for a few hours, into a fairy-tale world of fantasy that was normally reserved for grown-ups.[1]

If it takes an effort of imagination to recapture the sense of contrast that separated this sort of special occasion from daily routine, even fifty years ago, how much more difficult is it to project oneself back in historical time to a point where the spectator was denied even the freedom to choose either between one performance and another, or the day of the week on which to see it—indulgences that have been permitted to audiences ever since the art of acting in Christian Europe came to be recognized as a regular profession exercised on working days as well as holy days.* Yet throughout the Middle Ages drama was recognized as both a community event and as an activity restricted to those few days in the year generally acknowledged to be public holidays; and in such circumstances it could scarcely escape being

*See p. 161 below.

elevated into an almost mystical category of experience, a world of marvels.*

This is no less true of all primitive societies where a close relationship existed (in many places still does) between festival and the expression of it in dramatic games and rituals; a relationship, based in its turn, on that between the religion of a tribe or nation and its particular holy days or holidays. In other words, days deemed to be 'holy' demanded celebration; and that in turn demanded a ban on normal work. In many instances the celebration was itself a form of commemoration; in others it marked temporary release from normal, social restraints; in others again it was defensive and protective. And where drama is recognizable within this broad context, it can be seen to exist in part as an expurgation of fear, in part as a rebellion against authority, and in part as an idealization of the actual; in the language of more sophisticated societies the first of these three energizing forces comes to be associated with tragedy and melodrama, the second with comedy and farce, and the third with pastoral and fantasy.

This, at least, is how the relationship was viewed and described in ancient Greece from the fifth century B.C. onwards:[2] and it was a view which learned bookmen in English schools and universities during the sixteenth century A.D. sought to rescue from oblivion and to reimpose upon the theatre of their own time, a theatre which seemed to them to lack any respect for dramatic genre, and which appeared to have transformed its stages into wayside pulpits. William Crawshaw, when preaching in London at St Paul's Cross on 14 February 1607, and arguing the case for the suppression of all plays and playhouses in scientific vein, supplied a significant derivation for this state of affairs:[3]

'The ungodly Playes and Enterludes so rife in this nation: what are they but a bastard of Babylon, a daughter of error and confusion, a hellish device (the divels owne recreation to mock at holy things) by him delivered to the Heathen, from them to the Papists, and from them to us?'

In his opinion, therefore, as in that of other Puritan divines of his day, drama in England did not *begin* with the Mass, but already existed among the inhabitants of these islands before they were ever converted to Christianity, and was thus doubly offensive. It behoves us, therefore, not to neglect this viewpoint when attempting to comprehend how the art of drama reached Elizabethan and Jacobean audiences in the forms it took then.

*See 'device', p. 66 below.

4

It can remain an open question whether fear of death or zeal for life is the more powerful agent in human affairs; but, distanced as we are in time both from Tudor England and ancient Greece, we still recognize fear, joy and nostalgia to be among the most intense of human emotions. Manners have changed, and it is no longer considered respectable to weep in public either for joy or grief; yet this was once considered the natural response to these emotions; and in simpler communities than our own urban society it still is. Few of us, however, can say with truth that we have never 'laughed till we ached', 'shaken with fear' or 'shivered with fright': and the yearning for contact with a vanished yesterday, when life seemed to be simpler and more enjoyable, is as strong today as ever it was in the past. These areas of thought and feeling are properly the concern of psychologists, social anthropologists and theologians; but critics and historians of the drama cannot avoid contact with them if they wish to explain the paradox that is present wherever actors and audiences devote time and energy, either as performers or spectators, to participate in a corporate act of make-believe, an imitation of an action, a play. However irrational human beings may at times reveal themselves to be, it is difficult to suppose that they would continue to indulge in this particular activity, world-wide and over the centuries, unless they had reason to believe that it satisfied a persistent, social requirement. Admit it to be a game, and one moreover that supplies pleasure for its own sake, and still one must acknowledge that by playing this mimetic game both actors and audience are enabled in some measure both to explore and explain society to itself, the nature of the human condition. Shakespeare's Shylock, although pleading for himself and other Jews, speaks also for all oppressed individuals and minorities in saying,

'Hath not a Jew eyes? hath not a Jew hands, organs, dimensions, senses, affections, passions? fed with the same food, hurt with the same weapons, subject to the same diseases, healed by the same means, warmed and cooled by the same winter and summer, as a Christian is? If you prick us, do we not bleed? If you tickle us, do we not laugh? If you poison us, do we not die? And if you wrong us, shall we not revenge?'

(M. of V. III. i. 48–55)

No one can hear those lines spoken from a stage and not apply those questions to himself. And once this is recognized, it becomes possible to understand that the play-game establishes itself in a primitive society not only because it is innately entertaining, but also because it serves to instruct. Profit and pleasure thus go hand in hand, and this at once

5

raises the whole question of what has come to be called 'sympathetic magic'.[4]

It is impossible to determine in terms of historical data at what precise moment any given society becomes conscious of the dual role that mimetic games are playing in their lives; but the way in which this phenomenon has repeated itself in widely varying cultures and at different times suggests strongly that this awareness springs from an intuitive response to a felt need: and fear, from the cradle to the grave, provides the most powerful of incentives to action in the interest of self-preservation. The inescapable fact of death becomes a universal threat and cause of anxiety and provokes an immediate and instinctive response which is common to every individual in any group, tribe or community.[5] How can death be avoided? How can survival be guaranteed? Since neither question can be answered with certainty, recourse has to be taken to surmise and hypothesis; and here intelligence is called upon to assist instinct; but the first step must always be in the direction of death's opposite, towards the observed source of energy that is life. The evidence of natural and supernatural phenomena within the local environment is then called into play. Drought is thus opposed against rain, day against night, summer's heat against winter's cold, male against female, and so on, with the object of separating the hostile and threatening elements in our surroundings from those regarded as friendly and propitious.

Somewhere in the course of this elementary reasoning it becomes apparent that the sun takes precedence over all other forces in nature in determining whether human beings shall or shall not survive in the natural course of events. Excess of it will bring death by drought and famine; loss of it will bring death by cold and famine. In short, the progress of the sun—the source of energy—determines whether human beings, shall, or shall not, eat and live. Once this has been remarked, those particular points in the year when the sun's annual course can be said to be in doubt become endowed with special significance: the winter and the summer solstices and the vernal and autumnal equinoxes. All four are moments of critical ambiguity where the balance between human and superhuman powers over destiny is in question (see Appendix B; also the quotation from *Hick-Scorner*, p. xvii above).

No less self-evident than the relationship of the sun in the heavens to mankind on earth is that of the moon; but where the sun is associated most closely with active energy and the doings and functions of men in society, the moon, with its monthly phases mysteriously linked to the menstrual cycles of women, comes just as naturally to be associated with female functions and with more passive, contemplative and gestative behaviour.* The moon's effect upon the flow of the tides is also noted, more especially by peoples who dwell near the sea, and whose prosperity is directly affected by its erratic behaviour. Thunder, lightning, meteors, storms and floods, observed as interruptions to the smooth flow of the natural cycle, come inevitably to be interpreted as direct interventions by these two superhuman forces in human affairs, as do such disasters as plague, infertility (whether in crops, animals or human families) and defeat in battle.

Fear of these interventions and their attendant miseries consequently provokes a desire to prevent, or at least to tame or deflect the power of the supernatural to defeat human survival; but it is also possible to acknowledge the existence of such powers and to accept their suzerainty in lyrical expressions of well-being that assume their support and encouragement. It is at this point that instinct, coupled with the childlike reasoning powers of primitive peoples, directs that these feelings be met by imitating the observed behaviour patterns of the supernatural and invokes the forces of magic and religion, however tentatively, on the assumption that this behaviour will promote communication between the community and those invisible powers in nature that are recognized to outstrip man's own powers to control his own destiny whether for good or ill.[6] And once any serious attempt has been made to do this, the individual deemed likely to do it best, whether viewed as sorcerer or priest, becomes singled out for special respect and privilege within the community. No less important, in the context of the genesis of drama, is the fact that this individual, in any action or ceremony which the tribe may require him or her to initiate or undertake, will be assured of an audience, since the action in question is being undertaken on behalf of the community and not privately on his or her own account. By rationalizing these invisible and undefined powers—defined by Sir James Gordon Frazer as 'the unattainable good, the inevitable ill'—in terms of visible and tangible aspects of man's environment, intelligence directs an anthropomorphic interpretation of them that results in the postulation of gods and goddesses who manifest themselves, at least partially, in all natural phenomena that threaten, challenge, aid or promote man's survival; and once viewed in this perspective a battle of wits ensues between the tribe and its gods to prognosticate what price the god or goddess most directly concerned requires for his or her support.†

*Indeed, the English words 'lunacy' and 'lunatic' are derived from the Latin *luna*, moon. Cf. mooncalf, moonshine, moonstruck.

†In ancient Greece the word *theos* (which we, having no alternative, translate invariably as 'God') was often used of any power, physical or moral, which was regarded as a fundamental fact of life.

This reasoning, of course, assumes the possibility of an elementary form of communication between the magician, or priest, on the one hand and the gods directly invoked on the other. The missing link is dialogue, a link that must hopefully be supplied in movement, gesture, rhythm, melody, dance and prayer around an altar or image. At Delphi this link was supplied by the oracle.

The prognostic imitations, once they are attempted within the behaviour patterns familiar to a particular tribe or community, are *a priori* dramatic; and Aristotle is correct in claiming, in this context, that drama as he knew it was dependent for its existence on the imitation of an action, and not on character or 'diction' (i.e. verbal dialogue). The prognostic or propitiative actions imitated thus involve not only elements of disguise, but also the giving of gifts (including sacrifice) and rituals that are both mystical and metaphysical, while often containing an element of combat expressive of the ambiguity of the season being celebrated. This dualism generates, in its turn, notions of supernatural beings who are as positively malign and hostile as others are positively well-disposed and helpful. At times, therefore, it becomes difficult to determine whether greater importance should be attached to warding off evil spirits than to inviting the assistance of benign ones, an idea that gives rise to those figurative expressions of combat, vestigial reminders of which survive to us in many fairy stories, and in much folklore, as well as in some mimetic folk-customs that descend from earlier dramatic rituals.

Alongside of these mimetic games that figure so prominently in primitive religions go the athletic games that frequently took place as adjuncts to the same festivals; these were in themselves both expressive of a release of energy in action, and more nearly resembled challenging demonstrations of human prowess in taxing circumstances intended to exhibit men as demigods through strength, skill and endurance than servile acts of worship prompted by fear. Nevertheless, these assertive, not to say heroic, activities and attitudes are linked to the more reflective mimetic ones by a common interest in survival, since most of the forms chosen to exhibit trials of strength (wrestling, boxing, swordsmanship, archery, running, jumping and horsemanship) were those needed to win battles.

In Greece athletic games were closely associated with the shrines and religious festivals of Apollo at Delphi and Delos, and took precedence over everything else at Olympia.[7] Games, both athletic and mimetic, formed just as regular a feature of the festivals dedicated to Artemis, Demeter and Dionysus in Athens itself. In Rome, similarly, mimetic games (*ludi scenici*) and athletic games (*ludi circensis*) formed a natural accompaniment to all major religious festivals. Significantly, they also figured prominently in funeral rites both in Greece and Italy.[8] The most striking characteristic of the Greek athlete was his complete nakedness which was as obligatory as the particular dress associated with tennis, golf, football or horse-racing today, and was matched only by the competitive spirit in which the athlete strove to win the victor's crown. Thus nothing emerges more clearly from surviving accounts of Greek athletic games than the concept of *arete*, or excellence—the mark of the superman, the demigod, who pits himself against all comers regardless of his own safety.*

By contrast, mimetic games in their earliest forms sought, in one important sense at least, to reach beyond heroic defiance and to induce into mortal man some portion of the power, even the presence, of the deity whose help was needed. To the rational mind, direct communication with the supernatural is impossible: it can only occur as the product of faith and belief, not of scepticism. In other words, natural disbelief must be temporarily suspended. One means to this end is provided to us all at birth in the gift of imagination, as is obvious to anyone familiar with children at play. Another is trance, induced by some form of external stimulant—hypnosis, hunger, rhythm, alcohol and so on. Granted these conditions, the individual can become possessed of 'perceived truth', and in the light of it his faith can, almost literally, move mountains—a message that lies at the heart of Euripides' *The Bacchae*.

For anything meaningful to come out of this experience, the moment must be right, propitious: so must the environment—what the witches in *Macbeth* so neatly describe as 'place fit and time agreeing'. In short, all concerned must be possessed of a sense of occasion. Granted 'occasion', as thus defined, it is no less imperative that it should be celebrated appropriately—that is to say with fitting solemnity and in an approved order—and it is these demands that create the need for a liturgy or ritual. The word 'festival' combines both ideas, occasion and ritual, into a single concept, in default of which the desired end is unobtainable.

At the moment in time deemed to be special, sacred and thus 'holy', the normal routines of life must be suspended; the community, thus released from its mundane preoccupations, must assemble together; the individual recognized to be endowed with special suitability to conduct the ceremony appropriate to the particular occasion must be correctly attired, and perform the agreed rites, aided by other representatives of the community, also correctly

---

*This aspect of the heroic was subsumed in early Christian iconography within the image of Christ's triumphant defeat of Satan in the Harrowing of Hell.

dressed, in choric dance and chant. With these incantatory overtures completed, the time is ripe for the sacrifice to be made (if any be thought to be demanded); the gifts must then be presented; some manifestation of the god must be consumed; or some other physical action must be executed that is itself indicative of communion with the god.[9] These actions, if correctly performed, will then have served in their consummation to produce a cathartic result, replacing the fear that provoked the rite with joy and thanksgiving.

Frequently the feast (*festum*) or festival (medieval Latin: *festivalis*) is itself prefaced by a period of self-denial and watchfulness, matched in respect of athletic games by anticipatory training exercises; no less frequently, that final release from the anticipatory tension which is found within the festival itself is celebrated by a brief period of uninhibited licence which concludes the holy day, and the release which it has brought from daily stress and toil.[10]

Constant repetition of these mimetic and athletic rituals, year in, year out, engenders within the community a sense of tradition that carefully preserves all three major features—anticipatory preparation, enactment and release—a pattern still familiar to all actors today in the form of rehearsal followed by performance, followed by critical acclaim or abuse, and to all sportsmen in the form of training, game and victory celebration. Just as significantly this pattern closely parallels in simple, human terms that of courtship, wedding ceremony and fulfilment in the begetting of children, where death is seen to be defeated by life in the next generation.

A spectacular example of the whole process can still be experienced today by anyone who cares to attend the celebration known as the Palio in Siena. There, religious and civic rituals combine with a competitive horse-race that engages the minds and energies of the whole city for weeks beforehand in elaborate preparations. The event itself, prefaced by ceremonial blessings of horse and jockey in every parish church, and by spectacular displays of flag-waving outside the residences of the principal civic dignitaries, is a public holiday and a major tourist attraction. The Palio—a banner depicting a biblical subject—is then paraded round the great market square that is shortly to serve as the race-track in a cart drawn by white oxen with gilded horns and harnessed in traces of bay. Bands play; flags are thrown high in the air and are caught again; and the crowd, some standing in the centre, some seated on scaffolds on the outer edge of the sanded race-track, and some leaning out of windows and balconies that are hung with silks and carpets, cheer the representatives of every parish who surround their own competing horse and rider and who collectively escort the Palio on its circuit of the square. The race itself is swiftly over; heavy bets are won and lost: but revelry takes over, and the victorious parish plays host to all who wish to see the cherished prize—the Palio—and to congratulate the horse until the small hours of next morning.

To prescribe precisely which features of this extraordinary ceremony are religious, which civic, which athletic, which Christian and which pagan defies human powers of divination. No one who has been received into it, even if only as a witness, can ever forget it, explain it, or even describe it to his own satisfaction. It is like Bottom's dream.

'The eye of man hath not heard, the ear of man hath not seen, man's hand is not able to taste, his tongue to conceive, nor his heart to report, what my dream was. ... It shall be called Bottom's Dream, because it hath no bottom.' (M.N.D. IV. i. 206–10)

Yet if it defies explanation, it nevertheless still serves to define occasion, celebration and festival in senses that link the present to the mysteries of Demeter at Eleusis and Apollo at Delphi, and both to the *Visitatio Sepulchri*, the *Officium Stellae* and *The Play Called Corpus Christi* in medieval England.

2 Seasonal festivities

Archaeologists, anthropologists, antiquarians, psychologists and theologians have all devoted some of their energies during the past hundred years to collecting and classifying the residual evidence of particular tribal customs, and their antecedents, religious rites and games, that were practised by Celts, Franks, Greeks, Norsemen, Romans, Teutons and other inhabitants of Europe in pre-Christian times. It is not therefore my purpose to attempt to provide here, as W. Creizenach did in *Geschichte des neueren Dramas* (1893), or as Sir Edmund Chambers ten years later did in *The Mediaeval Stage*, a blow by blow account of how all these varied rites came into existence, of the particular forms they took in one place and another, or of the many dislocations and transferences that overtook them as a result of the substitution of urban for village life, or in the wake of conquest and occupation, or in consequence of the superimposition of one culture upon another as century succeeded century. Britain is in any case a notoriously difficult area of field study in which to hope to separate Celtic from Graeco-Roman observances, and both from Nordic and Teutonic ones in the years before St Columba, St Augustine and their missionary brothers arrived respectively in Northumbria and Kent. But it is also rather pointless to try to do so where the drama of the high Middle Ages is concerned, provided always that we recognize that Christianity established itself everywhere in Europe on pre-Christian religious foundations. Nor must we forget that its first missionaries adopted very similar methods to those of its predecessors in adapting what they found on arrival to what the executive, policy-making councils of the Christian Church in the Roman and Byzantine Empires took to be essential to the propagation of its own gospel. A fair example of the approach in question is provided by St John Chrysostom in a sermon preached in Antioch late in the fourth century in which he praises and congratulates his congregation on their response to the Kalends:[11]

'Yesterday, being a satanic festival, you turned into a spiritual festival. ... Wherefore the double benefit has accrued through you in this sense: that you changed the undisciplined chorus of drunkards, and celebrated in festivities of the spirit that were very well ordered: and you passed round the wine-bowl so that it did not pour forth unadulterated wine, but was filled with spiritual teaching; and you became the flute and the lute to the Holy Ghost; and while others were dancing for the devil, you gave your souls to the Spirit to refine.'

What then did the missionaries find on their arrival in Britain some two centuries later? First, they found buildings—temples, household shrines, stone circles, and altars erected for the worship of other gods; farther afield, and closer to nature in their setting, they found holy wells, sacred groves, caves and fires, and 'round tables'.[12] All this was familiar and recognizable, if not to each individual missionary, then at least to their mentors in Rome, since the same buildings, the same deities and the same rites appertaining to them had formerly confronted the fathers of the Church throughout the length and breadth of Italy itself.[13] Thus Prudentius, c. A.D. 348, speaks of December/January and the Christmas season:[14]

'And during the month offerings are made to Janus, honoured with full ceremony [celebri], with taking of auspices and sacred actions which the wretches conduct, alas, with the age-old observances; and they carry on the festal celebration of the Kalends.'

The missionaries thus found that the seasons of the year which they most wanted the inhabitants whom they had come to convert to regard as special occasions were already hallowed time out of mind, but to purposes directly related to an agrarian way of life rather than to specifically Christian speculations and convictions. The adoption, moreover, of Latin as the official lingua franca of the Christian Church in the West had served to aggravate this situation in literate circles by perpetuating the memory of such celebrations in the forms described and venerated by the Roman poets: St Jerome, *c.* 388, felt strongly enough about this to lay the blame for it squarely on the elders of the Church.[15]

'The bishops and presbyters appoint those who educate their children in secular literature, and make them recite comedies, and sing the shameful compositions of the mimes—scholars it may be maintained at the expense of the Church; the offering that a virgin or a widow, or some poor man giving away all his possessions, had made to the treasury for forgiveness of their sins [*pro peccato*], this the grammarian and the orator (receives as) a present for the Kalends,* the gift basket of the Saturnalia,† and the gift on Minerva's account,‡ (and) turns either to expenditure on his household, or to donations for the temple, or to the fee for a filthy whore.'

That the old customs did not die quickly is clearly revealed in the remarks of Pope Gregory III, 400 years later, about the penalties and penances attached to their continued observance.[16]

'If anyone ... as a brother [*ut frater*] had been guilty of taking part in festivals in honour of Jupiter or Belus or Janus, following the pagan customs, it was agreed under the old constitution that they should perform six years' penance [*poeniteant*]. (Now) with more leniency, they have judged three years to be more humane.'

Any attempt, therefore, to make radical changes in these behaviour patterns was certain to encounter resistance, and to generate conflict unless gently handled. Christianity, if it was to be the victor in the battle for loyalty that ensued, must prove itself to be as effective in meeting popular needs as its rivals; and to do this it must try both to seem to retain what it found, and yet to endow that with a new significance aligned with the new faith. Since the Church had already achieved this in Italy, and to some extent in France and Germany, the methods adopted in Britain were not new. Thus Pope Gregory the Great could write to the mission in Canterbury in A.D. 601 instructing his servants there to retain pagan buildings and re-dedicate them; to cherish devotional customs, but change their character.[17]

Another answer to these problems offered itself in abrogating heathen temples and shrines to Christian use while permitting at least some of the rituals formerly associated with them to continue

---

Kalendariam strenam: *strena* means literally a sign or omen, hence '*a new year's present* given for the sake of the omen' (cf. the French *étrenne*).

†*sportula*, literally a little basket, came to mean the gifts distributed by a great man to his clients in such a basket.

‡*Minervale munus*: a fee given by a scholar to his teacher.

in other environments. In summer almost any outdoor alternative would serve as well; but in winter, if the old customs were to survive, the shelter of friendly walls and a roof against the weather was essential, and recourse would have to be made to halls and refectories instead of the church. It is for this reason that we find Anglo-Saxon scôps and gleemen like Widsith and Beowulf entertaining their lords and followers in their tents and mead-halls and Christian reformers of the tenth century like King Edgar, St Oswald and St Dunstan rebuking the undiscriminating hospitality accorded to them and their less dignified companions, the mimes, in religious houses:[18]

'ut iam ... domus clericorum putentur, ... conciliabulum histrionum ... mimi cantant et saltant.'

(The house of the clergy is to be cleansed forthwith of minstrels as a place of assembly where mimes sing and dance.)

Such reforms as they attempted, however, had small effect, since it is again in a hall or a refectory in later centuries that we find Madame de Chini inviting young English knights to sing and dance at Chauvenci (1285), Edward II being made to laugh by his jester falling off his horse (1320), Richard II entertaining the mummers of London at Kennington (1377), and such entries in monastic account books as,

'Et solvit Johanni Andrewson et sociis suis operantibus pro nova tectura unius camerae vocatae le Playerchambre.' (Durham Priory, 1464-5)

(And paid out to John Andrewson and his fellows working on the new roof of a room called the Playerchamber.)

and,

'In rewardo dato ludentibus in aula domini in festo sancti Stephano hoc anno.' (Selby Abbey, 1496)

(In reward given to the players in the lord (Abbot's) hall at the Feast of St Stephen this year.)

It is in the moot-halls and guildhalls also that wealthy merchant-burghers of the fourteenth century imitate the manners of the lords spiritual and temporal in holding their own feasts and commissioning their own entertainments.* Thus by the fifteenth century Lydgate can as easily prepare an entertainment 'of mommers desguysed to fore the Mayre of London, Eestfeld, upon the twelffethe night of Cristmasse, ordeyned ryallych by the worthy merciers, citeseyns of London'

---

*See Ch. VIII, pp. 191–3 below.

as he can present 'the devyse of a momyng to fore Kyng Henry the Sixst, being in his Castell of Wyndesore, the fest of his Crystmasse holding there'.*

The evidence, fragmentary though it is, that reaches us from Anglo-Saxon Britain and the centuries immediately following the Norman Conquest, reveals that both methods—removal of use from *basilica* to *aula*, and continuity of use, but with changed meaning —were employed to combat dramatic ceremonies of pre-Christian origin, with the result that drama took root in Christian Britain simultaneously within two separate environments, connected by shared calendar festivals, but largely independent. In one sense the Roman Church dictated those dates in the calendar that were to be celebrated as Red Letter Days: yet that apparent freedom was in fact sharply curtailed by the decision to respect the existing festival days and endow them with a new significance. Thus room was left for two forms of festive celebration to coexist, frequently on the same day, or within a given group of days, but in different locations. The Feast of Fools and that of the Boy Bishop supply examples of an es- pecially questionable nature, since in both cases Christian practice reflected Roman use in point of date and form, while the actual cere- monies associated with both feasts were split between churches, refec- tories and streets, and incorporated a liturgy, a banquet, inversion of social hierarchy, buffoonery and a house-to-house collection.†

This arrangement was much easier to accommodate in towns than in small villages where practically the only place of public assembly boasting a roof was the parish church; and there, the Christian and the pagan expressions of the same holiday frequently continued to meet each other face to face within the same building. It is this situation which leads ultimately to the indignant expostulations of Philip Stubbs in his *Anatomy of Abuses* (1583) concerning Lords of Misrule and their hobby-horses whom he observed 'dauncyng and swingyng their handkercheefes over their heades, in the Churche, like Devilles incarnate, with suche confused noise that no manne can heare his owne voice' (sig. 6b).‡ Another face of the same coin is exposed by Bishop Latimer some twenty-five years earlier in a sermon preached before King Edward VI. He there explains that, knowing he had to ride from Oxford to London, he sent word ahead to a church that he would like to preach there on 1 May. Discomforted to find the church locked on his arrival, he was even more dismayed when a parishioner

---

*See *EES*.i. 191–6: on the word 'devyse' see Ch. IV, pp. 65–82 below.

† See Ch. VIII, pp. 182–8 below.

‡ See *EES*.ii(2). 33.

explained that the congregation had opted instead to go to the woods to pay homage to Robin Hood and the King and Queen of May.[19]

'It is no laughynge matter my friendes, it is wepyng matter, a heavy matter, a heavy matter [sic], under the pretence for gatherynge for Robyn Hoode, a traytoure, and a thefe, to put out a preacher, to have hys office lesse estemed, to prefer Robyn hod before the ministracion of Gods word.'

In between the conversion of the British peoples to Christianity in the sixth century and these and other attacks on village festivals during the sixteenth century lies the long succession of references to village 'games', 'church ales' and 'ridings' that survive in churchwardens' account books and episcopal injunctions alike.

What may be said with confidence, therefore, is that throughout Britain peasant communities of the early Middle Ages never forsook the dramatic ceremonies derived from the major festivals of the agricultural year, even though, as Sir Edmund Chambers remarked, it was the customs of which they were tenacious, not the meaning, so far as there was still a meaning attached to them.[20]

'Leave them but their familiar revels, and the ritual so indissolubly bound up with their hopes of fertility for their flocks and crops, they would not stick upon the explicit consciousness that they drank or danced in the might of Eostre or Freyr. And in time, as the Christian interpretation of life became an everyday thing, it passed out of sight that the customs had been ritual at all.'

Two phrases stand out from this explanation that call for further comment. The first is 'familiar revels'. While it would be imprudent to ignore the fact that superstitions die hard and provoke, in any deliberate breach of their routine observance, both a sense of profanity and a premonition of possible reprisals, 'familiar revels' suggests powerfully that the principal reason for the survival of the customs, despite divorce from their religious roots, lay in the fact that they were too enjoyable in their own right to forsake: in short, so long as repetition of them, in no matter how mongrel and debased a version, was rewarded by cakes and ale for the performers bought with money gathered from spectators (as is still the case today with the so-called Mummers' Play), the customs were always likely to survive.[21] The second point that calls for comment is 'the Christian interpretation of life'; for this, in deriving much of its appeal from its claim to make sense of life at every level in all its quirks and seeming contradictions, and above all in its optimism, created an atmosphere especially congenial to the comic spirit, and one that could thus comfortably

16

accommodate revelry of several kinds within its own calendar of festive events.* An astonishing example of the way this was in fact done survives from York; and as it has only recently been discovered, it is worth citing at some length.

On 15 November 1572, the Archbishop and the Dean of York wrote to the Mayor and Aldermen requiring them in the name of the Ecclesiastical Commission in the North to suppress the riding of Yule and Yule's wife, habitually undertaken on 21 December—the winter solstice; alternatively St Thomas's Day—time out of mind. They are explicit in their reasons for issuing this injunction.[22]

'Wheras there hath bene heretofore a verie rude and barbarouse custome mainteyned in this citie, And in no other citie or towne of this Realme to o(u)r knowledge, that...two disguised p(er)sons called yule and yules wief should ryde thorow the cite verey undecentlie and uncomelie Drawinge great concurses of people after them to gaise, often times co(m)mittinge other enormities. fforasmuche as the d [sic] said Disguysed ∧ [rydinge] and concourse afforesaid besydes other enco(n)venient(es) tendeth also to the prophanynge of that Daie appointed to holie Uses and also w(i)th drawethe great multitudes of people frome devyne S(e)rvice and Sermons...'

This wording clearly parallels that of the injunctions directed in earlier times against the Feast of Fools:† yet a broadside, dating from c. 1570 and recently discovered in the Bodleian Library, provides both the text of a carol particular to this riding and a Christian interpretation of both text and riding. As this is given in full in Appendix A, it suffices here to note that the carol glosses the word 'Yule' as derived from the Hebrew *Yulath*, meaning 'he is born': the shoulder of mutton and the cakes carried by the riders are glossed emblematically to signify Christ as Lamb of God and Bread of Life.[23] What the archbishop, however, appears to have recognized in deciding to issue his injunction, is that these glosses, if not complete fabrications, merely veil the revelry and gifts once offered to Ceres (or to her Teutonic equivalents) at the winter solstice.[24]

The no less surprising presence of a *Rex Autumnalis* honoured within the walls of the church itself at both Bath and Wells in the fifteenth century proclaims the same kind of confusion born from the same tolerance, albeit with the autumn equinox rather than the winter solstice as the dog beneath the skin. An entry in the City of Wells *Convocation Book* under the year 1498 records:[25]

*See Ch. VIII, p. 188 below.
†See Ch. VIII, n. 18, pp. 293–4 below.

'Pecuniae ecclesiae ac communitatis Welliae ... videlicet, provenientes ante hoc tempus de Robynhode, puellis tripudiantibus, communi cervisia ecclesiae, et huius modi.'

(Monies belonging to the church and city of Wells, ... namely, collected previously from Robin Hood, girls dancing, church ales, and suchlike.)

Mention of church ales in this context should alert us to the possibility that by this relatively late date a play may have been toward in Wells during 'this time of Robin Hood'. This is clearly the case in the so-called 'Reynes Extract' that contains the Epilogue to a play, and which ends:

> Sovereyns alle insame,
> ȝe that arn come to sen oure game,
> We pray ȝou alle in Goddys name
> To drynke ar ȝe pas;

> For an ale is here ordeyned be a comely assent
> For alle maner of people þat apperyn here þis day,
> Unto holy chirche to ben incressement
> Alle that excedith þe costys of our play.

The vernal equinox protrudes just as obviously from the May-Game of Robin Hood that caused Bishop Latimer, as already noted, such distress in 1549.* Equally conspicuous is the ancestry of those 'Midsummer Watches' which, although apparently sanctified by choice of St John the Baptist's Day (24 June) and St Peter's Day (29 June) for their annual celebration, proclaim in their bonfires, torches, giants and monsters a continuing respect for the summer solstice and the harvest months ahead.[26] John Stow recalled this riding as it was practised in London during his youth in the sixteenth century.[27]

'On the Vigil of Saint *John Baptist*, and on Saint *Peter* and *Paule* the Apostles, every mans doore being shadowed with greene Birch, long Fennel, Saint Johns wort, Orpin, white Lillies, and such like, garnished upon with Garlands of beautifull flowers, had also Lampes of glasse, with oyle burning in them all the night, some hung out braunches of yron curiously wrought, contayning hundreds of Lampes light at once, which made a goodly shew, namely in new Fish street, Thames streete, &c. Then had ye besides the standing watches, all in bright harnes in every ward and streete of this Citie and Suburbs, a marching watch, that passed through the principal streets thereof .... The Sheriffes watches come one after the other in like order, but not so

---

*See pp. 15–16 above.

large in number as the Mayors, for where the Mayor had besides his Giant, three Pageants, each of the Sheriffes had besides their Giantes but two Pageants, ech their Morris Dance, and one Hench man their Officers in Jacquets of Wolsted, or say party coloured, differing from the Mayors, and each from other, but having harnised men a great many ... '

If there is now almost no means of knowing what the pageants that Stow mentions consisted of (I suspect tableaux only), it is worth noting that in Chester, following the suppression of the Whitsun (Corpus Christi) plays, the guilds, in celebrating the Midsummer Watch, continued to display some at least of the pageant-wagons formerly used to stage the plays, together with some of their characters including God and the Devil.[28]

Just as treacherous, where interpretation and derivation are concerned, are those many innocuous-sounding phrases like 'in festo natalis Domini' or 'in Transitu Sancti Germani hoc anno' which litter the account rolls of medieval priories and churchwardens' parish registers in conjunction with payments to *histriones*, *lusores*, 'pleyers' and 'gamesters'. In 1494, for instance, the village of East Harling in Norfolk grossed 'xviij^s ij^d', 'Rec[eive]d of a Chirchale, made the Sunday before Medsomer when Keningale and Lopham came hither'.* From other entries in the same register it is clear that the villagers of Keningale and Lopham each brought their respective 'game' with them; indeed it was probably these games that raised the money, but the fact that they brought it on a Sunday does not mean that either 'game' was necessarily a Christian, religious play: it means only that the inhabitants of East Harling were not working and were thus free to watch the game. Indeed the most famous of these 'games' were the May-Game and its aliases, the King-Game and Plough-Play, all of which were variants of the so-called Mummers' Play with either the Green Man, Wildman, St George or Robin Hood as its protagonist, and with maypoles, morris dancers, wreaths and swords so much in evidence.[29] Again, the links with pre-Christian celebration of the vernal equinox and the end of winter, if imprecise, are clear enough, and have sufficed in their profusion to fill several books. One example (much fuller than most) is Lydgate's charming *Mumming at Bishopswood* (c. 1425), the full title of which is 'Nowe here nexst folowyng ys made a balade by Lydegate, sente by a poursyvant to þe Shirreves of London, acompanyed with þeire breþerne upon Mayes daye at Busshopes wod, at an honorable dyner, eche of hem bringginge his dysshe'.[30] This is a highly stylized May-Game in the form of a pastoral

*See *EES*.ii(2).33.

fête champêtre at which the sheriffs and their friends were to be greeted by Flora, Ver, and a personification of May: yet the deviser and author was himself a Benedictine monk.

Nor must fairs be forgotten. The English word 'fair' is derived from the Latin *feriae* meaning 'holiday', and in republican Rome *feriae* were normally accompanied by both mimetic and athletic games as we have already seen.* 'Fair' is defined in the *Oxford Dictionary* as a 'periodical gathering for the sale of goods, often with shows and entertainments, at a place and time fixed by charter, statute or custom'.[31] As it was pointless to offer goods for sale or barter when no one was free to inspect or buy them, fairs in the Middle Ages inevitably became attached to holidays, and thus to Christian calendar festivals like St Bartholomew's Day (24 August), St Giles's Day (1 September) or Martlemas (St Martin's Day: 11 November).[32] Yet, as the Roman *feriae* had been accompanied by festive plays and sports, so this custom also survived from pre-Christian into Christian times and gave itinerant mimes, minstrels, puppeteers and gamesters a chance to compete with stall-holders in attracting customers by plying their dramatic wares, or feats of skill and strength, in return for goods or cash. Fairs thus contributed substantially to establishing both circuits for professional actors to tour and the stigma of vagabondage which, by the sixteenth century, had come to be indelibly stamped upon acting as a profession.†

I hope I have now supplied examples enough to illustrate the point chiefly at issue: English festivals of the Christian Middle Ages, while virtually exclusive to Christian calendar feasts,‡ retain many of the ideas common to festivals that had fallen at approximately the same points in the calendars of pre-Christian religions, together with many of the customs initiated in the course of celebrating them. Sanctified they may have been by the saint or martyr whose name-day occasioned the festival, or by the event in Christ's life that was distinguished in the same way and by the traditional observance of them; but beneath this veneer lay primitive, instinctive responses to the recurrent, cyclic struggle for survival apparent in all four seasons of the year, and in the impact of these seasons upon the staple diet of farming and fishing communities throughout the British Isles. Representatives of these communities, in their mimetic games, bore witness to the existence of their gods; in their athletic games other representatives exhibited themselves defiantly as demigods and potential protectors of the community; and in both activities they discovered dramatic means to

*See pp. 8–10 above.
†See *EES*.ii(1).80.
‡See Appendix B.

20

communicate these ideas to one another. In doing so, they succeeded in transforming isolated collections of frightened individuals into much larger societies, each more secure in its attitudes to life within a common culture that acknowledged men to be less than gods, yet capable of finding common-sense solutions to their problems. In time they came to label the sort of drama that reminded them of this as comedy. Yet they also accepted the possibility of occasional clashes between human and divine will which, if not capable of resolution in human terms, inevitably brought disaster in their wake; and these situations they came to describe in literary and dramatic terms as tragedy. Folk custom itself, with its annual reminders of a life-style even more heavily dependent on the vicissitudes of climate and the seasons than that of urban society in medieval England, came to be transformed into plays extolling the simple life among flocks and meadow flowers and in the shelter of the forest that were later to be known as pastorals. All three processes were gradual and formulated, as I shall try to show, as much by shifts in Christian philosophy as by archaeological memories or manuscript accounts of former Graeco-Roman or Celto-Teutonic practice. Thus, in the high Middle Ages, men who defy the gods may still be said to fall at Fortune's whim, and be encouraged to cultivate Fortitude as the supreme, protective virtue; but they may also be said to have brought damnation upon their own heads through sin, and be encouraged to repent while time permits. Likewise, if things turn out well, while that might still be regarded as the product of chance, it is more often attributed to divine saving grace as expressed in love, mercy or forgiveness than to fortuitous circumstance or human ingenuity. And so long as festival and drama continued to support and nourish each other, they served between them to propagate and establish these views among the inhabitants of every town and village in the land together with a common code of conventions (first ritualistic and then theatrical) through which to communicate them in imitative action. At the Reformation, however, many of the festivals withered or were suppressed, a change which the triumph of professionalism in dramatic art, in the form of regular weekday performances presented for exclusively commercial reasons, served only to accelerate.* The plays devised to meet these changed circumstances reflect this tension between the old and the new attitudes to drama adopted by actors and public alike and are the greater for it; but consciousness of this division that had been opened between a sense of festive occasion and the expression of it in drama proved irreversible

In Ben Jonson's England, under the double pressure of the Puritan

---

*See *EES*.ii(1).100–21; also Ch. VIII, p. 183 below.

onslaught on the spirit of festivity itself (and thus on fertility) and the attack of scientific opinion on the poetic imagination (and thus on that kind of creativity), active measures were being taken both in Parliament and in city halls to cut the remaining links with the past, as Jonson himself sought to warn those still willing to listen in *Bartholomew Fair* and *The Sad Shepherd*. Yet so long as Lord Mayors paraded through their cities on the day of their installation and were met in the streets by their electors with salutatory pageants; so long as the King and his family were welcomed on progress through the country with entertainments; and so long as masques continued to entertain the Court at Christmas, at Shrovetide, and to mark weddings, the idea that drama had once existed to celebrate occasion could not wholly disappear. So long as that was true, drama could still claim to be a genuinely representative national art rather than the diminished toy of leisured minorities. The fact that it forfeited its earlier right to claim to be the former between 1642 and 1660 during the Civil War and the Commonwealth, and its re-emergence in the latter guise following the Restoration, provides one measure of what was lost and what was won in that round of the enduring struggle between the followers of Dionysus and their opponents. Drama survives today in plays, films and television; precious little 'sense of occasion' still attaches to it. In other words the commercially sponsored drama that we continue to support is itself coming to resemble folk-custom: revels tenaciously retained either to pass time and alleviate boredom, or to propagate social and political causes, but from which the original meaning and significance has almost wholly disappeared.

II

DRAMA OF THE CHRISTIAN CALENDAR

1 Festivals of the Christian year

ONE helpful fact that research has now placed beyond dispute is that all drama of a recognizably Christian character from the tenth century to the thirteenth was a product of the festive celebration of an event in Christian history deemed worthy of annual commemoration. Every play that survives to us from this period is thus directly related to a particular feast, or Red Letter Day, in the calendar of the Roman Catholic Church. Each was created, moreover, as an act of witness to a miraculous event with the establishment of faith in the actuality of that event as its primary function. This of itself explains why the earliest liturgical music-dramas should have come into existence in the context of Christ's Resurrection from the dead and be particular to Easter Sunday.*

The primacy of Easter and Christmas among feasts in the Christian calendar has never been in dispute, but the questions of which took pride of place and of whether they should be linked in ritual time to the solar or the lunar year occasioned long and vexatious controversy among the Church's founding fathers both in Rome and in Constantinople.[2] With the triumph, however, of the Roman liturgy over all other liturgical forms in Western and Northern Europe in the course of the sixth and seventh centuries, Easter became irrevocably attached to the lunar year and thus a 'floating' rather than a 'fixed' feast, with acknowledged primacy over Christmas. The latter was attached to the solar year and thus became a 'fixed' feast falling regularly on 25 December.[3] Easter remains a 'floating' feast, so called because of the variability of the paschal full moon as the Book of Common Prayer explains in its 'Table to find Easter Day'.

*The word 'Easter' is derived from the Old English *Eostre*, an anglicized version of the Teutonic mother-goddess Freya merged with the Anglo-Saxon fertility-goddess Erce.[1]

'This Table contains so much of the Calendar as is necessary for the determining of *Easter*; to find which, look for the Golden Number of the year in the first Column of the Table, against which stands the day of the Paschal Full Moon; then look in the third column for the Sunday Letter, next after the day of the Full Moon, and the day of the Month standing against that Sunday Letter is *Easter Day*. If the Full Moon happens upon a Sunday, then (according to the first rule) the next Sunday after is *Easter Day*.'

With Easter determined in this fashion, all other feasts that in point of time are measured from it, whether forwards or backwards, must inevitably be floating feasts also. These embrace all the events of Passion Week, the forty days of Lent, Shrovetide (or Carneval)* and the Sundays leading up to it, measured backwards in time and towards Christmas; moving forward from Easter itself they cover Whitsun (Pentecost), the Ascension, Trinity Sunday and, ultimately, from the start of the fourteenth century, the new Feast of Corpus Christi. With the exception of Lent (including Passion Week) all these festivals attracted celebrations cast in dramatic form: the idea of Lent, as a period of obligatory abstinence and penitential reflection in preparation for the rejoicing of Easter, militated positively against any form of display or festive celebration.[4] Lent nevertheless provoked an annual festival of great importance to drama that had little justification in religious ritual: Shrovetide or Carnival. Besides Lent itself there were other 'Days of Fasting, or Abstinence' in the year, notably 'The Ember Days at the Four Seasons' and 'The three Rogation Days'. The word 'Ember' is derived from the Old English *Ymbreu* (*ymbm*, about; *ryne*, course) which, in the connotation of the calendar, refers to the solstices and equinoxes. The word 'Rogation' is derived from the Latin *rogare*, to ask, and was used in the calendar to describe the litany of the saints chanted before Ascension Day and devoted to intercession. Both groups of days, therefore, were likely, more especially in country districts, to attract customs derived from earlier, pre-Christian prognostic and propitiatory rituals. 'Carneval' (the literal meaning of which is 'to put away meat'), with no good religious reason to justify its existence as a major festival, must be regarded as a final feast in the literal and secular sense of banquet (even extended to orgy) before the long, Lenten fast began. The Church strove to endow it with respectability under the name of Shrovetide, a time for the hearing of confessions and the assignment of penances; but historically there can be no question that laymen viewed this season in the spirit of 'eat, drink and be merry, for tomorrow we must die'. Shrovetide covered the three

*The modern spelling is normally Carnival.

days from Quinquagesima Sunday (fifty days before Easter) to Ash Wednesday (the first day of Lent): Carnival was particular to the Tuesday only, and is now better known in Catholic countries as Mardi Gras and in Protestant countries as Pancake Day.* Like the Ember and Rogation Days this period too, since it lacked specifically Christian justification for festivity, attracted to itself customs derived from pre-Christian rituals, notably those permitting inversion of normal social hierarchy, temporary freedom from normal moral restraints, and even parody of religion itself.

Christmas being a fixed festival, all other feasts directly related to it were also celebrated on fixed days. These stretch backwards in time through St Thomas's Day (21 December), St Nicholas's Day (6 December) and St Andrew's Day (30 November) to the beginning of Advent (the last Sunday in November), itself a period of sustained preparation, standing in respect to Christmas as Lent does to Easter, but with the important difference that the emphasis on the relationship of prophecy to penitence is reversed. (See Appendix B.) Again, however, the feasts appointed to follow Christmas like those following Easter are all celebrations: St Stephen (26 December), St John the Evangelist (27 December), Holy Innocents (28 December), Circumcision (1 January) and Epiphany (6 January). Collectively they make up the Twelve Days of Christmas, terminating with Twelfth Night. Here both the preparatory feasts and the celebratory feasts directly parallel the change in the sun's course at the winter solstice (21 December).

From this brief analysis of the Christian calendar it will be noticed that compared to the autumn, winter and spring months those of high summer are distinguished by a dearth of festivals, as any churchgoer will know who recalls the seemingly interminable sequence of uneventful Sundays after Trinity varying between twenty-two when Easter falls at its latest date (25 April) and twenty-seven when it falls at its earliest (22 March). If the August festivals particular to the Virgin Mary still observed in Roman Catholic countries are omitted, this long, three to four month period is punctuated by only a few saints' days: St Swithin, St Margaret, St Mary Magdalene, St James and St Anne in July; St Lawrence and St Bartholomew in August; St Giles, St Matthew and St Michael in September; St Luke and St Simon and St Jude in October. Nevertheless, before the Reformation all of these days were public holidays in England and must be thought of as likely to have been celebrated with mimetic games and plays, at least in

---

*For the status of this festival in England c. 1599, see Thomas Dekker's *The Shoemaker's Holiday*, V. i. 44–50 and V. 2. 180–216.

places where the saint in question was held in special esteem; thus guilds or churches dedicated in the name of one of them frequently regarded the name-day of the patron saint as among the most important in the calendar and marked it with the production of a play depicting aspects of the life and works of the saint. In these cases the motivation could be strictly devotional—a thank offering—or it could be commercial—a fund-raising effort. Sometimes it combined both. Either way what matters is that these plays existed to celebrate the feast day in question and were justified as praiseworthy activities on that account until the Reformation brought the whole question of images and imitation into conjunction with idolatry and superstition and thus invited a change of attitude in England to both saints and plays.[5]

2 The drama of Easter and its vigil

The famous opening lines of Shakespeare's *Richard III*

Now is the winter of our discontent
Made glorious summer by this sun of York;
And all the clouds that low'red upon our house
In the deep bosom of the ocean buried ...

provide as apt an expression as any imaginable of the impact of the earliest Easter drama of the Christian Church upon the worshippers to whom it was presented.

Angel	Whom seek ye in the sepulchre, O followers of Christ?
The Maries	Jesus of Nazareth, which was crucified, O celestial one!
Angel	He is not here; he is risen, just as he foretold.
	Go, announce that he is risen from the dead.
The Maries	Alleluia! The Lord is risen today,
	The strong lion, the Christ, The Son of God!
	Give thanks to God! Huzzah!
Angel	Come, and see the place where the Lord was laid.
	Alleluia! Alleluia!
The Maries	The Lord is risen from the sepulchre,
	Who for us hung upon the cross.
The Choir	We praise thee, O God.[6]

St Ethelwold, Bishop of Winchester from 963 to 984, tells us in his *Regularis Concordia*, written to reform and regulate the forms of worship practised in all Benedictine monastic houses within his diocese, that at Mass on Easter Sunday, following the third reading from Scripture, four of the brethren are to vest themselves, one in an alb and the others in copes, in preparation for the singing of these verses. The verses are to be sung in front of a tomb, sculpted and reserved for that purpose.[7] (See Plates I and II.) The brother representing the angel is to seat himself in front of this tomb with a palm in his hand; the other three are to approach, carrying in their hands censers filled with incense, '*ac pedetemtim ad similitudinem querentium quid*' (lit: 'and slowly, simulating seeking something'). There can be no doubt about the mimetic nature of these actions since the rubric is quite specific at this point.

'Aguntur enim haec ad imitationem angeli sedentis in monumento atque mulierum cum aromatibus venientium ut ungerent corpus Jhesu.'
(These things are done in imitation of the angel seated in the monument [i.e. sepulchre],* and of the women coming with spices to anoint the body of Jesus.)

Yet this short play is patently a component part of the *officium*, or service, for Easter morning commemorating Christ's Resurrection from the dead. The concluding *Te Deum*, led by the prior, joined by everyone else present, and accompanied by the ringing of all the bells in the tower proclaims no less clearly that all concerned are committing themselves to an act of thanksgiving, praise and jubilation.

What purpose then is this simple play designed to serve, set as it is so firmly within the order of worship prescribed for this outstanding feast? One answer is that it commemorates the historical event by re-enacting it; but that answer is evasive since it avoids a direct answer to the ancillary question 'Why re-enact it?' To answer that question I think we have to ask ourselves another, more disturbing question: how can anyone *re-enact* an action that defies reason since no mortal man, once dead, can rise physically from out of the grave? In other words, if this event occurred at all in the first century A.D., was it by supernatural rather than by natural means? If it was a miracle, then it has remained one ever since; and if reason rejects this possibility, acceptance of it can only be attained through faith. What dramatic re-enactment is called upon to do, therefore, is to nourish and sustain faith. In other words the mimetic actions are intended to supply in three-dimensional, realistic, visual images an outward, theatrical figuration of an abstract concept. It exists to help us to see the events in the same circumstances and in the same emotional mood as they were first experienced by the women and men who claimed to have witnessed them. The brothers representing the angel and the Maries in the play (also the disciples in later, extended versions)

*Cf. *Romeo and Juliet* and *Antony and Cleopatra* for Shakespeare's use of this word.

are thus performing the actions prescribed in the rubrics of the liturgy to help us to believe the unbelievable through the witness of the senses—ears, eyes and touch. Historical time is dissolved in ritual time: we are transported back to Jerusalem on Easter morning in the year A.D. 33 as if it were today: we *hear* what the angel and the Maries tell us: we *see* the empty tomb: we are *shown* the abandoned shroud: and finally we are invited to add our testimony, as were the original disciples, to the actuality of this event, and then urged to go out and announce it to others (see Plate III). The ringing of all the bells symbolizes this last expectancy, carrying the message received within the church out over the surrounding countryside. Mosaic, fresco, stained glass, candlelight, incense, music and movement are all released suddenly and simultaneously upon our senses after the long Lenten vigil of fasting and abstinence to help us to transcend the barriers of historical time and incredulity, and thus to perceive in our hearts the spiritual truth of what the three Maries are asserting to be the evidence of their eyes, ears and hands; and if we identify ourselves with them in their expressions of joy we too have become believers. Faith has triumphed over reason, like life over death. It is in this spirit that we are then asked to join in the *Te Deum*: 'We praise thee, O God, we acknowledge thee to be the Lord.'

We can never be certain how effective this method proved to be in its principal objective: all we can be sure of is that it added greatly to the *joy* of Easter, since mimetic re-enactment of event came to be applied to other commemorative festivals in the Christian calendar, as well as being extended to other events immediately before and after the encounter of the three Maries with the angel at the sepulchre. Examples of the latter include the *Ordo Paschalis* from Klosterneuburg (early thirteenth century), and the Benediktbeuern *Ludus, Immo Exemplum, Dominice Resurrectionis* (late thirteenth century), both of which preface the scenes of witness and belief with a scene of positive disbelief anticipating by some 600 years the style of a Jacobean anti-masque.[8] This scene embraces Pilate, the high priests and the soldiers who, when surrounding the sepulchre, sing, 'Non credimus Christum resurgere ... ' (We do *not* believe ...). It is followed by the blinding of the soldiers by angels carrying the insignia of Christ the King singing the antiphon,

Alleluia
Resurrexit victor ab inferis ....

This in turn leads on to the Maries' purchase of spices from the merchant and their pilgrimage to the sepulchre. The Benediktbeuern play breaks off with the astonished soldiers 'going to Pilate and the Priests and the

Jews, and announcing what they have seen and heard' (quod viderunt et audierunt). The longer but more confused Klosterneuburg text embraces not only a fully developed visit to the sepulchre that includes Christ's appearance to Mary Magdalene but also the Harrowing of Hell. An even longer *Ludus Paschalis* from Tours as well as including these events jumps forward in time to finish with Christ's appearance to all the disciples including doubting Thomas; but here again, through the translation of Thomas's disbelief into belief, the play's concluding episode becomes one of reiterated witness and affirmation, culminating in Christ's final words to Thomas:

'Quia vidisti me, Thomas, creditisti; beati, qui non viderunt et crediderunt, alleluia.'

(You, Thomas, believed because you saw me; blessed are those who have not seen and yet have believed, alleluia.)

The entire statement made through the mimetic action of re-enacted event is thus again turned outwards to the audience who, as a chorus of witnesses and believers, are required to join in the singing of the *Te Deum*.[9]

The first distinct, additional play within the Easter season, as opposed to an extension of the Easter Play itself, is the *Peregrini*: it depicts Christ's appearance to the disciples on the road to Emmaus.[10] This was an evening play particular to Vespers either on Easter Monday (as at Rouen, Padua and in Sicily) or on the first Sunday after Easter (as at Beauvais), or on evenings throughout that week: at Fleury it was presented on Easter Tuesday. In England we know that it was performed at Malmesbury in 1125, at Lichfield in the thirteenth century; and a fragmentary version survives from Shrewsbury (fifteenth century).[11]

The simplest of these plays conclude with the disciples' recognition of the risen Christ and the singing of the *Magnificat*: the more extended versions add the conversion of Thomas. All of them, however, belong to their liturgical context, and in doing so exist to celebrate this particular, commemorative calendar feast: divorced from this context, they become irrelevant and thus virtually meaningless. Such is also the case with plays for two other 'movable feasts' related to Easter—Ascensiontide, and Pentecost (or Whitsun).

The day prescribed in the calendar to commemorate the Ascension had to be the fortieth day after the Resurrection, and so it was celebrated on the Thursday following the fifth Sunday after Easter. The introit for that feast included a trope very similar to that used on Easter Day itself.

'Quem creditis super astra ascendisse, o Christicolae?'

(Whom do you believe to have ascended above the stars, O Christians?)

'Jesum qui surrexit de sepulchro, o coelicolae.'

(Jesus who rose from the tomb, O heavenly ones.)

'Iam ascendit, ut praedixit.'

(He has ascended already, as he prophesied.)

However, although this simple nucleus of chanted question and answer is clearly as capable of dramatic development as the Easter *Quem quaeritis in sepulchro?*, it does not appear to have been extended into a play either as uniformly or as swiftly as the Easter introit. In fact only one fully developed play-text has thus far been discovered: it exists in an *ordinarium* (normal service book) of the fourteenth century, from the South German town of Moosburg, and is prescribed as a preface to Vespers.[12] The manuscript is now in the Staatsbibliothek in Munich. Fifteen priests are required to represent Mary, the twelve disciples, and two angels. Another is needed to speak the lines given to Christ; but he is concealed from public view, and Christ is represented as an image or effigy within a cloud-like mandola that is drawn up into the bell-tower on ropes. Indisputably a play, and with as specific a location (Mount Sinai) as the sepulchre of the Easter Play, the text is nevertheless as formal as it is liturgical, and exists, yet again, as an act of witness to, and belief in, an incredible event that pits faith against reason.

Evidence survives throughout Europe to prove that the Feast of the Ascension was celebrated in churches with special ceremonies of a mimetic kind centred on the symbolic raising of a cross or an effigy, but very little is known about how they were presented[13] (see *EES*. i, Plate XXXI, No. 50).

The Feast of Pentecost, marking the descent of the Holy Ghost and the gift of languages to the disciples, appears likewise to have been only fitfully dramatized; indeed, in this case, as Karl Young observed, it would perhaps be more accurate to describe those ceremonies of which record survives as 'not lacking in theatrical effects' rather than as 'impersonation and drama'. The most popular of these effects was the release of a dove, either real (as in London) or fabricated (as in Florence), coupled with pyrotechnical effects that symbolized in fireworks and incense the tongues of flame and gift of languages described in the Bible. One such ceremony as practised in London at St Paul's Cathedral early in the sixteenth century is vividly described by the antiquarian William Lambarde.[14]

'The like Toye I my selfe (beinge then a Chyld) once saw in *Poules* Churche at *London*, at a Feast of *Whitsontyde*, wheare the comynge downe of the *Holy Gost* was set forthe by a white Pigion, that was let to fly out of a Hole, that yet is to be sene in the mydst of the Roofe of the great Ile, and by a longe Censer, which descendinge out of the same Place almost to the verie Grounde, was swinged up and downe at suche a Lengthe, that it reached with thone Swepe almost to the West Gate of the Churche, and with the other to the Quyre Staires of the same, breathinge out over the whole Churche and Companie a most pleasant Perfume of suche swete Thinges as burned thearin.'

Thus in every instance the feast of Easter and those both of its related vigil and subsequent festivals precipitated celebrations that were dramatic or theatrical and sometimes both. They were conceived as 'shows' in the simplest and original sense of that word, demonstrations, acts of witness, statements of faith and belief. All of them proclaimed that Christ, although incarnate in mortal form as man, is God, the Conqueror of death, the Redeemer of sinful men and King of souls. As plays they are living icons which, taken collectively, may be regarded as lyric dramas of praise and thanksgiving donated by believers as an annual tribute to Christ, their king.

3 Christmas, its vigil and its aftermath

As at Easter and Ascension Day, the introit for the Nativity included a trope cast in antiphonal form.[15]

'Quem quaeritis in praesepe, pastores, dicite.'

(Whom seek ye in the manger, O shepherds? Tell us!)

'Salvatorem Christum Dominum, infantem pannis involutum, secundum sermonem angelicum.'

(The Saviour, the Christ, the infant Lord wrapped in swaddling clothes, according to the words of the angel.)

'Adest hic parvulus cum Maria matre sua, de qua dudum, vaticinando, Isayas dixerat propheta':

(The baby is here with Mary his mother, of whom long ago in prophecy spoke the prophet Isaiah.)

'Ecce virgo concipiet at pariet filium.'
Et nunc euntes dicite quia natus est.

('Behold a virgin shall conceive and bear a son.' And now as ye go forth, announce that he is born.)

By the eleventh century this trope had been elaborated into a play imitating in its action and dialogue the Easter *Visitatio Sepulchri* with one important exception: here mortals respond to mortals, not to spirits, the questioners being the midwives attendant upon Mary and not angels; but the purpose is the same. The play exists to attest the fulfilment of prophecy in a miraculous birth. In the fully developed *Officium Pastorum*, as at Rouen, we find the midwives instructed in the rubrics to 'show the child' (puerum demonstrent) and then 'expose to view the mother of the boy' (hic ostendant Matrem Pueri).[16] The shepherds respond mimetically by saluting and worshipping the child with bowed heads (Tunc, eo viso, inclinatis cervicibus, adorent Puerum et salutent); convinced, they then turn to the congregation and bear witness to what they have just seen by singing the hymn, 'Salve, virgo singularis': 'Hail, virgin unparalleled!'

Celebration of Christmas, however, was not confined in the Middle Ages to the day of the Nativity alone. As everyone knows, it was a twelve-day holiday starting on 25 December and ending at the Epiphany, 6 January. In between lay four important calendar feasts, two of which were dedicated to the commemoration of St Stephen, the first martyr (26 December), and St John the Evangelist (27 December). The other two, like the Nativity itself, were particular to children—Innocents' Day (28 December) and the Circumcision (1 January)—which goes some way to explaining why, in the later Middle Ages, the whole twelve-day season comes to be so closely associated with inversion of status, folly and misrule.* There is small reason to believe, however, that this development was ever the Church's original wish or intention: rather does it suggest the forceful intrusion in the course of time of external, secular factors upon existing, devotional feasts that succeeded in translating holy days into holidays in a literal sense (see Appendix B).

The key to this paradox, in my view, lies in the dramatic development of the liturgical office for Matins at Epiphany, the *Officium Stellae*, sometimes known as the *Trium Reges* or 'Coming of the Magi'; for this play, in the course of its development, not only brings the shepherds into conjunction with King Herod, the Magi, and the children whom Herod seeks to kill and their mourning mothers, but in doing so within the limits of twelve days effected some confusion in the choice of day most appropriate for its performance, and created in the character of Herod a dramatic persona of an ambiguous and controversial nature.†

---

*I say 'some way' since recollection, and possibly even customs associated with the Roman Saturnalia, almost certainly played some part also.

†See Comedy, Ch. VIII, pp. 175–6 and 182–5 below.

The nucleus of this play was the same as for those already discussed, but scripted in terms of a new set of characters—the Magi, or three kings, who follow the new star to Bethlehem and there offer gifts to the Christ-child and acknowledge him to be divine.[17]

> 'Gaudete, fratres,
> Christus nobis natus est
> Deus homo factus est.'

(Rejoice, brethren! Christ is born to us! God is made man!)

There is of course a correspondence between this Christian re-enactment of the presentation of symbolic gifts by the Magi to Christ on Twelfth Night and the pre-Christian habit of offering gifts both to the Roman goddess Fortuna and domestically among friends at this same season of the year:* and herein lies one important area where secular custom could and did impinge upon doctrinal rite.

Another was the contrast, implicit in the biblical account of both the Nativity and the Epiphany, between two kinds of kingship, Christ's and Herod's. Homage is paid to Christ in a feudal sense, first by simple shepherds, then by temporal rulers who humble themselves, and who then in this meek state of mind and heart perceive the truth of Christ's divinity and proclaim it to the world. Herod does the opposite. Not only does he deliberately reject the word of the prophets and the advice of his counsellors, but in blind pride he attempts, like Lucifer, to destroy God. Thus, as with Pilate and the soldiers in developed versions of the *Visitatio Sepulchri*, text and rubrics of developing versions of the *Visitatio Praesepe* and *Officium Stellae* had to provide for conduct and behaviour representing disbelief as well as that indicative of belief: and this could not be done without incorporating some measure of *indecorum* and even absurdity into Herod's words and actions. So here, too, lay another area of dramatic representation in which secular rather than doctrinal example was likely to be deployed to meet the need. This problem could only be aggravated by the further extension of the *Officium Stellae* (motivated by the proximity of Innocents' Day in the calendar to Epiphany) to include the slaughter of the Innocents by Herod's soldiers since this of itself necessitated the substitution of grief and militant and murderous conflict for joy and devotional calm and meditative contemplation in respect of stage action. Richard Axton observes in writing about the earliest plays—in my view, correctly—that the actor[18]

'is partly an officiant; his job is merely to point, offering the congrega-

*See p. 12 above, and Plate II, No. 3.

tion visible proof of the holy mysteries by means of traditional ceremonial objects.

Such a filtering of historical action through the prism of liturgical
ceremony and gesture as well as language is characteristic of the liturgical drama.'

This cannot be said of Herod who is not an officiant and who does
not share the approach of the worshippers to the mysteries; his attitude
is contrary in every sense, a fact that the actor could not ignore.

The effect of these changes is to be seen in the introduction of
armour and weapons, of sadistic soldiers and terrified women, and
of a tyrannous megalomaniac into the basilica and its services, made
explicit by the texts and rubrics of many thirteenth-century versions
of the play and by the rising tide of official condemnations of them.*

These aspects of the extended *Officium Stellae* which, while integral
to the story of the events commemorated, were so contrary to the
gravitas of a liturgical office, recurred at the other end of the twelve-
day Feast of Christmas in another liturgical drama that was particular
to Advent, the *Ordo Prophetarum*. This sought to assemble the major
prophets of Christ's Nativity from Moses to John the Baptist so that
each might in turn re-enact his particular vision and act of faith, and
concluded with a hymn celebrating the predestination of Christ's
coming. Its primary purpose, like that of the other plays considered
in this chapter, was essentially an assertion of faith, appropriate
in its character to this season of confession and contrition preparatory
to the joy of Christmas. Some of the prophets, however, notably
Daniel and Balaam, invited treatment in terms of their adversaries
so that belief might be the better displayed when contrasted with
disbelief. As a result the episodes of Daniel and Balaam became
detached and enlarged into separate plays that incorporate animals
as well as tyrants and soldiers in their cast-lists. These plays, however,
can be more conveniently considered in association with another
group which appear to owe as much to academic, and even secular,
initiatives as to strictly liturgical and monastic ones.†

4 Commemoration of saints, prophets and martyrs

A hundred years, by any standards, is a long time: long enough at
least for parents to become great-grandparents, and for their children
to take for granted customs that their great-grandparents had regarded

---

*See Ch. VIII, pp. 175–6 below for examples.
†See pp. 39–41 below.

as shockingly new and innovative. Thus by the close of the eleventh century, if we take St Ethelwold's *Regularis Concordia* of *c.* 975 to mark the start of the regular use of the *Visitatio Sepulchri* on Easter Day in Benedictine monasteries in England, the idea of dramatic re-enactment of historical events as a normal adjunct of worship on major feast days had come to be widely accepted. From Easter the practice had by then undoubtedly been extended to embrace Christmas, Epiphany, the Ascension and Whitsun. Where was it to stop? Difficulties about the impersonation of Herod and his soldiers were raising questions about the propriety of according a place to such mimetic ceremonies within the sacred confines of liturgical offices; but these questions did not in themselves invalidate re-enactment, more especially when the practice was so self-evidently successful in generating enthusiastic imitators. Efforts were made to control abuse, but not to stop extension of it to other festive events,* and chief among these were the days reserved for the commemoration of saints. The earliest to receive such attention was St Nicholas whose feast day was 6 December. Other figures whom we know to have attracted similar attention during the twelfth century are St Catherine, St Paul, the prophets Daniel and Balaam, Anti-Christ, the Wise and Foolish Virgins, Lazarus, Rachel, Joseph and Adam.[19]

It forms no part of my purpose here to discuss the dramatization of any of these familiar, biblical and eschatological stories beyond remarking the occasions that gave rise to the choice of these particular subjects. The texts have been edited and printed in an exemplary manner by Karl Young in *The Drama of the Mediaeval Church*, and this work has subsequently been reinforced by much helpful critical commentary by O. B. Hardison, Junior, in *Christian Rite and Christian Drama in the Middle Ages*, Richard Axton in *European Drama of the Early Middle Ages* and in other shorter essays. What has thus far escaped critical attention is the specific relationship of all these plays to the holidays that occasioned their composition. It is into this relatively dark corner, therefore, that I hope to direct a little light in this present study.

Disparate as all these plays appear at first glance to be, both in terms of subject and of treatment, they do possess three factors in common: their liturgical form, an absence of that emphasis upon witness which characterizes all their precursors, and at least one indication in each case of some influence other than monastic devotion upon their composition.

As well as being the earliest of these subjects to attract attention,

*See Ch. VIII, pp. 179–85 below.

St Nicholas also received much the most frequent and fullest dramatic treatment. The abnormality in this case is the lack of any biblical source material whatever, either to commemorate or dramatize. Yet by the twelfth century the legendary life of this historically obscure man who became Bishop of Myra in the Province of Lycia (now southern Turkey) in A.D. 325 had become as popular as any story in the Bible, and the saint himself a cult-hero for prisoners, sailors, scholars, children, and the poor and the needy.* Venerated for his miracles both before and after his death, he could be said to have eclipsed most of the Apostles in general familiarity and popular appeal. We should therefore expect to find external pressures at work in elevating the feast held in honour of his name-day into a festival of abnormal significance, more especially as he seems to have become the patron saint of clerks and goliards at about this time—in other words, to find the Church acknowledging that faith in the saint, and his powers to assist those in almost any form of distress, could only be established the more firmly by re-enactment of some of his earliest miracles. The subject-matter actually chosen for dramatic treatment embraces four particular legends: his rescue of the daughters of a bankrupt father from prostitution; his raising from their death-beds of three scholars murdered by a greedy innkeeper and his wife; his posthumous rescue of goods stolen from an unbeliever whom he converts to Christianity; and the restoration to his parents of a Christian youth abducted by pagans. Of one play at least we know the author, Hilarius, himself a wandering scholar and not a cloistered monk.† All the plays that survive, however, were composed—as is clear from the rubrics—for performance on the saint's day, and more probably within the basilica than outside it.[20]

By contrast the Fleury play of the conversion of St Paul sticks closely to St Luke's account in Acts 9: 1–27. It too treats of a miracle, and calls on the Apostles to rejoice that their enemy who hitherto had behaved like a ravening wolf is now their friend and as gentle as a lamb. This introduces the *Te Deum* which concludes a play clearly designed to celebrate the feast day at Matins on 25 January.[21] What this play shares in common with the Herod plays is the indecorous behaviour of Paul as Saul (and his armed knights) in his role of chief persecutor of Christians.

Another play with far greater biblical authority than any play of St Nicholas is the *Ordo Representacionis Adae*, more commonly known as the *Jeu d'Adam*; but this, likewise, is characterized by a two-fold abnormality. In the first place it is scripted almost wholly in Anglo-

*The saint's tomb is in the cathedral at Bari in southern Italy.
† See p. 181 below.

Norman instead of Latin, and in the second it is intended for performance in the churchyard rather than within the church itself.[22] This play combines the account given in Genesis of Adam's fall and Cain's murder of Abel with an *Ordo Prophetarum* of Jewish patriarchs and prophets starting with Abraham and ending with Isaiah. Critics used to explain this play as a normal *Ordo Prophetarum* of the Advent season whose author had simply extended its scope backwards in time to embrace the two earlier sections covering Adam and Eve and Cain and Abel: they do not appear to have considered the consequences of trying to perform it in the open air in December. More recent critics, however, including Grace Frank, Lynette Muir and Richard Axton, have noticed that the case could as easily be reversed since, in Axton's words, 'liturgically speaking, Adam and Cain belong to Sexagesima, the pre-Lenten period of emphasis on the necessity for atonement for sin'.[23] Lynette Muir goes further in saying,[24]

'the lections and responsories in *Adam* belong to the opening chapters of *Genesis* which was begun at Septuagesima and continued into Lent: the pericopes included the stories of Noah, Abraham and the Patriarchs, including Moses; in Passiontide the prophecies of Jeremiah led up to Easter. This sequence seems to have been in the mind of the author of *Adam* and to have suggested the general pattern of the play.'

If then, what the play, taken as a whole, actually reflects is the sinful state of man coupled with a stirring call for repentance, it becomes entirely appropriate in a liturgical sense to Shrovetide, more particularly to Carnival, the vigil of Ash Wednesday.[25] If this assignment of the play, arrived at by relating its content to its proper place in the liturgical year, is correct, then its purpose becomes as evident as that of the other liturgical plays discussed: re-enactment provides testimony not only of original sin, but of the redemption bought through atonement and repentance. It is for this reason that Isaiah is made to argue with the unbelieving Jew and to proclaim the name of Jesus

> ' ... who shall be our Saviour
> and bring Adam forth from torment;
> To Paradise He will restore him.'
> (ed. Muir, II. 920–2)

It is also for this reason, in my view, that the play is devised for presentation in the churchyard so that Jeremiah may urge the audience to learn to repent and, in doing so, to make themselves worthy to enter the church itself.[26]

> Hear the sacred word of God,
> All you who are on his side:

37

The great lineage of Judah,
All the members of his household!
Do you seek to pass this gateway
And go in, our Lord to worship? [my italics]
The Lord of Hosts, he does command you,
The God of Israel in High Heaven,
Prepare ye, and make good the paths;
Let them be as straight as furrows.
And let all your hearts be cleansed now
That no harm may come upon you;
Let your intentions all be good,
And no evil-doing in you.
If you do thus, God will come,
And with you will make his home;
The glorious one, the Son of God,
Will come down to you on earth here.
The Lord on High, the Heavenly One,
As mortal man will dwell with you;
Will bring Adam forth from prison,
His own Body give for ransom. (*ibid.*, II. 851–72)

Figuratively speaking, no fitter exhortation can be imagined to put the forty days that O. B. Hardison has called the Lenten Agon, starting on the morrow, to full use in order to win back the chance of salvation promised by God, made possible by the events of Good Friday and to be fulfilled in Christ's reunion with his followers on Easter Day.

Another play which, in my opinion, properly belongs to Shrovetide is that of the Wise and Foolish Virgins from Limoges, called, simply, *Sponsus* in the St Martial Troper.[27] This too contains abnormalities suggesting external influences. One of these is the mixture of Latin with Romance dialect mirrored also in the music which mixes liturgical with troubadour styles; the other is the novel appearance, shared with the *Jeu d'Adam*, of hell and devils in the final stage-direction.

'Modo accipiant eas Demones, et precipitentur in infernum.'

(Forthwith let demons take hold of them [i.e. the Foolish Virgins], and let them be thrown into hell.)*

The choir announces that Christ, as Bridegroom, is coming 'to wash away our stains of evil through his death upon the cross'. It is not a time for sloth and idleness (Gaire noi dormet!); rather is it a time for watchfulness and repentance. The Wise Virgins are ready for the Bridegroom; the Foolish Virgins are not, and pay the price. This

*On the treatment of hell in the *Jeu d'Adam* see Ch. VI, pp. 154–5.

play, moreover, could as readily be performed in the refectory at Carnival as in the church since there are no rubrics or canticles to link it to any specific office.

Even vaguer in direct affiliation to the calendar is the single surviving play of Joseph in Egypt from Laon.[28] The story in Genesis 37 provided the lesson for the octave of Ash Wednesday. The play itself is incomplete, leaving us with no clues to its specific liturgical placement; but again it would seem safer, in view of its content, to assign it to Shrovetide than to any other calendar feast.

It remains to glance briefly at five other subjects dramatized late in the eleventh century or early in the twelfth; all of them belong to the Christmas season and its vigil rather than to Easter or Shrovetide. They embrace two plays devoted to Daniel (one composed by the young clerks of Beauvais and the other by Hilarius); two to Lazarus (one from Fleury and one by Hilarius); a fragmentary treatment of Isaac and Rebecca from Vorau in Austria; an exceptionally elaborate play of Anti-Christ from Tegernsee in Bavaria;* and the famous *Festum Asinorum*.†

The two plays on the raising of Lazarus from the dead seem neither more nor less appropriate to St Lazarus's Day (17 December) than are the plays of St Nicholas already discussed to his feast day, and may thus be said to have come into being to mark and adorn that holiday.[29] The fragmentary nature of the *Ordo de Ysaac et Rebecca* makes it much harder to assign to a particular festival with any assurance; yet even here the allegorized chorus suggests a typological drama designed to prefigure Christ's nativity. Advent Sunday or Christmas Eve would thus be appropriate occasions for its performance.[30]

It has usually been held that the Daniel plays represent independent dramatic treatment of a single episode in the *Ordo Prophetarum*, and that the *Festum Asinorum* represents a similar separation and expansion of the episode relating to Balak, Balaam and his ass. Karl Young challenged this view some fifty years ago in respect of the latter, arguing that the reverse is nearer the truth, the ass having first come to be associated with the Feast of Fools and then been added to the *Ordo Prophetarum* at Rouen.[31] Young's view strikes me as the more probable of the two, but insufficient evidence survives to establish either with certainty. There is, however, another approach to this question that is suggested to me by what I have already said about *Isaac and Rebecca*; this serves to explain the existence of both plays and, as far as I know, is advanced here for the first time. This approach

*Discussion of this play is postponed to the end of this chapter in the Postscript, pp. 46–7 below.
†See Ch. VIII, pp. 182–4 below.

involves considering the expansion and separation of both episodes in terms of typology.

It is known that the story of the prophet Habakkuk's feeding of Daniel in the lions' den was generally regarded in the Middle Ages as prefiguring Christ's feeding of the disciples at the house in Emmaus.[32] Since the latter had already received dramatic treatment at Eastertide in the *Peregrini*, was it not a logical corollary, in Advent, to accord the same treatment to the story of Daniel—more especially since both surviving plays devoted to that subject end with a prophecy of Christ's birth, and with the singing of a Christmas hymn, *Nuntium vobis fero*, followed by the *Te Deum* or the *Magnificat*? And if this seems likely, then, by the same reasoning, it would have been just as acceptable to dramatize the Old Testament story of Balaam as a prefiguration of Christ's appearance to doubting Thomas.

This explanation must in both cases remain speculative; but it does possess the advantage of according with the facts as we know them, and of reinforcing the liturgical rectitude of both performances by explaining the choice of subject-matter in each case in terms of its appropriateness to the festive season celebrated, and vice versa.

In concluding this discussion of Romanesque liturgical dramas composed between the tenth and the thirteenth centuries, it is worth remarking that the word 'miracle' is a singularly apt one to use in this context, since it is a supernatural event in every case which each play exists to acknowledge and celebrate: the Resurrection, Christ's subsequent appearances to his disciples, the Incarnation and its appreciation by the shepherds and the Magi, the advance knowledge of these events vouchsafed to the prophets, and the marvels achieved through faith by the disciples' successors, the saints and martyrs.

Some of these plays, however, at least among the later ones, add to the testament of fact and belief encompassed in re-enactment of event that is common to them all a suggestion that the gateway to faith is preparation, without which it is impossible to perceive the truth of these miraculous events. Liturgically this is acknowledged in the seasons of Lent and Advent: dramatically it begins to make an appearance in plays proper to Shrovetide in exhortations to admit man's fallen nature and repent: the *Sponsus* and the *Jeu d'Adam* are the prime examples. A third is the Anglo-Norman *La Seinte Resureccion* of about 1180. The subject-matter of this play covers events from the Deposition from the Cross to the Ascension.[33] If, however, the idea of original sin related to the possibility of subsequent redemption is to be fully deployed, it must be extended to embrace the idea of atonement; and if this is to be achieved in dramatic art, ways must be found to figure all three ideas in visual images of the Fall and of Doomsday with Christ's Passion at the centre. This became the prime concern of clerical play-makers in the fourteenth, fifteenth and sixteenth centuries, and its triumphant achievement in epic dramas of astonishing proportions is one of the crowning glories of the Gothic era.

5 Corpus Christi and its sequels

V. A. Kolve's *The Play Called Corpus Christi*, first published in 1966, opened the way to an understanding of the importance of the promulgation and institution of the new festival of Corpus Christi to the development of a new style of drama destined ultimately to carry the name of the feast. In England this feast is known to have been widely observed by 1318 and continued to be so annually until it was abolished in 1548 by Edward VI;* revived briefly by the Catholic Mary I between 1553 and 1557, it was finally removed from the calendar of the Church of England by Elizabeth I.

The new drama that came into being to celebrate this feast day of the early summer could not ignore its theatrical antecedents pioneered during the Romanesque era within the liturgical offices for other festivals. Indeed, it owed its very existence to the fact that the Eucharist had come to be regarded in the preceding century as itself possessed of miraculous quality and power.[34] To that extent this drama necessarily remained one that existed to affirm the factual quality of supernatural events in Christian history with the re-enactment of particular acts of witness. This it did in part by repeating and in part by enlarging the repertoire of events selected for re-enactment; and to that extent there is some justification for the long-established critical belief that the English cycles of miracle plays are best accounted for in terms of some evolutionary process.[35] Yet what that school of criticism ignored was the no less important break with tradition represented in the switch of doctrinal emphasis within the new drama away from Christ's divinity and towards his humanity; away from a primary concern with establishment of faith and towards a no less urgent concern with repentance.† In performance this carries with it an important shift in emotional participation for the audience: for if each individual spectator is to be required to examine the condition of his or her own soul, then all of them must be supplied with a more realistic form of representation of re-enacted events in order clearly to communicate and reinforce the changed emotional responses solicited by the play-maker.

*See *EES*.i. 121–2, 130–3 and ii. (1). 69.
†See *EES*.i. 117 ff. and 314 ff.

As I have argued in *The Medieval Theatre* (1974), this change of
direction is expressed in theatrical terms through a shift away from a
drama of Christ the King towards a drama of Christ crucified. The
message is clear: Christ died to redeem sinful man—a message
repeated every time Mass was sung or said. Incorporation of this idea
into the drama is the greatest single change made manifest in the
French and German Passion plays of the fifteenth century, in the
English cycles, and in the morality plays and many of the later saint
plays that grew up alongside them. Scripted throughout in the vernacular instead of in Latin; spoken, not confined to the clergy; realistic
rather than formal in the representation of particular events—all
these plays find their visual equivalents in the frescoes, altar paintings,
sculpted roof-bosses and rood-screens that adorned the churches of
Europe built in the Gothic style (see Plates IV–VI).

The Old and New Testaments, including the Book of Revelation,
were regarded as a single historical entity with the events recorded in
the former prefiguring those related in the latter, a view that play-
makers were required to take into account when selecting their source
material for dramatization. In the words of *Deus Pater*, introducing
the New Testament at Wakefield:

> I wyll that my son manhede take,
> ffor reson wyll that ther be thre,
> A man, a madyn, and a tre:
> Man for man, tre for tre,
> Madyn for madyn; thus shal it be.*
> (X. lines 29–33)

The resulting drama proceeds in three broad movements from the
Creation and Fall, via Christ's Passion to the Harrowing of Hell,
Resurrection and Final Judgment; a pattern succinctly summarized
in the division of the Cornish Cycle into *Origo Mundi*, *Passio* and
Resurrectio, with one whole day reserved for each.[36] Chester ordered
its plays on the same basis; but the time-scale could be compressed,
as at York, into a single day; or it could be expanded, as at London,
to cover a whole week. It could be shifted to suit local convenience,
at least marginally, backwards in liturgical time to Whitsun as at
Chester, or forwards to St Anne's Day (26 July) as was probably the
case at Lincoln:[37] either way it would remain a summer festival,
and no objection could arise on account of inappropriateness since it
could be argued that the obligatory procession sufficed for Corpus
Christi Day itself, while the plays, as adjuncts to it, might fare better

---

*Cf. the Cornish *Origo Mundi* with the infant Christ cradled in the branches of the
Tree of Knowledge; see pp. 84–5 below.

if presented separately. Moreover, since the festival had been created to honour the Eucharist, plays composed to celebrate its miraculous qualities like *The Play of the Sacrament* from Croxton, or devised as affirmations of Christian belief like the *Creed Play* at York, or the *Paternoster Play* at Beverley, Lincoln and York, were just as appropriate to the occasion, and could be used as alternatives to a cycle, if only for variety.

Since I have examined the organization, management and production of these plays in the first volume, and since in the meantime other scholars—notably Emily Prosser, A. C. Cawley, V. A. Kolve, Arnold Williams, David Bevington, Stanley Kahrl and the late Rosemary Woolf—have all added greatly to our previous knowledge of the plays themselves, I do not propose to translate a limited discussion of the plays' relationship to the festival they existed to mark into a discourse on their other qualities. Suffice it here to say, therefore, that their success in this respect, both as a form of popular worship and as community events, led inevitably to their becoming primary objects of attack from Protestant reformers throughout Europe, Spain only being excepted, as the sixteenth century advanced.[38]

Just as relevant to Gothic concern with Christ's humanity was the *Mater Dolorosa* and the procession of martyrs who had imitated Christ's example in facing death with humility, resignation and fortitude. Given the model of the early liturgical saint plays of St Nicholas and St Paul, it was easy to improve upon them by adding other Christian heroes to the list, by communicating the events re-enacted in the vernacular and by extending the number of them by recourse to respected, legendary sources, since fiction, depending on its significance, was accepted as often being more useful than fact—a view hotly contested by Wyclif and his followers.* Plays thus burgeoned during the fourteenth and fifteenth centuries on the feast days particular to the Virgin Mary and to the patronal feasts of many minor local saints. In England the St Anne plays in *Ludus Coventriae*, the Digby plays of *Mary Magdalene* and *St Paul*, and the Cornish play of *St Meriasek* supply us with virtually the only surviving examples of a much wider range of plays that once existed but all texts of which were destroyed as part of the general iconoclasm of the early years of the Reformation. As appropriate for a founder's day as to celebrate a feast proper to a patron saint of a church, a guild or a school or college, these plays flourished in a variety of locations in both summer and winter and could be used to raise funds to restore the fabric of buildings, or to assist the poor and the sick, if not simply for their own sake.[39]

*See pp. Ch. VI, pp. 128–9 below.

Particularly helpful in this respect are the account books of Magdalen College, Oxford, where a clear distinction is made between expenses for dramatic performances in the chapel and in the hall from 1481 onwards.[40] Expenses are incurred in the chapel in connection with St Nicholas's Day in 1482–3 and again in 1484–5 together, that year, with an *Ordo Prophetarum* at Christmas, while in 1486–7 'xij^{d}' is laid out for the Easter Sepulchre in the chapel and 'iij^{s} iiij^{d}' for plays in the hall at Christmas. In 1488–9 'v^{d}' is spent on providing a Service Book for a Boy Bishop in the chapel and in 1506–7 a play of St Mary Magdalene appears in an unspecified location. Christmas 1512–13 was marked by 'interludes' presented on St John's Day at night and on the octave of the Epiphany; and by 1530–1 the scribe is entering payments to professional players. Almost invariably the date is recorded in terms of the feast day, and the feast itself (or its vigil) is celebrated with an appropriate play.

At Cambridge plays were given regularly in several colleges at Christmas during the sixteenth century, but records for most colleges are lacking before the Reformation.[41] At Christ's College a play was surprisingly performed on Ash Wednesday in 1532–3 and as late as 1568–9 the accounts of Jesus College record payment of £4 6^{s} to Messrs Day and Wood, 'Spent at the playes in the chappell'. In 1577–8 the same accounts record payment of '23^{s}/2^{d}' 'towards the stage & other charges of y^{s}comoedie played publiklie in the hawlle in Christm(as)'. At King's 'le disgysyns' graced the Feast of the Purification in 1484–5, and at St John's College plays appear to have been given on St John's Day (27 December) and at Shrovetide from time to time.

Another facet of Gothic concern with Christ's humanity was a new kind of play more closely aligned with sermons than with either readings from the Old and New Testaments or the legendary lives of saints. Described as 'morals' or 'moralities', these plays set out to convince spectators of their sinful natures; to illustrate how Satan and his agents toiled to bring even the best-intentioned of men to ruin; and to prove that Christ's mercy and forgiveness were boundless, provided sinners would recognize the folly and error of their ways and repent.* A sermon, however, may be preached at any time; neither is it so directly dependent upon a particular calendar feast as is the Gospel or any other part of the Proper (as opposed to the Ordinary) of the Mass for that day. The call to repent, moreover, being urgent, is admissible at any time. Development of this kind of play, therefore, carried within itself a loosening of the bonds that had hitherto tied drama to occasion.[42] That these bonds could not be completely cut is

*See *EES*.i.229–34.

obvious from the fact that throughout the fourteenth and fifteenth centuries, and for much of the sixteenth, no play could hope to find an audience without a public holiday to release performers and spectators alike from the obligations of their routine occupations and obligations to their masters.* Nevertheless the gist of the subject-matter of a play like *Wisdom* or *Everyman* is as suitable for presentation on one feast day as another. If the author is aware that he is required, in a commissioned sense, to prepare a play for a particular festival, it is always likely that this awareness will colour particular incidents in it. In choosing to parody a Christmas song, the author of *Mankind* thus makes it clear to readers of the play that he intended it to be performed at some point in the twelve-day feast. He also makes his play topical by singling out familiar local worthies as targets for his vices to hustle and rob. Nearly a century later the author of *Respublica* declares himself to this same effect in his Prologue.

> 'We, that are thactours, have ourselves dedicate
> With some Christmas devise your spirites to recreate.'†

Unlike *Mankind*, however, this play contains nothing by way of songs or incidents specific to the Christmas season; yet it remains highly topical. Almost certainly the first play to be presented at Court following the accession of the Catholic Mary I, it sets out to ridicule the Reformation and presents the Queen herself in the role of Nemesis as *deus ex machina*. The Queen's Warrant to the Revels Office (dated 26 September 1553) happily survives:

'Wee will and co(m) maunde yowe upon the sighte herof forthw(ith) to make and delyver owte of ow(r) Revells unto the gentillmen of o(wr) Chappell for a playe to be played before us at the feast(es) of o(wr) coronacyon as in tymes paste haithe bene accustomed to be done by the gentillmen of the Chappell of o(wr) p(ro) genito (u)rs all soche necessary garment (es) and other thing (es) for the furniture therof as shalbe thowghte meete and convenyente by bill betwyxte yowe and toe of the seide gentillmen.' (*RO* (*E&M*), 149)

Another document survives intimating that 'by reason of a newe determynacion of appoyntement the playe [*was*] to s(er)ve att (chr)istmas nexte foloing' (*ibid.*, 150). It thus stands firmly within the long tradition of plays composed to celebrate an occasion.

---

*Much of the antagonism of London's merchant class to the professional theatre in the sixteenth century is directly attributable to absenteeism among employees. (See also Appendix C.)

† For editions see Ch. IV, n. 12 below.

A postscript

Some at least of the external characteristics of the morality play are to be found at a very early date in the formidable *Anti-Christus* from Tegernsee in Bavaria (late twelfth century). Although scripted in Latin and as ritualistic in its presentation as any liturgical *officium* of the Romanesque era, it is described as a *ludus*, mixes abstract personifications freely with named, historical characters and might be mistaken on that account for a play of much later date.[43] It also contains four battle-scenes; moreover, the subject-matter is so organized as to convince all modern critics that the play was composed as propaganda for the Emperor Frederick Barbarossa's campaign to launch the Third Crusade. The play is thus as political in its content as it is liturgical in its form: the *aula* would seem a more likely locality for its performance than the *basilica;* and a gleeman-clerk a more likely author than an ordained priest. It merits comparison therefore with the French *entremets* of 1377–8 and 1389 described in the next chapter (pp. 50–1), where propaganda for a crusade is again the objective of the entertainment in at least one of them. If the Tegernsee *Anti-Christus* defeats all scholarly attempts to categorize it or determine its auspices because of the paradox implicit in its early date and liturgical form when contrasted with its advanced subject-matter and dramatis personae, a possible pointer to its origin may lie in the fact that not only scholars and minstrels roamed Europe in the twelfth century, but also the younger sons of the nobility in search of land, heiresses and booty. In his essay on 'Youth in Aristocratic Society' in *The Chivalrous Society*,* Charles Duby says of nomadic, knightly *juvenes*, 'These formed "the spearhead of feudal aggression", enjoying lives of high mortality and low morals, celebrated by jongleurs and deplored by monks.' One could do worse therefore than search for a sponsor if not the author among their ranks. By then the tournament, which was destined to grow steadily more spectacular and ultimately to find its way into stage-plays like *Pericles* or *The White Devil* and into Ben Jonson's Masques at Barriers, was already in the ascendant, notwithstanding papal efforts to ban it.†

Medieval tournaments revived the athletic rather than the mimetic aspect of Graeco-Roman *ludi* in the first instance, and as battle-schools were directly concerned with survival. Yet on those counts alone their relationship to the calendar festivals of the Church was non-existent. Knights, as often as not, simply suited their own wishes

---

*Trans. Cynthia Pugh, 1977.
†See *EES*.i.13ff., and pp. 87–93 below.

and convenience in determining where and when these martial festivals should be held. By the twelfth century, however, attempts were being made to tame them within a chivalric code of personal honour and service to Christ.[44] (See Plate III, No. 5.) What we should note, therefore, is that tournaments (which were, of course, the prerogative of the aristocracy) served to pioneer the idea of festive occasions of a secular and theatrical character outside the traditional bounds of either agricultural or Christian calendar festivals long before any break appears in the bonds linking drama to occasion in terms of the *ludi scenici* of either the folk or the Church. It is these non-recurrent festivals celebrated under secular auspices, therefore, that must concern us next.

III

NON-RECURRENT COURT
AND CIVIC FESTIVALS

A striking way of regarding all such festivals in medieval England would be to view them as fertility cults; and in one sense at least this would not be far removed from the truth, since all of them celebrate royal engagements, weddings, births and coronations; or the election of a new mayor, a master or warden of a livery company; or a ruling monarch's symbolic marriage with his or her subjects when on progress through the provinces: as James I told his first Parliament, 'I am the Husband, and all the whole Isle is my lawfull Wife.'[1] At first sight the celebration of a military victory, or of an alliance, may seem an exception; but as survival, and the defeat of the enemy that threatened it, provides the occasion for the festivities it clearly is not. Such was the case with Henry V's victorious return from Agincourt and the welcome accorded to him by the citizens of London in 1416 when John Lydgate supplied the device and accompanying texts.[2] It was so again in 1520 when Henry VIII met Francis I at the Field of the Cloth of Gold.[3]

As I have already analysed most of these pageants, mummings, disguisings and entertainments in the first two volumes of this book, I shall only be concerned in this chapter with the methods adopted by their creators to fit their festive devices to suit the occasion celebrated both visually and verbally, and thus to make their significance apparent to auditors and spectators whether or not they could read and write. To this end survey by example will suffice, rather than by complete but inevitably repetitive coverage of every recorded celebration.

A useful starting-point is a festivity that combined both a religious and a secular celebration, and involved both royal and civic participation: the mumming at the Palace of Kennington where Richard II was spending the twelve-day feast of Christmas in 1377.* That it took place on 1 January or at Epiphany (6 January) may be presumed

*See *EES*.i.197–8.

from the fact that the principal objective of this elaborate masquerade was gift-giving:* it thus bears witness both to the Roman tradition of presenting offerings to Fortuna and to friends at this season of the year, and to the Christian belief derived from Scripture that the Magi honoured the new-born Christ at Bethlehem in this same way on Twelfth Night. On this occasion London's city fathers rode out to the palace by night disguised as a pope, an emperor, cardinals, knights and African or Eastern ambassadors. Once arrived they dismounted and carried three precious gifts into the hall, like the Magi—a bowl, a cup and a ring of gold—all intended for the King, and several smaller ones for his mother and other members of his family. They said nothing; but after dancing in the hall they used loaded dice to ensure that the gifts would pass into the young king's hands. Indeed, the significance of this gesture, quite apart from the pleasure this surprise visitation must have occasioned, is patently obvious from the nature of the disguises chosen and the gifts offered when associated with the calendar feast in question.

Comparison may be made of this dumb mumming with another some fifty years later devised by John Lydgate to assist the Mercers' Company to entertain their own most distinguished brother, the Mayor of London. This mumming is specifically stated to have been prepared for Twelfth Night and is equipped with a long, introductory speech spoken by a presenter disguised as a herald which serves to usher three ships into the hall with merchants from the East aboard them.[4] Lydgate then allegorizes this visual spectacle by combining the idea of the visit of the Magi with the miraculous draught of fishes to enhance the actual presentation by the mummers of their gifts to their mayor.

In one sense both of these mummings should properly be regarded as celebrations of the same calendar feast, Epiphany, and tied, by reflection of the oblations of the Magi in the gifts presented respectively to King Richard II and Mayor Eastfield, to that liturgical festival. Yet both the environment—streets and hall—and the descriptive tone of both mummings place them just as firmly within a context of social revelry where religious meditation is clearly secondary to popular recreation in dancing, dicing, charade and carousal.

This delicate balance is preserved in at least one other Christmas mumming which Lydgate prepared for the young King Henry VI when spending Christmas at Eltham.[5] This allegorizes the presentation of gifts of wine, wheat and oil in terms of Bacchus, Ceres and Juno. In four other entertainments, however, described variously by Lydgate

---

*See Ch. V, p. 123 below.

as mummings or disguisings, the liturgical festival provides little more than an excuse for secular revels; and in one more, the mumming on May Day at Bishopswood, even this link is cut.

At Bishopswood the Sheriffs of London were visited by Flora, Ver and the Lady of May: the entertainment thus exists to celebrate the occasion and does so very prettily.[6] The verse is lyrical, dwelling largely on flowers, song-birds and the verdant wood, and is didactic only in so far as it contrasts 'noblesse' and 'rightwysnesse' in civil government with the sweetness of spring, and the 'derknesse of al extorcyoune' among rulers with the 'hevynesse and trouble' of winter: and no one wants more than that when relaxing at a *fête champêtre*.

The Goldsmiths' mumming was prepared for 'Candelmasse day at nyght, after souper' (2 February); another, for 'the great estates of this lande, thane being at London', lacks a date; but, as it concerns Dame Fortune herself, it seems likely to have been prepared for 1 January.[7] The *Mumming at Hertford*, with its argument about the balance of 'maistry' between husbands and wives, looks likewise to have been prepared as a New Year entertainment for the King: this is discussed at length in Chapter VIII under comedy.* Suffice it to say here, therefore, that this mumming exists purely to entertain: it does little or nothing to tie the subject-matter specifically to the occasion celebrated, and could as easily have been presented for recreational purposes on any other holiday in the year. The same may be said of the mumming at Windsor which, apart from its educational motive in supplying the young king with an explanation of the French blazon in his coat-of-arms, exists simply to pass time agreeably.†

Two French entertainments of substantially earlier date need to be taken into account in this context. The first was given by King Charles V of France for his uncle, the Emperor Charles IV, at dinner on 6 January 1377–8 and depicted Geoffrey of Boulogne's 'Conquest of Jerusalem' in 1099. The date is Twelfth Night, Epiphany; but this entertainment, instead of allegorizing gift-giving in terms of the Magi's gifts to Christ, concentrates, like the play of Anti-Christ at Tegernsee 200 years earlier, on the idea of a crusade. As L. H. Loomis has demonstrated, the French *entremet* is just as politically slanted to the same end as its German predecessor. Writing about its author, Philippe de Mezières, she says: 'Such an excursion into secular history, divorced from all religious legend, was a bold innovation. ... '[8] If it was not as innovatory as Mrs Loomis appears to think, since she neglects to cite the Tegernsee *Anti-Christus*,‡ she is correct in asking

*See pp. 194–5 below.
†See *EES*.i.205–6.
‡See pp. 46–7 above.

her readers to reflect on the links between subject-matter and occasion of performance provided in this instance, and thus in inviting us to regard this *entremet* as an *exemplum* to be imitated in the form of a new crusade.

Eleven years later King Charles VI of France married Isabella of Bavaria and entertained her at dinner with an *entremet* depicting the siege of Troy.[9] I have failed to decipher any particular connection between choice of this subject and the occasion in question; but this choice shares with that of 'The Conquest of Jerusalem' a common interest in secular history as a legitimate topic for drama, and suggests that from this time forward modern history is likely to be allegorized along with scripture and legend as a mirror for magistrates. The idea of deploying analogue mimetically for political and social rather than strictly religious purposes conforms nevertheless with Roman Catholic doctrine in respect of history, which was grounded on the notion of 'recurrence' *sub specie aeternitatis*, in sharp contrast to later Protestant insistence upon 'remembrance' and, with it, a determination both to separate fact from fiction and to order events if not exactly chronologically, then cyclically; and for so long as Christian Europe was content to accept papal insistence upon the real presence within the Eucharist every time Mass was celebrated anywhere within Christendom, this could scarcely be otherwise.[10]

In England, Lydgate took these ideas out of the courtly environment of the banquet hall and deployed them before popular and largely illiterate audiences in London and provincial streets. This he did in his reception for Henry VI on his return to London from his coronation in France in 1432.* He chose as his device the Jesse Tree, familiar to all and sundry in countless stained-glass windows.† Two such trees were supplied: the first, springing from St Louis of France and from St Edward the Confessor, supported, at the top, Henry VI himself; the second sprang from Jesse and supported Jesus in its topmost branches.[11] Pictorially, Lydgate thus contrived not only to establish the legitimacy of Henry's claims to both kingdoms in mortal terms of reference, but also to show that they were no less divinely ordered and blessed than Christ's claim to be God's only begotten Son. (See *EES*.i, Plate XVI.)

Although no character from 'modern' history appeared in the London pageants which Lydgate prepared thirteen years later to welcome the King's bride, Margaret of Anjou, Fabyan states in his chronicle that they represented 'resemblaunce of dyverse olde hystoryes', and there is good reason to believe that the texts were

*See *EES*.i.62–3, 75–8 and 90–1.
†See *EES*.i, Plate XVI

51

devised as political propaganda for peace and, with it, an end to the
Hundred Years War.[12] When Margaret, evidently pregnant, journeyed
to Coventry in 1456, John Wedbury related his pageant-welcome just
as firmly to topical circumstance.[13] Like Lydgate he included Edward
the Confessor among his dramatis personae, making him address the
Queen in *oratio recta*. 'I, King Edward, welcu(me) you w(i)t(h)
affeccion right cordial ... ' Isaiah and Jeremiah prophesy that her
child will be a blessing to the whole nation. Here Wedbury copies
Lydgate in linking topical event with the Will of Heaven: he does so
by placing the Queen's pregnancy within the context of the familiar,
liturgical *Ordo Prophetarum*,* thus linking the anticipated birth of her
child to the saving grace of Christ's nativity. Coventry also presented
her with a show of the Nine Worthies; but the city had in fact been
anticipated in this respect by the Parisians in 1431 who had not only
presented them to Henry VI, but also greeted him with a show of their
female counterparts.[14]

Bristol offered William the Conqueror to Edward IV in 1461;
Coventry, 'Kyng Richard w(i)t(h) xiij other arrayed lyke as Dukes(,)
Mark'es(,) Erles(,) Viscounts and Barons and lordis ...' to Prince
Edward in 1474; and both York and Bristol their legendary founders,
King Ebrauc and King Bremius, to Henry VII in 1486.† In the course
of the fifteenth century, therefore, it was thus becoming as customary
in the provinces as in London to mix recognizable characters from
modern English history with both biblical characters and the abstract
personifications of appropriate virtues and vices in civic pageants,
and to allegorize one in terms of the other in order to emphasize the
significance of the occasion to ruler and citizens alike.

This process accelerated during the sixteenth century until at the
coronation of Elizabeth I in 1558 we find the Wars of the Roses
presented in a pageant entitled 'The uniting of the two howses of
Lancastre and Yorke' some thirty years before Shakespeare turned
his attention to the depiction of 'York and Lancaster's long jars'.[15]

An especially interesting Tudor example is the welcome accorded
to the Emperor Charles V in London in June 1522, since this enables
us to catch a brief glimpse of the sort of men employed to prepare such
festivities. On this occasion they included Sir Thomas More, John
Rastell, William Lyly and Garter King at Arms.[16] Both Henry VIII
and his nephew, the Emperor, appeared in two of the pageants, as did
many of their ancestors. Classical mythology was also tapped on this
occasion for a pageant of Jason and the Golden Fleece, an obvious

*See pp. 34 and 39–40 above.
†See *EES*.i.71 ff.

compliment to the Emperor and the Burgundian Chivalric Order of Toison d'Or. This innovation appears to have met with approval since, eleven years later, when Anne Boleyn passed through the city to her coronation she was greeted almost exclusively by classical deities.[17] In Fenchurch Street she met with Apollo and the Nine Muses seated on Mount Parnassus: the Three Graces confronted her at Leadenhall: and in Cheapside she was treated to a re-enactment of 'The Judgment of Paris', but with a surprising and flattering new conclusion. When Paris was on the point of giving the ball of gold to Venus he caught sight of the approaching Queen and gave it to her instead.* This idea was destined to be taken up again fifty years later when George Peele adapted it to fit Anne's daughter, Elizabeth I, in *The Arraignment of Paris*, but this time in a full-blown stage play.

With Edward VI's coronation in 1547 the rising tide of Protestantism brought a reaction against things Roman and Italian, and with it a reversion to the heavy-handed moralizing of earlier times; this is as evident in civic pageantry as it is in the interludes of that time.† Nevertheless the habit of dramatizing the occasion itself remains intact: if the event is such as to warrant celebration, then the aim must be to figure that event in verbal and visual images which will give concrete form to the ideas that it embodies; and that this could best be done theatrically is made abundantly evident by the repetition of the same devices, dressed in varied guises, in city after city, century by century, from late in the fourteenth until well into the seventeenth. As Robert Withington shrewdly noted in *English Pageantry*,[18]

'Certain blanks are filled with new names, as the years pass; but the formulae remain pretty nearly the same. The station, rather than the individual, is of importance—while the crowds in the streets, unchanging from age to age, give these "triumphs" the continuity of an institution. Kings, queens, archbishops, and mayors may come and go; but the companies and the citizens are always there to greet their successors.'

It is that last sentence to which I would wish to call attention; for in my view it is the idea of life in succession, as opposed to disturbance and death through the lack of it, which is common to all these celebrations and which caused them to take the form they did. No matter how cunning the machinery employed to operate these devices, or how sophisticated the allegorizing of the Bible, of Christian ethics, or of legendary and modern history into dramatic *tableaux vivants*,

*See *EES*.i.80–1 and 90–1.
†See *EES*.ii.(1), Ch. I.

all these ceremonies serve primarily to ornament a folk-ritual that at heart is concerned with survival, and thus with tomorrow rather than today.

Another institution related to processional pageantry was the royal progress. Initiated by Henry VII to bolster his still contested claim to the throne, it developed sluggishly and did not really come into its own until late in the sixteenth century when poets were quick to seize on the opportunity it offered to focus the sovereign's attention directly upon their own abilities as purveyors of occasional 'entertainments'. Whether by chance, or by design, Elizabeth I made the first of many such excursions among her subjects to the universities of Cambridge and Oxford and to the Inns of Court. In each instance the visit was marked by the presentation of a play. The choice at Cambridge in 1564 was a revival of Plautus' *Aulularia* presented in King's College Chapel.*

At Oxford, two years later, two new plays—*Damon and Pithias* and *Palamon and Arcite*—both by Richard Edwards, were presented in the hall at Christ Church.† In 1567–8 the play given at the Inner Temple was *Gismond of Salerne* which was addressed more particularly to Elizabeth's maids of honour than to the Queen herself.‡ The production of a play was an obvious enough way of celebrating a royal visit within these academic centres since all the facilities needed in terms of play-makers, actors, stage and auditorium were already to hand. It was a far less obvious method in the context of midsummer visitations to country estates; yet the owners had both to ensure that the Queen was not bored, and that she was duly impressed with their own sense of the honour bestowed on them by her, and of their devotion to her, no matter how much the visit cost them personally. And here the knowledge of her own predilection for plays must have affected their choice of entertainment. Precedent was set in 1575 when the Queen visited the Earl of Leicester at Kenilworth, and where George Gascoigne's imaginative improvisations in dialogue on the local environment, ennobled by the Queen's temporary presence, provided successors (including John Lyly and Ben Jonson) with a theatrical form ideally suited to this kind of occasion.

One key ingredient of the recipe supplied by Gascoigne was surprise; another was the allegorizing of the local topography into pastoral personages; a third was the transfiguration of the landscape by the Queen's presence; and a fourth was a tangible token of gratitude in the form of appropriate gifts. The entertainment thus borrowed

*See *EES*.i.248 f.
†See *EES*.i.250–1.
‡See pp. 248–51 below.

something from both civic pageantry and mummings; but it added a new dimension of its own, the arcadian welcome. Pools, woods, streams and boscages were peopled with nymphs, satyrs and the wild men of the folk, and gave convenient cover for hidden choirs of naiads and dryads. At Kenilworth, Gascoigne placed Sibilla in an arbor, disguised the castle gatekeeper as Hercules, and made the Lady of the Lake appear to glide from a pool adjacent to it. While in residence the Queen encountered gods and goddesses, tritons and wildmen and, on her departure, Gascoigne himself disguised as Sylvanus.[19]

Later that year the Queen visited Woodstock where her host, Sir Henry Lee, prepared an entertainment of *Hemetes the Heremyte* for her, in the course of which she was visited by 'the Queen of Fayry drawen with 6 children in a waggon of state' who gave her a new gown. That this entertainment was highly topical and created both for and out of the occasion cannot be doubted since the author, George Gascoigne, is described as having shown[20]

'great proofe of his audacity, in which tale if you marke the woords with this present world, or were acquainted with the state of the devises, you should finde no lesse hidden then uttered, and no lesse uttered then shoulde deserve a double reading over ... '

Three years later the Queen was at Wanstead on May Day 1579 where she was entertained with Sir Philip Sidney's *The Lady of May.** There she met shepherds, foresters and the Lady May herself. Again music figured prominently in the entertainment.[21]

What, therefore, all these entertainments and those which succeeded them served to do was to open up country life, just as civic pageantry had opened up modern history, as legitimate territory for the playmaker. None of the interludes that survive from before the opening of the Theater and the first Blackfriars in 1576 employs pastoral settings and characters in this way; but thereafter they begin to make their appearance in romantic comedy and thus to supply Peele, Nashe, Greene, Shakespeare and Jonson in the following decades with a new storehouse of material with which to surprise and delight their audiences in public and private playhouses alike, and greatly to enrich the texture of their plays.†

If royal progresses provided enterprising poets with new opportunities to dramatize these visitations, civic pride was no less vigorously engaged during the sixteenth century in turning drama, or at least

---

*She was also there 13–16 May 1578, and this entertainment may have been presented then; but it would have been less appropriate on that occasion than on May Day itself.

† On George Peele's *The Arraignment of Paris*, see p. 53 above.

theatricality, to its own uses. In London the principal opportunities for this dramatizing of occasion were provided by the annual Mid-summer Watch and the election of new masters and wardens to the headship of the livery companies:* from 1535 onwards another was added in the show that marked the taking up of office by a new lord mayor and sheriffs on the day following that of SS. Simon and Jude (28 October) each year. The Midsummer Watch, however, appears to have been dropped by 1546, probably in deference to Protestant sentiment, since attempts to revive it proved unsuccessful. The last of them was in 1558; but by then the pageantry formerly associated with it had been transferred to the Lord Mayor's Show.[22]

At the livery company feasts, the Drapers' Company regularly paid professional players to entertain them until about 1540. Thus in 1515 the Drapers paid 'xiij^s iiij^{d}' 'to John Slye and his company for ij plays. Monday and Tuysday', and in the following year 'xv^s viij^d to the King(e)s players for monday and tuysday for ij plays'.[23] The Goldsmiths and the Merchant Taylors also employed players, including the choirboys of St Paul's and Merchant Taylors' School, but not on a regular basis.[24] Other companies to engage players in-cluded the Armourers', the Bakers', the Carpenters', and the Weavers'; and some companies hired out their halls to players.† At the Reforma-tion, however, the companies seem to have been persuaded that the Mayor and Sheriffs could hardly conduct a campaign against actors who used taverns and other places of public assembly in the city for performances of stage-plays—a campaign which started in earnest c. 1545—and welcome them at the same time into their own halls. No certainty can attach to whether the plays performed in those circum-stances were specially written to celebrate the occasion in question since not even the title, let alone a text of a play, has survived which is known to have been performed to mark such festivities.[25] I suspect myself that the professional companies, called on to perform for reward, offered only stock plays from their standard repertoire with, at best, a few lines added or adapted in the manner proposed by Hamlet to the players from Wittenberg in respect of *The Murder of Gonzago* to give that performance a topical flavour, or in that actually used by the authors of *Gismond of Salerne* to compliment Elizabeth I when she attended the play at the Inner Temple in 1567–8.‡

A further reason supporting this argument lies in the readiness with which the Companies seem to have complied with the dropping of plays by professional actors to celebrate their feasts, since this suggests

* On the Midsummer Watch see Ch. I, pp. 18–19 above.
† See *EES*.ii.(1).185–6 and Plate VII.
‡ See Ch. IX, n. 41, p. 307 below.

that the plays performed, amusing though they may have been, were not organically related in a topical sense either to the membership or to the life-style of the Companies who paid the actors. Very different was their attitude, by marked contrast, to the Midsummer Watch and the subsequent Lord Mayor's Show in both of which the vested interests of the participating Companies were carefully nurtured and flamboyantly displayed. Professional authors were hired to compose the speeches and professional craftsmen were engaged to design and construct the pageants and costumes; but as both tasks were put out to tender and the final choice was made by the officers, a major criterion of success incumbent upon competitors continued to be the appropriateness of the devices submitted to the occasion.* Thus, in 1561, the Merchant Taylors' Company honoured their Master, Sir William Harper, on his election as Lord Mayor by agreeing 'w(i)th John Shutte That he shall make for this company ageynst the feaste of S. & Jude next a pageant accordying to suche a patterne as shalbe Devised to answer the speches also [here] devised'. The speeches have survived: all are given to famous 'harpers' of antiquity— David, Orpheus, Amphion, Orion and Topas. They conclude with the lines

> Wherefore reioyce ye londoners
> and hope well of yo(u)r mayre
> ffor nev(er) did a mylder man
> sitt in yo(ur) chiefest chaire.

Five years later it was the Ironmongers' turn, and they selected George Peele's father, James: 'Also it is agreed that Mr. Pele shall have xxx^s paid him for the devising of the pageant besides the mony w(hi)ch he hath disburside.' In 1568 when the Lord Mayor elect was again a Merchant Taylor, Richard Mulcaster was commissioned to devise not only the verses but the scenic illustration of them and was paid the large sum of £10 13s. 4d. to that end.[26] Certain features, moreover, were strictly traditional such as the giants, the King of Moors and his morians (replaced later by wildmen or greenmen with clubs and firecrackers) and heraldic beasts and the city waits:[27] these have the mark of folk-custom stamped upon them, and only morris-dancing appears to have been killed off by the Reformation. That loss, however, was more than compensated for by the steady growth in the number and complexity of the pageants, and by the calibre of the professional play-makers called upon to devise them. They thus come to occupy the same status and function in the life of the City as the New Year and Shrovetide masques in that of the Court. This competitive feature

*See EES.i. 51–111 and ii (1). 206–44.

does not begin in earnest until the accession of James I, but the seeds of it had been sown at least two decades earlier.[28] Its importance lies in the fact that despite the progress of professional acting on a regular, weekday basis from 1574 onwards, the tradition of dramatizing occasion took on a new lease of life at both popular and courtly levels, thus obliging the most successful and sought-after authors to acquire the necessary skills to work in both genres rather than to prefer one and let the other die.[29]

Where the corresponding festivities of the Court are concerned, it is a sad fact that between the lavish disguisings presented to Prince Arthur and Catherine of Aragon to celebrate their wedding in 1501* and the death of Elizabeth in 1603 no complete text of any such Court entertainment has survived.† That disguisings (later known as masques) were very popular is clear enough from such household accounts as have survived, from chronicles, diaries and letters, and from ambassadors' reports to their governments; but lavish as the costumes and scenic items listed in the Privy Purse, Controller's and Revels Accounts may be, and full as eye-witness descriptions sometimes are, it is a hazardous occupation indeed to try to determine from this information alone how pertinent the subject-matter of any of these many masques was to the occasion celebrated.

According to the chronicle of Edward Hall, the first entertainment to be presented at the English Court and described as a masque formed part of the Twelfth Night revels, 1511; but what interested Hall was the innovation of male masquers choosing female dancing partners from the ranks of the spectators and the Venetian cloaks worn by the former, not the story nor its emblematic significance, if any.‡ Still more daringly, this situation was reversed in 1532 when Anne Boleyn led her ladies out to pick their own partners from the men in the auditorium; but again Hall, in his description of the event, fails to dwell on the nature of the text. At Epiphany 1559, we catch a glimpse of the allegorical quality of that masque from the Venetian ambassador's disapproving description of 'the mummery performed after supper ... of crows in the habits of Cardinals, of asses habited as Bishops, and of wolves representing Abbots'.[30]

Thereafter, eight more masques were given during the year: two to mark the coronation in January, two at Shrovetide, and four during the summer, of which two were presented in London and two on progress in the country. Conquerors and Moors were the primary figures in the coronation masques; Hungarians, Almayns and Swart

*See *EES*.i.224–5.
†For an exception see p. 59 above and n. 32, pp. 278–9; also Appendix D below.
‡See *EES*.i.218.

Rutters appeared in the first of the Shrovetide masques (in the course of which the Queen's maids of honour seem to have been besieged and then rescued); market wives and fisher wives appeared in the second. Astronomers greeted the Constable of France on 24 May in the first of the summer masques; shipmen and country maids greeted the Queen in the second of the provincial masques at the home of the Lord Admiral; no details of settings or costumes survive in respect of the other London and provincial masques.[31]

The pattern established in this first year of Elizabeth's reign was, broadly speaking, repeated throughout the next decade, with weddings and visits from foreigners providing the occasions for masques over and above those given in the Christmas and Shrovetide holidays. Several of them were directly linked with tilts and jousts.

The year 1572 brings us tantalizingly close to a complete under-standing of the Elizabethan masque. The double wedding of the son and daughter of Lord Montague to those of Sir William Dormer was marked by a masque of Venetians, with introductory and concluding speeches for the presenter by George Gascoigne which have survived.[32] Another wedding, that of Sir Henry Unton, provides us with a pictorial illustration of a masque in progress in a country house.* The proposed meeting between Elizabeth I and Mary Queen of Scots at Nottingham provided Secretary Cecil's draft of the devices for three consecutive masques cited in Chapter IV, p. 81 below.† From these three separate items a composite, if generalized, picture emerges of an entertainment surprisingly similar to Lydgate's mummings and disguisings of the 1420s in its shape and content, with due allowance made for the change of fashion in the choice of dancing partners, and the more extra-vagantly luxurious provision made through the Revels Office for its spectacular aspects.

Topicality would still appear to have been a prime requirement, equalled only by the continued excuse for dancing that this form of entertainment existed to provide. An element of surprise in the shape of friends disguised in exotic costumes, together with a presenter equipped with speeches to relate the deviser's choice of costumed characters to the occasion celebrated, appears also to have been mandatory. Torchbearers and musicians were no less obligatory and had to be integrated with both the entry of the masquers and the subsequent dancing. The Queen, when present, participated either as principal spectator or as a dancer, but, unlike her father, never as a performer if the records speak truth.[33] Gifts continue to figure pro-

*See *EES*.ii(1), Plate V, No. 6.
†See also Appendix D.

minently in the New Year and Twelfth Night masques and almost invariably in those accompanying the progresses, while copies of the introductory speeches were frequently presented by the masquers to the Queen.

During the 1580s masques became less frequent, possibly on account of Elizabeth's own instinct for thrift, but more probably on account of the steadily mounting threats of war and rumours of plots aimed at the Queen's life. Whatever the reason, such details of those masques that were given throw no further light on the form or content of these lively, choreographic entertainments during her reign.

One startling feature of dramatic festivities in the latter half of the Tudor era remains to be considered: the rapid decline of creative initiative in the provinces. Something has already been said about the suppression of public holidays in honour of local saints and of the Feast of Corpus Christi in consequence of the Reformation.* To this must now be added a brief comment on its effects. Paramount among them was the loss of a *raison d'être* for most local plays, scripted, rehearsed, mounted and performed by and for the local community. Chester, Coventry, Wakefield, York and some other larger cities defied the Corpus Christi injunction issued from London, at least until the 1570s; but the majority of towns possessed of a cycle complied, especially in southern counties, with Cornwall excepted. Saint plays disappeared swiftly and completely.† Moral interludes supplied by professional actors replaced the longer moralities of local amateurs. As this paralysing blight settled on country districts, so local practitioners with centuries of local expertise in play-making, acting, and production techniques behind them were trapped into having either to abandon these pleasurable and dignified social pursuits, or else to transfer to London, on a full-time professional and commercial basis, taking their skills with them. This is something of an overstatement, since the process by which this change took place in English society between the 1530s and the 1580s was slower and more piecemeal than that form of words may suggest. Yet the provincial records, which local archivists and the Malone Society have between them done so much in recent years to make available for inspection, reveal quite plainly both how steady and how real the decline in local theatrical activity actually was during the five decades in question. Superficially it may appear to have been rather less severe in terms of the total number of payments made to players year by year from

*See also p. 183 below. It is relevant to add that even today where we in England have eight public holidays a year, Italy and Spain still have sixteen and seventeen respectively.

†See pp. 216–17 below.

municipal or parish funds; but the shift to items recording monies received from the sale of costumes, properties and pageant houses, and of payments made to visiting professionals is unmistakable.[34] Occasionally a local schoolmaster or histrionically-minded artisan makes a brave attempt to stem the flowing tide and make yesterday return. The Queen's progresses helped to keep this flame burning and to preserve the memory of celebrating a special occasion in terms of a play as a mirror image of earnest as the visits to Bristol, Worcester and Norwich bear witness;[35] but these opportunities were rare, and the attempts proved ineffectual, leaving only the residual folk-customs associated with the agricultural year as pale shadows of the epic dramas and memorable theatrical occasions that formerly had been the common heritage of the whole nation—'bare, ruined choirs/where late the sweet birds sang'.

Before this collapse occurred, however, non-recurrent festivals, both in the provinces and in the capital, had contributed substantially to the growth and variety of dramatic experience in England. Lacking the repetitive quality of Christian calendar feasts which, between the tenth century and the sixteenth, served to establish the association of drama with occasion as a habit of mind, they nevertheless made their own contribution to this situation precisely by being exceptional and thus deserving of special celebration in ways that brought together the leaders of society and the communities they served or represented within a common understanding of the event and of its significance to them all.

What the collective evidence of the surviving texts and eye-witness accounts of all such drama, recurrent and non-recurrent, described in the preceding chapters reveals is that the prime requirement imposed upon those responsible for inventing and organizing these mimetic spectacles was to find a device (or devices) that accurately reflected the occasion, both in pictures (stage images) and in words (speeches or dialogue), and that was thus intelligible—at least in essentials—to everyone who had been released from the normal restrictions and tensions of daily work to witness these events and to participate in the celebration of them. These devices must thus be our next concern.

BOOK TWO

Emblems of Occasion

IV

PLAY-MAKERS AND DEVICE

W HEN the vivid and fruitful partnership between Ben Jonson and Inigo Jones that began with the creation of *The Masque of Blackness* in 1604 broke up some twenty years later following the performance and publication of *The Masque of Augurs*, the eye of the storm lay in the poet's and the painter's respective claims to control 'the device' on which both text and scenic realization of it were ultimately based.* This dispute was by no means a new one, nor particular to Jonson and Jones although in their case it was both more acrimonious and more serious in its consequences than it had ever been before. John Lyly, indeed, had put it to use as early as 1598 to provide the framework for his *Entertainment at Mitcham*.[1] There a poet and a painter dispute not only the superiority of their respective arts in terms of what each can depict without the assistance of the other, but which of them derives most from the other. It is a line of argument which Lyly received from Petrarch and which Petrarch in turn derived from Horace. It is an argument, moreover, that Shakespeare deployed to open *Timon of Athens* when making his Painter discuss the depiction of Fortune with his Poet.

> *Painter* A thousand moral paintings I can show,
> That shall demónstrate these quick blows of Fortune's
> More pregnantly than words.
>
> (I.i.93–5)

What then was a 'device' that responsibility for its 'invention' should have occasioned such serious contention and debate?

Defined in the *Oxford English Dictionary* as 'an emblematic figure or design, *esp.* one borne by a particular person etc., as a heraldic bearing, etc.: usually accompanied by a motto', the word possessed several Tudor and medieval synonyms, or near equivalents, of which the commonest were 'impresa', 'insignia', 'emblem' and 'ensign':[2] when

*See *EES*.ii(1).245–75.

Thomas Dekker wrote about 'speaking pictures' and 'dumb poesie' in the context of the pageants being prepared for James I's triumphal entry into London, he too was assuming that his readers were acquainted with 'device'.* So did Ben Jonson. Describing his own contribution to the pageants in *Part of King James's Entertainment*, he says:

'The nature and property of these devices being, to present always some one entire body, or figure, consisting of distinct members, and each of those expressing itself in its own active sphere, yet all with that general harmony so connexed, and disposed, as no one little part can be missing to the illustration of the whole: where also is to be noted, that the symbols used are not, neither ought to be, simply hieroglyphics, emblems or impresses, but a mixed character, partaking somewhat of all, and peculiarly apted to these more magnificent inventions: wherein the garments and ensigns deliver the nature of the person, and the word the present office.'

A fuller and more accurate definition of 'device' would be hard to find. Take the phrase 'and peculiarly apted to these more magnificent inventions' away, and what is left still provides an excellent description of what those whom he goes on to describe as 'the sharp and learned' expected of a good stage-play. The concept is a difficult one to define precisely in words, largely because the visual element formed so crucial a part of it. Moreover, it incorporated a striking paradox; for while the visual component was designed to arrest attention and boldly to proclaim an idea, the form in which it was cast was as often designed, like a riddle, to contain a secret. Thus a device could at once be highly personal and at the same time, depending on the individual, socially or politically significant: seals and signet rings offer obvious examples.† Livery and heraldic blazon extend this idea not only to the whole outward appearance of the individual, but to his entire household, or fraternity of fellow-craftsmen. It could be stretched to incorporate a written text—a 'scripture', a motto, a poem—of an explanatory character: but to be truly itself a device had to be something more (even other) than it seemed to be, and to be fully possessed of its meaning viewer or reader had to own, or be supplied with, the key that alone would release the secret and reveal its full significance.‡ By this means, in real life, a lover could declare his identity to the beloved as 'her servant'—using her livery colours, her special flower, her badge—while still leaving everyone unfamiliar with this

*See *EES*.i. 82 and 102. For a very early use of the word see Ch. I, p. 15 above.

†The famous Essex ring provides a notorious Elizabethan example.

‡For such use of 'device' in civic pageantry and mummings in the fifteenth century, see *EES*.i.102–3. See Plate XII.

combination of colours and objects in ignorance of his intentions;[3] and in the world of the theatre, it is knowledge of this fact that supplies Maria, Sir Toby Belch and Fabian with the means to revenge themselves upon Malvolio in *Twelfth Night* by persuading him to parade in yellow stockings, cross-gartered, in front of Olivia. It is in this sense of something concealed from the immediate view of the undiscerning that Lawrence Humphrey employs the word 'device' in his description of George Gascoigne's *Hemetes the Heremyte*, quoted in the preceding chapter, when remarking, 'If you ... were acquainted with the state of the devises, you should finde no less hidden then uttered ... '.[4] Onwards from 1531, when Andreas Alciatus published his *Emblematum Liber*, English interest in the artistic uses of 'devices' burgeoned rapidly; for devices, as presented within its pages, incorporated several, particular visual emblems, so chosen and interrelated as to comprise a composite allegorical picture, accompanied by an expositional poem.[5] The component pictures might represent familiar objects, persons or even scenes, and were normally framed by an appropriately decorated border not unlike a proscenium arch: the poem beneath served to comment on the individual, visual emblems, to expound the allegory, and thus to supply the key to the composite pictorial riddle.

Within its widest embrace the concept of 'device' comes thus to incorporate allegory, parable, typology, analogue and paradigm, as well as costumes, animals, precious stones and other objects; and in this guise it is of special value to the author of stage-plays, masques and pageants, for he, like the painter, is catering for a public who have eyes in their heads as well as ears; yet, like the poet, he is also feeding his audience with a succession of verbal images, metaphors and similes, as well as visual ones. The play-maker, moreover, enjoys the advantage of being able to juxtapose, and to contrast or complement, his verbal with his visual images since he is dealing with actions, and thus with events in motion. And therein lies the vital difference between 'game' and 'earnest' as articulated in miracle cycles, moralities and interludes; for there, 'earnest' is deemed to be physical and spiritual actuality (as revealed by God and perceived by the play-maker) while 'play' or 'game' is the 'device' that he has selected as being best fitted to reflect it accurately in the make-believe action presented by actors on a stage. Skelton illustrates the point in *Magnyficence* by inverting it to characterize his principal vice, Counterfeit Countenance.

> 'To counterfeit I can by pretty ways:
> Of nightés to occupy counterfeit keys,
> Cleanly to counterfeit new arrays,

Counterfeit earnest by way of plays.'
(Stage 2, scene 8, ed. Henderson, ll. 22–5)

He makes the point again, and in its proper context, in his Epilogue.[6]

Magnyficence   This matter we have movéd, you mirthful to make,
Pressly* purposéd under pretence of play,
Showeth wisdom to them that wisdom can take,
How suddenly worldly wealth doth decay,
How wisdom through wantonness vanishes away.

(ed. cit., p. 244)

The author of *Jack Juggler* (*c.* 1555) proceeds more colloquially, but on the same assumption, when making the unfortunate Careaway respond to Jack's threats of violence by asking, 'But speak you all this in earnest, or in game?' and later, self-protectively,[7]

'For ought I se yet between earnest and game:
I must go seek me another name!'

The impact of a well-articulated device on spectators is vividly illuminated by R. Willis's recollection in his seventies of a play called *The Cradle of Security*, a typical moral interlude, which he had seen performed in Gloucester, *c.* 1570. After describing the plot which concerned a king brought to ruin after being ensnared by vices (masquerading as usual as his counsellors) Willis concludes,

'This Prince did personate in the morall, the wicked of the world; the three Ladies, Pride, Covetousnesse, and Luxury; the two old men, the end of the world and the last judgement. This sight tooke such impression in me, that when I came towards mans estate, it was as fresh in my memory, as if I had seen it newly acted.'

(*Mount Tabor, or Private Exercises of a Penitent Sinner*, London, 1639)†

The point at issue is that it was what he saw, not what he heard or read, that stamped the play's plot, characters and moral meaning so indelibly upon his mind that he could recall them clearly some fifty years later: and it is by the same token that Marlowe's Tamburlaine, Kyd's Old Hieronimo, and Shakespeare's Ophelia were to provide the next generation with archetypal images of pride, grief and pathos against which to measure and judge such emotions in others.

For Shakespeare and his contemporaries device remained the keystone of the dramatist's craft, though we need to recall that the word 'dramatist' was at that time still unknown in the English language:

pressly: expressly.

†Quoted in full by J.P. Collier, *History of English Dramatic Poetry*, 1831, Vol. II, pp. 274–5.

nor, when James I arrived in London in 1603, was it customary to regard the authors of plays presented on common stages as men of letters. This was a distinction reserved for writers of history, philosophy, poetry and theology. By the end of the reign, however, Ben Jonson, largely through his own efforts, had succeeded in changing that—a fact avouched as much by the publication of his own *Works* in 1616 and the Shakespeare First Folio in 1623 as by his own literary standing as poet laureate. From then onwards it became steadily more normal for the public to regard playwrights as men of letters, and for playwrights to take as much care to please a reading public at home as to make their scripts acceptable to actors and audiences in playhouses.

That some writers of plays in Elizabethan England aspired to be recognized as men of letters, at least by their patrons, is also true; but they, for the most part, were the writers of closet dramas who made no pretensions to win the sort of public acclaim that relied upon professional actors—still less the applause of men and women of 'grounded judgment'—but who sought rather to express their thoughts in a manner self-consciously imitative of Italian *commedia erudita*; these authors included university dons like William Gager and Thomas Legge, and patrician courtiers like Sir Fulke Greville and Edward De Vere, Earl of Oxford.

Another kind of writer for the stage existed, however, in Tudor England who succeeded the private chaplains and clerical tutors of medieval and early Tudor times, and who found themselves in charge of groups of boys and youths in schools, choir-schools and universities (including the Inns of Court) whose profession offered them a chance to see their own work performed by their pupils. As amateurs these writers could not only afford to experiment in ways that neither professional writers, nor individual poets isolated from contact with actors, could hope to do, but they could also be sure that no one would intervene between themselves and their texts to cut or mangle them in the supposed interest of the lowest denominator in the auditorium. Such men included John Heywood, Nicholas Udall, William Hunnis and John Lyly; as pace-setters, John Marston, Ben Jonson and the other writers for the boy-companies in the private playhouses were their direct heirs in Jacobean London.

These men were sometimes referred to as 'stage-poets' and sometimes as 'authors'. Richard Edwards described himself as the author in the Prologue to *Damon and Pithias*, as do both Udall (?) and Ulpian Fulwell in the Prologues to *Respublica* and *Like Will to Like:* but the normal designation for a dramatist who offered his plays for acting by professional companies was 'play-maker' or 'maker of enterludes'.

Writing on playbills in public playhouses *c.* 1583, Sir Philip Sidney remarked, 'Perchance it is the Comick, whom naughtie Play-makers and Stage-Keepers, have justly made odious.'[8] The anonymous author of *Jack Juggler* some thirty years earlier describes himself twice in his Prologue as 'this maker': and it is as 'makers of enterludes' that dramatists are usually referred to in edicts, proclamations and statutes emanating from Westminster or city councils. George Walpull in *The Tyde Taryeth no Man* (1576) speaks of having 'some shew to make' (l. 1148): likewise the title-page of *Like Will to Like* (*c.* 1568) states that the play has been 'made by Ulpian Fulwell'.[9]

These designations clearly recognized that a play was an artefact, a combination of visual stage tableaux on the one hand and spoken dialogue on the other, that must either support and reinforce what the audience was observing with its eyes, or else undercut, or even contradict, these impressions verbally.*

A play-maker, or maker of interludes, working for a professional or quasi-professional company of actors in the late fifteenth century and in the sixteenth was therefore expected to possess both sufficient imaginative ability to externalize in sequences of visual and verbal images those abstract ideas and arguments that gave rise to the festive celebration of any special occasion, and sufficient technical skill to find a device that would serve to bring them into an harmonious conjunction, and thus mirror 'earnest', or ultimate reality, in terms of a mimetic 'game' or 'play'.† As the literal narrative or debate advanced horizontally, so to speak, in terms of story-line, so the moral argument, whether ethical, political or social, must advance vertically in terms of added, emblematic texture.

Lewis Wager in his Prologue to *The Life and Repentaunce of Marie Magdalene* (*c.* 1558) reminds his audience of one of these expectancies.[10]

> We desire no man in this poynt to be offended,
> In that vertues with vice we shall introduce;
> For in men and women they have depended:
> And therefore figuratively to speak, it is the use.

Some two years later William Wager addresses his audience in similar vein and reminds them of another.[11]

> Our title is *Inough is as good as a feast*,
> Which Rhethorically we shall amplyfye:
> So that it shall appeer bothe to moste and leaste
> That our meaning is but honestie.

The picture is conveniently completed by this couplet from the Prologue to *Respublica* (1553).[12]

*See pp. 73–4, 104 and 160–2 below, and *EES*.ii (1). 121–32.
†See Chapter VIII, pp. 196–200 below.

We, that are thactours, have ourselves dedicate
With some Christmas devise, your spirites to recreate.

In the process of formulating the device around which to construct a
play, fiction and fantasy can be as useful to the play-maker as fact;
the physical personification of abstract concepts as important as
human portraiture; graphic combat a prelude to verbal debate or
vice versa: to the play-maker all are equally valid as visual emblems,
explicable within the accompanying dialogue. Beyond this he can still
add an expositor, prologue or chorus, or frame his play within an
induction or a sequence of dumb-shows if he thinks it necessary to
supply his audiences with yet clearer signposts to the meaning of his
device—the signification that is 'earnest', or actuality, *sub specie
aeternitatis*. It is on these foundations that the fabric of the whole
emblematic tradition of medieval and Renaissance dramaturgy rests.
In our own times we have gone far towards recognizing once again
these fundamental differences that distinguish dramatic art from
literature; but we still have much to learn.

For the medieval play-makers and actors, 'device' formed the
starting-point of their scenarios, a concrete image or figure that
mirrored the ideas that were to be exhibited and portrayed in action
on the stage. The active nature of the 'play' or 'game' obliged them to
search for and select either a story or a developing argument that
would illustrate the ideas in question. Thus the author of *Jack Juggler*
states blandly in his Prologue that Plautus has provided the datum
point for his own play.[13]

> Wherefore this maker deliteth passinglie well
> Too folow his [i.e. Plautus'] arguments and to draw out the same,
> For to make at seasuns co(n) venient, pastims, mirth and game:
> As now he hath don this matter, nor worthe an oyster shel,
> Except percace it shall fortune too make you laugh well.
> And for that purpose oonlye this maker did it write.

Once he had his story or argument, the play-maker could then
activate it partly in terms of the dramatis personae or cast-list, and
partly in terms of the order of these characters' entrances and exits,
coupled with their deeds, words, or both in conjunction, when present
in the *platea*, 'place' or acting-area.* With these salient structural
foundations laid, the play-maker could proceed to elaborate his
'device' or 'invention' by specifying in his stage-directions the minimal
scenic items required to identify the locality of his action, the essential
items of clothing needed to distinguish one character visually from

---

*See Ch. V, pp. 85–6 and Ch. VII, pp. 162–7 below.

another, and the minimum number of actors needed to perform all the roles. With this done he could then proceed to amplify his device with a text and, if necessary, descriptive dumb-shows. A frame for the whole device could be supplied in the sentiments and apologies put into the mouth of an expositor, or prologue and epilogue. It is thus within this frame that the author of *Thersytes* (1537) alerts his audience in the Epilogue to the proverb that supplied him with his device:[14]

> Maysters, ye maye see by this playe in sighte
> That great barking dogges do not most byte.

The maker of *Respublica* is still more explicit:

> Oure meaning is—I say not, as by plaine storye,
> But as yt were in figure by an allegorye.
> (Prologue; EETS (1952))

This account covers only 'device' or 'invention', as applied to the stage at its simplest. Variety and complexity, with a corresponding enrichment of texture, grew naturally out of the stage's most important asset: the actor's ability to transform his outward appearance through disguise from one character into another. A man could thus not only play a woman's role, as in the earliest liturgical drama (where priests are required in the *Visitatio Sepulchri* to represent the three Maries), but by assuming virtues that he did not possess could deceive other characters and, catching them off their guard, cause them to betray themselves as Lucifer does Eve in the English cycles, or as the Vice does the protagonist in all moral interludes.* As Juventus warns the audience in *Lusty Juventus*, 'Credite not al thynges unto the outward shew' (*MSR*, l. 1132). Lewis Wager in *The Life and Repentaunce of Marie Magdalene* extends this image considerably by making his vice, Infidelity, inform the audience,[15]

> 'Beware of me, Infidelitie!
> Like as Faith is the roote of all goodnesse,
> So am I the head of all iniquitie,
> The well and spring of all wickednesse.

> Mary, syr, yet I convey my matters cleane!
> Like as I have a visour of vertue,

> So my impes, whiche unto my person do leane,
> The visour of honestie doth endue.'

This is a game that Shakespeare still delights to play when contrasting worldly behaviour and appearances with spiritual motivation and inner reality. As Hamlet observes,

*See Ch. VIII, pp. 197 ff. below.

> ''Tis not alone my inky cloak, good mother,
> Nor customary suits of solemn black,
> ....
> Together with all forms, moods, shapes of grief,
> That can denote me truly. These indeed seem,
> For they are actions that a man might play;
> But I have that within which passes show:
> These but the trappings and the suits of woe.'
>
> (I.ii.77–86)

or the Macbeths, immediately following Macbeth's instructions to the murderers to dispose of Banquo:

> *Lady Macbeth* Gentle my lord, sleek o'er your rugged looks;
> Be bright and jovial among your guests tonight.
> *Macbeth* So shall I, love; and so, I pray, be you.
> Let your remembrance apply to Banquo;
> Present him eminence, both with eye and tongue:
> Unsafe the while that we
> Must lave our honours in these flattering streams,
> And make our faces vizards to our hearts,
> Disguising what they are.
>
> (III.ii.27–35)

or King Lear:

> 'Let them anatomize Regan: see what breeds about her heart.'
>
> (III.vi.73)

Another and still more subtle variant offers itself to the play-maker through the opportunity which stage action provides of contrasting what the spectator is seeing with what he is hearing, thus making it possible to juxtapose visual images with verbal ones. At its simplest, this technique may be seen at work in the character of Herod in the miracle cycles where, crowned and sceptred, he boasts and blasphemes: the stage-direction *pompabit* exactly catches the double image of tyranny and absurdity incarnate. He is thus at once frightening and ridiculous; the more he brags in alliterative, bombastic verse, the more comic his behaviour becomes.* This game too was one which Elizabethan and Jacobean play-makers still delighted to play with their audiences. Thus, when Thomas Lupton describes his play *All For Money* (c. 1578) as 'a Moral and Pitiful Comedie' he is not being naïve, but literal: his theme is human greed; his hero is to be brought to ruin by greed; but the agents of this vice who accomplish this serious, not to say tragic, conclusion are not only entertaining in themselves,

*See Ch. II, p. 33 above, and Ch. VIII, pp. 175–6 below.

but also in their methods. Some ten years later Marlowe makes his Tamburlaine, after all his earthly conquests, wage war against heaven itself only to find that his erstwhile servant, death, is now his master; his former chariot is now his hearse; his own whip has become a spear aimed at his own heart.

> 'See, where my slave, the ugly monster Death,
> Shaking and quivering, pale and wan for fear,
> Stands aiming at me with his murdering dart,
> Who flies away at every glance I give,
> And, when I look away, comes stealing on!'
> (II *Tamburlaine* V.ii.67–71)

Combining the Petrarchan visual images of the Triumph of Jove with the Triumph of Death in a new vision of the old dance macabre, Marlowe here superimposes a text that alternates rhetorical threats with cringing fear to secure an ironic effect that fits the climactic moment of his dramatic epic.* I do not wish to suggest that Marlowe borrowed this image from the author of *The Pride of Life*; but I do wish to remark that the latter had already turned it to fine theatrical effect at least 150 years before Marlowe used it; for in that interlude we find the King of Life claiming to be immune from Death.[16] Warned by his queen that this is not so, yet confirmed in his own belief by his knights, Health and Strength, he boasts:

> '3e, þes be kni3tis of curteisye
> And doghti men of dede;
> Of Deth ne of his maistrie
> Ne have I no drede.'
> (ll. 259–62)

Thus assured, he sends his herald to challenge Death to a joust to prove the point (ll. 451–70). Unfortunately the latter half of the play is lost.†

In comic vein Jonson achieves the same kind of shock effect in *The Alchemist* when Sir Epicure Mammon arrives at Subtle's laboratory to claim his gold. On his first visit (Act II, scene 1) he had said to Surly,

> 'Come on, Sir. Now, you set your foot on shore
> In *novo orbe*; here's the rich Peru:
> And there within, sir, are the golden mines,
> Great Solomon's Ophir!'

On Face's entry, which starts Act II, scene 2, he asks,

---

*See Plate IX, No. 13.
†See *EES*.i, Frontispiece and Fig. 3, p. 32.

Mammon   Do we succeed? Is our day come? and holds it?
Face   The evening will set red, upon you sir;
             You have colour for it, crimson; the red ferment
             Has done his office. Three hours hence, prepare you
             To see projection.
Mammon   Pertinax, my Surly,
             Again, I say to thee, aloud: be rich.

On his third visit (Act IV, scene 5) when 'the red ferment has done his office' in earnest, the furnace explodes. As the smoke and soot subside, Mammon is left standing, no longer glittering in crimson silks and cloth of gold, but a blackened ruin barely able to speak. 'O my voluptuous mind! I am justly punished.'

No less effective is Jonson's handling, in association with Inigo Jones, of the volte-face in *The Masque of Queens* when the witches' invocation to Hecate that is the climax of the antimasque is answered by the scene-change in which the 'ugly hell, which flaming beneath, smoked unto the top of the roof . . . quite vanished . . . scarce suffering the memory of such a thing' only to be replaced by*

'a glorious and magnificent building figuring the House of Fame, in the top of which were discovered the twelve masquers [including Queen Anne] sitting upon a throne triumphal erected in form of a pyramid and circled with all store of light. From whom a person, by this time descended, in the furniture of Perseus, and expressing heroic and masculine virtue, began to speak.'

Most late Elizabethan and Jacobean plays are so richly textured with such variety of particular devices that it is difficult to unravel one from another and thus to return to the initial figures on which the play is built. However, a convenient example of the way in which device is used to underpin an entire play is offered by John Redford's *Wit and Science* (1530). The story-line is very simple, and, with its wooing and winning of a lady who has been saved from a monster, stands squarely between medieval romance and late Elizabethan romantic comedy.

Reason hopes his daughter, Science, will marry Dame Nature's son, Wit, once he has successfully completed his schooling. Wit sets out to win her, but is deflected, first by Tediousness and then by Idleness: Shame and Policy come to his rescue and enable him to woo and win his bride.

To dramatize this story Redford employs a device constructed from three principal 'figures'—the mock death and resurrection of the

The Yale Ben Jonson, ed. Stephen Orgel, 1969, pp. 123 and 134.

Mummers' Play, a startling change of name and clothes, and a public whipping—and four minor ones—a gown, a mirror, a miniature and a sword.

Equipped with a scholar's gown, the emblem of his quest, Science's portrait to encourage him, and a mirror in which to take the measure of his own progress, Wit sets out. This completes scene 1, as it were. The next scene or sequence of the scenario is lifted straight from the Mummers' Play. Wit meets the Giant Tediousness (who swears by Mahomet), fights with him and is left for dead, but is then revived by Honest Recreation, Comfort, Quickness and Strength (who swear by St George). Wit resumes his journey. The third scene involves Wit's meeting with Idleness (fresh from the tavern), his casting off of his academic gown, and a sequence of word-games that end with Wit being vested in a fool's cap and coat and having his face blacked. Translated thus into Ignorance, he meets Lady Science. The fourth scene exploits this change of identity, with Wit attempting to woo Science and she refusing to recognize him: the mirror then alerts him to what has happened. Punished for his folly by Shame with a whipping and given a sword by Confidence, Wit embarks on his second encounter with Giant Tediousness. This time he wins and is rewarded with a graduate's gown in which to plight his troth to Lady Science.

In this way Redford transforms his simple fable of 'a student's progress', notwithstanding a cast-list made up exclusively of abstract personifications, into a sequence of vivid and instantly recognizable visual images. The dramatic economy is exemplary: no expositor is needed; and the text, despite its necessarily didactic character, supports and forwards the action without digressions or loss of emotional tension. In short, it is a well-made comedy with a moral that succeeds in its objective of mixing profit with pleasure; or, in the language of its own time, an entertaining 'play' that mirrors the 'earnest' of academic life with great clarity.[17]

A no less skilful but much more sophisticated handling of device is illustrated in *Jack Juggler* (*c.* 1555).[18] Here the author is dealing with subject-matter so dangerous at the time of its first performance that it would expose him to charges of heresy and sedition if it were not carefully protected.* Like Redford's play, this too is written for boys to perform, and for an academically minded audience to see and hear. It was Professor C. M. Gayley who first noticed, some seventy years ago, that the play 'in spite of its avowed aesthetic intent . . . is a subtle attack upon the Roman Catholic Church'. I would go further and suggest that it is a satire specifically directed against the

---

*See *EES*.ii(1). 54–97; also p. 68 above and pp. 203–4 below.

spearhead of the Counter-Reformation, the newly founded Jesuit order and the casuistry in argument for which its members became a byword in Elizabethan and Jacobean England. To have attempted this, even within the relative privacy of a school, under the government of Mary I when St Ignatius Loyola was himself writing to Cardinal Pole asking him to supply English recruits for his Roman and German colleges to train as Jesuits, must have needed as much artistic self-confidence as courage;[19] and for the former the author trusted to his 'device'.

He pleads repeatedly in his lengthy Prologue that with Plautus as his model and Cicero to support his case his purpose is only to provide entertainment at Christmas. His plot, moreover—an anglicized and vulgarized adaptation of *Amphitruo*—supports this case. Jack Juggler, to pay off old scores with Jenkin Careaway, disguises himself as his rival's double, and then leads him into a series of encounters that provoke such a torrent of verbal abuse and physical beatings from his mistress, her maid and his master that he finally succumbs to believing that he cannot be himself: the situations could not be more absurd, nor the treatment of them, despite the perceptive characterization, more farcical. Yet Jack opens the play with a declaration of who he really is and what he intends to do.[20]

> 'I am called Jake Jugler of many an oon,
> And in fayth I woll playe a jugling cast a non.
> I woll cungere the moull,* and god before!
> Or elles leat me lese my name for ever more.'

In other words his 'game' is going to be to deceive in earnest, to juggle black into white, or lose his reputation if he fails. Spectators who suppose that he will lose have a shock in store for them. He wins, very convincingly and very amusingly; but then the Epilogue turns to the audience and remarks,

> ' ... this trifling enterlud th(a)t before you hath bine rehersed,
> May sygnifye some further meaning, if it be well serched.'

Further hints are then given on how to 'search' it. Jesuits are indeed jugglers, the casuistry of whose talk, backed by force and recourse to torture, will make normal men betray their friends and themselves into behaving in ways totally alien to their own nature and conscience.[21]

> 'Such is the fashyon of the worlde now a dayes,
> That the symple innosaintes are deluded,
> And a hundred thousand divers wayes

---

*moull : the devil; 3rd ed. 'mole'. Cf. *Hamlet*, ed. Dover Wilson, I. v. 162.

By suttle and craftye meanes shamefullie abused,
And by strenth, force, and vyolence oft tymes compelled
To belive and saye the moune is made of agrene chese
Or ells have great harme, and percace their life lese.'

Some fifteen years later the sentiments expressed within this stanza will be developed by Nathaniel Woodes in *The Conflict of Conscience* into an entire play that warrants description as a tragedy since it incorporates a heresy trial and the collapse of the defendant under torture.*

In the light of these two examples of the importance of device and its uses for Tudor play-makers, it is perhaps useful, by way of a final illustration, to take the case of an author who appears to have thought that moral zeal coupled with a modicum of literary skill was all that was needed to *make* a play: I refer to the writer of *King Darius* (*c*. 1565).[22] This piece seeks to compound a conventional morality with two biblical incidents and thereby to create a drama of anti-Catholic polemic. It fails dramatically and theatrically on all three counts because from start to finish it is a crashing bore. The morality takes the form of a debate between the vice, Iniquity, supported by his companions, Importunity and Partiality, and the virtue, Charity, supported by Equity and Constancy, which consistently disappoints in its repetitiveness and inconclusiveness. If the latter group can be said to survive this contest, it is because of their intolerable self-righteousness, Iniquity being much the more sympathetic character. Yet he too disappoints in his interminable threats to chastise his opponents which never materialize. The victory accorded to Charity (alias hospitality in the Darius story), Equity (alias impartiality) and Constancy (alias faithful service) is a pyrrhic one. King Darius likewise and all his Court, including the foreign rulers whom he befriends and Zorobabell, the loyal counsellor and the victor in the next disputation, are cardboard figures lacking all semblance of genuine personality. Regarding the polemic, Iniquity is loosely equated with the Pope and Anti-Christ, and Zorobabell's oration on the supremacy of love and of women in human affairs is just as loosely directed towards Queen Elizabeth I and her council; but in neither instance is the case made out by means other than bald, verbal statement. What is altogether lacking is any command of device, either as a frame around which to construct the play as an entity, or in terms of those visual components through which the author's abstract ideas and arguments can be projected to the audience in forceful, figurative images. The morality lacks the realism of either physical combat or any genuine unmasking; the biblical disputation

*See Ch. IX, pp. 235–9 below.

lacks the excitement of a wager or prize attaching to it, or any change of consequence in the status or fortunes of the contestants; the polemical element remains fragmentary, instead of providing the spectator with a memorable satirical image. However, *King Darius* still serves one useful purpose: it serves as an object lesson in the essential difference between 'making' an interlude and merely writing one.

This was a lesson that the young poets emerging from the universities in the 1580s who wished to earn a living as play-makers were going to have to learn the hard way—by trial and error—before their work was likely to satisfy popular audiences. As Professor Ewbank has remarked, when discussing the dramatic writings of George Peele,[23]

'The men writing for the London theatres in the 1580s and early 1590s were particularly strongly subjected to pulls in two directions: towards the word, in the shape of exuberant and/or horrific rhetoric, and towards spectacle in every sense, from the significant grouping to the bloody banquet or the coronation pageant. They responded, not with the schizophrenia of contemporary British theatre, but with a happy eclecticism.'

A similar viewpoint is expressed by D. H. Zucker in respect of Marlowe's plays.[24]

'The language spoken by the actors serves to present visual actions and pictures that in their turn comment on the language .... When the stage images are related to the verbal images either complementarily or ironically, they can be said to be emblematically related.'

And this is what Shakespeare had in mind, judging by his own work, when making Hamlet exhort the players from Wittenberg 'to suit the action to the word, the word to the action'—the thing said to the thing done—so that the audience might amplify what it was actually seeing with the word-pictures to which it was listening.

It is in this vital area of Tudor drama that the long and continuing tradition of tournaments, civic pageants and disguisings made its most vital contribution to the play-maker's art: for the problem that confronted the devisers of all these occasional entertainments was to achieve a satisfactory balance between static tableaux, set speeches and the combative, processional or choreographic actions which they adorned and explained. From Lydgate's day to Gascoigne's and Peele's there is rarely any dialogue in the texts of these entertainments: set speech follows set speech, with each speech constructed as an explanation of the pictures, and with most of the pictures selected specifically to link time-present either to the heroic past or to future expectancies, or to both; and in this way the creator of the entertainment aspired to connect its several, seemingly disparate components into a composite emblematic whole—a device.

Thus the Princess Elizabeth, on her journey to her coronation in 1558, saw first, in Gracious Street, 'The uniting of the houses of Lancastre and Yorke' by her ancestors, surmounted by a mirror image of herself portrayed by a child dressed as the new Queen.[25] The accompanying speech, delivered by another child, expounds the tableau by stating, in effect, that London expects the daughter of Henry VIII and Anne Boleyn to provide the nation with that same peace and unity achieved by the marriage of her grandparents, Henry Tudor and Elizabeth of York.

> 'Therefore as civill warre, and shede of blood did cease
> When these two houses were united into one
> So now that jarre shall stint, and quietnesse encrease,
> We trust, O Queen, thou wilt be cause alone.'

The next major tableau, at Cornhill, tackled the highly controversial issue of religion, and did so in terms of personified virtues and vices recognizable by their costumes and accoutrements. Each verse in the accompanying speeches describes the defeat of one of the vices depicted in the tableau by its counterpointed virtue. What is remarkable here is that the virtues and vices presented are those same figures which recur in virtually all the interludes that survive to us between 1558 and 1570. The vices (all directly associated with Roman Catholicism) include Superstition, Idolatry, Folly, Hypocrisy, Insolence and Rebellion; among the virtues were Pure Religion (Protestant), Wisdom and Justice.

In Cheapside, another pageant, while playing on Elizabeth's personal cipher, *Temporis Filia Veritas*,[26] presented a messianic vision of the Triumph of Truth, figured in terms of a triptych—a ruined republic, a prosperous republic, and a cave from whence emerged Time leading his daughter Truth by the hand to present Elizabeth with a copy of the Bible in English.* The last pageant, erected in Fleet Street, figured Elizabeth as Deborah, judge and restorer of Israel.

Thus the author and artists manage to span some 2,000 years of history in this sequence of pictures and explanatory speeches (a method not unlike that adopted by Thomas Preston in his 'Lamentable tragedie mixed full of pleasant mirth', *Cambises*, some three years later),† and to endow the entertainment as a corporate whole with

---

*See *EES*.ii(1), Plate XXIII, and *EES*.i, Plates XIII–XVII.
†See p. 93 below.

religious, political and social significance through the particular emblems chosen to make up the device.

Unfortunately, no texts of disguisings, masques or jousts at barriers have reached us from the central decades of the Tudor era, 1530–70; but one manuscript does survive in the autograph of Secretary Cecil (BM MS. Lansdowne 5) which covers the sequence of masques planned for the proposed meeting of Queen Elizabeth I with Mary Queen of Scots at Nottingham in 1562.[27] The meeting never materialized; but the draft of the devices reveals clearly that the required approach of this essentially choreographic and chivalric form of entertainment was similar to that adopted by civic pageanteers. As the three 'Devices [sic] to be shewed before the quenes Ma(jes)tie by waye of maskinge' so vividly illuminate the means adopted to fuse picture, speech and topical moral into a single, coherent entertainment, I have supplied the complete text in Appendix D; here it suffices to quote briefly from the device for 'the first night'. The scenic picture was to consist of an empty prison named Extreme Oblivion. In this prison, the vices Discord and False Report, led captive into the hall by the virtues Prudence and Temperance riding on gold and red lions respectively, were to be confined by its gaoler, Circumspection. The explanatory speech was to be committed to Pallas, riding a Unicorn and carrying a banner depicting 'ij Ladyes hand(e)s, knitt one faste w(i)thin thother, and over thand(e)s written in letters of golde— ffides'. Pallas was then to declare

> in verse, that the goddes understandinge the noble meteinge of those ij quenes, hathe willed her to declare unto them, that those ij vertues Prudentia and Temperantia have made greate and longe sute unto Jupiter that it wold please hym to gyve unto them false Reporte and discorde to be punisshed as they thinke goode.

With the vices safely under lock and key, the trumpets were to blow 'and thinglishe Ladies to take the nobilite of the straunger [i.e. the Scots] and daunce'. The concluding dance was thus itself to provide the expression of the burial of past wrongs in new-found amity.

It is to be doubted whether anyone concerned in the preparation of this entertainment was so naïve as to suppose that so simple an initiative would automatically bring an *entente cordiale* into existence overnight; but, as a means of making future possibilities explicit to mutually suspicious autocrats, there are worse ways of proceeding than to allow both sides to sample at first hand the prospective fruits of friendship, on three successive nights.[28]

The continuity of this emblematic tradition in court masques and civic pageantry, carried forward into the seventeenth century by

Jonson, Middleton, Heywood, Milton and others, goes far towards explaining why English drama, despite strong pressure to make it conform to principles derived from classical antiquity, remained so stubbornly loyal to native, medieval traditions of play-construction and theatrical conventions.

In the light of these illustrations of the methods employed, I turn now to an examination of the principal figurative devices invented by medieval and Tudor play-makers, and handed on from one generation to the next as a common storehouse of visual and verbal emblems for use (with such variations and additions as the imaginative power of each newcomer could supply) in one play after another.

V

DEVICE AND VISUAL FIGURATION

In Volume One I have explored, and charted by example, the elaborate codes of ecclesiastical iconography, heraldic blazon and trade-symbolism that grew up in the early Middle Ages around the liturgy, tournaments and civic pageantry, and which formed the foundations on which play-makers based their earliest essays in the use of visual, figurative device. Here I wish to illustrate how play-makers came to deploy the visual aspect of device and expand its possibilities as they became more fluent in its use.

1 Superimposition and typology

One of the earliest examples known to me occurs in *Ludus Danielis* where time is drastically foreshortened by the superimposition of the announcement of Christ's Nativity to the prophet Daniel immediately after his release from the lions' den.[1] By this means the youthful authors at Beauvais sought to link the Advent office of the *Ordo Prophetarum* from which their play is directly derived to the Christmas season which provides the occasion for its performance. Here the device is a typological one serving to relate prophecy to its fulfilment and to bring both into visual conjunction at the calendar festival reserved for the celebration of that fulfilment.

A simpler example, involving superimposition in the form of repetition, not typology, occurs in fully developed versions of the earliest of all liturgical music-dramas, the *Visitatio Sepulchri*. Since what matters there is the act of witness to a miracle, one such affirmation is superimposed upon another, thereby lengthening the play and adding new characters but in no way changing the nature of its content. Thus, in the Dublin version, the initial testament of the angel concerning Christ's Resurrection comes to be repeated, first by the three Maries, then by the Apostles Peter and John, and culminates in the final affirmation by the whole choir in unison, 'alta voce quasi gaudentes et exultantes'.*[2]

It is typology, however, that directs the authors of the vernacular Corpus Christi cycles to select the stories of Abraham and Isaac and of Noah's Flood for re-enactment, the one prefiguring the Crucifixion, the other, Doomsday. The play of Noah's Deluge has come to be regarded not only as a comedy bordering upon farce, but as indicative of the growing 'secularization' of English religious drama. Substance is given to these beliefs by the treatment accorded to the character of Noah's wife and her gossips; and indeed, the play is still a very amusing one in performance. Yet critics who only notice how realistically Noah is defied by his shrewish wife in the York, Newcastle and Chester texts betray their ignorance of 'device' and its operation in the hands of a skilled play-maker;[3] for the first requirement, if this play is to fulfil its typological purpose, is an image that will relate God's purging of the earth by deluge (as recounted in Genesis) to the Last Judgment awaiting Noah's posterity. The fitting image is one of disorder, more especially disorder resulting from disobedience; and it is just this image that the play-makers discovered and exploited in Mrs Noah's refusal to acknowledge her husband's 'mastery': only when order has been restored between husband and wife can God's will be fulfilled, and the rainbow, as the sign or emblem of his peace, appear in the heavens to signal a return to normality on earth.[†]

Another very striking example of the superimposition of one image upon another—this time both visual—occurs in the *Origo Mundi*, the first play of the Cornish trilogy, when Adam sends his son Seth back to the Paradise Garden.[4] On his arrival Seth meets a cherub at the gate and tells him that his father 'is old and weary' and hopes for news

> Of the oil promised to him
> Of mercy in the last day.
> (ll. 736–42)

The cherub tells him to look into the garden. There he sees the tree of knowledge and,

> High up on the branches
> A little child newly born;
> And he was swathed in cloths,
> And bound fast with napkins.
> (ll. 805–8)

---

*See pp. 27ff. above.

†For a similar juxtaposition of ideas in Old Testament contexts see Plate IV, No. 6 and accompanying note, p. 309 below.

This child has been cradled in those branches throughout the play. Next day, in *Passio*, the child will appear full-grown as Jesus the man entering Jerusalem, and one of the seeds of that same tree of knowledge, now also fully grown, 'on Kedron lying ... that is accursed' will provide the cross for His crucifixion (11. 2534–72). For the Middle Ages all time was one time. Thus the point here, as with the stage-business between Mak and the shepherds in the Wakefield *Secunda Pastorum*, is that Christ was born into a world we all know, as the world of Noah and his wife is known.

An example of superimposition in repetitive scenic terms is the 'erbyr', or arbour, of the Digby *St Mary Magdalene*. At line 568 in Part I, scene 2, it exists for Mary to entertain her lovers in and thus to serve as an emblem of her corruption: at line 1078 in Part II, scene 25, it has become the environment for her redemption, for it is there that she mistakes the risen Christ for the gardener, watering it with her tears.

What matters in all these examples is the flexibility which this device gives the play-maker in his approach to questions of space and time. Uninhibited by any obligations to respect the irksomely restrictive unities of time and place that were later so to mesmerize playwrights of the high Renaissance, medieval play-makers learned to impose unity of action upon short interludes and long epic dramas alike, by respecting the natural laws of the acting-space, and by treating time-present ritualistically as a mere adjunct to historical time within universal time. The story of Abraham's sacrifice of Isaac in the historical past prefigures Christ's crucifixion, but the crucifixion recurs daily in time-present in the suffering imposed by men upon their fellow men throughout the world: fifteenth-century England, if Henry Bolingbroke usurps Richard II's crown, will itself become another 'field of Golgotha and dead men's skulls' and so will Elizabethan England if Elizabeth is deposed or the question of succession is not swiftly and securely resolved.* These dramaturgical techniques of typological analogue and superimposition of images developed within the religious drama of the Middle Ages were revivified in the course of the Reformation by John Bale and his fellow polemicists.†

Bale's most brilliant, innovative device was to create an equation between the pope and Anti-Christ, Roman Catholic priests and the diablerie, and any English monarch who opposed their tyranny over subjects' lives and the prophets and Christ himself. This equation is made explicit in *Kyng Johan* (1536) where Pope Innocent III is depicted in the false usurper's role of Anti-Christ, King John in the heroic martyr's role of St John Baptist, and Imperial Majesty (alias Henry VIII) as

*See pp. 90–1 below.
†See pp. 206ff. and 228–9 below.

Messiah; Widow England, divorced from Christ and his Gospel by seditious clergy, pleads with John for restitution of conjugal rights; but despite his efforts on her behalf she will not regain them until the architects of the Reformation (Bale's friends, Archbishop Cranmer and Lord Chancellor Cromwell) restore the glorious time of the Gospel in England's churches and cathedrals under the leadership of Henry VIII. Bale may have been an indifferent poet, and often as crude in his language as he is bullying in his tone; but he was self-evidently the master of both dramatic time and theatrical space. Fact and fiction, abstract personification and historical character, first-century Jerusalem, thirteenth-century Rome and sixteenth-century London are all successfully compounded to point a single, topical moral of overriding political consequence to every individual spectator.* Similar techniques are employed to bring the Law of Nature, the Law of Moses and the Law of Christ into conjunction in *Three Lawes* (*c.* 1538), where the cast-list, the particular doubling of the roles stipulated for the actors, the costuming and the dialogue combine to argue that all three laws have been overthrown by the schemes and depravity of the Roman Catholic Church.

Dynamite in its own time, Bale's use of device survived the attempts of Henrician, Marian and Elizabethan licensing authorities to suppress it; nurtured through difficult and dangerous times by university dons and divines like Martin Bucer, Nicholas Udall, Nicholas Grimald and William Wager, it was handed intact, if refined, via Sackville and Norton's *Gorboduc* to Lyly, Marlowe, Peele and Shakespeare at the end of the century.

It is by these means at a humbler level that the author of the seemingly innocuous *Godly Queen Hester* attacked Cardinal Wolsey, the authors of *Respublica* and *Jacob and Esau* blasted respectively the Protestant reformers and Catholic reactionaries, and John Lyly discussed relationships between the Earl of Leicester, Elizabeth I and Mary Queen of Scots, in *Endimion*.† One Shakespearean example must suffice here, and I choose *The Winter's Tale* because all the supporting documentation is already supplied in an essay I contributed to *Elizabethan Theatre*, III. (ed. David Galloway, 1973), entitled 'Romance and Emblem: A Study of the Dramatic Structure of *The Winter's Tale*'. There, the inherited formula serves to equip Shakespeare with a device that will translate the story offered by Robert Greene in *Pandosto* into an analogue of the popular belief that his patron, James VI and I, was the fulfilment of Merlin's prophecy of a second Brutus who would reunite the British Isles and open a new era of peace,

*See Chs VII and IX, pp. 206ff. and 228ff. below.

†For detailed discussions of these plays see pp. 229ff. below.

prosperity and imperial destiny. Time, in this play, assumes the importance of an actual character. First and second Brutus are figured respectively in the jealous and vicious Leontes of Acts I to III, and the patient and pious Leontes of Act V. Between them lies the united kingdom of 'Great' Britain at first fragmented by the divorce and death of Hermione, but then miraculously recovered in the animation bestowed on her statue in the chapel. That which was lost, Perdita, is now found; 'the happy time that was' is recovered; and with her marriage to Florizel (alias Henry Stuart born Prince of Scotland, made Prince of Wales and heir to the English Crown) the prophecy can reach its fulfilment with the shepherd reunited with his flock, the bridegroom with his wife, a united kingdom ruled by one sovereign and his lady; or, as Ben Jonson put it in Epigram V,[5]

> When was there contract better driven by Fate?
> Or celebrated with more truth of state?
> The world the temple was, the priest a king,
> The spoused pair two realms, the sea the ring.

2 *Combat*

The device on which *The Castle of Perseverance* is structured is implicit in its title; for this castle both shelters Humanum Genus and is placed under siege by World, Flesh and the Devil as in that form of tournament known as a *pas d'armes*.* The assaults of this triumvirate are repelled not by arrows and blazing pitch-balls, but by rose petals, an emblem of Christ's blood. The images are concrete, visual figurations of complex ideas, vivid and immediately intelligible with or without benefit of literacy.

Henry Medwall picked up these same images some eighty years later in II *Nature* where Reason likens Man's life to a castle besieged,

> 'Whom to impugn laboreth incessantly
> The world, the fleshe, the enemy—these thre—
> Hym to subdue and bryng into captyvyte.'

After describing first World's tactics and then those of Flesh, he turns to the devil.[6]

> 'The last of all ys our great enemy(;)
> Whyche ever hath us in contynuall haterede
> Of old enkankred malyce and envy
> That he oweth to us, and all the kyn(d)rede

*See *EES*.i. 22–30.

Of all the auncesters of whom we do succede(;)
Nor yet ceseth hys malyce(,) unto this day(,)
Us to endaunger in all that he can or may(.)'

Medwall here enjoys the advantage of employing verbal similes already familiar to his audience in terms of their visual representation in frescoes and tapestries as well as on the stage, just as the Wakefield master does when comparing the tormentors' raising of Christ on his cross into silhouette against the sky to esquires hoisting a knight in armour up onto his horse for a tilting, or as the author of *The Pride of Life* contrives to do with his device of a joust between the Kings of Life and Death.[7]

In *Fulgens and Lucres*, however, Medwall turns directly to the tournament for an image within which to parody the rivalry of Publius Cornelius and Gaius Flamineus for Lucres' hand by making the servants A and B joust with mop and broom for the favours of her maid Joan.[8]

Fighting, of course, on the stage as in life, not only serves to resolve debates which words fail to conclude, but appeals directly to sadomasochistic instincts innate in human kind. Fights attract crowds: some lay bets, others just gloat, whether it be at a cock-fight, a boxing bout, or a pub brawl! As a component in device, therefore, fights have an irresistible appeal for play-makers since they can provoke mirth and ribaldry as easily as arouse fear and pity. The antagonism between the houses of Montague and Capulet in *Romeo and Juliet* and its bitter consequences is structured on fights—Sampson and Gregory versus Abraham and Balthasar; Tybalt versus Mercutio; Romeo versus Tybalt; Romeo versus Paris: it is a figure that serves to mirror the antipathy between Tudor England and Stuart Scotland, or between English Catholic and Protestant families following the Reformation, just as readily as it highlights Juliet's predicament in Gothic Verona. However, in John Heywood's *The Pardoner and the Friar*, and in *Gammer Gurton's Needle*, *Ralph Roister Doister*, *Thersytes* and *Twelfth Night* fights are used for comic effect to deflate pretensions. The fight between the Pardoner and the Friar, joined later by the local vicar and the sexton, like that between Gammer Gurton and Dame Chat (the first in English drama between two pantomime dames), serves to provoke mirth while ridiculing both priests and women for behaving in so indecorous a manner. *Roister Doister* provides an amusing variant when Dame Constance and her women take on Ralph and his men, and put the latter to flight. In *Thersytes* precedent is set for the mockery of a tribe of braggart-cowards by the picture of Thersytes in full armour and equipped with club and sword, yet turned into a quivering jelly by the sight of an outsize snail with its horns advanced.[9]

'But what a monster do I see nowe
Cominge hetherwarde with an armed browe!
What is it? ah, it is a sowe!
No, by God's body, it is but a grestle,
And on the backe it hath never a brystle.
It is not a cow—ah, there I fayle,
For then it should have a long tayle.
What the devyll! I was blynde, it is but a snayle!
I was never so afrayde in east nor in south,
My harte at the fyrste syght was at my mouth.
Mary, syr, fy! fy! fy! I do sweate for feare!'

(ll. 388–98)

What more natural therefore than for Shakespeare, some sixty years later, when creating a 'deformed and scurrillous Grecian' outside the walls of Troy to name him Thersites?

Enter Hector

Hector   What art thou, Greek? Art thou for Hector's match?
             Art thou of blood and honour?

Thersites No, no. I am a rascal, a scurvy railing knave,
             a very filthy rogue.

Hector   I do believe thee. Live.   (*Exit*)

Thersites God-a-mercy, that thou wilt believe me, but
             a plague break thy neck for frighting me!

(V.iv.24–30)

It is the same voice: both audiences laugh: the allusion holds.

In *Twelfth Night* Aguecheek's pretensions to the chivalric qualities of knighthood and virility are as amusingly deflated as Viola's efforts to impersonate an adolescent male: the wings of two birds of very different plumage . are here clipped simultaneously with the same device by Maria, Fabian and Sir Toby.

Another emotive image grounded on combat is the test of manly skill and strength with a wager, or a prize, attaching to the outcome, like Wit's two fights with Giant Tediousness in Redford's *Wit and Science*,* the wrestling bout in *As You Like It*, or the fencing match in *Hamlet*. Again this image can be used for comic or tragic effect at the play-maker's convenience. Either way the spectacle creates its own theatrical tension and the outcome supplies the desired dramatic effect.

In *Hamlet* the fencing match serves to conclude the play. There the duel provides the catalysis that, like a *deus ex machina*, brings divine retribution down on all the principal offenders against the moral

---

*On *Wit and Science* see pp. 75–6 above.

laws of society still alive: Gertrude is punished for her adultery, Laertes, Hamlet and Claudius for their respective murders.

In *As You Like It* the wrestling match serves by contrast to spark the play into action. After learning that Oliver, jealous of his younger brother Orlando, is maintaining him in ignominious idleness and poverty, the audience is introduced to the professional wrestler, Charles, who with the best of intentions approaches Oliver to persuade him to ask Orlando to withdraw from the impending contest and thus escape inevitable disgrace. It is a variant on the device that Shakespeare had already used successfully to launch *Richard II* with the combat *a outrance* in the lists at Coventry.* In *As You Like It* Oliver turns Charles's information to his own advantage, maligning his brother and persuading Charles to let events take their course. 'I had as lief thou did'st break his neck as his finger' (I.i. 122–3). To this Charles replies,

'If he come tomorrow, I'll give him his payment. If he ever go alone again, I'll never wrestle for prize more.'

The scene ends with Oliver, solo, saying,

' . . . this wrestler shall clear all. Nothing remains but that I kindle the boy thither, which now I'll go about.'

The audience is thus made witness to a framing of Orlando, and its interest is swiftly caught in consequence. In the next scene this same device serves to introduce Rosalind to Orlando and to cause her to exclaim (in an aside), 'O excellent young man!' (I. ii. 177). The wrestling proceeds and Charles is beaten; but Orlando receives as prize a chain from Rosalind's hands together with a broad hint:

'Sir, you have wrestled well and overthrown More than your enemies.'

(ll. 219–20)

To this Orlando responds (again in an aside), 'O poor Orlando, thou art overthrown!' From this point forward the audience knows that it is to be treated to a comedy and is fairly sure of its principal drift:† a game is afoot that is destined ironically to turn the tables on the vicious and scheming older brother.

Another variant of the fight that proved no less useful to the playmaker was the joust with its ritualistic aura and heraldic ornament. The time span from Medwall's parody in *Fulgens and Lucres* to Shake-

---

*See p. 91 below. It is also used in this sense by Ben Jonson to open *The Alchemist* to characterize and distinguish Subtle, Face and Dol by means of a furious quarrel among thieves.

†See p. 173 below.

speare's *Richard II*, Webster's *The White Devil* and Jonson's *Masque at Prince Henry's Barriers* covers more than a hundred years; yet the device holds, transmitted through the sixteenth century in sequences of disguisings in the reigns of Henry VII and Henry VIII and of Ascension Day tilts under Elizabeth I, as an instrument of dramaturgy possessed of exceptional theatrical value. Shakespeare exemplified this in his handling of the quarrel between Mowbray and Bolingbroke which opens *Richard II*. There the device serves to exhibit the king in his capacity as the ultimate arbiter of earthly justice, supported by the solemnity of the law and the panoply of the College of Arms: at the same time it mirrors the perilous proximity of civil war in the microcosm of this feud between noble houses with murder of the previous heir apparent as the *causus bellandi*. Ironically, as the action proceeds, the audience perceives that it is the king himself who is on trial rather than the combatants; and when, unsure of how to act in a crisis, he petulantly interrupts this ritualistic form of trial that he has himself promoted and authorized and calls it off, he can be seen to be inviting his own overthrow. Three acts later when Bolingbroke, in his turn, is confronted with a similar situation, he displays no such indecisiveness and survives.

When Jonson uses the device, it is for chivalric purposes, as archaic as nostalgic. In *Hymenaei* (1607) his object is the celebration of marriage. On the second night of this extended masque he takes recourse to the traditional disputation, choosing Truth and Opinion to argue the respective merits of married and single life. When they fail to reach agreement Opinion protests,

> 'These are but words; hast thou a knight will try
> By stroke of arms the simple verity?'

Truth replies,

> 'To that high proof I would have daréd thee.
> I'll straight fetch champions for the bride and me.'

And Opinion answers, 'The like will I do for Virginity' (ll. 765–9). Immediately the two teams of sixteen gorgeously dressed noblemen 'armed with pikes and swords' enter the hall. Truth and Opinion are given a few more lines to cover the setting up of the barrier.* Then follows the stage-direction:

'Here the champions on both sides addressed themselves for fight, first single, after three to three; and performed it with that alacrity and vigor as if Mars himself had been to triumph before Venus and

---

*See *EES*.ii(1), Plate XX and pp. 229–41 and 341 ff.

invented a new music. When on a sudden (the last six having scarcely ended) a striking light seemed to fill all the hall, and out of it an angel or messenger of glory appearing.'

This *deus ex machina* arrives to 'end with reconciléd hands these wars', thereby linking the device directly to the noblest spectator present, the King himself, by fulfilling the precepts of *Beatus Pacificus*.

In *Prince Henry's Barriers* (1610) Jonson turns to Arthurian legend and selects Merlin and the Lady of the Lake as his contestants, a device particularly appropriate to Henry Stuart's forthcoming investiture as Prince of Wales since Prince Henry himself was to lead the knights to the combat at the barrier. Jonson accordingly casts him as Meliadus, Lord of all the Isles, and lets Merlin wind up the proceedings with a prophecy relating to the three royal children. Turning to James he concludes,

> 'Whilst you sit high,
> And led by them behold your Britain fly
> Beyond the line [i.e. horizon], when what the seas before
> Did bound, shall to the sky then stretch his shore.'

For all the nostalgic fantasy that informs this device, the prophecy was shortly to be fulfilled in the colonizing of Nova Scotia by James's Scottish subjects.

When Webster uses the device, he does so in a sinister context to give lustre and theatrical excitement to the cynical and cold-blooded murder of Duke Brachiano in *The White Devil* (V. iii). His actual stage-direction parallels Ben Jonson's in *Hymenaei*: 'Charges and shouts. They fight at barriers; first single pairs, then three to three. Enter Brachiano and Flamineo with others.' Preceded, as it has been, by Flamineo's spiteful murder of his brother, Marcello, in a travesty of a formal duel of honour, this formal combat at barriers fails to reach its climax; although it has been invested with all the pageantry of the robes and insignia of the Knights of Malta, Brachiano succumbs to the poisonous unguents pasted on to the lining of his helmet and visor, and collapses before he can begin his own bout with the mysterious Moor, actually his arch-enemy, the Duke of Florence in disguise. This in its turn serves as prelude to the blasphemous parody of the last rites in the course of which Webster arranges for Brachiano to be strangled in one of the most chilling scenes in all Jacobean drama.

Most potent of all dramatic and theatrical uses of the device of the combat, however, is the battle-scene. Deployed in *The Castle of Perseverance*, *The Blessed Life of St Meriasek* and doubtless in many other saint plays now lost, it went out of fashion with the advent of professional acting companies since troupes of 'four men and a boy' could not hope to present one; but as the companies stretched their numbers to twelve late in the sixteenth century, and later to sixteen, the battle-scene rapidly recovered its popularity among audiences at a time when the men among them wore swords in daily life.* Indeed, without the battle-scene the chronicle play could not have become the staple diet of the public playhouses from 1590 to 1610.

As spectacle it has everything: flags, trumpets, drums, armour, archers, scaling ladders, camouflage, pikes, swords, cannons, smoke and blood. Emotionally it can be manipulated to provoke pride, fear, horror and pity in the auditorium; even laughter, as is the case with Falstaff and Thersites. The battle-scene could easily degenerate into the sort of 'inexplicable dumb shows and noise' and drearily repetitive 'alarums and excursions' that pricked Ben Jonson into satirizing them in the Prologue to the folio edition of *Everyman in his Humour*:

> ... or, with three rusty swords,
> And help of some few foot-and-half-foot words
> Fight over York and Lancaster's long jars;
> And in the tiring-house bring wounds to scars.

but in the hands of a skilful play-maker battle-scenes offered the best of opportunities for illustrating and contrasting character under extreme stress. Examples abound in Shakespeare: the differences of attitude to the chivalric values of honour and knighthood adopted by Henry V depicted as a general in battle and as a human being among fellow soldiers in the stillness of the night, between Coriolanus' military virtues and civil vices. A battle provides Macbeth with his finest hour, Achilles and Cleopatra with their meanest.

Of course not every fight in Tudor drama was designed to fulfil these lofty aesthetic ideals, but simply to meet some practical need as the author of *The Tyde Taryeth no Man* makes clear at line 1215 where Hurtful Help and the vice are instructed to fight 'to prolong the time, while Wantonesse maketh her ready'.[10] Yet in most scenes involving fights, jousts and battles it was the explicit visual realism of the action, transcending every level of literacy, that made this device so attractive and so useful to the professional play-maker, granted a company large enough to stage them.† Especially relevant here are some of the stage-directions in Thomas Preston's *Cambises* (*c.* 1561), George Peele's *The Battle of Alcazar* (1589) and Robert Greene's *Orlando Furioso* (1591).[11]

---

*See Ch. VII below, pp. 162–6.
†See Ch. VII, p. 162 below, and *EES*.ii (1). 114–18.

3 The tavern

In I *Nature* Henry Medwall selects a familiar verbal image of a voyage to reflect Man's journey through life to open his play—

> *Nature*   I let the wyt, thou arte a passanger
>   That hast to do, a great and longe vyage *
>   and through the world, most be thy passage(.)

—but he does not exploit its visual possibilities: these were left virtually untouched by the early makers of interludes for Elizabethan writers of theatrical romances to develop.† Instead, Medwall turns quickly to images of the tavern and clothing. Presented naked to the audience, Man is ritualistically vested by Reason, Innocency and Sensuality to protect him against climate and seasons.[12]

> 'Take thys garment. man, do as I you byd(!)
> Be not ashamed hardely to do yt on.
> So lo! now thys gurdell have gurd yt in the myd;
> And thys for your hed(!) go set yt upon;
> By the charge of me! You be a goodly on
> As ever I saw syth y(a)t I was borne.'

These clothes meet his daily needs until Worldly Affection introduces Man to Pride. Pride scorns their modesty and promises to acquire better ones. When, eventually, they arrive and Man has put them on, his servants fail to recognize him until Gluttony realizes what has happened.

> *Gluttony* I cry you mercy! I se yt well now;
>   Byfore(,) I knew you not(,) I make God avow!
>   In ernest nor in game.
> *Man*   Why? Bycause I have chaunged myne aray?
>   (Rastell's ed., sig. Gii)

It is at this point that they all repair to the tavern. The tavern, as the common rendezvous of all the deadly sins, is an image used again and again by the makers of interludes throughout the sixteenth century to depict the concept of Hell in worldly terms. Sloth, Wantonness or Lechery, and Gluttony are its habitués. Drink and gambling provoke Wrath and Envy, while Pride promotes both and finds its satisfaction in the companionship of all of them at once. Covetousness alone is regarded as solitary, a vice of old age rather than of youth.

It is to the tavern that Mankind, in the play of that name, repairs

---

vyage: voyage.
† See Ch. VIII, pp. 216–18 below.

once he has been persuaded by Titivillus to abandon farming and church-going:

> 'Adieu, fair masters! I will haste me to the ale-house,
> And speak with New Guise, Now-a-Days, and Nought:
> A(nd) get me a leman [*woman*] with a smattering [*kissable*] face.'
>
> (ll. 610–12)

Once there, the vices amuse themselves (and the audience) with a mock-trial during the course of which the play-maker seizes upon the clothes image to reveal the deterioration in Mankind's character by first shortening his gown into a coat (1. 1673 ff.) and then cutting it down again into 'a jolly jacket' (1. 702–27).

Likewise in *The Four Elements* (*c.* 1517–25), when Sensual Appetite wishes to corrupt Humanity, he says,[13]

> 'Well then will ye go with me
> To a tavern(,) where ye shall see
> Good pastaunce(,)* and at your liberty
> Have whatsoever you will(?)'

In this play the device of the tavern is deployed as the central image of depravity and moral degeneration with the taverner himself making a notable personal appearance. When he does so, it is to extol the virtues of his menu and his wine-list with all the jargon of the *bon viveur*: that done, however, he then proceeds to take this chance to inform his clients that his establishment offers more than food and drink, for discreetly annexed to the dining-rooms is a thriving brothel which is as well stocked with wenches as his cellar is with wines.

Sensual Appetite	Then we will have little Nell,
	A p(ro)per wench(,) she danceth well,
	And Jane with the black lace(;)
	We will have bouncing Bess also,
	And two or three proper wenches mo
	Right fair and smotter † of face.
Humanity	Now be it so! thou art *sans* peer.
Taverner	The(n) I p(er)ceive ye will make good cheer.
Humanity	Why, what should I else do(?)
Taverner	If ye think so best, then will I
	Go before, and make all things ready
	Again ye come thereto.

Humanity tries to break free of his wastrel companions, but he is weak-willed and has to be warned by Nature, his protector, that if he refuses to learn either by study or experience,

*pastaunce: pastime, sport.

†*smotter*: smooth.

'... thou shall dure then
Despised of every wise man
Like this rude beast Ignorance.'

Another and earlier example of the taverner treated as the prime agent
in the corruption of innocence is supplied in the Digby play of *St Mary
Magdalene*. Scene 9 of Part I starts with the stage-direction,

Here takyt mary hur wey to Ierusalem with Luxsurya, and þey xal
resort to a taverner, þus seyy(n)g þe taverner.

'I am a taverner witty and wyse,
that wynys have to sell great plente.
of all þe taverners I bere þe pryse
that be dwellyng with-inne þe cete;
of wynys I have grete plente,
both whyte wynne and red þat (ys) so cleyr.'

He then lists the specialities of his cellar at some length. Luxuria
then directs Mary's attention to 'þe comford and þe sokower' obtainable
from drinking wine, and is backed up in her views by the taverner
himself.

'here, lady, is wyn, a re-past
to man, and woman a good restoratyff;
ʒe xall nat thynk your mony spent in wast,
from stodyys and hevynes it woll yow relyff.'
(ed. EETS, ll. 485–8)

Mary succumbs to the temptation thus blandly proffered to her and
promptly falls a victim to the lecherous desires of a male visitor to
the same tavern, a young gallant called Curiosity. Satan and his devils
then congratulate themselves on the success of their plan.[14] This
variant of the device is thus dramatically as successful as this method
of attempted seduction has proved in life to be unchanging. In *The
Interlude of Youth* (*c.* 1520) it is Riot who appropriately says to the hero,

'... to the taverne let us go[,]
And we will drynke divers wine[,]
And the cost shal be myne[;]
Thou shalt not pay one peny, i-wis
Yet thou shalt have a wenche to kysse
Whan so ever thou wilte.'
(sigs Bi and Biib)

Having picked up Pride and Lechery on the way there, they never
actually reach this tavern, becoming distracted instead by the game of
clapping Charity and Humanity into the stocks; but the point has
been made.[15]

Similarly in *Hick-Scorner* there is no formal tavern-scene; but when Freewill appears and says, 'Syrres, I was at the taverne and dronke wyne' (ed. Manly I, p. 649), the tale he then tells of his thieving, his arrest, his imprisonment and release by recourse to bribery amuses its hearers by its extravagance and impertinence, but occasions no surprise.[16]

By the middle of the century this device has been used so often as to have become a cliché: a mere reference or allusion to a tavern will suffice. Thus the author of *Impatient Poverty* (*c.* 1560) has only to warn his hero within this idiom for the audience to be aware of what is afoot.

> Play nor at cailes, cards, nor dice;
> Also from miswomen,* for by them mischief may rise,
> As it doth often; this daily is seen;
> Haunt no taverns . . .
>
> (ll. 226–9)

Impatient Poverty (now re-named Prosperity) ignores this warning, needless to say, and succumbing to the blandishments of Envy and Misrule paves the road to his own ruin at 'The Fleur de Lys'.[17]

Nicholas Udall likewise, in *Ralph Roister Doister* (*c.* 1550), familiarizes his audience in the opening speech of the play with the sort of company that will provide the 'mirth' promised in the Prologue. Mathewe Merrygreeke confesses that his 'living lieth here and there' among such companions as Lewis Loiterer, Watkin Waster, Davy Diceplayer, Tom Titivile (an especially significant acquaintance), Sir Hugh Pye (an ancestor of Falstaff?), and Nichol Neverthrives, all recognizable denizens of the alehouse. We meet none of them, but the device serves itself to establish Merrygreeke as the Vice.[18]

Similarly in *Gammer Gurton's Needle* of the following year, it is the Vice Diccon who repairs to Dame Chat's abode 'to feele how the ale doth taste'. Once there he conjures the devil, plays cards, and sets up the brawls between Chat and Gurton and the trap to discomfort the vicar, Dr Rat: in short, this tavern becomes the focal point of the play's comic action.[19]

In both these cases low-life comedy of realistic incident—so like the rural scenes painted by the Breughels and written in the manner of John Heywood—takes precedence over homiletic intention. The latter, however, despite the ever-tightening pressures of stage-censorship, was by no means dead, and indeed received a new lease of life from the Protestant exiles who returned to England from Calvin's Geneva following Elizabeth's accession in 1558.

Such a play is *New Custom* (printed 1573 but performed *c.* 1560). No

miswomen; prostitutes.

tavern-scene is included, but the only persons to recognize its existence are two of the Roman Catholic vices, Perverse Doctrine and Ignorance.[20] At the end of Act II, scene iii, the former says,

Perverse Doctrine But come, Ignorance, let us follow after apace,
                For we have abiden all too long in this place.
Ignorance Let us go then, but, by the mass, I am vengeance dry,
                I pray let us drink at the alehouse hereby.
Perverse Doctrine Content, in faith, thither with speed let us hie.

Here the mere allusion suffices: yet in *Nice Wanton* (an attack on sentimental and lazy parents rather than on youth) it is once again the tavern that leads Dalilah to prostitution and her brother Ismael to gambling and murder under the tutelage of the vice Iniquity, despite the warnings of their good, elder brother, Barnabas.[21]

Barnabas Come, let us go, if ye will to school this day;
          I shall be shent for tarrying so long.
Ismael Go, get thee hence, thy mouth full of horse-dung!
          Now, pretty sister, what sport shall we devise?
          Thus palting to school, I think it unwise:
          In summer die for thirst, in winter for cold,
          And still to live in fear of a churl—who would?
Dalilah Not I, by the mass! I had rather he hanged were
          Than I would sit quaking like a mome for fear.
          I am sun-burned in summer; in winter the cold
          Maketh my limbs gross, and my beauty decay;
          If I should use it, as they would I should,
          I should never be fair woman, I dare say.
Ismael No, sister, no! But I can tell,
          Where we shall have good cheer,
          Lusty companions two or three,
          At good wine, ale and beer.
Dalilah O good brother, let us go
          I will never go more to school.

                          (ll. 54–72)

The most notable of many treatments of this device, however, is to be found in that most famous of all stage-taverns, the 'Boar's Head' in East Cheap, with Falstaff as its lord of misrule and Mistress Quickly as its bawd.[22]

The tavern as an emblem of hell on earth was so well established among Protestants in Elizabethan England as to make choice of an inn the natural habitat for the corruption of the heir apparent. Even the name chosen for this lord of misrule, Sir John Falstaff, is a pun compounding two emblematic names associated with vicious behaviour—'Sir John', and 'false-staff'—familiar to every actor of Tudor interludes and to most playgoers schooled in this insistently repetitive tradition. It thus only requires a few deftly sketched allusions to hell and the devil within the dialogue for audiences to relate everything that passes within the walls of the 'Boar's Head' to this tradition. Such are Hal's two remarks in *1 Henry IV*, Act II, scene 4.

> 'There is a devil haunts thee in the likeness
> of an old fat man'
>
> > (ll. 393–4)

and

> 'That villainous abominable misleader of
> youth, Falstaff, that old white-bearded Satan.'
>
> > (ll. 407–8)

or Falstaff's own remarks about Bardolf in Act III, scene 3, and *2 Henry IV*, Act II, scene 4.

> 'I never see thy face but I think upon hell-fire and
> Dives that lived in purple; for there he is in his
> robes, burning, burning'
>
> > (ll. 25–6)

and

> 'The fiend hath pricked down Bardolph irrecoverable;
> and his face is Lucifer's privy-kitchen, where he
> doth nothing but roast malt-worms.'
>
> > (ll. 295–7)

or the Chief Justice's rebukes in *2 Henry IV*, Act I, scene 2, and Act, II scene 1:

> 'You follow the young prince up and down, like his evil angel.'
>
> > (l. 148)

and

> 'Sir John, Sir John, I am well acquainted with your manner of
> wrenching the true cause the false way.'
>
> > (ll. 93–4)

It was by equivocation that Lucifer tempted Eve and Christ: as precedent it suffices for the testing of tomorrow's king. The 'earnest' behind the 'game' is thus clearly signposted; but the game itself is so amusing that it can easily enmesh the unwary spectator.

4 Changes of name and costume

Justice	Yet(,) besyde that(,) thou seemest of manhode frayle
	Because so abused is thy lyght apparaile.
Injury [alias	Apparell, good syr, what faulte is that(?)
Manhood]	Though grey be her cote why blame ye the wild cat(?)
	Why shuld ye hym deme of nature frayle
	Though as wyse as ye wolde were a Fox tayle(?)
	Or a cote after the common usage(?)
	Or have by nature a mad vysage(?)
	These be no wytnesse for Justyce to dyserne
	Nor certayne knowledge of nature to lerne(,)
	And christ taught you(,) syr(,) how ye shuld judge men(,)
	Sayenge *Nolite judicare secundum faciem.*
	And yet in nature better knowledge shuld bee
	Then is apparell ye know(,) perdie.
Justice	O yet in apparell is great abusion
	If it be framed without dyscretion(;)
	For in apparell there may a great token bee
	Of fraylenes, of pryde, and instabylytie,
	If com(m)on assye therin use no mesure
	For then is apparell a wanton foolysh pleasure
	And foly(;) best mede is presumpcyon
	When nature of reason used resumpcyon(;)
	And therefore Chryst taught a great wyse prose
	Sayenge *Ex fructibus eorum cognoscetis eos.*
Injury	Yet with the same text I pray you wipe your nose(!)
	Hee said not *Ex vestibus eorum cognoscetis eos.*

(Albion Knight, ll. 13–38)

While it is evident that the anonymous play-maker is here causing the devil (the Vice) to quote Scripture,* this controversy sums up the attitude of almost every English dramatist from Medwall to Shakespeare to changes of name and costume as a theatrical device:[23] a hundred years later, Hamlet will translate Injury's last line into: 'Tis not alone my inky cloak, good mother', etc.

Medwall opens I *Nature* with the elaborate, ritualistic vesting of Man by Reason (his father), Sensuality (his mother) and Innocency (his Nurse) already quoted on page 94. He is given a simple coat and belt to protect him against the weather. This simple apparel, however, is

---

*Some eighty-five lines later Injury soliloquizes,

'Now here begynneth a game, y-wys(;)
For manhode they wene my name is(,)
But, trust mee syrs if I shuld not lye,
My name is called Injury.'

(Albion Knight, ed. cit., ll. 126–9)

made an object of jest and scorn by Pride shortly afterwards who, on taking Man to the tavern promises him new clothes. There they meet five of the other deadly sins, all of whom rapidly change their names. Pride assumes the pseudonym of Worship; Wrath becomes Manhood; Envy takes the alias of Disdain; Gluttony that of Good Fellowship; Sloth translates himself into Ease and Lechery into Lusty. This done, all of them solicit Man to take them into his household as his servants. When he finally gets his new clothes his new servants fail to recognize him.*

This device is again elaborately deployed by the anonymous author of *Mundus et Infans*.[24] When the Child is first presented to World he lacks clothes.

Mundus	These garmentes gaye I gyve to the;
	And also I gyve to the a name
	And clepe the Wanton, in every game,
	Tyll xiiij yere be come and gone,—
	And than come agayne to me.
Infans	Gramercy, Worlde for myne araye;
	For now I purpose me to play.

(ed. Manly, ll. 67–73)

Altogether Infans is given seven changes of costume, corresponding with the seven ages of man, and thus setting the precedent for a practice that Ben Jonson, a century later, was to ridicule in the Prologue to *Everyman in his Humour* when castigating play-makers with so little talent and sense of style as

> To make a child, now swaddled, to proceed
> Man, and then shoot up, in one beard and weed,
> Past three score years.

Skelton appears to have been the first play-maker to slant this device in a new direction, that of political corruption. In *Magnyficence* his vices seek preferment at Court in order to ruin the Prince and thus claim the State for their master, Satan. To this end they deem it necessary to change their names and outward appearance. The most elaborate treatment of these several transformations is accorded to Courtly Abusion in Stage 2, scene 14 who adopts a lyrical attitude to his new clothes.[25]

> 'What nowe? Let se
> Who loketh on me
> Well rounde aboute,
> Howe gay and howe stoute

*See p. 94 above.

That I can were
 Courtly my gere:

My heyre bussheth
 So plesauntly,
My robe russheth
 So ruttyngly,
 Me seme I flye,
I am so lyght
To daunce delyght;

Properly drest
 All poynte devyse,
My persone prest
 Beyonde all syse
 Of the newe gyse,
To russhe it oute
In every route.

Beyonde Measure
 My sleve is wyde,
Al of Pleasure
 My hose strayte tyde,
 My buskyn wyde,
Ryche to beholde,
Gletterynge in golde.

Abusyon,
 Forsothe I hyght;
Confusyon
 Shall on hym lyght
By day or by nyght
That useth me—'
 (ed. EETS, ll. 829–61)

Having drawn the audience's attention thus forcibly to the outward
deception of his new Court clothes, Abusion turns in the next scene to
the question of a new name to match them.

	Ye(a), but what shall I call my name?
Fancy	Cockes harte! tourne the, let me se thyne aray.
	Cockes bones! this is all of John de Gay!
Courtly Abusion	So am I poynted after my Consayte.
Fancy	Mary, thou jettes it of hyght.
Courtly Abusion	Ye(a), but of my name let us be wyse.
Fancy	Mary, Lusty Pleasure, by myne advyse,
	To name thyselfe; come of, it were done!

102

Courtly Abusion Farewell, my frende.
Fancy   Adue tyll sone.
                                   (*ibid.*, ll. 959–67)

Abusion and his fellow vices thus insinuate their way into Magnyficence's service and succeed swiftly in emptying his exchequer and
bringing him to Despair. It is then Magnyficence's turn to be redeemed
by Redress, Circumspection and Perseverance. This too is accomplished visually when Redress says to Magnyficence,

> 'Nowe shall ye be renewyd with Solace;
> Take nowe upon you this abylment,
> And to that I say gyve good advysement.'

Taking the garment Magnyficence replies,

> 'To your requeste I shall be confyrmable.'
> (*ibid.*, Stage 5, scene 43, ll. 2404–7)

In *Hick-Scorner* name and costume-changes are held back to the end of
the play to figure the reclamation of Freewill and Imagination.[26]
'Holde here a newe garment,' says Contemplation to Freewill, 'And
here-after lyve devoutly'; no change of name is deemed necessary.
When Imagination is converted shortly after, he is renamed 'Good
Rembraunce', and Perseverance offers him 'better clothynge', just
as Everyman twenty years earlier had been given 'the garment of
sorrow' by Knowledge, symbolizing Contrition, before proceeding
with Good Deeds to meet his Maker.

In the hands of John Bale this device is given a further twist, this
time to serve the interests of Protestant propaganda. In *Three Lawes*,
as T. W. Craik has remarked,[27]

'Bale can be seen turning metaphor and simile into dramatic allegory
by his use of costume-changes, and amplifying Tyndale's rhetorical
hints (*An Exposition upon the V. VI. VII chapters of Mathew*) by means of
invented detail calculated to make a powerful effect on an audience.'

The importance that Bale himself attached to the visual impact of his
characters may be judged from his own detailed costume instructions
appended to the play.[28]

'Late Idolatry be decked lyke an olde wytche, Sodomy lyke a monke
of all sectes, Ambycyon lyke a byshop, Covetousness lyke a pharyse
or spyrituall lawer, false doctrine lyke a popysh doctour, and hypo-
cresy lyke a graye fryre. The rest of his partes are easye enought to
coniecture.'

In *Kyng Johan* he carries this technique a step further, making one character, Dissimulation, describe his own costume to the other actors on stage and interpret its significance.

> 'Nay, dowst þou not se how I in my colours jette?
> To blynd þe peple I have yet a farther fette.
> This is for Bernard and this is for Benet,
> This is for Gylbard and this is for Ihenet;
> For Frauncys this is, and this is for Domynyke,
> For Awsten and Elen, and this for seynt Partryk.
> We have many rewlles, but never one we kepe;
> Whan we syng full lowde owr hartes be fast aslepe.
> We resemble sayntes in gray, whyte, blacke and blewe,
> Yet unto prynces not one of owr nomber trewe.
> And that shall kyng John prove shortly, by þe rode!'
>   (ed. Adams, ll. 724–34)

In this play he has again made a virtue of necessity, carefully arranging the doubling of parts to correspond with the manner in which his characters are going to advance his argument. The actor who has played Usurped Power up to line 983 thus reappears at line 1025 as the Pope, thereby reinforcing Bale's equation of the Pope with Anti-Christ: Private Wealth simultaneously becomes a Cardinal, and Sedition is translated into Stephen Langton, Archbishop of Canterbury. This change of name and costume is at once physical and metaphorical, and prepares the way for the Pope to excommunicate King John and lay England under interdict: for this conspiracy to proceed one further change of name and costume is necessary and this is covered by the stage-direction at line 1061, 'Here go out [Cardinal] and dresse for Nobylyte'. Bale thus succeeds in equating Nobility with Private Wealth in a way that spectators can remark with their eyes. The whole device is completed when married to the subsequent dialogue since what these characters then say becomes instantly recognizable as the hypocritical and seditious cant that Bale intends it to be. In short, visual and verbal image are here so juxtaposed as to contradict each other flatly.*

A similar technique is used in *The Temptation of Our Lord* when Satan presents himself to Christ in the wilderness dressed as a hermit in a monk's habit, having informed the audience that

> 'Subtlety must help; else all will be amiss;
> A goodly pretence, outwardly, must I bear,
> Seeming religious, devout and sad in my gear.'

This choice of costume places a wholly different complexion on the whole of the subsequent dialogue; and once again the satiric effect is achieved by contrasting the verbal with the visual image.[29]

*See p. 70 above.

Lewis Wager adopts the same technique in his *The Life and Repentavnce of Marie Magdalene* (*ed. cit.*, ll. 397–400) when making Infidelitie say,

> 'Prudence before Marie my name I will call,
> Which to my suggestions will cause her to fall.
> A vesture I have here to this garment corresponde(n)t:
> Lo, here it is, a gowne, I trowe convenient.'

Shortly after, Wager adds the stage-direction, 'Puts on a gowne & a cap'. Thereby, however, he creates a problem for himself since he knows full well that, iconographically, Prudence ought to be possessed of either a third eye in the back of her head, or a hand mirror. He meets it by turning this omission to comic effect in the ensuing dialogue.

By the middle of the century this device, at least in these terms of reference, had become so familiar to audiences as to be platitudinous: but Nicholas Udall (supposing him to have been the author of the anti-Protestant *Respublica*) glimpsed fresh possibilities within it which he exploited in his depiction of the vice, Avarice.* He is the most engaging fellow, possessed of wit, vitality and charm. These are characteristics which he shares with Diccon in *Gammer Gurton's Needle* and Idleness in *The Marriage Between Wit and Wisdom*; but he inhabits a much more sophisticated social world than either of them and in many respects anticipates that arch-Venetian mountebank, Volpone.

In an ingratiating opening soliloquy Avarice takes the audience into his confidence.[30]

> 'But nowe, what my name is, *and* what is my purpose,
> Takinge youe all for frendes, I feare not to disclose.
> My veray trewe unchristen Name ys Avarice,
> which I may not have openlye knowen in no wise;
> For though to moste men I am founde Commodius
> yet to those that use me, my name is Odius.'

He goes on to say that need impels him to disguise it, and so will he call himself Policy.

> 'The Name of "policie" is of none suspected:
> Polycye is ner of any cryme detected.
> So that under the Name and cloke of policie,
> Avaryce maie weorke factes† & scape all Jelousie.'

Thus disguised he hopes to prevail upon the Lady Respublica to take him into her Privy Council. He succeeds, and in that capacity (in the

*See Ch. VIII, n. 76, p. 301 below.
†*Sic*; but more probably a misprint for 'feates'.

name of Reformation and with the help of Oppression, Insolence and Adulation) he sets about dissolving monasteries, accusing landowners of heresy and sequestering their estates for himself and his friends. A whole scene of nearly one hundred lines is then devoted to finding appropriate new names for the vices to shelter behind: they emerge from a scene of high comedy as Honesty, Authority and Reformation. With that achieved they switch attention to their clothes.

> *Avarice (to Adulation)* Ye muste have other garmentes, and soo muste ye
> all:
> Ye muste for the season, counterfaite gravitee.
> *Oppression and Insolence* Yes, what els?
> *Adulation* And I muste counterfaite honestie.
> *Avarice* And I muste tourne my gowne in & owte, I wene,
> For theise gaping purses maie in no wyse be seen.
> I will tourne ytt een here; come helpe me, honestye.
> (I.iv.417–22)

The irony of this device becomes apparent in Act II, scene 3 when Respublica issues them with her instructions to 'destroy Avarice' and 'vanquish Oppression and Adulation/For those three have nighe wrought my desolacion', and is then reminded by none other than Avarice (alias Policy) that she has omitted 'Lucifers sonne, called Insolence'!

> *Respublica* Ye saie truth, and manye Naughtie ones moo
> then he.
> *Insolence and Oppression* If ye dare truste us . . .
> *Insolence* all . . .
> *Oppression* all shall reformed bee.

The deception holds, and with a sigh of relief and a song to celebrate their success they scamper off to work their envious and avaricious worst on their fellow-countrymen with the full blessing of the law behind them!

Money and lands pour in, just as they will into Mosca's and Volpone's coffers half a century later.

> *Avarice* Come on, swete bags of golde: come on with a good will;
> I on youe soo tendre; & ye soo frowarde styll?
> Come forewarde, I praie youe, swete bags: ah, will ye soo?
> Come, or I must drawe youe whether ye will or noo.
> I knowe your desire; ye woulde faine bee in my chest.
> When the bealie is full, the bones woulde bee att reast.
> Bee contente awhile; I will couche youe all up soone,
> Where ye shalnot bee spied neither of Sonne nor Mone.
> (III.iv. 751–8)

In Act III, scene 6 Avarice is carrying his money bags again, but this time they are all labelled as the proceeds 'of leasses encroched and foorthwith solde again', bribes, church goods, etc.

When retribution comes, it is at the hands of the Four Daughters of God; and it is Truth, the daughter of Time,* who conducts the examination: the unmasking of Avarice is handled in terms of his money bags and his cloak.

> Verity   Now doe of thie gowne, & tourne the inside outwarde.
> Avarice Leate me alone[,] and an Angell for a rewarde.
> Verity   Come of at ons;† whan? come of. No more gawdies or iapes.
>
> (V.ix.1752–4)

Once the cloak is off, the gold lining is revealed together with all the purses stitched into it. Quite literally it is a spectacular 'discovery' and forms the theatrical climax of the play.

The anonymous author of *Impatient Poverty* (*c.* 1560) uses this device with a similar degree of flexibility and wit.[31] Early in the play Peace provides Impatient Poverty with sober, simple clothes and re-names him Prosperity: Envy, Peace's rival, does the same by Misrule before introducing him as Mirth to Prosperity: these vices then attack Prosperity's clothes.

> Envy   Off with this lewd array!
>   It becometh you nought by this day.
> Prosperity By my troth, even as ye say.
>   Yea, marry now am I well apaid
>   Methinketh I am properly araide.
>
> (ll. 685–9)

This costume change is so swift as to imply the stripping off of the outer garment given to him earlier by Peace and an immediate reversion to his own more ostentatious dress.

However, after he has lost all his savings to Colhasard at dice and been beaten up in the ensuing fight, he reappears in a much more tattered outer garment provoking Envy into cracking a sly joke.

> Envy   Marry so methink, you have changed your coat;
>   But now ye have one vantage.
> Prosperity What is that?
> Envy   Your executors shall not strive for your goods another day,
>   Nor thieves shall not rob you going by the way!
>
> (ll. 880–4)

*This was also Queen Mary I's personal device: she, later, is figured in the character of Nemesis. See Ch. IV, n. 26, p. 280 below.

†I.e. come off at once.

So much of a stage-convention had the changing of name and costume become when Elizabeth I came to the throne in 1558 that it is hard to find a play from *Impatient Poverty* onwards that does not make use of this device in the first two decades of her reign.

The great advantage of this situation from the play-maker's standpoint is that he can turn his audiences' familiarity with it to his own advantage. Thus Francis Merbury in *The Marriage Between Wit and Wisdom* (*c.* 1575–9) uses it ironically when Wit first meets Idleness.[32]

Wit   Thou art a merry fellow and wise and if thou keep thyself warm.
Idleness In faith, I have a mother-wit, but I think no harm.
Wit   I pray thee, what is thy name?   (*EMI*, ll. 147–9)

Wit's first line arises directly out of Idleness's beggar's costume which is itself sufficient pointer to his name and character for every spectator; only Wit is naïve enough to need to ask him what his name is. This joke enables Merbury to extend it over the next ten lines and to make it easy for Idleness to assume a sudden honesty and thereby persuade Wit, notwithstanding the visible lie of his costume, that his real identity is Honest Recreation: it is then just as easy for him to make Wit accept Wantonness as Mistress Modest Mirth. Having lulled Wit asleep in her lap, she puts a fool's coxcomb on his head and blacks his face while Idleness relieves him of his purse.*

Merbury then inverts the device to discomfort Idleness, letting Catch and Snatch rob him of the contents of the purse and tie him up in a sheet as if he were a mummer disguised, whom Wit can shortly mistake for a ghost when he returns with the genuine Honest Recreation as his escort. Idleness can thus only escape from imprisonment in the sheet by betraying his original deception on Wit, unless of course he can succeed in changing his identity again. This he does, claiming now to be Due Disport. When he next appears it is disguised as a rat-catcher, armed with a crutch: one scene later he presents himself as a ruffler—'Now I am a bold beggar—I tell you, the stoutest of my kin' (1.584). Three scenes later he has changed his costume yet again and appears as a priest, claiming that he cannot and will not be detected:

> 'I am of that condition
> That I can turn into all colours like the chameleon.'
>   (ll. 688–9)

It is therefore fair to claim that Merbury has structured his whole play on the device of changing names and costumes and that by doing

---

*This scene is of course a simple variant of Redford's original in *Wit and Science*; see pp. 75–6 above.

so he has created something approaching a comedy of mistaken identity: it is at least only the shortest of steps from Merbury's treatment of Idleness in this interlude to the comic confusion arising from the creation of identical twins, and from the use of boys dressed as girls pretending to be young men. Nor does it take much imaginative effort to turn Idleness's claim to 'play the purveyor here on earth for the devil' into men and women who, like Macbeth and Lady Macbeth, can 'look like the innocent flower, But be the serpent under't', and for whom 'The false face must hide what the false heart doth know'. *

This image was pictured in Whitney's *Choice of Emblemes*, published in 1586, as a snake coiled beneath a strawberry plant; but it had figured in drama nearly twenty years before that in *Gismond of Salerne*, where it is used as a warning against Cupid. 'What she snake lurkes under those flowers gay.'[33] The probable dramatic source is Lucifer's equivocal shape as seen by Eve in the Garden of Eden.†

Thus, after more than a century of continuous use, the device of changed names and costumes, with its special appeal to the actor's temperament and skills, developed into a vehicle for the remorseless stripping down of masks and outward appearances to reveal the inner springs of human nature and behaviour that inform the masterpieces of the Elizabethan and Jacobean dramatic repertoire. It was a technique that depended in very large measure on the willing collaboration of spectators who were as well trained in the theatrical iconography of stage costume and disguise as were the play-makers and the actors themselves, and who entered a playhouse expecting to 'read' a play with their eyes as well as with their ears. The point is made explicit by the anonymous author of *Liberality and Prodigality*, performed before Queen Elizabeth I in 1601, when to start the play Vanity enters '*solus*, all in feathers' and says:[34]

'In words, to make description of my name,
My nature and conditions, were but vaine,
Sith this attire so plainely shewes the same,
As shewéd cannot be in words more plaine.
For lo, thus round about in feathers dight,
Doth plainely figure mine inconstancie,
As feathers, light of minde, of wit as light,
Subjected still to mutabilitie.
And for to paint me forth more properly,
Behold each feather decked gorgeously,
With colours strange in such varietie
As plainly pictures perfect Vanitie.'

*See p. 111 below for the same image in *Wisdom*.
†See Ch. VIII, p. 197 below, and Plate X, No. 14.

5 Revels, games and plays within plays

Like the other visual figurations of complicated ideas discussed above, the device of a game or play as a mirror image of earnest within the frame of an interlude enjoys a long history. The tradition stretches in unbroken line from the three mummings in *Wisdom* (*c.* 1460) to 'The Murder of Gonzago' in *Hamlet* and beyond. Strictly speaking the combative games of fist-fights, wrestling, fencing, jousts and battles ought to be included in this account; but as they have already been discussed (pp. 87–93 above) they are excluded here.

The maker of *Wisdom* deploys the device so skilfully and on so large a scale that it is hard to believe that he can have been the first to do so; yet lacking any text surviving from an earlier date it must serve as the starting-point of this enquiry. It appears in two forms: as song in the guise of an elaborate *planctus*, or lament, in scene 4, and as dance in the mould of three separate but interrelated mummings in scene 3.[35]

The *planctus* is used to illustrate the reclamation of the soul, Anima, from the disfigurement of possession by devils.* This elaborate, processional exit serves both to demonstrate Anima's change of heart and behaviour, and to impress the sincerity of her conversion upon the audience by recourse to the power of the music with its special and familiar associations with Holy Week.

The author is no less explicit about his objective in the stage-directions covering the entries of the three groups of dancers in the preceding scene. Again he wishes to display Anima's spiritual condition, control of which at this time has been wilfully deflected from Wisdom's hands into those of Lucifer.

Anima's composite companions—Mind, Understanding and Will—introduce in turn a group of dancers, each group wearing the livery of its respective leader and presenter. 'Here entur six dysgysyde in þe sute** of MYNDE, wyth rede berdys, and lyouns rampaunt on here crestys, and yche a warder† in hys honde; her‡ mynstrallys, trumpes. § Eche answere for hys name' (1. 692).

Mind immediately introduces the retainers whom he maintains—Indignation, Sturdiness, Malice, Hastiness, Vengeance and Discord. The stick-morris that they then perform (a variant of the sword-dance) to the accompaniment of trumpets (the musical emblems of battle)

---

*See Ch. VI, p. 152 below.
** *sute*: livery.
† *warder*: staff, wand, morris-stick.
‡ *her*: their.
§ *trumpes*: trumpeters.

figures war, the product of Pride, Envy and Wrath in the world: 'þis ys þe Devllys dance'. Understanding caps this with a mumming of Jurists representing 'fair speech and falsehood in one space' figured by faces cloaked in lawyers' hoods. 'Here entrethe six jorours in a sute, gownyde, wyth hodys abowt her nekys, hattys of meyntenance* þerupon, vyseryde dyversly;† here mynstrell, a bagpype' (1. 724).

He too introduces his troupe by name—Wrong, Slight, Doubleness, Falseness, Robbery and Deceit—a gang of opportunists with one eye always on the main chance, now in the livery service of Perjury and Covetousness. Their dance over, Will introduces 'a sprig of Lechery': 'Here entreth six women in sut, thre dysgysyde as galontys and thre as matrones, wyth wondyrfull vysurs congruent; here mynstrell, a horne-pype' (1.752). The girls disguised as gallants are Carelessness, Idleness and Surfeit-cum-Greed; the wenches Adultery, Mistress and Fornication. Their music is again appropriate, since the horn sounds soft and sensuous, but is itself ugly to look at and the emblem of cuckoldry.

A quarrel then follows between Will, Understanding and Mind about who actually maintains this troupe which leads to a fight between them; but this is soon patched up in a diabolic consortium:

Mind Ther ys no craft but we may trye yt.
(1. 861)

Will Now go we to þe wyne!
(1. 868)

In production these 'plays', or revels, within the play provide vivid theatrical contrasts to the gravity of the sermon that surrounds it; yet while supplying the audience with lively variety, they are self-evidently just as *serious* as the other more verbal and didactic scenes which precede and follow them. As a device the *planctus* succeeds splendidly in smoothing the transition from theatrical 'game' to dramatic 'earnest'.

When, some forty years later, Medwall uses this device in II *Fulgens and Lucres* it is partly to supply variety according to his own evaluation of audiences' tastes, and partly to compliment his patron's guests, the Flemish and Spanish ambassadors.[36] He admits that such

> . . . trifles be impertinent
> To the matter principal;
> But nevertheless they be expedient
> For to satisfy and content
> Many a man withal.

*I.e. livery hats indicative of their being Understanding's retainers.
†I.e. wearing different face-masks, needed to translate schoolboy faces into those of adult barristers.

> For some there be that looks and gapes
> Only for such trifles and japes.
>
> (ll. 25–31)

There are no stage-directions describing the mumming which Publius Cornelius offers to Lucres for her entertainment, only Lucres' questions about it and B's rather scurrilous answers to them supplied in the dialogue. From these we learn that the minstrels and dancers had Flemish accents and bizarre costumes.

Less formal than this 'play', but more cleverly integrated with the advancement of the plot, are the carol-singing incident in *Mankind*, and the subsequent conjuring of Titivillus, in both of which devices the audience is required to participate. When Nought says to the spectators,

> 'Now, I pray all the yeomanry that is here,
> To sing with us a merry cheer'—
>
> (ll. 332–3)

their acceptance of this invitation to join in the innocent pastime of community singing is immediately used to degrade them to the level of the vices by fouling their lips with the same obscene parody of sacred music that the play-maker is employing to reveal their vicious language and conduct.[37]

In the other 'play' he translates the spectators into accomplices in blackmail and then employs them as the Devil's personal financiers when the vices refuse to make Titivillus materialize without cash in advance:

> 'We shall gather money unto;
> Else there shall no man him see.'
>
> (ll. 456–7)

This device not only exploits the traditional invisibility of Titivillus, but succeeds in 'building' his entrance in a highly theatrical manner.*

The author of *The Four Elements* follows Medwall with a 'play' designed as much to offer the audience light relief as to advance the plot.[38] Humanity is bored.

> ' . . . I had much merrier company
> At the tavern than in this place.'
>
> (sig. Eiib)

Sensual Appetite then offers to bring a troupe of minstrels and dancers to cheer him up.

> 'And I will go fet hither a company
> That ye shall hear them sing as sweetly

*See p. 123 below.

112

> As they were angels clear;
> And yet I shall bring hither another sort
> Of lusty bloods to make disport;
> That shall both dance and spring,
> And turn clean above the ground
> With friskas and with gambawds round,
> That all the hall shall ring.'
>
> (sig. Eiii)

While he is fetching them Ignorance serves as spokesman for the author in telling Humanity,

> ' . . . so shalt thou best please
> All this whole company;
> For the foolish arguing that thou hast had
> With that knave Experience, that hath made
> All these folk thereof weary.'

He then adds, tauntingly, that what audiences 'love principally' is

> 'Disports, as dancing, singing
> Toys, trifles, laughing, jesting;
> For cunning they set not by.'
>
> (sig. Eiv)

In time, Hamlet will speak just as disparagingly about Polonius's theatrical tastes.

When the mummers arrive, the author takes care to cover his actors against the contingency of there being no minstrels available; so what is offered is a species of morris or clog-dance thumped out rhythmically to words sung, unaccompanied, by Ignorance. Stage-direction: 'Then he singeth this song and danceth withal, and evermore maketh countenance according to the matter; and all the others answer likewise.' Having provided his audience with this diversion, the play-maker then returns to the serious matter in hand of the catechizing of errant Humanity by his good angel, Nature.

In the hands of the Reformation polemicists the device was turned towards parody. Thus John Bale uses it twice in *Kyng Johan* to pillory Roman Catholic ritual, taking as his examples the ceremonial rites of cursing with cross, bell, book and candle, and of confession and absolution. In performance both these scenes (ed. Adams, ll. 1030–61 and 1212–37) are very colourful and highly entertaining in a shockingly satirical vein.

By the middle of the sixteenth century at least one scene or incident of this kind had become almost obligatory. The author of *Misogonus**

---

*Harbage and Schoenbaum in *Annals of English Drama*, while setting 1560–77 as outside limits for composition, date this play firmly as 1570; yet to me the whole character of the text suggests a much earlier provenance.

meets this challenge by providing one of the liveliest tavern-scenes
in English drama prior to Shakespeare's 'Boar's Head', with a very
elaborate dicing sequence followed by a riotous country dance.[39]
At the centre of both these eloquent, visual games he places the rector,
Sir John, who when reminded in Act II, scene iv, that he should be
officiating at Evensong, remarks,

> 'By God! I thank you, Sir; my parishioners, I am sure, be content
> To miss service one night, so they know I am well occupied.'
>   (ed. Farmer, p. 182; ed. Bond, p. 211, ll. 219–20)

The dicing concludes with Sir John stripped of his cassock. Thus
lightened, he is ready to partner Melissa in the dancing.

> 'Priest! keep your sink-a-pace and foot it o' the best sort;
> Now close, quod currier; come aloft, Jack, with a whim-wham!'

Environment, company and activities are here all carefully orches-
trated to exhibit the degeneration of Misogonus's character in a
manner that makes this point by entertaining rather than preaching.

Two other examples that are just as original in their treatment of this
device occur at about this time in Richard Edwards's *Damon and
Pithias* (1566) and the anonymous *Trial of Treasure* (*c.* 1565) : a shaving
tableau and the bridling of a horse. Edwards uses the former to great
comic effect in making his parasite's servants, Jack and Will, strip the
ingenuous coal-merchant, Grim, of his money and his sacks while he is
submitting himself to what they have induced him to believe is a
fashionable Court hair-cut and beard-trim. This is one of the earliest
examples of a straightforward 'gulling' that survives to us.[40]

In *The Trial of Treasure* the author's purpose is more traditional,
but his method is as amusing as it is original; the moral he is pointing
is that if a man is to be just, he must discipline his natural instincts.[41]
This is figured in the play by the seizure of the vice, Inclination, on
two occasions: first by the virtues, Sapience and Just, and then by
Just on his own, who throws a halter round his neck, a bridle over his
head and sticks a tail on his backside. When Greedy-guts returns, he
fails to recognize his friend.

> 'Why, what have we here? Jesus, benedicite!
> I holde twenty pounde it is Baalam's Asse!
> Nay, 'tis a Coolte, I see his tayle, by the masse!'
>   (sig. Ciii)

The precedent for the treatment later to be accorded by Oberon to
Bottom the Weaver is here made as obvious as the ancestor of the
device itself in the early liturgical music-drama of the *Ordo Pro-*

phetarum and the Feast of Fools. At the end of the play, when Just is instructed in a stage-direction to 'lead him out', Inclination retorts with spirit,

> 'What, softe, I saye, me-thinke ye go a shamefull pace;
> Was there ever poore, colte thus handled before?
> Fie upon it, my legges be unreasonablye sore;
> Well, yet I will rebell, yea, and rebell againe,
> And though a thousand times you shouldest me restrain.'
>
> (sig. Eiv)

Is this a case of 'he who laughs last laughs longest'? No sooner has he been led off than Time appears 'with a similitude of dust and rust'. These must be either two painted placards or, more probably, Lust and Treasure still recognizable as their earlier selves but freshly costumed to correspond with the stage-direction.*

The first play-maker, as far as we know, to have carried this device beyond 'games', mime, song, dance, disguise and other revels into the fully structured play-within-a-play was Thomas Kyd in *The Spanish Tragedy*. When the brain-sick Hieronimo finally decides how to revenge himself upon his son's murderers in terms of a play that re-enacts the murder, the method chosen is the play-maker's own, 'device' itself.

Once given definitive shape in this context, this game flowers in all the rich variety of Elizabethan and Jacobean imaginative genius as fully-fledged masques, mummings, bergomasques, pageants, May-Games, dumb-shows and scripted plays within a long succession of plays from *Love's Labour's Lost* and *A Midsummer Night's Dream* to *The Two Noble Kinsmen* and *The Maid's Tragedy* until, by 1624, the child subsumes its parent in Middleton's *A Game at Chess*. The wheel has there returned full circle to *The Play of Wisdom* with the English Court explicitly equated with the White House and its pieces, and the Spanish and Jesuit causes just as explicitly associated with the Black, and with the proposed marriage of Prince Charles to the Spanish Infanta represented in terms of the Black Knight's Pawn's attempt to seduce the White Queen's Pawn: indeed, so explicit was this use of 'game', and so completely had the notion of a play-within-a-play as a 'game' to mirror the 'earnest', or moral significance of the play surrounding it usurped the earnest of real life, that it occasioned the arrest and examination of the actors.[42] In short, they had broken the rules of 'device', jettisoning the secret, the riddle and the thrust-oblique in favour of the thrust-direct; they were lucky to escape with a fine and a brief injunction against playing, thanks to the Lord Chamberlain's intervention on their behalf. These examples, however,

---

*Cf.Dalilah's change of costume and make-up in *Nice Wanton*; see pp. 116–17 below.

take us into a world of far more sophisticated usage of this device than anything attempted before 1576. While English play-makers before then were fully aware of how to put the 'game' convention to use within a play as a pointer to the moral sense in which they wished their audiences to receive it, their actual uses of it were experimental: a play-within-a-play, moreover, requires a stage audience as well as stage players and is thus much easier to handle given a company of twelve actors than one of merely six or eight. Nevertheless, their experiments prepared the way for Kyd, Peele, and their successors to exploit the device to its fullest extent.

6 Divers other devices

If 'device', from the Tudor play-maker's standpoint, may be regarded as an active incident that gives physical and visible form to abstract concepts, it is obvious that some devices were likely to be of more general use than others. Those that were regularly employed through-out the sixteenth century have been discussed individually in the preceding sections of this chapter; but there were others which, if used less frequently, were nonetheless serviceable in special circum-stances, and these can be examined collectively in this section.

One such device is closely related to changes of name and costume, but was the concern of the make-up specialists rather than the ward-robe: this is disfigurement of faces.

The origin of this device is, presumably, the change that overtook Lucifer on falling from heaven,* since its invariable purpose is to exhibit moral degeneration. In the Tudor era it is first used by John Redford in *Wit and Science* in the context of the classroom.[43] There Wit, following his wilful flirtation with Idleness, is translated into Ignorance by having his face blacked while he is asleep; Lady Science meets him in this condition and understandably refuses to recognize him; only after he has seen his own face in the hand mirror which he had received as a gift from Reason does he realize what has occurred. This incident is retained with only minor variants by the anonymous author of *The Marriage of Wit and Science* (1568) and by Francis Merbury in *The Marriage Between Wit and Wisdom* (*c.* 1575–9) in their respective redactions of Redford's play.

Thomas Ingelend in *Nice Wanton* (*c.* 1550) adapts the device to demonstrate the fate that overtakes Dalilah following her decision to quit school and haunt the tavern. A stage-direction at line 260 instructs

*See pp. 196–7 below.

her to enter with 'her face hid,* or disfigured': this image then becomes the subject of immediate comment.[44]

> 'My sinews be shrunken, my flesh eaten with pox.
> . . . .
> Where I was fair and amiable of face,
> Now am I foul and horrible to see.'

Yet it was because she believed that the sun's heat in summer and 'in winter the cold' would make her 'limbs gross' and her 'beauty decay' that she first decided to play truant. The dramatic irony of her situation is thus accurately reflected in this striking device.

> 'Alas, wretched wretch that I am!
> Most miserable caitiff that ever was born!
> Full of pain and sorrow, crooked and lorn:
> Stuff'd with diseases, in this world forlorn!
> My sinews be shrunken, my flesh eaten with pox;
> My bones full of ache and great pain;
> My head is bald, that bare yellow locks;
> Crooked I creep to the earth again.
> Mine eyesight is dim; my hands tremble and shake;
> My stomach abhorreth all kind of meat;
> For lack of clothes great cold I take,
> When appetite serveth, I can get no meat.
> Where I was fair and amiable of face,
> Now I am foul and horrible to see
> All this I have deserved for lack of grace;
> Justly for my sins God doth plague me.'
>
> (ll. 261–76)

Robert Wilson in *Three Ladies of London* (1581) advances the device by incorporating it into his stage-action.[45] There Lucre and her servant Usury, who have persuaded Conscience to work as their bawd, pay her her wages; but while doing so Lucre dips her finger into a bottle of ink and soils every feature of Conscience's face with a black spot as she lists them.†

> 'This face is of favour, these cheeks are reddy and white;
> These lips are cherry red, and full of depe delight:
> Quicke rowling eyes, her temples hygh and forhead white as snow,
> Her eye-browes seemly set in frame, with dimpled chinne below.'

Thus pock-marked with nine black spots, Conscience's 'face of favour' has become as grotesque as her degraded way of life. (See Plate XII.)

*John Bale similarly hides the face of Law of Moses in *Three Lawes* behind a veil to indicate corruption by Scribes, Pharisees and Roman Catholic priests.

†Cf. the 'black and grainéd spots' that Queen Gertrude sees in her soul in *Hamlet*, III.iv,88–91.

It is this device again which Shakespeare employs when causing Regan and Cornwall to gouge Gloucester's eyes out in full view of the audience. Gloucester, in the play's opening scene, has rejoiced in 'darkness' and in the 'sport' which accompanied it in the begetting of Edmund: only when he has been condemned to live in physical darkness for the rest of his life does he recognize the spiritual blindness that has brought this fate upon him.

> 'O my follies! Then Edgar was abused.
> Kind gods, forgive me that, and prosper him.'
> (III. vii. 89–90)

An interesting inversion of the device is used by Marlowe to great comic effect in *Dr Faustus* immediately following the summoning of Mephostophilis. Shocked by the grim vision that greets his eyes on Mephostophilis's entrance, Faustus says:

> 'I charge thee to return, and change thy shape;
> Thou art too ugly to attend on me:
> Go, and return an old Franciscan friar,
> That holy shape becomes a devil best.'
> (First Quarto, 1604, ll. 257–60)

The verbal image is thus juxtaposed with the visual picture to obtain the maximum ironic effect possible for the audience at this crucial moment. Mephostophilis promptly obeys, thereby reinforcing the impact of this device.

Related to the disfigurement of countenance and physique is the figure of the witch. This makes its first appearance in drama in *Calisto and Melibea* (*c.* 1525) when Calisto's friend, Parmeno, describes Celestine as 'that old bearded whore' and as

> 'Yet worse than that, which never will be laft,*
> Not only a bawd, but a witch by her craft.'

Both attributes are repeated later.[46] Parmeno refers to her again as 'yonder old witch', and Melibea actually addresses her as 'Thou bearded dame, shameless thou seemest to be!' This association between witches and procuresses is made explicit by the parasite, Sempronio.

> 'Therefore lo! it is an old saying
> That women be the devil's nets, and head of sin;
> And man's misery in Paradise did begin.' †

He reaches this conclusion after observing that 'seeming to be sheep'

---

laft: left.

†Cf. Leonatus Posthumus's outburst on this theme in *Cymbeline*, II.v.

they are 'serpently shrewd' and that they use 'witchcrafts and charms to make men to their love'. In short, they are the supreme equivocators. It is thus a natural equation for John Bale to make in *Three Lawes*, some eight years later, when deciding to costume Idolatry 'like an old witch'.*

If Celestine was the first witch to make a personal appearance on the English stage, the ideas which she figures emerged in drama at least a century earlier in Chester and Wakefield where Christ in both cycles is accused by the Pharisees of using witchcraft to effect his miracles.[47] It is on these grounds, likewise, that the first Jewish doctor in the *Ludus Coventriae* Passion Play I begs Caiaphas to keep Jesus in custody because,

> 'With his fals wichcraft þe pepyl to blynde
> He werkyth fals meraclis Ageyns all kende.'
> (EETS, ll. 64–5)

One of the earliest definitions of the word as used in this context occurs in *Dives and Pauper*, and is there so similarly phrased as to suggest that the author of *Ludus Coventriae* was acquainted with it.[48]

'Every craft þat man or woman usyth to knowyn ony þyng or to don ony þyng þat he may nouȝt knowyn ne don be weye of reson ne be werkynge of kende it is wychecraft' (Commandment I, Cap. XXXIX, ll. 3–5).

Witchcraft, so we are given to understand, is 'fiend's' craft, or 'devil's' craft; the craft of equivocating to the point of making black seem to be white, or effecting changes which no mortal can achieve. It is by this means that Satan entered Paradise.†

The introduction of the figure of the witch to the stage thus admits double development either as one of Lucifer's most material agents, the prostitute, and her exploiters, the pimp and the procuress, or as a more mystical being endowed with supernatural powers to divine the future and even to influence it. The latter image, in its turn, leads directly to the 'game' or 'play' of conjuring. This idea is put to comic use in *Gammer Gurton's Needle* where Diccon assumes these powers for himself and so frightens Hodge as to make him urinate in his torn trousers. When Marlowe and Shakespeare come to use the device, it is for far more serious ends; but it is to be noticed that beards on women's faces serve just as effectively to convince Macbeth and Banquo that the three creatures whom they encounter on the heath are witches as Celestine's beard persuades Parmeno and Melibea to regard her as a witch.

*See p. 103 above.
†See Ch. VIII, p. 197 below.

Another form of disfigurement, or at least of submitting an individual to physical indignity, is to set him in the pillory or the stocks. Pillories seem to have been avoided by play-makers, possibly because they were too large and clumsy for their actors to store and handle. Stocks, however, appear early in *Hick-Scorner* where they are used by the vices to humiliate Pity.[49] Imagination first invents false charges to justify this action. Freewill then arrives carrying the stocks.

> *Freewill*　A, se! a, se, syrres, what I have brought!
> A medycyne for a payre of sore shynnes.
> At the Kynges Benche, syrres, I have you sought;
> But, I praye you, who shall were these [*rynges*]?
> *Hick-Scorner*　By God, this felowe that maye not go hence,
> I will go gyve hym these hose-rynges;
> Now, yfaythe, they be worth forty pence,
> But to his hondes I lacke two bondes.
> *Imagination*　Holde horesone, here is an halter!
> Bynde hym fast, and make hym sure.
>
> > (ed. Manly, ll. 511-20)

Use of the device in *Youth* (*c*. 1520) parallels that in *Hick-Scorner* closely. Pride, Riot and Youth take the places of Imagination, Freewill and Hick-Scorner, and Charity is substituted for Pity. Both victims accept their ill-fortune philosophically and warn their tormentors that time will bring its own revenge.[50]

In mid-century the author of *Impatient Poverty*—a rather tentative play-maker—arouses his audience's expectations that the device will be used, but disappoints them; so it is not until we arrive at *King Lear* and *Bartholomew Fair* that we find it fully deployed again. Shakespeare's use of it is the more traditional of the two. The figure placed in the stocks represents the virtues of constancy and fortitude in the person of the loyal Kent; his tormentors, the vices of pride, covetousness and lechery in the persons of Cornwall, Oswald and Regan.

> *Cornwall*　Fetch forth the stocks! As I have life and honour,
> There shall he sit till noon.
> *Regan*　Till noon! Till night, my lord, and all night too.
> *Kent*　Why, madam, if I were your father's dog,
> You should not use me so.
> *Regan*　Sir, being his knave, I will.
>
> > (II.ii.125-9)

In scene iv the pain and indignity of the image evoke the traditional sympathetic response from Lear and his Fool. 'Ha, ha!' remarks the Fool, 'he wears cruel garters'; to Lear 'such violent outrage' is 'worse than murder'. When Jonson comes to use the device, however, he turns it inside out by reversing the roles of victim and tormentors. It is the Puritan spoil-sport and hypocrite, Zeal-of-the-Land-Busy, who is placed in the stocks for overthrowing and damaging a stall of fairground ginger-bread dolls and knick-knacks—'the merchandize of Babylon ... the prophane pipes, the tinkling timbrels; a shop of reliques!'—alongside of Justice Over-doo, whose desire to hear good spoken of himself has landed him in this plight, and Waspe for assaulting the Watch. Waspe escapes by putting his shoe on his hand to make it look like his foot, and then 'slips' it out of the stocks, leaving his two companions to start fighting in this ludicrous posture. Audience sympathy is thus manipulated towards Waspe for his wit and practical common sense in an emergency, and against Busy and Over-doo who are so preoccupied in advancing their own self-righteousness as to have failed to notice that the Constable, distracted by Trouble-All, had never turned the key that locked the stocks; it is thus some eighty lines later that they realize what has happened and make their escape.

A device which from one viewpoint resembles the fight under a referee, and from another the 'play' within a play, is the trial. Again, use of it spans the sixteenth century from *Mankind* to *Liberality and Prodigality* and *The Merchant of Venice*. In *Mankind* it appears as a parody of a magistrate's court and is intended to amuse; but with Mischief in the Judge's seat, Nought as his Clerk and Mankind as the Defendant, the overriding image of corruption and disorder in the device constrasts sharply and ironically with the gravity of the model that it mirrors.

In *Gammer Gurton's Needle* the device serves simply to tie up the play's loose ends in a neat knot. All the feuding parties are summoned before the Bailey; with infinite patience and great tolerance, he picks his way through the confused skein of charges and counter-charges to reach a humane judgment that quite fortuitously results in providing the play with its farcical dénouement.

Thomas Ingelend amalgamates both techniques in the closing sequence of *Nice Wanton* and adds his own piquant variation—the casting of his vice, Iniquity, as the Council for the Prosecution coupled with his subsequent unmasking during the Defendant's plea for mitigation of sentence.

The trial scene in R. B.'s *Apius and Virginia* (1564) tamely and ineptly imitates Ingelend's example. This is another case that illustrates the difference that already existed, following the accession of Queen Elizabeth I, between the skilled professional play-maker and the amateur writer of plays.* Both *Nice Wanton* and this play end with

*See Ch. IV, pp. 78–9 above.

executions; but where Ingelend successfully contrives to balance the wit and surprise implicit in his device with the serious moral conclusion that he wishes to imprint on spectators' minds, R. B. mingles heavy-handed humour with melodramatic sensation and funereal gloom that merely draws spectators' attention to the artificiality of his conclusion.[51]

However, with the appearance of *Liberality and Prodigality* the trial-scene emerges with the potential of earlier examples fully realized, as the stage-direction which opens the final scene attests.[52] 'Enter Tipstaves, Liberality, Equity, Sherife, Clerks Cryer, Prodigality, and the Judge.' Here is the full panoply of the law courts, formally advanced and ritualistically presented.

Tipstaff	Roome, my Masters, give place, stand by.
	Sir, Equity hath sent me to let you understand,
	That hither he will resort out of hand,
	To sit upon the arraignement of Prodigality.
Liberality	In good time.
Tipstaff	Behold, he comes.
Liberality	Now, Equity, how falles the matter out?
Equity	That Prodigality is guiltie of the fact, no doubt.
	And therefore for furtherance of Justice effectually,
	My Lord the Judge comes to sit upon him presently:
	Wherein we crave your assistance.
Liberality	Ile wayte upon you.
Tipstaff	Roome, my masters, roome for my Lord: stand by.

The Judge placed, and the Clerkes under him.

(ll. 1230–44)

There can be no possible mistaking the tone set in the opening moments of this scene. It commands attention. Dramatic and theatrical as it is, this picture is also realistic in its attention to detail, more especially as the trial proceeds, being accurately observed from life. This play also ends with a death sentence.

Judge Thou, Prodigalitie, by that name haste bin indited and arraigned here, of a robbery, murther, and felonie, against the lawes committed by thee: the inditement whereof being read unto thee here, thou confessest thy selfe to be guilty therein: whereupon I Judge thee, to be had from hence, to the place thou camst fro, and from thence to the place of execution, there to be hangd till thou be dead. God have mercy on thee.

(ll. 1289–95)

Yet as the play confesses itself, on its title page, to be 'A Pleasant Comedie' it cannot end on this note; and, indeed, its unknown maker deftly turns the prisoner's plea in mitigation of sentence into an opportunity for an active display of mercy.

When Shakespeare comes to use the trial scene in *The Merchant of Venice*, it still exists as a singular device, but there it serves the much larger purpose of providing an environment in which the major device of bonds and rings can be played out, thus linking Venice organically to Belmont, and Shylock—no less symmetrically via Leah, Jessica, Antonio and Bassanio—to Portia; Old Testament justice to New.

Gift-giving also figures so prominently in many medieval and Tudor plays, from those presented to the infant Jesus by the shepherds in *Secunda Pastorum* to the tennis-balls sent by the Dauphin to Henry V and the basket of figs given to Cleopatra, as to give grounds for supposing that this too was a familiar device in the play-maker's workshop. Its origins are clearly to be discerned, as discussed in Chapters II and III, in New Year customs of the Roman Empire and the Christian extensions of them dramatized in the Visit of the Magi to Bethlehem and Lucifer's gift of the apple to Eve; but it would be useful to explore other possible sources such as the prizes awarded at tournaments and examples drawn from classical mythology. It continues to figure prominently in early Elizabethan entertainments. I find it difficult, however, to trace any consistent development of this device to any particular theatrical ends in early Tudor plays. This comment also applies to the device of invisibility although its use stretches across two centuries from Penitentia in *The Castle of Perseverance* to Prospero in *The Tempest* via Titivillus in *Mankind* and Godly Admonition in *The Longer Thou Livest*.

Another important device in many plays was song; but as the handling of this involves words as well as music, it is more convenient to discuss it in the context of verbal figures in the next section.

VI

DEVICE AND VERBAL
FIGURATION

---

1 Speaking pictures

T HE verbal devices of medieval drama were shamelessly absorbed
from the Latin Bible, compilations of English sermons and religi-
ous treatises, proverbs, and the textbooks of the schools of rhetoric.
Borrowers in Tudor England came to lean more heavily on Latin and
Greek authors, principally Cicero and Quintilian for rhetoric;
Plautus, Terence, Seneca and Horace for drama; Ovid, Seneca,
Aristotle and Plato for philosophy; but as the Reformation took root a
reversion to the Scriptures in the form of Tyndale's English New Testa-
ment of 1527, Archbishop Cranmer's *Book of Common Prayer* of 1552, the
Elizabethan *Book of Homilies*, Foxe's *Book of Martyrs*, and the Geneva
Bible of 1561 becomes just as noticeable.

Some Englishmen, if they were fortunate enough to have been
singled out for the privilege of a clerkly education and a sojourn at
university or at the Inns of Court in London, acquired a knowledge
of the classical authors; but most of them (including many priests)*
did not. Yet all of them, obliged to go to church as they were at least
once every week and frequently more often, were constantly exposed to
readings from the Scriptures and to sermons expounding them and
commenting upon them. After 1569 it became incumbent upon heads
of Protestant households who were literate to own a copy of the Bible
and familiarize their families with its contents by daily readings. When
classical authority supported biblical sentiments this was to be welcomed and turned to use by quotation; but where it did not, it could be
dismissed either as pagan superstition, or as heretical, superstitious
and casuistical like the reasoning of the Jesuits or the morality of
Machiavelli.† Play-makers, therefore, whose primary concern was the
schooling of choristers and students were free (within the bounds of

*See pp. 213–15 below.
†See pp. 205–7 and 215–16 below.

Christian orthodoxy as interpreted by governments of alternating Roman Catholic or Protestant persuasion) to search the works of classical authors for appropriate stories, debates and *sententiae* on which to build their own texts since they might reasonably expect their audiences to be equally familiar with them. Play-makers, however, who opted to write for professional actors whose economy rested on pleasing popular audiences had perforce to prefer the much more familiar traditional sources of literary *exempla* and analogy— the Bible, chronicles and popular proverbs.

Both types of play-maker possessed a further storehouse of such source material in a wide variety of visual representations of both biblical and classical stories and debates; and this 'dumb poesie', because it short-circuited literacy, could safely be regarded by play-makers as common to courtier, clerk and countryman alike. The frescoes, roof-bosses, altar-pieces and shrines that adorned every church in the land before the Reformation, and were gazed upon (even prayed to) almost every day of life—nativities, crucifixions, pietas, dooms, together with Old Testament subjects ranging from the Creation and the Fall of Lucifer to King Solomon and Daniel in the lions' den—familiarized old and young, men and women, priest and congregation with every aspect of scriptural history. Many of these subjects recurred in the tapestries, arrases, and other hangings and wall-paintings that furnished the halls and other public or 'open' rooms of all the larger houses in the land; but so did many of the more famous stories of classical antiquity as represented in the *chansons de gestes*—Hercules and Orpheus; Juno and Dido—together with Roland and Arthur and troops of virtues and vices ranging from Dame Fortune with her wheel and Dame Sapience with her looking-glass to Justice, Mercy, World, Flesh and Death.*

The three-dimensional *tableaux vivants* of civic pageantry and *tableaux morts* of the confectioner's art called 'subtleties' served only to endow these same images with greater realism and thus to make them the more useful as datum points for play-scripts. All of these visual figurations of stories from romance and Scripture, moreover, had to be painted, woven, carved, or modelled by men and women who were themselves not necessarily literate, but who had to familiarize themselves with the properties, costumes, and colours by which these characters could be identified.†

Lastly, the play-maker had access to the treasure-trove of language and all the amusing games associated with the Latin word *jocus*:

*See *EES*.i, Chs V and VI. See also Plates IV, No. 6 and V, No. 7.
†See *EES*.i, Chs II and III. See also Plate V, No. 8.

anecdote, alliteration, rhyme and what Ian Maxwell has called 'reduplication of sounds, peppered with puns'. From antiphonal chant and the *planctus* the vernacular play-maker learned soliloquy and aside; and with the confidence derived from experience he slowly came to jettison the regularity of stanzaic form to gain the flexibility of speech needed to differentiate character in stage dialogue. These aspects of dramatic development, culminating in the invention of blank verse, at least *were* evolutionary, since they were the products of trial and error, all of them being matters of technique.[1] Success provoked repetition, repetition bred familiarity, and familiarity paved a way towards variation and extension. It was in this fashion that Skelton learned from Medwall, Heywood from Skelton and his French contemporaries, Bale from Heywood and Skelton and so on throughout the century, thus explaining how Marlowe, Shakespeare and Jonson came to move so freely in a world of language and dramatic idiom that is at one and the same time unique to the end of the Tudor era and yet so reminiscent of the start of that era and of the play-makers who adorned it.

As it is obviously impossible here to follow these developments of verbal technique play by play throughout the century I propose to adopt the same method as I have used to discuss visual figuration in the theatre, and thus to treat the principal aspects of technical development in terms of selected examples under specific, but broad headings.

2 *Narrative: incident and story-line*

Although the central dynamic of the art of drama is action—an action imitated by actors in deeds, deportment, gesture and facial expression —little of this activity will be intelligible to spectators unless it is so organized as to advance a story or to conduct an argument effectively. Both the habit of story-telling, therefore, and a readiness to receive and respond to stories are well-nigh indispensable forerunners of the successful development of an organized, scripted drama; and if a story is to be narrated, or a debate conducted, in a manner that can be understood and enjoyed by an audience, a common language both of words and signs is essential. The signs, or theatrical conventions, may suffice (provided the story is a very simple one) to communicate the gist of the story or of the argument, even if the verbal code in which they are couched is foreign and unintelligible. Such was the case for most laymen of the early Middle Ages with liturgical music-drama, the texts being wholly in Latin. Adoption of the vernacular made comprehension easier and gave the play-maker much greater flexibility in handling points of detail both in straightforward narration and, more especially, in debate.

It is hardly surprising, therefore, that the art of story-telling should have been cultivated and systematically developed throughout Western Europe, first by the *trouveres* of Northern France and the troubadours of Provence in a context of social recreation, and then by the mendicant friars in the didactic and expositional context of preaching, long before its techniques became available to play-makers. Once, however, these techniques were sufficiently advanced in the form of *narracio*, *exemplum* and *disputatio* to be recognized as such, they were quickly adapted to theatrical use in the service of dramatic texts.

Provence was so situated geographically as to be the cross-roads of Western Christendom, and it was there that the writers and entertainers of the Latin South met the authors and reciters of saga and epic romance from the Gothic North.* Slowly the exchanges of mode and method of composition, and of form and style of presentation, resulted in the creation of a new literary language—Provencal—and of a new poetry—the *chansons de geste*, partially superseded in the twelfth century by the romances—which convinced educated society that a modern language was as suitable for composition as an ancient one. The new verses conveyed old stories from classical antiquity in a familiar tongue that was as intelligible to laymen as it was to clerks, and to women as it was to men; the romances also added an incentive to embellish contemporary exploits of Christian heroism undertaken for the Church Militant in its constant struggle with Islam. (See Plate III, No. 5.) Lying between classical epic with its tales of Priam, Ulysses, Aeneas and Queen Dido, and tales of modern chivalry pertaining to the crusades, were those of the Bible, and the Christian saints and martyrs. These too found their way into the new literature and, by the thirteenth century, were readily available in single copies and collections for the preachers to quote from, or to refurbish for their own instructional purposes.

The most important of these purposes was the provision of examples through which both to illustrate exposition of Scripture and doctrine, and to serve as mirrors in which to reflect those standards of conduct deemed to be admirable or, conversely, to be so reprehensible as to invite damnation. Although this kind of literature was not unknown in England during the eleventh and twelfth centuries, it was largely confined to works in Latin.[2] However, its vernacular equivalent reached these shores from two very different quarters almost simultaneously, early in the thirteenth century. On the one hand it accom-

*See *EES*.i. 181–2.

panied the minstrel troupes who escorted Eleanor of Provence to England on her marriage to Henry III in 1236, and who quickly won reputations that sufficed to earn them a living as entertainers both at Court and in the palaces of the lords temporal and spiritual. On the other hand it was also the most formidable instrument of evangelism that the recently founded mendicant orders of preachers brought with them on arriving at Canterbury to obtain Archbishop Langton's leave to work in England. The Dominicans (Friars Preachers) arrived in August 1221, and the Franciscans (Friars Minor) in September 1224;* both set up houses in Oxford where Robert Grosseteste became a lecturer in the Franciscan convent.[3] Their success was sensational as may be judged from Grosseteste's own account of their work in a letter to Pope Gregory IX, c. 1238.[4]

They illuminate the whole country with the light of their preaching and learning ... If your Holiness could see with what devotion and humility the people run to hear the word of life from them, for confession and instruction in daily life, and how much improvement the clergy and the regulars have obtained by imitating them, you would indeed say that 'upon them that dwell in the light of the shadow of death hath the light shined'.

How then did they preach to win so glowing a testimonial from so stern a taskmaster as this famous Bishop of Lincoln, and in so short a time?

By the fourteenth century sufficient written evidence of their technique survives to give us a clear answer to these questions. They translated preaching from dry, and inevitably rather dreary, scholastic exegesis into a lively art form that entertained as it instructed, and made marvels seem credible. In short, they made themselves masters of the spoken monologue in English, not only in churches, but in wayside pulpits and at market crosses, just as the *trouveres* were doing in the banquet halls of the nobility and the livery halls of the princes of commerce.†

Much the most effective weapon in the histrionic armouries of these preachers was the illustrative or exemplary story known as *narracio* or *exemplum*; no less important in its impact on the emergent art of drama was their notion of 'mirrors of conduct', or tracts specially prepared for the laity employing similar narrative techniques. Neither was original to the friars; what was new was their application of them in vernacular languages, coupled with the greatly extended range of

*From the colour of their habits the Dominicans were known as Black Friars and the Franciscans as Grey Friars.

† See *EES*.i.179–90.

tales and allegorized interpretations. What, therefore, we are confronted with is a popularizing movement that revolutionized vernacular literature, giving it a vocabulary of formal, verbal conventions hitherto undreamed of, and thenceforward shared by speaker and listener alike; and it was during this period (i.e. the late thirteenth and early fourteenth centuries) that goliardic literary traditions came to be fused with those of the preachers within the universities for the simple reason that both these groups of rhetoricians were seeking to win the allegiance of the same audience. As Robert Mannyng of Brunne observed, there were many people[5]

> þat talys and rymys wyl bleþly here;
> Yn gamys, & festys, & at þe ale,
> Love men to lestene trotëvale.

This competition between preacher and play-maker remained a constant source of rivalry and contention until the Puritans in Parliament closed the playhouses in 1642.

By the start of the fourteenth century the friars' sermons had acquired a distinctive shape that included at least one *exemplum*, and often several; these could take the form of either an extended story or a brief incident. Robert of Brunne dates his own manual of sermons 1303. John Myrk, although not himself a friar, compiled his Shropshire *Festial* at the other end of the century; its appearance is thus contemporaneous with that of Chaucer's *Canterbury Tales*. John Bromyard's *Summa Predicantium* became available midway between the two (*c.* 1350–60) and thus at least a decade before Langland tackled *Piers Plowman*.

These sermons usually start with a text appropriate to the occasion which is first expounded and then illustrated by an appropriate tale; further glosses frequently follow, and the whole is rounded off with a summary not unlike the literary *envoy*. In many sermons not only did a single *narracio* or *exemplum* proliferate into several, but it often eclipsed in length the whole of the rest of the sermon in its subject matter, and frequently became very fanciful, dramatic, or both: so much so, indeed, as to cause John Wyclif to denounce such preachers, who 'techen openly fablys, cronyklis and lesyngis,* and leven cristes gospel and þe maundementis of god'.[6]

Thus Robert of Brunne opens his homilies on the Ten Commandments with 'The Tale of the Tempted Monk' to illustrate the first, and with 'The Tale of the Bloody Child' and 'The Tale of the Vine-Storms and the Saturday half Holy-day' to illustrate the second and third. Each

---

lesyngis: lit. releasings, i.e. comic incidents.

of them is protected by careful authentication. Thus the first is introduced with:

> And þat may wel (i)prevyd be
> Wyþ a tale of auctoryte.
> þe tale ys wrytyn, al and sum,
> In a boke of 'Vitas Patrum':—

It ends with the following justification:

> By þys ensample may ȝe see
> þat god ys ever ful of pyte;
> þogh a man hym onys forsake,
> Eft wyl god aȝen hym take
> Ȝyf he with herte wyl mercy crye
> And do penaunce for hys folye.
> (ed. cit., ll. 167–70 and 329–34)

It is of course in just such words as these that the makers of fifteenth-century moralities address their audiences in their prologues and epilogues: the action of the play itself provides an even more forceful example than the tale since it is received by the eyes and ears instead of by the ears alone. Many of these tales could be dramatized without difficulty. Thus Robert of Brunne illustrates the deadly sin of Sloth with his 'Tale of the English Squire who put off his Repentence till too late', followed by 'The Tale of the Father that would not chastise his Child'.* He illustrates the sin of Covetousness with 'The Tale of the Hard Judge'.

Myrk similarly attaches an appropriate tale (sometimes two or three) culled from the legendaries of saints' lives to each of the sermons he provides for saints' days in the calendar. Nor, in the telling of these tales, does he shrink from the need to command at least three voices, two for characters in a dialogued exchange and one for the intervening narrative. Such is the case in the *narracio* attached to his sermon for St Andrew's Day where the preacher is required to speak lines given to a young man in conversation with St Andrew, and again in that for Septuagesima Sunday where Adam, Eve and Lucifer, as well as the narrator, are all required to speak.[7]

In such cases the preacher is unselfconsciously assuming for himself the triple role of actor, author and teacher, just as the *trouvere* was doing in the banquet halls when reciting epics, romances and *fabliaux* for the entertainment of his princely patrons (see Plates VIII and IX). Thus in Chaucer's and Lydgate's lifetimes the histrionic techniques of poet and preacher alike were being so regularly exercised that at any

---

*Cf. *Pride of Life*, *Mundus et Infans*, *The Disobedient Child* and *Nice Wanton*.

moment it would become possible for actors to collaborate with both in acting out the story, thereby relieving them of the need to assume any voice other than that of the expositor who introduced and concluded the active, three-dimensional *exemplum*.*

Granted this vast storehouse of biographical and incidental narrative, therefore, together with a convenient formula for applying any item in it to moralistic ends a full century before any English dramatic texts survive to us,† it is inconceivable that play-makers of the fifteenth century should not already have been well schooled in narrative techniques, and should not have found the application of *exempla* indispensable to the verbal aspect of their art. And even in later plays the inclusion of an *exemplum*, recited in the manner of a play-within-a-play, proved to be an acceptable device as may be instanced by the sailor Hick-Scorner in the play of that name, with his twin tales of the Ship of Virtue that sailed from Ireland to England and sank with all hands, and the Ship of Vice (or Fools) which carried him safely back to England, or by the incidents of the dispossessed tenant and the unbeneficed priest in *All for Money*.[8]

John Heywood in *John, Tyb and Sir John* dispenses altogether with both introductory text and concluding commentary, allowing his domestic and cautionary *exemplum* to stand on its own and to speak for itself. Three actors, each impersonating a single character, have there taken over the preacher's role of impersonator; the narrator's role has been translated into the dramatic action of the baking of the pie, the laying of the table, the summoning of Sir John the priest to supper, the mending of the bucket for water, and the final cuckolding of the hungry and stupid husband by the scheming wife and the lecherous priest; and the teacher's role of providing the text and its exposition has been incorporated emblematically into the combination of visual and verbal images of which the play is 'made', or compounded.

Of the several 'mirrors of conduct' assembled by the preachers, that collection of illustrative stories known as *Jacob's Well* and prepared for farmers and men of commerce early in the fifteenth century affords a good example.[9] Divided into ninety-five sections, or chapters, this work sets out 'to make a deep well of a shallow pit'. The pit is the human body: this lacks natural grace, and through five senses constantly admits into itself the foul water of 'the great curse'; beneath this lies 'a deep ooze, the seven deadly sins'. The author then declares his purpose:

'My werk & labour schal be to tellyn what is þis wose [ooze] of þe

*See *EES*.i. 191 ff; cf. a century later Baleus Prolocutor in *Kyng Johan*.
†The one exception is *Interludium de Clerico et Puella*, *c.* 1300.

vii dedly synnes, & how ȝe schul caste out þis wose, ffirst w(y)t(h) a skeet of contricyou(n), and aft(er) w(y)th a skavell of confessio(n), and þa(n)ne schovelyn out clene þe cru(m)mys, w(y)t(h) þe schovele of satisfaccyou(n).'

(ed. EETS, p. 2, sig. B)

With that accomplished, the watergates of the senses must be blocked up.

'More-ov(er), be-cause þi pytt is no ȝt depe in p(er)feccyou(n), but schelde in frelte and in febylnes, it muste be dolvyn depper(e) w(y)t(h) þe spade of clennesse, and þe(re)-w(y)t(h) castyn out þe sande & þe gravel þ(a)t lay under þe wose of synne, þ(a)t is, all þe circumsta(n)cys of synne ; and þa(n)ne delve dou(n), w(y)th þe spade of clennes(e), depe in þe grou(n)d of v(er)tewys, contrarye to þe vii dedly synnes, tyl þ(o) fynde vii sprynges of watyr) of g(r) ace, þ(a)t is, vii ȝiftes of þe holy gost. And þa(n)ne þi welle is depe ynow in p(er)-feccyou(n) for to springe watyr of g(r)ace.'

(*ibid.*)

The process of the actual building and furnishing of this new well is then elaborated in the same imaginative allegorical style. This is followed by a brief *exemplum*: an incident in the life of Alexander the Great indicative of the fact that time is at a premium since life itself is very short. The second chapter proceeds along the same lines expounding the nature and dangers of 'the great curse', and concluding with two much longer *exempla* retailed in vivid yet homely language—'The Vision of the Clerk Ode's Man' and 'The Contrite Scholar of Paris'. The latter illustrates the virtues of confession: the former provides a terrifying example of retributive justice. Clerk Ode, being ill, sent his servant to fetch a doctor; while on this errand the servant fell asleep and dreamt his master had died and that his soul had been brought by devils in a red-hot iron basket before the King of Hell who said to him, ironically,

'Ode, þ(o)u hast lovyd wel ese & reste, tendyrnesse to lyn & to gon in softe & delycat beddyng & clothyng, & in swete bathys, & to slepe longe in bedde. þ(er)fore þ(o)u schalt now tendyrly ben bathed and wasschyd!'

(ed. EETS, p. 9, sig. 8b)

He is then promptly stretched out on an iron grid over a fire, and roasted with brimstone heated by bellows: 'wha(n)ne he was al for-rostyd, fryed, & scaldyd, & þus for-brent, he roryd as a devyl for peyne'. Because, alive, he was a glutton and a drunkard, he is now made to drink molten metal till it runs out of his nose, eyes and ears. When his body is black all over, the Devil kisses him and 'þe feendys þrewe him dou(n) to þe pytte of helle'. On returning home the servant 'fonde his mayst(er) deed & blak as pych' (sig. 9). (See Plate VII, No. 11.)

This sensational and sardonic *exemplum* could be dramatized just as it stands.*

No less relevant to later habits of medieval and early Tudor dramaturgy is the method used throughout this book of allegorizing familiar objects in frequent use in daily life. An excellent example is offered in the chapters on 'Idleness of Thought, Word and Deed' (nos 35–7). Referring back to the advice offered in the first chapter about the equipment needed to dig the well, the author says to his readers,

'The oþ(er) day I teld ʒou how ʒe schul castyn out of ʒo(ure) pytt gravel & sand of ydelnes, þ(at)t is, of ydel thouʒtys, woordys, & dedys, to makyn ʒo(ure) pytt depper(e) in p(er)feccyou(n); for it is to scheld.†
Now schal I telle ʒ(o)u of þe spade wherew(y)t(h) ʒe schul delve ʒour(e) pyt depper(e).

þ is spade muste be cle (n) nesse. þe scho‡ þ(er) of is clene thouʒtis, þe heved§ þ(er) of is clene woordys, þe handyl þ(er) of is clene werkys. To þe firste loke þe scho of þi spade be a clene herte! lete þin herte delve depe & scharpe to thynke what seharp peyne & deth c(r)ist sufferyd for þe. (ed. EETS, p. 233, sig. 74b)

No one reading these chapters who is familiar with *Mankind* can fail to be struck by its author's parallel use of the spade, first as an emblem of Mankind's physical and spiritual health, and then, following its seizure by Titivillus, as indicative of the cause of the sudden disintegration of Mankind's character in thought, word and deed. It is to be noted moreover that *Mankind* begins *as a sermon*: it is about the separation of corn from chaff at Doomsday and it is being preached by Mercy while carrying out the function of Prologue who is then rudely interrupted by a member of the congregation (i.e. auditory), namely Mischief:

> 'I beseech you heartily leave your calc(ul)ation!
> Leave your chaff! leave your corn! leave your dalliation!
> Your wit is little; your head is mickle; ye are full of
>   predication [i.e. preaching].'

The play that then unfolds is, in effect, the *exemplum* attaching to Mercy's sermon.

*Indeed it is possible that plays like *Dux Moraud* and *The Pride of Life* originated in just this way.

†*scheld*: shield, protect.

‡*scho*: blade.

§*heved*: shaft.

This same relationship between prologue (exposition of text), the play (*exemplum*) and epilogue (moralized summary and application) characterizes far too many morality plays and Tudor interludes to be dismissed as a matter of mere chance; rather it is the case that it was from such sermons and related religious tracts of the fourteenth century that the play-makers of the two succeeding centuries, *who were so often skilled preachers themselves*, derived those methods of story-telling and plot-construction that support the 'plays' and 'games' that they devised to mirror 'earnest' for popular audiences.

G. R. Owst has already demonstrated convincingly how many characters in the English miracle cycles were shaped and made recognizable as contemporary human beings, rather than merely presented as remote figures of biblical history, from this colloquial sermon literature by men who were both highly educated and very close to the people in their daily work.[10] The common shepherds and speculative philosophers who are humble enough to enquire into the miracle of Christ's birth in Bethlehem and to pay homage to Him there, the arrogant and hypocritical bishops and magistrates who condemn Christ to death; the weeping mother, penitent prostitute, sullen withholder of tithes, shrewish housewife, and many other denizens of English town and country life populate these plays, often speaking the same language, and employing the same imagery while doing so, as was coined in sermon and tract.* Both, therefore, deserve a worthier place in histories of English literature and of the theatre than they have hitherto been given.

3 Disputation: argument and polemic

It was in the universities that the other major instrument of plot-construction was forged that underpinned so much of medieval and Tudor drama; for it was there that the young students, or 'general sophisters' as they were called, were required in their third year to devote their time to 'disputing, arguing, and responding' as part of the normal curriculum in Logic and Grammar. In his fourth year the sophister was advanced to the status of a 'questionist', namely a person officially entitled to respond to a question put to him by a Master of Arts. The question day was marked by feasts and drinking; but luckily for the student a reasonable interval of time was allowed for the preparation of those arguments to be offered on his 'determination day', or day prescribed for responding to the question. The

*See Ch. VIII, pp. 189–93 below.

questionist then had to argue his response against a Bachelor of Arts in the presence of at least one Master of Arts.[11]

Determination day was a great occasion in the life of the schools, and in many respects a theatrical one, since the *disputatio* was not only conducted with all the ritual of a formal ceremony in public, but the auditorium was packed by the determiner's own contemporaries and by senior scholars. The master sat on a raised dais surrounded by the audience: the bachelor and the determiner stood in the centre throughout the contest. Thus both judge and disputants were presented to the audience in the same relationship as judges, challengers and defenders tourneying in the lists,* or as actors *in platea*. A point lost stirred apprehension among the listeners; a point gained deserved applause, since the outcome would determine whether or not the determiner was awarded his degree.[12]

It was in this hard and highly theatrical school that men learned to recognize the everlasting combat between God's will and man's, between the four cardinal virtues allied with the Four Daughters of God and the seven deadly sins, and its extension in the form of Prudentius' *Psychomachia*, to their struggle for possession of human souls, and to handle the many, subtle twists and turns of argument that each side—good angels and bad—would resort to in attacking its opponent's claims and in defending its own positions.†

It is the more significant, therefore, that of the two public spectacles prepared for Queen Elizabeth I when she visited Cambridge in 1564 one should have been a play, and the other a disputation: the former was Plautus' *Aulularia*, performed in King's College Chapel; the latter was presented in St Mary's Church 'on a great and ample stage'.‡

The point at issue is that throughout the 200-year period 1377–1576, the literate public at Court and elsewhere appreciated and enjoyed public debate as keenly as physical combat, and surrounded both recreations with elaborate rituals of a recognizably theatrical character, and that accordingly they welcomed the inclusion of such verbal disputations within stage-plays as warmly as wrestling-matches, fencing-bouts and the cruder forms of buffeting and slap-stick fight— and as much for the methods and techniques of debate displayed as for the subject-matter. If Shakespeare's Queen Gertrude could tell Polonius to use 'more matter with less art' it was the habit of employing 'indirection, to find direction out' acquired in the dis-

---

*See *EES*.i.31–8.

†It is in the context of such debates as these that plays were fashioned out of the Creed, the Lord's Prayer, and the Ten Commandments, as well as the more obvious moralities with their confrontations between teams of virtues and vices.

‡For full descriptions of both events see *EES*.i.248–52.

putations at the university (where he played the part of Julius Caesar with the dramatic society) that she is criticizing.

That clerical play-makers should have preferred to debate theological issues as in *Wisdom*, *Everyman* and *Mundus and Infans* before the Reformation, or *Jacob and Esau*, *New Custom* and *The Life and Repentaunce of Marie Magdalene* after it is understandable, just as the schoolmen clearly preferred to debate educational questions, as John Redford does in *Wit and Science*, Thomas Ingelend in *The Disobedient Child*, or William Wager in *The Longer Thou Livest the More Fool Thou Art* who boldly states in his Prologue,[13]

> In deede, to all men it is most evident
> That a pleasaunt Rose springeth of a sharpe Thorne;
> But commonly of good seed procedeth good Corne;
> Good Parents in good manners to instruct their childe,
> Correcting him when he beginneth to grow wilde.
>
> (ll. 23–7)

and then goes on to state (1. 68): 'To extoll Vertue, without faile, is our devise.'

Other play-makers preferred social and domestic issues as is the case with John Heywood in *The Four PP* or *Gentleness and Nobility*, or the anonymous author of *Calisto and Melibea*; others again preferred political polemic, Skelton and Bale being the pioneers of this school. In every case, however, circumstance and occasion combine to provide the context for the choice, and the resulting play is accordingly serious (at times even tragic) in tone, despite comic and sometimes farcical treatment of particular incidents.[14]

John Heywood was probably the most committed of Tudor play-makers in his use of the fully dramatized *disputatio* since at least three of his plays consist of little else—four, if *Gentleness and Nobility* is credited to his invention. Where the mechanics of plot-construction are concerned, *Witty and Witless* is the most informative. This consists of a double debate, the first between James and John (which is heard by Jerome) and then the second between the loser, John, and Jerome who shows him how he could have won. In both cases the subject-matter lies within the question: 'Who is in the better case? The Fool (Witless) or the Wise Man (Witty)?'[15]

James (in the role of determiner) states that it is better to be Witless ('the sott/The natural foole calde(,) or th'Ydeot') whose basic natural wants are met gratis than Witty (the wise worker) whose labour and experience are acquired 'By muche payne of body or more payne of mynde' (ll. 1–23). John (in the role of the Bachelor of Arts) retaliates by stating that if pain is to be taken as the differential, then the poor fool who is mocked, beaten and taken advantage of by others is certainly the loser. With the debate firmly established on these lines James is able to prove that since Witless is not subject to mental stress, he suffers less pain than Witty. This John admits, but parries the thrust by then claiming that Witty, by inverse proportion, gets far more pleasure out of life; James counters by arguing that Witty's pleasures are material ones, while Witless, being too simple-minded to know what sin is, is assured of eternal bliss. To this John has no answer and admits defeat.

> 'I gyve upp my part, and your part playnly
> Of wytty and wyttles I wyshe now rather,
> That my chyld may have a foole to hys father!
> The pythe of yowr conclewsyons be all so pewr,
> That better be a foole than a wise man sewr.'
>
> (ed. Fairholt, p. 16)

At this point Jerome intervenes assuming the role of the Master of Arts.

> 'Not so! althowgh yowr fancy do so surmyse;
> Not better for man to be wytles then wyse.'

James, as the successful determiner, then retires from the fray with a final crack aimed at them both and at the audience. 'Better be sott Somer [i.e. Henry VIII's jester] than sage Salamon!'

Jerome then rebukes John for having failed to defend his case adequately and makes him admit that he would rather be a man than a beast; with this granted, Jerome presses home his advantage and argues that (the King's fool apart) just as Christ had said, 'In the house of my father ther are/Dyvers and many mantyons', so the degree of bliss awaiting a man in heaven will depend on how, while alive, he has used 'gods gyfts of grace'. John then recants, saying to the audience,

> 'Where my mate, my lords, sayd that ys gone,
> Better be sot Somer than sage Salaman,
> In forsakyng that I would now rather be
> Sage Saloman then sot Somer I assewr ye!'
>
> (*ibid.*, p. 27)

That the play was intended for production before a Court audience is apparent from the stage-direction that follows two stanzas later: 'The thre stave next followyjng in the Kyngs absens, ar voyde.' This stage-direction reveals as little else could do what made so severely abstruse a debate acceptable to its original audience; for it served, in effect, to contrast the King with his fool—hence the reiterated references to Will Sommers—and thus to be at once personal yet

137

flattering in a daring and sophisticated fashion (see Plate X, No. 15).

In *The Play of Love* the structural relationship between the play and the disputation is revealed early on when 'The Lover not Beloved' is challenged by the woman 'Beloved, not loving':

> 'Ye be a lover no whyt lovyd agayne(,)
> And I am lovyd of whom I love nothyng(;)
> Then standyth our question betwene these twayne(,)
> Of lovyng not lovyd, or lovyd, not lovyng
> Which is the case moste paynfull in sufferyng(?)'

(MSR, ll. 81–5)

This debate is then enriched with the counterpoint of a second debate between 'Lover loved' and 'Neither lover nor loved'.

Thomas Lupton, when he wrote *All for Money*, c. 1578, must have been familiar with Heywood's play since the long debate between 'Learning with Money', 'Learning without Money' and 'Money without Learning' is similarly constructed, and again enriched with the addition of two more vices, 'Moneyless and Friendless' and 'All for Money'.[16] There, however, the debate only forms one item within an extended *exemplum*, as is the case with all Tudor plays other than Heywood's, which incorporate a *disputatio*, with the exception of *Wealth and Health* (c. 1554).[17] *Horestes* thus includes two short debates, one on the ethics of regicide and revenge at the outset, and another halfway through on those of matricide.* *John Evangelist* (or *Johan the Evangelyst*) starts similarly with a debate between Irisdision and Eugenio on the relative merits of direct and indirect action; but this peters out before it really gets launched.† The author of *Impatient Poverty* (c. 1560) begins his play with a debate between Peace and Envy.[18]

> *Envy*   A syr(,) here was a longe predication(!)‡
> Me though(t) ye sayd in your communication
> To every man peace was most behoved.
> *Peace*   Forsoth(,) and so sayde I.
> *Envy*   That shalbe proved contrarye by and by (;)
> For by peace moche people are undone.

(ll. 23–8)

Matters of religious controversy like transubstantiation and the relative value of faith and works lend themselves readily to this kind of treatment and are to be found thus handled in *Jack Juggler* and *New Custom* respectively.[19] Nathaniel Woodes in *The Conflict of Conscience* debates the contrast between earthly and spiritual joy, and the

---

*See pp. 241–2 below.
†See p. 146 below.
‡*predication*: sermon, preaching.

technique was still regarded as acceptable enough in the early years of the seventeenth century for Shakespeare to use, albeit sparingly, in *Troilus and Cressida* to discuss the pros and cons of continuing the war as seen both by the Greeks and the Trojans, and in *Measure for Measure* as the central device around which the whole play is constructed. Mary Lascelles recognized in 1953 (*Shakespeare's 'Measure for Measure'*) that the whole play takes the form of 'a long-drawn-out contest between Angelo and Isabel...a single, unremitting trial of strength, suspended and renewed, but never relinquished'. She went on to observe,

'It is clear that Isabel sets out with no thought of calling the law in question. Indeed, she and Angelo are at first of the same way of thinking about it, and never so far apart but that one can see the other's position. In their several situations, each has professed a stricter adherence to the principles which all Vienna acknowledges than is customary in Vienna. And, it should be observed, Vienna does not question the good faith of either. Thus, they are to dispute a matter from a shared standpoint.' (pp. 64–5).

Nevertheless, it is obvious that by James I's accession most professional play-makers had come to regard the *disputatio* as too sophisticated an element of dramaturgy to be employed at any length in plays intended for public playhouse audiences unless suitably disguised in comic incident (as in Hamlet's discussion of death with the grave-diggers) or concealed within extended action as is the case with Prince Hal's training for kingship, and with *Measure for Measure*. Disputation, moreover, possesses the awkward corollary of suggesting further questions which it was never the play-maker's intention to raise or answer: these loose ends, therefore, float provocatively around the play to tease and worry us long after the performance is over.

As early as 1497, Henry Medwall shows himself to have been aware that even a courtly audience might jib at a disputation if offered as an entertainment at a banquet unless it was appropriately tempered with farcical incident or other 'merry disports'.[20]

Recalling Part I of *Fulgens and Lucres* at the start of Part II, he makes A say,

> 'This was the substance of the play
> That was showed here today,
> Albeit that there was
> Divers toys mingled in the same
> To stir folk to mirth and game
> And to do them solace.

The which trifles be impertinent*
To the matter principal;
But nevertheless they be expedient
For to satisfy and content
Many a man withal.
For some there be that looks and gapes
Only for such trifles and japes;
And some there be among
That forceth† little of such madness
But delighteth them in matters of sadness ‡
Be it never so long!
And every man must have his mind,
Else they will many faults find
And say the play was nought.'

(ll. 19–38)

This is a principle that even Heywood thought it advisable to follow in advertising *Gentleness and Nobility* (supposing the play to be his) to his public.[21]

A dyalogue betwen the merchau(n)t(,) the Knyght(,) and the plowman dysputyng who is a verey gentylman(,) and who is a noble man(,) and how men shuld come to auctoryte; compiled in maner of an enterlude with divers toys and gestis addyd therto to make mery pastyme and disport.

Sometimes (if rarely) a play is stated by its author to exist only to celebrate a festival or to provide honest recreation: such are Heywood's *The Play of the Weather*, the anonymous *Thersytes* and Udall's *Ralph Roister Doister*. Yet frequently such disavowal of any serious purpose serves as a protective device for the play-maker himself to distance a message that might otherwise bring the play to an end with a prison sentence for the author instead of with applause: *Godly Queen Hester* and *Jack Juggler* illustrate this point.§

However, the author of *The Four Elements*—clearly a schoolman—is fully aware that if a play is to be well received, its maker must take the intellectual calibre and tastes of its likely audience into account, and that concentrated verbal debate, while delightful for those schooled in its techniques, can be dull and meaningless for those who are not. He therefore reposes his trust in his actors, not only authorizing them to make heavy cuts, but even suggesting where these may most conveniently be made in his opening stage-direction:[22]

impertinent: irrelevant.
†*forceth*: careth.
‡*sadness*: seriousness.
§See pp. 76–8 above, and 229–31 below.

140

which interlude, if the whole matter be played, will contain
the space of an hour and a half; but, if ye list, ye may leave
out much of the sad [i.e. *serious*] matter, as the Messenger's
parte, and some of Nature's parte, and some of Experiences parte, and
yet the matter will depend conveniently [i.e. still flow smoothly], and
then will not be past three quarters of an hour of length.

This advice reveals that a consciousness existed quite early in the
sixteenth century of a division between what already might be described as 'private' and 'public' theatrical occasions, and of a growing
need to cater specifically for 'sophisticated' and 'common' stages.
This division grew steadily sharper and more contentious as the professional acting companies came to assert their hegemony over the
amateurs, whether representing town or gown; by the end of the
century it had come to ensure that if *disputatio* was to retain its traditional place in the art of play-making, it must demonstrably be clothed
in the garments of the extended, illustrative *exemplum* and those of
visual 'device'. This was a lesson that university graduates who sought
to earn a living within the professional theatre after 1576 would have
to learn the hard way by surrendering copyright in their scripts to
the company managers, and by recognizing that the managers would
not release these scripts for publication (and thus for use by other
companies) until they were certain that the play had outlived its
usefulness in earning money for its owners. Authors who could not
bring themselves to accept this situation would have to fight their
battles through the alternative schools of the private playhouses and
the Court masques.

4 *Word games:* ludus *and* jocus

In Southern Europe the Latin *jocus*, originally confined in meaning to
verbal games and tricks, came to subsume within itself all the wider
recreational meanings of *ludus*; thus, in the later vernacular languages,
the French *jeu*, the Italian *gioco* and the Spanish *juego* (together with the
personalized forms of each word) came to cover all forms of specifically
theatrical entertainment. In Northern Europe this was not the case;
and in England, while *jocus* was anglicized into 'joke' and 'joker', these
new words continued to be kept separate from *ludus*, 'game' or 'play',
and to retain their original verbal connotations.[23]

As an active ingredient in dialogue, however, jokes or *truffe*, could still
fulfil an important role within stage-plays, as could the sort of character
whose overriding propensity and predilection for playing tricks
and practical jokes on other people singled him out from the crowd, and

distinguished him as a merry-minded, if vicious, individual. With the development of an organized, scripted drama in Christian society it was inevitable that this kind of character should come in time to be allied with Lucifer and his major agents, World and Flesh, as 'The Vice'. Naturally he shares some characteristics with his classical predecessor, the parasite; but it is his association with Lucifer and sin that gives him his special English quality of an athletic equivocator, stigmatized by his wooden dagger and forearmed with a special, if hellish, grace to excel in inventive disguise of person and voice. In *Dives and Pauper*, Dives explains this quality at length to Pauper in reply to the latter's question: 'Syth þer ben so many maner of wyche-craftis þat mon nouȝt ben told in special, Y preye þe tel me in general what is wychecraft?'[24]

Not surprisingly, therefore, it is normally through the Vice that the play-maker conducts his own experiments in verbal games and tricks. This character starts to make his appearance in such persons as Mak the sheep-stealer, Garcio, and Titivillus in the Towneley Cycle, and only lacks a wooden dagger to be wholly manifest in the person of Mischief in *Mankind*. Significantly, in that environment, Mischief together with his three henchmen, Nought, Nowadays and New Guise, are also working in the service of Titivillus. Once he has come into existence as a recognizable stage-type, the Vice becomes a virtually indispensable instrument of the play-maker's craft since he solves two technical problems simultaneously within his own person; for he can both serve as Devil's advocate in any disputation (as Envy does in *Impatient Poverty* or Avarice in *Respublica*), and at the same time provide the necessary mirth from his repertoire of tricks and jokes to keep the less alert and erudite spectators awake and attentive to the instructional quality of the play as a whole, as Hick-Scorner does in the play of that name and as Iniquity does in *Nice Wanton* some fifty years later.

The subsequent history of the Vice has been treated often enough and fully enough for it to be unnecessary for me to retail that story again here;[25] but there are a number of purely verbal devices that were developed into conventions of the play-maker's craft which deserve attention for their own sake. These include alliterative abuse; re-duplication of synonymous adjectives and nouns; misheard, mis-quoted or mispronounced words and phrases; puns; inordinate boasting and grovelling sycophancy; and, of course, *double entendre* —usually infused with sexual innuendo or social satire. These games also include devices that are not particular to the Vice: *exempla* in the form of short anecdotes; *sententiae* in the form of popular proverbs and pithy sentences from Scripture or the classical authors; and the whole range of verbal imagery embracing simile, metaphor and parody. Song must also be regarded as an extension of these word games, as must diction itself, and the varied uses of rhyme, blank verse and prose to create atmosphere and distinguish character.

John Heywood was particularly fond of 'worrying' words. Thus to the Pardoner's question in *The Four PP*,[26]

> 'I pray you tell me what causeth this:
> That women, after their arising,
> Be so long in their apparelling?'

the Pedlar replies,

> 'Forsooth, women have many lets,
> And they be masked in many nets:
> As frontlets, fillets, partlets and bracelets;
> And then their bonnets and their poignets:
> By these lets and nets the let is such,
> That speed is small when haste is much.'
> (ed. Farmer, p. 36; ed. Manly, ll. 254–62)

In *The Play of the Weather*, Heywood lets Merry Report ring the changes on alliterative place-names,

> 'At Louvain, at London, and in Lombardy
> At Baldock, at Barfold, and in Barbary', etc.—

for fourteen consecutive lines concluding,

> 'The devil himself, without more leisure,
> Could not have gone half thus much, I am sure!'
> (ed. Farmer, pp. 99–100; *MSR*, ll. 204–19)

This device is particularly effective in verbal slanging matches like that between Merry Report and the Laundress in *The Play of the Weather* (p. 125) and in Neither-lover-nor-Loved's dismissal of all women in *The Play of Love*, where the text resembles a Gilbert and Sullivan patter-song.

> 'I am at one point with women all—
> The smothest, the smirkest, the smallest,
> The truest, the trimmest, the tallest,
> The wisest, the wiliest, the wildest,
> The merriest, the mannerliest, the mildest,
> The strangest, the straightest, the strongest,
> The lustiest, the least, or the longest,
> The rashest, the ruddyest, the roundest,
> The sagest, the sallowest, the soundest,
> The coyest, the cursest, the coldest,

143

The busiest, the brightest, the boldest,
The thankfullest, the thinnest, the thickest,
The saintliest, the sourest, the sickest—
Take these with all the rest, and of everyone,
So God be my help I love never one!'
(ed. Farmer, p. 150; *MSR*, ll. 356–70)

Thirty years later the author of *Respublica* employs the same technique when letting his vice, Avarice, tell the audience how he intends to fleece the State:

'Noble dame Respublica, she and none other
of the offalles, the refuse, the Ragges, the paring(es)
The baggage, the trashe, the fragment(es), the sharing(es)
The od end[es], the Cr[u]mes, the driblet(es), the chipping(es)
The patches, the peces, the broklett(es), the dripping(es)
The fliettance, the scraping(es), the wild wai[v]es and straies
The skymmyng(es), the gubbins of booties and praies
The glenyng(es), the casualties, the blynde excheat(es),
The forginge of forfayct(es), the scape of extraict(es),
Thexcesse, the waste, the spoile, the sup(er)fluities,
The windefalles, the shridding(es), the flycyng(es), (the) petie fees
with a Thowsaunde thing(es) mo w(hi)ch she maye right well lacke,
woulde fyll all these same purses (that) hange att my bakke.'
(ed. EETS, 1952, ll. 92–104)

These and other games played with words for their own sake led play-makers quickly to use them to describe and delineate development of character, and to sketch scenic and atmospheric background in a theatre that regarded heaven, earth and hell as its oyster, and rejected tiresome and artificial rules of unity of place and time as irrelevant to its purposes. Thus not only can the author of *Mankind* reveal through the actual language used by the title-role the deterioration in his character that follows upon the exchange of Mischief for Mercy as his mentor, and Skelton reveal the different characteristics of his several vices in *Magnyficence*, but actors can clothe the stage itself with words to depict day or night, Court or country, tavern or domestic hearth: in short what Thomas Dekker will later describe as 'speaking pictures'.[27]

In this context I have already called the reader's attention to the sense of actuality supplied by Worldly Affection's use of the fireplace in the hall in Henry Medwall's *Nature*, and by the purposeful use of table, candles, bread and wine in Heywood's *John, Tyb and Sir John*.* Another example occurs in *Hick-Scorner* when Freewill and Imagination want Hick himself to appear.[28]

*See p. 131 above.

Freewill   Ye, but where is Hycke-scorner now?
Imagination   Some of these yonge men hath hydde hym in
                Theyr bosomes, I warraunt you,
                Let us make a crye, that he may us here!

They then cry his name through the hall and he appears from the audience.

Half a century later William Wager in *Enough is as Good as a Feast* makes Covetousness describe the corrupting effects of wealth and power in conjunction as realistically as Shakespeare does in *Cymbeline* and *Timon of Athens*;[29] but for straightforward, artistic control of 'speaking pictures', or verbal scene-painting, little can eclipse, in Elizabethan tragedy, the Queen's description of Ophelia's suicide or, in comedy, Titania's description of a disastrously wet summer.*

It was not, however, until play-makers had acquired the confidence to use prose in conjunction with a variety of verse forms that they equipped themselves with a language of sufficient flexibility to create atmosphere, and thus with an instrument to manipulate audiences' emotional responses through contrast, juxtaposition and modulation of language alone. It is mastery of this technique, achieved during the last three decades of the sixteenth century, which above all else separates Shakespeare and his contemporaries from their predecessors as makers of plays. Thus, when Shakespeare in *All's Well That Ends Well* wants to equip Helena and the King during their first encounter in Act II, scene i with an aura of mystery mixed with majesty, he moves stealthily from the free prose given to Parolles in his remarks to Bertram (ll. 39–55) via blank verse in Lafeu's cautious introduction of Helena to the King (ll. 56–95), into rhymed couplets as confidence grows between them (ll. 127–206). Rhymed couplets emerge no less subtly and strikingly from other forms of dialogue in *Measure for Measure* to alert the audience to the linking by the Duke of the *sententiae* that underpin the disputation to the play's story-line.†

The path towards this singular achievement can be charted through the cruder experiments of the authors of the Digby *Conversion of St Paul* (*c.* 1500) and *John Evangelist* (or *Johan the Evangelyst*) (*c.* 1520) in the form of sermons, and through the use of proverbs and *dicta* of classical authors by Lewis Wager, Richard Edwards, Ulpian Fulwell, George Walpull and Thomas Kyd.

This device originates within religious moralities and is grounded in the desire to interpret familiar biblical texts from Psalms, Wisdom and the Books of the Proverbs. A late example of this treatment of

---

*Hamlet, IV.vii.165–83; *A Midsummer Night's Dream*, II.i.81–117.
†See III.ii. 163–6 and 231–52, and the song that starts Act IV.

Latin texts occurs in *John Evangelist*[30] and is worth quoting since it provides a useful gloss on Shakespeare's handling of the character of Polonius in *Hamlet*.

Eugenio	But what callest thou this way(?)
Irisdision	*Via recta*, fedyng [*sic*.? leading] to lyfe(;)
	So David named it his daye
	Spes mea stetit in via recta.
Eugenio	Passeth all men by this journeye(?)
Irisdision	Nay, and the more pytie(,) verely(,) I saye
	. . . .
Eugenio	Why(,) is there no other way but this(?)
Irisdision	Yes(,) on the lefte syde another there is(,)
	That is called (*via obliqua et via circularis*).
Eugenio	And whyder draweth this(?)
Irisdision	Even ryght to dethe(;)
	Who so walkes that way, hym selfe he slethe
Eugenio	Syr(,) who gothe that way so yll(?)
Irisdision	All they that worketh the devels wyll,
	As (*Omnes iniqui in circuitu impii ambulantes*).

Such then is the likely end awaiting those who admit to 'going round to work' and who 'by indirection find direction out'.

Wager, in *The Life and Repentaunce of Marie Magdalene*, uses Latin *sententiae* (with an immediate translation into English) to equip his Vice, Infidelity, with the means to corrupt Marie.[31] He first reflects on women's proverbial frailty and the power of flattery.

> '*Verba puellarum foliis leviora caducis*
> The promise of maidens, the Poet doth say,
>> Be as stable as a weake leafe in the wynde;
> Like as a small blast bloweth a feather away,
>> So a faire word truly chaungeth a maiden's mynd.'
>> (ll. 121–5)

Proceeding next to flatter her, he pretends to have been long acquainted with her family in order to ingratiate himself and thus gain her good-will. Then follows the next *sententia*.

> '*Puella pestis, indulgentia parentum*
> Of parents the tender and carnall sufferance
>> Is to young maidens a very pestilence.
> It is a provocation and furtherance
>> Unto all lust and fleshly concupiscence.'*
>> (ll. 174–8)

*Cf. Thomas Ingelend's *The Disobedient Child* and *Nice Wanton*, both of which are constructed around this sentiment.[32]

George Walpull uses the title, *The Tyde Taryeth no Man*, as a kind of ground-base frequently reiterated within the dialogue and as a running reminder to the audience of the play's moral significance.[33] Thomas Kyd improved on this when grafting the *sententia* at the heart of Hieronimo's dilemma in *The Spanish Tragedy* directly to soliloquy. Debating whether to choose revenge and break the fifth commandment or to observe the latter and incur dishonour, he quotes from the Vulgate.

> '*Vindicta mihi.*
> I, heaven will be revenged of every ill,
> Nor will they suffer murder unrepaide:
> Then stay *Hieronimo*, attend their will,
> For mortall men may not appoint their time.'

Against this he balances a line from Seneca's *Agamemnon*—

> *Per scelus semper tutum est sceleribus iter.**
> Strike, and strike home, where wrong is offred thee,
> For evils unto ils conductors be.
> And death's the worst of resolution.
> For he that thinks with patience to contend,
> To quiet life, his life shall easily end.

—and then a line and two half-lines from Seneca's *Troades* (ll. 510–12) rewritten as a couplet:

> *Fata si miseros juvant, habes salutem:*
> *Fata si vitam negant, habes sepulchrum.*
> If destinie thy miseries doo ease,
> Then hast thou health, and happie shalt thou be.
> (*MSR*, 1592 ed., III. xiii, ll. 1977–91)

He concludes the debate by deciding to revenge Horatio's death.[34]

Another word game or verbal device constantly repeated throughout the sixteenth century is that of misquotation and misunderstanding; this takes two forms—obstinacy or ignorance, and deliberate innuendo—and is almost invariably used for comic effect or for purposes of disguise, and is more often employed in the depiction of vicious than of virtuous characters. Henry Medwall's comic servant B inaugurates this device in II *Fulgens and Lucres* when given a verbal message by his master Publius Cornelius to convey to Lucres. Told to remind her that at their last meeting they'd seen a bird sitting on the stump of a hollow ash tree, and that Lucres had lent Cornelius her musk-ball to toss into the tree (ll. 180–215), B conveys the message in a garbled form so misquoted as to seem impertinent and vulgar (ll. 251–300),

---

*l. 115. lit: The safe way for crime is always through crime.

thus alienating Lucres against his master rather than endearing him to her.

John Redford in *Wit and Science* improves upon this by making misquotation follow immediately upon first statement in the catechizing of Ignorance who cannot spell his own name.[35]

Idleness	Where was thou born?
Ignorance	Chivas-i-bore in England mother said.
Idleness	In Ing-land?
Ignorance	Yea!
Idleness	And what's half Ingland?
	Here's *Ing*; and here's *land*. What's 'tis?
Ignorance	What's 'tis?
Idleness	What's 'tis? Whoreson! What's 'tis?
	Here's *Ing*; and here's *land*. What's 'tis?
Ignorance	'Tis my thumb.
Idleness	Thy thumb? *Ing*, whoreson! *Ing!*
Ignorance	*Ing, Ing, Ing, Ing!*
Idleness	Forth! Shall I beat thy narse, now?
Ignorance	Um—m—m—
Idleness	Shall I not beat thy narse, now?
Ignorance	Um—um—m—
Idleness	Say *no*, fool! Say *no*.
Ignorance	*Noo, noo, noo, noo, noo!*
Idleness	Go to, put together! *Ing!*
Ignorance	*Ing*
Idleness	*No!*
Ignorance	*Noo.*
Idleness	Forth now! What saith the dog?
Ignorance	Dog bark.
Idleness	Dog bark? Dog *ran*, whoreson! dog *ran!*
Ignorance	*Dog ran, whoreson! dog ran, dog ran!*
Idleness	Put together: *Ing*
Ignorance	*Ing*
Idleness	*No!*
Ignorance	*Noo*
Idleness	*Ran!*
Ignorance	*Ran*

and so on for another twenty lines.

The author of *Respublica* varies the device to suit his own ironic purpose by making his vices forget the new names they have assumed to deceive the Lady Respublica and acquire office in her government. It is then cleverly used to satirize the aims and methods of Protestant reformers ending with a sol-fa scale sung by the vices to the syllables Re-For-Refor-Reformation and conducted by Avarice.[36] The device

148

is given a new dimension in *Ralph Roister Doister* in terms of the faultily punctuated letter which, when correctly punctuated, reads quite differently, an idiom which Shakespeare adapts to his own ends in the misdirected letters of *Love's Labour's Lost*, in the trick-letters of *Twelfth Night* and *Much Ado About Nothing*, and most obviously in *A Midsummer Night's Dream* in the play within the play.

A further variant is used by the author of *The Trial of Treasure* (*c.* 1565) which is then repeated and expanded by Francis Merbury in *The Marriage Between Wit and Wisdom* (*c.* 1575–9) in the following form.[37] Constable Search spots the Vice, Idleness, disguised as a rat-catcher.

> *Search*   What shall I give thee to cry a proclamation?
> *Idleness*   For half a score pots of beer I will cry it after the best fashion.
>   *Here shall Search reach a chair, and Idleness shall go up and make*
>   *the proclamation.*
> *Search*   Come! get up here; you must say as I say.
> *Idleness*   Ho! and you say I am a knave, then I must needs say Nay.
> *Search*   First, cry 'Oyez' a good while.
> *Idleness*   Very well.

After crying 'oyez', first interminably and then much too fast, he gets it right.

> *Search*   That is very well said.
> *Idleness*   That is very well said!
> *Search*   What, I ween thou be'st drunk to-day!
> *Idleness*   Why? did you not bid me say as you did say?

Then, for the next twenty-five lines, he acts on this principle but by changing key words distorts the sense into nonsense (scene 4, ll. 492–535). When Shakespeare picks up this variant in *King Richard III*, it is to twist sense into a different sense in an aside. It is still the Vice, however, who does the twisting.

> *Prince Edward*   Methinks the truth should live from age to age,
>   As 'twere retailed to all posterity,
>   Even to the general all-ending day.
> *Gloucester*   So wise so young, they say, do never live long.
> *(aside)*
> *Prince Edward*   What say you, uncle?
> *Gloucester*   I say, without characters, fame lives long.
> *(Aside)*   Thus, like the formal Vice, Iniquity,
>   I moralize two meanings in one word.
>   (III.i.76–83)

Turn this technique inside out and one arrives at the well-intentioned, but absurdly assertive self-contradictions of Constable Elbow in *Measure for Measure* and Dogberry in *Much Ado About Nothing*. The bawdy *double entendres* that enliven Constable Elbow's accusations against Pompey Bum, the discourse of the clown Lavache in *All's Well that Ends Well* and other low-life characters, likewise stretch back to the servant B's miscarriage of Publius Cornelius's message to Lucres in II *Fulgens and Lucres*.* Notable examples occur in Lewis Wager's *The Life and Repentaunce of Marie Magdalene* and in John Lyly's *Mother Bombie*;[38] but, in general, there is a studied avoidance of this kind of word game in Elizabethan plays of religious polemic and in plays for schoolboys. When it recurs in late Elizabethan and Jacobean drama it does so most noticeably in tragedies where the play-makers are seeking to create an impression of duplicity and corruption as concomitants of luxury and power.

5 Song and atmospherics

The place of music in our drama is an honoured and all-pervasive one; for not only do payments to minstrels (in the musicianly sense of the word) vastly outnumber those made to actors in all early medieval account rolls relating to secular entertainments, but the drama of the Church was itself grounded on antiphonal singing.[39] By and large, moreover, singing, dancing and simple instrumental playing are all activities which amateurs can practise with greater ease and enjoyment than play production. In any social, recreational environment therefore music, song and dance, as well as providing pleasant pastimes with strong sexual overtones for both men and women, have themselves offered nuclei for development into more elaborate, lyric entertainments. Granted a relatively stable and sophisticated society on the one hand, and sufficient leisure and financial resources on the other hand, to permit the organization of vocal and choreographic ensembles, the challenge to expand them in the direction of dramatic art is both natural and likely to be exploited anywhere and at any time;† but the pace and direction of such development will be strictly governed by the musical forms and instrumentation currently available as well as by public taste. Thus when Bottom, in *A Midsummer Night's Dream*, responds to Titania's offer to provide him with music by expressing a predilection for the tongs and the bones, his philistinism is as much a comment on his social and educational background as it is on his personal taste. Bottom, however, can at least respond to music, however rustic its forms may be, and as a human being is thus deemed to be a

*See p. 147 above.

†See *EES*.i,Chs VI and VII.

better person than 'that man that hath no music in himself', whom Lorenzo condemns as untrustworthy in Act V, scene i of *The Merchant of Venice* on that very account.

This leads us to the heart of the matter, since music and harmony in the Middle Ages were regarded as the concomitants of divine order and concord. The abstract idea of the angelic soul is thus constantly figured in the concrete image of innocent children who sing and play instruments; and so music itself becomes an emblem of joy, decorum, peace, and harmony in human affairs. (See Plate VII, No. 10.) Thus God, in *Ludus Coventriae*, after creating heaven and the angels, says[40]

> 'Aungell(s) in hevyn evyr more xal be
> In lyth ful cler*e* bryth as ble*
> W*ith* myrth *and* song to worchip me
> Of joye þei may not mys.'
>
> (EETS, ll. 36–9)

This is immediately followed by the stage-direction, 'hic cantent angeli in celo. "Tibi omnes angeli tibi celi et universe potestates. Tibi cherubyn et seraphyn incessabili voce proclamant Sanctus, Sanctus, Sanctus, Dominus deus sabaoth"' (*Te Deum*, verses 3 and 4). By contrast, the opposite of harmony—cacophony—becomes an emblem of indecorum, disorder, the diabolic.

The presence of music in the texts or stage-directions of medieval drama is thus never wholly incidental or fortuitous. It is introduced for a specific purpose which is either to make a special point, or else to intensify the mood and tone of the entire work. Liturgical music-drama, therefore, of the tenth, eleventh and twelfth centuries, existing as it does to testify to the miraculous, and to God's constant care for men, is operatic in its style and constructed throughout from familiar tropes, antiphons, hymns and canticles, ending almost invariably with an invitation to the congregation to join in the singing of the *Te Deum* or the *Magnificat*. The words 'gaudentes et exultantes' of the concluding rubrics to the Dublin *Visitatio Sepulchri* thus exactly express the mood of the play, and explain why it must be sung throughout.

Tunc audita Christi Resurreccione, chorus presequatur alta voce quasi gaudentes et exultantes sic dicentes: Scimus Christum surrexisse a mortuis vere; tu nobis, victor rex, miserere.[41]

(Then after the announcement of Christ's Resurrection [lit: having been heard of], let the choir follow with high voice as if rejoicing and

*I.e. of brilliant colour.

exulting thus saying: We know that Christ has truly arisen from the dead; thou, O King conqueror, have pity on us.)

The Chester Play of Antichrist likewise ends with the stage-direction:

Tunc abducans eos [Elijah and Elishah] ad celos cantabit angelus Gaudete iusti in domino et cetera.[42]

(Then, leading them towards heaven, the angel shall sing, 'Rejoice in the Lord, o ye righteous ones, etc.') (See Plate VII, No. 10.)

If music can thus enhance expression of choric joy it is no less helpful to the individual in signposting moments of exceptional emotional stress. An outstanding example in liturgical drama is the aria sung by the prophet Daniel in the Beauvais *Ludus Danielis* just before he is flung into the lions' den; another is the famous *planctus*, or lamentation, of the Virgin Mary following Christ's crucifixion.[43]

Although the vernacular drama of the later Middle Ages makes much less use of music, it nevertheless continues to rely heavily upon it when seeking to achieve emotional and atmospheric effects that words *per se* are deemed incapable of supplying.[44] Thus the disconsolate Anima in *Wisdom*, when brought to acknowledge her sinful state, exits with Mind, Will and Understanding on the line, 'Wyth veray contricyon thus compleynnyng we' (1. 996), and sings lamentations prescribed for Maundy Thursday: 'Magna velud mare contricio, contricio tua: quis consoletur tui? Plorans ploravit in nocte, et lacrime ejus in maxillis ejus.'[45] The accompanying stage-direction specifies that the verses are to be sung 'in the most lamentabull wyse', and that this is to be accomplished by use of long drawn out notes as is customary in Holy Week.

When Anima returns redeemed together with her three companions, the change of state and feeling is again expressed by recourse to music.

Here entrethe ANIMA ... all in here fyrst clothynge, her chapplettys and crestys, and all having on crownys, syngynge in here commynge in:
Quid retribuam Domino pro omnibus que retribuit mihi?
Calicem salutaris accipiam et nomen Domini invocabo.

In this play, too, a singular care for appropriateness is evident in the musical instruments selected to accompany the spectacular entries of the three groups of mummers: trumpets for the emissaries of war; bagpipes for the jurors in the service of Covetousness, and horns for the servants of Sloth and Lechery. Lucifer enters without music, but roaring (1. 325). (See Plate VI, No. 9.)

In *Mankind* song is used to involve the audience in an obscene parody of sacred music. When Nowadays offers a Christmas song, Nought invites 'all þe yemandry* þat ys here to synge wyth us wyth a merry chere' and launches into a round sung in canon, the words of which are wholly scatological yet end with 'Holyke, holyke, holyke!'[46]

Medwall introduces music in II *Fulgens and Lucres* simply as a diversion to accompany the parody of Flemish folk-dances provided by Cornelius to entertain Lucres.[47]

By the start of the sixteenth century, therefore, play-makers have learnt to employ music for widely varied purposes ranging from the strictly incidental—what Medwall describes in *Fulgens and Lucres* as 'divers toys ... to stir folk to mirth and game and to do them solace' (ll. 22–4)—to serious ends that have been fully integrated with the characters and their emotions as in *Wisdom*. Granted this wide spectrum of possibilities, it is surprising that many plays thereafter appear to make little use of it. One reason for this is the economic restrictions which a nomadic existence imposed upon the resources of small professional companies; and in plays that formed part of the repertoires of such companies it is unusual to find provision made for any instrumental music other than that for pipe, fiddle or drum.† In baronial halls, of course, such companies could rely on the collaboration of the resident minstrels; and in guildhalls, livery halls and other civic settings they could call on the services of the local waits if the actors were willing to pay for them. Thus in *Mankind*, when the Vice, Mischief, calls in his assistants (Nought, Nowadays and New Guise), the last of them enters singing, 'Ande how, mynstrellys, pley þe common trace!' This is followed, ten lines later, with the stage-direction: 'Her þei daunce.'[48] No less casually introduced are the calls in the text for music in *Patient and Meek Grisell* and in *Damon and Pithias* some fifty years later; but in both of these cases provision is made for elaborate, instrumental accompaniment to the songs.

The author of *The Four Elements* (*c.* 1517–25), however, is careful to cater for the absence of minstrels as well as for their presence: hence his stage-direction, 'Then the dauncers without the hall sing this wise, and they within answer, or else they may say it for need.'[49]

Similar practical provision for both eventualities is made by Ulpian Fulwell in *Like Will to Like* in his stage-direction,[50]

'Nichol newfangle [*the Vice*] must have a gittern or some other Instrument (if he may) but if they have none they must daunce about the place all three and sing this song that followeth, which must be doon though they have an instrument.' (1587 ed.)

In general, however, it is evident that the plays which make the

---

yemandry: yeomanry.
†See Ch. VII, pp. 161–6 below.

fullest use of songs and music are those, as we would expect, which were composed for occasional performance by schoolboys or students where the play-maker could anticipate easy access to trained voices and skilled instrumentalists at no extra cost.[51] Such plays include Redford's *Wit and Science*, Udall's *Roister Doister*, Ingelend's *Nice Wanton* and R. B.'s *Apius and Virginia*; and in most of these plays the songs are so placed in the text as to provide atmosphere and heighten the emotional tension of the scene. John Phillip's *Patient and Meek Grisell* offers an excellent example with its three songs for the boy playing Grisell, its song for her husband, and its lullaby for the nurse.[52]

In stark contrast to this sweet singing in the choir is the militant roaring of the devils and the noisy clamour of their agents, the vices: the *clamant* as opposed to *cantant* of so many stage-directions in the cycles, and moralities alike. Thus in the *Jeu d' Adam* of the late twelfth century, following the death of Adam and Eve, a stage-direction at line 588 provides for a hell (*infernum*) out of which devils (*demones*) enter to carry them within, and states: 'A great smoke rises and there are noisy rejoicings and a clattering of pots and pans so that it can be heard outside.'[53]

Some three centuries later, in the Digby *Conversion of St Paul*, Diabolus's entrance at line 411 is covered by the stage-direction, 'Here to enter a dyvel with thunder and fyre' who introduces himself with the line,[54]

'Ho, ho, ho, be-holde me, the my ȝte prince of the partes in-fernall.'

Thirty lines later, 'Here shall entere a-nother devull callyd mercury, with a fyering, commyng in hast, cryeng and roryng' whose first words are 'Ho, ow ȝt, ow ȝt!' After thirty more lines another stage-direction reads, 'Here thei shal rore and crye ... ', and the scene ends spectacularly. 'Here thei shal vanyshe away with a fyrye flame and a tempest.'

Noise, violence, haste, oaths and clamour are thus the well-nigh invariable outward figurations of that general disorder and indecorum by which devils and their worldly agents declare themselves to audiences in their speech; and as in the play just quoted, sound effects of a cacophonous kind are added to enhance this effect where appropriate, and when resources permit. Thus in *Ludus Coventriae*, King Herod celebrates what he takes to be the death of the infant Christ with a drinking bout and the command,[55]

þerfore menstrell(s) round a-bowte
blowe up a mery fytt.'´

Ironically this rowdy orgy instantly provides the cue for Death and the

Devil to enter to strike Herod down and carry him off to Hell. In performance this scene, as I learned when presenting it in Tewkesbury Abbey, is one of the most chilling and dramatic in all medieval drama.

The same use of music to provide atmosphere appropriate to the mood of a scene and to enhance it where words or movement alone are deemed inadequate is evident in the dumb-shows which open each act of *Gorboduc*.* There violins are specified for Act I to accompany the entrance of the 'sixe wild men clothed in leaves'; 'cornetts' are pre-scribed for the entrance of 'a king accompanied with a nombre of his nobilitie and gentlemen' at the start of Act II; the first stage-direction for Act III specifies flutes for the 'mourners clad in black'; oboes are required for the fairies in Act IV; and the authors state that 'the drommes & fluites, began to sound' as 'the Hargabusiers and ... Armed men all in order of battaile' made their entrance in Act V. *Gorboduc* is an Inns of Court play for a special occasion where lavish musical effects might be expected; but it also provides a model at the start of Elizabeth I's reign for others to imitate as their resources permit in other, less exceptional circumstances in the years ahead. And as the economy of the professional players became more secure and their links with the Court closer, so too is greater and more consistent provision made by play-makers for songs, dances and incidental music. Nevertheless, despite these noticeable extensions of traditional uses of song and instrumental music, we must remember that one of the most remarkable innovative advances made by the later Elizabethan and Jacobean dramatists lies in their handling of language itself—most especially verse forms—to manipulate and control atmosphere and emotional tension in many scenes.

*On this play see Ch. IX, pp. 242–8 below.

VII

PRACTICAL
CONSIDERATIONS

I N this chapter I shall be concerned only with those practical considerations which directly affected the making of plays, and not
with those that governed theatres, stage-conventions, acting and
production. I have already covered stage-conventions and theatre
buildings to the best of my ability throughout the period 1377–1642 in
Volumes One and Two, and it is my intention to reserve serious discussion of acting and production for Volume Four since these are
subjects better treated retrospectively with all the evidence provided
by the stages, auditoria, plays and stage-directions to refer to, and since
both acting and production in my experience are modes which change
almost imperceptibly under external pressures exercised by changes of
taste and economic circumstances.

Much of the work relating to the influence of strictly practical
considerations upon the craft of Tudor play-makers has already been
tackled by T. W. Craik in *The Tudor Interlude* (1958), David Bevington
in *From Mankind to Marlowe* (1962) and Richard Southern in *The
Production of Plays Before Shakespeare* (1973); this chapter, accordingly,
is much indebted to their findings. No less helpful has been Richard
Axton's work in recent years on the earlier drama, especially where the
impact of popular traditions and the growth of cities upon religious
plays are concerned.[1] As a result, students of medieval and Renaissance
drama in England are today more keenly aware of the overriding
importance to the style of the surviving plays of the rise of the merchant-
bourgeois class on early drama, and of the emergence of professional
acting companies upon the later drama between 975 and 1576.
Another factor which my own studies have convinced me to be at
least as important in this context is the shifts in Christian philosophy
which must be held responsible first for the rise of the preaching
friars in the thirteenth century, then for the Lutheran Reformation
in the opening decades of the sixteenth century, and finally for the
growth of Calvinism as a political and social force in the latter half of

the century.[2] All three movements were radical in the changes they effected in attitudes to life and in the fabric of contemporary society; and all of them affected the drama profoundly in altering the nature of the 'earnest' (or perceived, ultimate reality) that the makers of stage-plays sought to capture and mirror in game'.

It would perhaps be useful, therefore, to start this discussion with a summary of those changes of approach forced upon clerical play-makers by these and earlier changes in Christian spiritual and philo-sophic attitudes, since the historical period under review spans a full 600 years, or three times that separating, say, the Romantics from ourselves. If it is granted that the earliest liturgical music-drama discussed at the start of Chapter II was one of witness to the miracles underpinning the Christian faith and of demonstration of their recurrence and abiding significance, then it follows that the only requirement imposed upon the composers of these dramas was famili-arity with the Latin biblical texts, and the anthems and canticles from which the subject-matter was selected and the plays constructed. It is to be doubted if the composers ever thought self-consciously about 'actors' in our sense of the word; rather did they think about the clerical singers, their fellow-choirmen, whom initially they were only asking to undertake certain simple variants on standard liturgical rituals on major feast days. Once they start using such words in their rubrics, however, as *quasi* (as if), *ad similitudinem* (in the likeness of), *ad imitationem* (imitating), or *quo modo* (in the manner of), it is evident that they are superimposing a new requirement upon the old ones, and that this innovation is visual. It concerns the way in which the direction of the rubric is to be carried out, and it is intended to convince the eye of the beholder rather than to attract the ear of the listener. Any reader of St Ethelwold's *Regularis Concordia*, where all these phrases occur, should thus notice that it is here that the play-maker's dis-tinguishing artistic task of juxtaposing visual or stage images with verbal ones finds its original authority. In other words, not only do the liturgical rubrics begin to imply impersonation but also to specify *behaviour*; and character plus behaviour equals acting. A subsequent addition, still well within liturgical practice, is identification of both character and locality of the required behaviour by recourse to em-blems and icons—sepulchre, crib, Mount Sinai, thuribles for the three Maries, a palm-frond for the angel, and so forth. Yet at the same time any extension of these practices must serve to deflect attention from the office *per se* towards the make-believe nature of the characters and their behaviour. For so long as the characters, and the behaviour required of them in the rubrics, remained decorous, and befitting disciples bearing witness to the reality of supernatural events in the course of a liturgy designed to celebrate a holy day, these changes were likely to have been imperceptible; but once they had been stretched to embrace unbelievers in contrast to believers, and thus to conduct that is in direct opposition to liturgical propriety and *gravitas*, they could not fail to be recognized for what they actually were —changes propelling mimetic re-enactment of event away from a liturgical *ordo* or *officium* and towards a histrionic *representatio*, *spectacula*, or *ludus*; in short, towards the make-believe actions of a stage-play or game. The catalyst would appear to have been King Herod in the extended *Officium Stellae* closely followed by Belshazzar in extensions of the *Ordo Prophetarum*. Both are unbelievers; both rejoice in their tyrannical pride; both defy prophecy and seek to kill anyone who opposes their will. No behaviour that an actor can devise to give credence to these qualities can hope to remain liturgically decorous (*honestus*) and still succeed in its aim. This dilemma and the Church's response to it is considered at length in Chapter VIII: it need not, therefore, be taken further here.*

I date this first major change of attitude by the medieval clerical play-maker to his task as occurring in the course of the twelfth century, and I believe it to have been accompanied by a decision on the part of the bishops to legitimize the new *ludi* on two conditions. The first was the separation of *honesti* (devotional) from *inhonesti* (unseemly)† *ludi* with corresponding changes in the liturgical timing and placement of the two sorts of drama; the second was the emphasis to be placed on the instructive quality of the *ludus* that was subsequently to justify continued tolerance of it under any ecclesiastical auspices. If, however, it was to instruct, it must perforce address itself much more directly than it had done hitherto to popular audiences rather than to those already dedicated to the faith by their monastic vows. And it is at this point in its history that the play-maker's craft underwent its next major change.

Whether in competition with or alongside of the *trouveres* and wandering scholars of the newly founded universities of Western Europe, clerical play-makers had to learn to accustom themselves to four novel conditions: use of vernacular languages; a spoken text as an alternative to chanted ones; to both the banquet hall and an outdoor environment as venues for performances; and to illiteracy as a major stumbling-block between crowds assembled in holiday mood at calendar festivals and the abstract, doctrinal concepts that the play-makers were required to expound in dramatic form. In short, the need to entertain while instructing became paramount if the attention of

*See pp. 178–86 below.
†I.e. in a devotional context.

audiences was to be captured, and if it was to be held for long enough for them to grasp what was being talked about. Plays like the Bavarian *Anti-Christus* from Tegernsee, Hilarius's play of St Nicholas and the Anglo-Norman plays of Adam and the Resurrection, all from the twelfth century, along with the slightly later French *Garçon et l'Aveugle* and the English *Interludium de Clerico et Puella*, give us tantalizingly brief glimpses of some of the ways in which play-makers learned to accommodate themselves to the requirements of their new audiences.* While they clung tenaciously to their original methods of establishing faith through the re-enactment and affirmation of the marvellous, they added, however tentatively, battle-scenes, contemporary low-life characters like prostitutes and clerks, devils, tricks and jokes, and even abstract personifications. The rise of cities, and of the merchant class whose wealth was fuelling this growth, could only expedite this process if the Church was to retain its often tenuous hold on the allegiance of this powerful yet restless new audience; and here, as G. R. Owst insisted nearly half a century ago, it was the preachers rather than the clerical play-makers who were most closely in touch with these audiences. As their daily work brought the preachers into direct contact with men and women in town and country, so they became acquainted with their tastes, their abilities, their faults, their fears and their sense of humour. The arrival in England of the Dominican and Franciscan friars in the first quarter of the twelfth century, and the impact of their preaching methods on people from all walks of life whether literate or not, has been discussed in Chapter VI;† so again it is unnecessary here to do more than remind the reader of the skills which they developed in transforming the English language into a flexible teaching instrument. By recourse to stories, incidents, analogues and other vivid, topical material of a figurative kind, they developed the art of monologue to a very high degree, sugaring their heavily moralized pills with entertaining anecdote. Frequently playing off one class in society against another, not shrinking from attacking hereditary power or newly acquired wealth in biting, satirical commentary, and by treating history as poetry—that is, as an invitation to participate directly in the single, great *historia* of which the prophets, Christ and the saints were all deemed to be a part, together with the preacher's own audience—the friars won the hearts and minds of their hearers to an extent that some of the severer clerics, like Wyclif and his followers, came later to regard as bordering upon idolatry.[3] In the relating of their varied *exempla*, or illustrations, moreover, they often found themselves obliged, like the reciters of *fabliaux*, to assume

*See pp. 179–82 and 189–92 below.
†See pp. 128ff. above.

the voices of several characters in conversation. In doing this they offered both play-makers and actors alike a splendid model for the construction of a didactic play: preacher's chosen text (prologue), first *exemplum* (play), second *exemplum* (sub-plot), and final commentary and exegesis (epilogue). What the preachers could not realize, at least initially, was that the play-maker, by sharing his didactic function with his actors, could colour every spoken word with a stage-picture; and that the play-maker, once aware of this, could so juxtapose his pictorial and verbal figures as either to reinforce the one with the other, or to contradict the validity of the word with the deed, or of the deed with the word. By the close of the fourteenth century, if not earlier, play-makers had learnt how to do this; and from that time forward they possessed an instrument more powerful and evocative than any devised by their mentors, the preachers, when it came to attracting audiences on public holidays. It is for this reason that the Wyclifite preachers couple writers and actors of miracle plays with friars whose *exempla* eclipse their texts, whose use of fiction submerges truth itself, and who encourage simple men and women to mistake signs for significance instead of using signs to disperse and expose the deceit and vanities of World, Flesh and the Devil; indeed such preachers and play-makers are both directly accused of doing the Devil's work for him in the well-known *Tretise of miraclis pleyinge, c.* 1390.[4]

Unabashed by these accusations which, it is only fair to note, were pressed by men deemed to be heretics by the orthodox clergy of the time, the play-makers consolidated their newly won advantage by creating those typological, cathedral-like structures in honour of the Feast of Corpus Christi, which we refer to as the English miracle cycles. In arriving at these monumental creations, however, the play-makers of the fourteenth and fifteenth centuries were also swayed by the drift in academic, theological circles away from a preoccupation with the divinity of Christ that had characterized Christian thought and liturgical practice during the Romanesque era, and towards a more pragmatic concern with Christ's humanity. The literalism of Gothic painting and sculpture, so expressive of the tenderness between smiling mother and the child at her breast or of the grief-stricken mother at the foot of the cross, or nursing the lifeless, tortured corpse of her dead son, extends into stage-plays not only in Nativity and Passion sequences, but in the lively, contemporary realism of the dramatic portraiture of Cain and Abel, Noah and his wife, Caiaphas and Pilate, and the depiction of devils.* And here too the preachers offered precedent in their constant harping on hypocrisy, greed and cruelty in high

*See *EES*.i, Plates XXIX–XXXI.

places in all walks of professional life as experienced by the helpless and exploited poor; for the latter, they argued, to be poor was to be like Christ and his family; but blessed are the meek, for they shall inherit the earth: blessed are they which do hunger and thirst after righteousness, for they shall be filled. Yet memorable though the epic miracle cycles must have been to everyone who participated in them or witnessed them summer by summer, the preachers still possessed the advantage of much more frequent and regular opportunities to address the people, and thus to polish their own rhetorical techniques; but that was an advantage that could not remain unchallenged for much longer. This was due partly to the fact that in the morality play English play-makers had found a dramatic instrument that did not owe its life to celebration of a particular occasion, but which, once it existed in the form of a prompt-copy, could be adapted for repeat performances on any other holiday anywhere, with only a line or two changed here and there to fit changed circumstances of presentation. The decline in the preachers' fortunes relative to the play-makers', however, must also be attributed to the rise of a new type of individual within English society in the course of the fifteenth century: the household servant and the civic minstrel possessed of exceptional mimetic talent who aspired to make acting their métier, mystery, or profession, and thereby to free themselves from economic and social serfdom within a country still governed by feudal barons and wealthy merchant-princes. Towards the middle of the century small bands of players begin to make their appearance in account rolls as recipients of financial rewards, travelling widely under the name of a noble patron, yet obviously free to seek employment as professional purveyors of entertainment wherever and whenever they could find an audience. This eventuality, and with it the emergence into prominence of the word 'interlude', provoked a further change in the attitudes adopted by play-makers towards their craft—a change so radical as virtually to force the play-maker to think of the resources of the acting company before setting one word or one stage-direction to paper, and thus to make the concept of 'scoring' a play for its players more appropriate than one of simply discussing an idea in dialogue. This change is perhaps best represented by Henry Medwall in the opening sequence of II *Fulgens and Lucres* in the passage already quoted on pp. 139–40 above where he admits the need to regard a play as entertainment.

Medwall was an ordained priest and chaplain to Cardinal Morton; but his primary concern here is how best to keep his audience—his patron's guests and personal household—amused. Yet before letting his prologue, the servant B, meditate publicly on this important point, he had clearly made two, prior decisions, the first being to make his moral social, topical and satirical, and the second to tailor the visual and verbal figuration of it to fit a company of five players, of whom one, possibly two, were boys.[5]

As luck would have it, English play-makers were granted another thirty years in which to come to terms with this situation, and to cast a critical eye on the early progress of the neo-classical dramatic revival proceeding in Renaissance Italy, before the Reformation forced them once again to reappraise the criteria that had hitherto governed their approach to play-construction. Within this period—the first three decades of the sixteenth century—play-makers had thus to make up their minds whether they were composing their scripts for amateurs or professionals. If it was for the former they could continue to rely on the availability of as many actors (and, usually, singers) as their cast-lists demanded; if it was for the latter, then while not necessarily restricted to the provision of only one character for each actor (i.e. five or six of each) they had to think very carefully how best to eliminate superfluous characters, and how to allow actors whom they required to double or even treble roles within a play adequate time to effect the necessary changes of costume. They also had to reflect on the time-factor, remembering that it would be difficult for a small company of players to sustain a play that lasted for more than an hour or so, more especially in the normally noisy and carefree atmosphere of a banquet hall, or tavern, or fairground. The penalty for boring an audience in those circumstances was to find no one left in the auditorium to applaud the play at the end or to contribute to the collection.* These obligations impelled play-makers to discover for themselves many new techniques that in the event operated in the interest of dramatic economy, and thus served to make the texture of their plays much richer than might otherwise have been the case.

The principles of this technique were first articulated by Robert Lee Ramsay as long ago as 1908 in his fine introduction to his edition of *Magnyficence* for the Early English Text Society, and subsequently expanded by David Bevington. First, priority had to be given to the compression of the cohorts of virtues and vices so lavishly deployed in amateur, occasional drama into a single representative of each of the warring parties.[6] Similar attention had to be given to the possibility, within the extended narrative, of suppressing characters once they had discharged their primary functions in order to release the actors cast in those roles to play new characters in later scenes. A further task of well-nigh equal importance was to reduce the scenic

*See Ch. VII, n. 16, p. 291 below.

requirements to the barest minimum that a travelling company could carry with it.

As an example of the simplest attempt to meet these new circumstances (and as the earliest to survive to us) let us look briefly at *Mundus et Infans*, alias *The World and the Child, c.* 1510.[7] This anonymous play contains a cast-list of nine characters. C. M. Gayley noted in 1903 two strikingly innovative features of this play, 'an iteration of crises in plot, and a sequence of changes in the character of the hero'. The plot is in fact traditional and follows the pattern, as Bevington remarks, 'of innocence corrupted by evil into a state of degeneracy, an encounter with God's grace resulting in conversion to goodness, then a relapse, and finally recovery to salvation'.[8] This pilgrimage, however, of the stock Everyman figure (Infans), is astonishingly accomplished with never more than two actors on the stage at once. A straight reading of the text suggests that the actor playing Infans is in fact required to play five roles—the Child, Wanton, Lust-and-Liking, Manhood and Age. Each of these characters is of course another, and older, aspect of the same single pilgrim; but as one is abandoned and the next assumed, so the actor is required to find the means to differentiate between them. This actor is consequently only off-stage for the time needed to change his costume and make-up for each new role.

The play-maker thus does precisely what Ben Jonson, a century later, said no actor or playwright should ever do:

> To make a child, now swaddled, to proceed
> Man, and then shoot up, in one beard and weed,
> Past three score years.
>   (Prologue to *Everyman in his Humour*)

Infans, however, does at least change his 'beard and weed'!

The second actor is confronted with a no less challenging role, for he must alternate between the pilgrim's good and evil angels, and thus assume four, clearly distinguishable characters. As the evil angel he must appear first as Mundus and then as Folly: as the good angel he must appear first as Conscience and then as Perseverance.

I have never produced this play, but I cannot believe that any talented actor would not welcome the many chances provided by this play-maker to exhibit his virtuosity and versatility in this multiplicity of cameo sketches. In fact the challenge is even more stimulating than I have depicted it as being, since the second actor has to alternate his stage-appearances between pilgrim's enemy and pilgrim's friend. The theatricality of this device is only heightened further by his meeting the first actor on each occasion in a new role. The only disadvantage from the audience's viewpoint is that pilgrim's friend and pilgrim's enemy can never meet, and so no direct confrontation is possible, verbal or physical. A further direct consequence of this alternating device is an alternation of mood scene by scene: seriousness contrasted with ribaldry, spirituality with worldliness.

As the story-line advances, so the play-maker suppresses characters no longer wanted. Mundus has done his work having once persuaded Child, Wanton, Lust-and-Liking and Manhood to seek material rather than spiritual advantages in life, and so can be dispensed with: the actor is thus freed to re-enter as Conscience and to sow doubts about this course of action in Manhood's mind. Having once converted Manhood, Conscience likewise can be dispensed with, and the actor is once more freed, while Manhood soliloquizes on the sacrifices he has been asked to make, to get ready to reappear as Folly and undo the good work that Conscience had done. Folly successfully completes the work begun by Mundus and then disappears from the play. Manhood is left to soliloquize again, this time deciding to commit himself fully to Folly's counsel. At this point Conscience surprisingly reappears and, finding Manhood in unconciliatory mood, decides to seek help from Perseverance. Here, for the first time, the stage is left empty for perhaps thirty seconds while the second actor dons a cloak and hood (or doffs the one he was wearing as Conscience) to reappear translated into Perseverance.* Manhood, meantime, is also changing his clothes, wig and beard to reappear as Age. The scene is thus set for the final reclamation of the errant Infans by Perseverance: and so the play ends with Age translated into Repentance.

From this brief synopsis it will be seen that this play is constructed like a sonata scored for two instruments. To achieve this within the thematic bounds of the traditional morality play, the unknown author has compressed the whole of the normal diablerie into two characters played by a single actor, Mundus and Folly. Mundus, as the engineer of corruption, represents World, Flesh and Lucifer: Folly represents all their agents, the seven deadly sins. As Conscience observes, 'These seven synnes I call folye' (1. 461). Folly confirms this identification by remarking,

> 'By my feyth, syr, into London I ran
> To the tavernes to drynke the wyne.'
> (ll. 585–6) †

The virtues are similarly compressed from the normal seven or eight to two. All in all, it is a remarkable technical achievement; more

---

*This gap can be eliminated, given two actors of similar build and height, if first and second actor switch roles at this point with the first actor changing from Manhood to Perseverance rather than to Age and vice versa. See Craik, *Tudor Interlude*, p. 41.

†See pp. 94–9 above.

especially since the play-maker succeeds in covering his tracks by seeming to expand the play's terms of reference by recourse to the frequent re-naming of the pilgrim, to additional pseudonyms, and to oblique allusions to other characters who do not appear, and to localities which are not shown. Actors can legitimately complain that their entrances and exits are often poorly motivated, and that the crude mechanics of suppression and compression at times obtrude at these points disconcertingly. Nevertheless this is a fault that experience can quickly set to rights in later plays.

One such, which may serve as an example of a more adroit technique within a more complex structure, is Skelton's *Magnyficence*.[9] Skelton wrote for a company of four adult actors and a boy instead of for two actors only, and expanded his cast-list from the nine in *Mundus et Infans* to eighteen. He restricted the boy, as Ramsay noticed, to the part of Fancy who is mocked by Folly at line 1076 as being so small that he cannot grow out of his boy's gown![10] Another actor was charged exclusively with the title-role. This left him three actors to play the sixteen other parts, an average of at least five roles each! As in *Mundus et Infans* these actors were expected to be versatile enough to play good and bad characters in swift succession. Thus one of them is required to present both Liberty and Circumspection as virtues, and Counterfeit-Countenance, Courtly Abusion, Folly and Mischief among the vices—a tall order by modern standards and one which opens up for us the prospect of a style of acting worlds removed from the naturalist techniques so assiduously cultivated by Stanislavsky, Lee Strasburg and their disciples in the film and television industries.

Skelton further restricts himself to permitting only four of his players to appear together in any one scene. Sir Edmund Chambers suggested with shrewd, theatrical perspicacity that this arose from the need to hold one actor free to keep the prompt-book and thus to serve both as prompter and stage-manager. I think this more than probable. At all events, Skelton reveals himself as a professional craftsman in the skill with which he manipulates the steady advancement of his plot to allow for the constant changes of costume required of his actors. That these costumes were anything but simple is evident from the use that Skelton makes of them to satirize the extravagance and vanity of the flamboyant Court fashions of his own day, an example of which is Courtly Abusion's narcissistic soliloquy on his 'courtly gere' already quoted (pp. 101–2 above).

Both Skelton and the author of *Mundus et Infans* used costume for another practical reason: to contrast a character's outward appearance with his or her inner nature and to reveal changes of heart and mind in the course of the action. This was achieved quite simply by making

165

characters adopt assumed names to suit their own purposes and with the change of name a change of costume. This aspect of the Tudor play-maker's technique has already been fully discussed in section 4 of Chapter V.* Suffice it here to remark therefore that this device, once mastered, could be extended at any time from the purely literal to the allegorical level. On the evidence of the plays surviving to us, John Bale was the first to grasp this opportunity in *Three Lawes* and to turn it to polemical use; but that was during the course of the Reformation when other attitudes to the craft of play-making were once again undergoing radical revision.[11]

Before the Reformation, however, play-makers found an unexpected foreign source of help in their new task of meeting the requirements of professional players. The Italian revival of interest in Roman drama that began late in the fifteenth century spread relatively quickly into England in the leading schools, at the universities and at Court.† At first interest centred on Plautus, Terence and Horace; and from these sources the idea of a concentrated scene became available as an alternative to the multi-locational, simultaneous settings traditionally used in English mystery, morality and saint plays. So too did the character of the parasite as a lively manipulator of stage-action. The latter corresponded with the English play-maker's need to suppress the multiple diablerie into a single agent of mischief and malignity; imitation thus almost certainly hastened the creation of the Vice (of whom Folly in *Mundus et Infans* is an early projection). Skelton was moving in the same direction in creating Mischief as the counter-part of Measure. As Felicity observes to Liberty at the close of Stage I, scene 3,

> 'For, without Measure, Poverte and Nede
> Wyll crepe upon us, and us to Myschefe lede;
> For Myschefe wyll mayster us yf Measure us forsake.'
>
> (EETS, ll. 152–4)

These words are deliberately prophetic and will be fulfilled by Adversity in the overthrow of Magnyficence in Stage IV, scene 31.

The idea of the concentrated scene, first encountered by English academics studying at Italian academies and subsequently publicized in illustrated editions of Terence's plays, assisted English play-makers further by suggesting to them how they might localize the stage-action of their plays.[12] In other words the *platea*, or place, of earlier plays comes to resemble the forum or street-scene of Roman comedy. Characters continue to meet in the *platea* as of old, but the place of

*See pp. 100–9 above.
†See pp. 201ff. below.

PLATE I

No. 1 Norman apsidal sanctuary: Copford, Essex

PLATE XII

No. 18 Fame and Infamy: an emblem of History forming the
frontispiece to Sir Walter Raleigh's *History of the World*, 1614

meeting becomes steadily more local and specific. In *Mundus et Infans* it is still generalized, but it is near enough to London for Folly to talk familiarly to Manhood about Holborn, Westminster, and the stews and taverns near London Bridge.[13] Skelton narrows his scene down still further; although he does not name it in his stage-directions, the dialogue consistently plants it squarely in 'An open place near the Palace of Westminster'. The palace is off-stage and out of sight, but never for long out of mind. No scaffolds, *domus*, *aedes*, mansions or other scenic *loca* are needed; and when scenic furnishings are called for, as in *Mankind* or *Hick-Scorner*, they are simple and portable. But the way is open, as with costume, to translate these furnishings from purely literal, visual emblems into allegorical ones, as Heywood does in *John, Tyb and Sir John*.*

The one essential scenic requirement was some place of concealment as nearly adjacent to the acting-area as possible for the actors to achieve the lightning-swift changes of costume and make-up required of them. In a hall, the nearby pantry or kitchen would serve; out of doors, a tent or booth: Roman example offered the curtained arcade.† In English halls, the existing screen could be adapted to this end with the additional advantage of supplying an upper level in the musicians' gallery directly above it.[14]

Granted amateur actors, whether in country towns, in colleges or at Court, play-makers were not subject to these constraints and could afford to experiment according to their fancy rather than within the limits imposed by economic pressures. Use of disputation is a case in point; elaborate provision for music is another. Heywood's *Witty and Witless* and *The Play of Love* (discussed on pp. 136–8 above) illustrate the former, Redford's *Wit and Science* illustrates the latter;[15] Redford, moreover, demands fairly elaborate scenic 'houses' for his play. Brevity, however, was coming to be regarded as the soul of wit: and this was a rule that was soon to apply as forcefully to plays written for amateurs as to plays written for professionals. And here it can scarcely be doubted that sophisticated audiences in colleges and at Court were the pace-setters. One solution frequently adopted by the play-makers was to divide their stage-action into two or more virtually self-contained sections which could be performed consecutively, but punctuated by substantial intervals of time, as Medwall did with both *Nature* and *Fulgens and Lucres*.[16] Skelton seems consciously to have experimented in *Magnyfycence* with five-act form.

By the time that Henry VIII was excommunicated and the Reformation in England had begun, most of these lessons had been well

*See p. 131 above.
†See *EES*.ii(1). 180, Fig. 10.

learned; play-makers, whether of Protestant or Roman Catholic persuasion, were thus ready to grapple with the new conditions that the break with Rome imposed upon the theatre. The most immediate of these was not so much doctrine *per se*, important though that was from a polemical and dialectical standpoint, but the dramatic metamorphosis of the Pope and the whole Catholic hierarchy from God's representatives on earth into those of Anti-Christ and Lucifer; and this was quickly followed by the imposition of stage censorship with all its implications for the play-maker.* Just as radical in its consequences for the play-maker was the sharp curtailment of the number of public holidays dedicated to saints and martyrs, the suppression of saint plays and cycles, and the struggle of the professional companies to take advantage of this situation to advance their own interests.†

Hitherto the play-maker, like the preacher, had only rarely felt impelled to extend his concern beyond moral teaching and social criticism into politics; from now on, however, he could scarcely tackle either issue without finding himself embroiled in the politics of the day, and had in consequence to learn to protect himself against accusations of heresy or sedition or both. As we shall see, means to this end had been found before the downfall of Cardinal Wolsey, when satirists elected either to use the morality form to avoid actual names and direct references, or else to distance the plot into biblical history;‡ and it was these means that John Bale and his followers polished and refined as the need for self-protection grew keener with the advance of the censorship. The result was in one sense strangely reactionary since it served to preserve at least the externals of traditional play-forms, and to delay the advancement of alternative neo-classical forms imported from Italy.§

More difficult to accommodate was the iconoclastic movement, spearheaded by Lord Chancellor Cromwell and Archbishop Cranmer, against Roman Catholic images and sacraments, since either one or the other had provided the basis of virtually every play written to celebrate a feast day in the Christian calendar. Saint plays, as I endeavour to show in Chapter VIII, were an almost immediate casualty, and the suppression of the Feast of Corpus Christi in 1548 brought with it the collapse of the annual cycles throughout England with the notable exception of the largely Catholic north. Mockery of Roman Catholic belief in the real presence in the Eucharist laid an even sharper axe to the roots of traditional attitudes to history. *In conspectu Dei* is not the

*See *EES*. ii(1), Chs III and IV; also pp. 206–8 and 228–36 below.
†See pp. 169–70 and 183 below.
‡ See pp. 204–6 and 235–8 below.
§ See pp. 201–4 below.

same thing as *sub specie aeternitatis*; as D. L. Jeffrey has shown, the reformists elected to 'remember' rather than to 'celebrate' God's several Advents in human history.[17] This, in my view, was the cruellest cut of all where the drama was concerned, sabotaging the very idea of catholicity, and with it the notion of community that had hitherto linked play-maker, player and spectators in the common celebration of events of universal concern. *The Play Called Corpus Christi* had done exactly that, as had the *Officium Visitationis Sepulchri* on Easter Day, throughout Christendom for centuries. Now that must end, and if the theatre was to survive it must find a new dynamic. Luckily, in England, some of the links between drama and occasion were preserved for at least another hundred years in the non-recurrent Court and civic festivals discussed in Chapter III. And, for a time, the Protestant reformers—so long, that is, as the drama provided them with a useful instrument of propaganda for their own cause—continued to use it for devotional and instructional ends. John Bale tried his hand at a Protestant cycle; the authors of *New Custom, Wealth and Health* and *The Trial of Treasure* likewise turned the moral interlude to Protestant uses.[18] The only other dynamic on the horizon, however, was commercial; and with the accession of Elizabeth I the play as entertainment, governed by the professional actor rather than by the clerical play-maker, was beginning to eclipse the play as celebration, both in London and in the larger provincial cities.

The Church, in the guise of Protestants of Calvinist persuasion, made one last, stalwart effort to regain control over the form and content of plays that were slipping from its hands. Led by Martin Bucer, Regius Professor of Divinity at Cambridge from 1549 to 1551, and supported later by the exiles returned from Geneva following the death of Mary I in 1558 (including John Bale), this important faction within the Anglican Elizabethan Settlement attempted to dramatize predestination; and it did so with considerable success as may be judged from the dramatic writings of Thomas Ingelend, Richard Wever and Nathaniel Woodes. Another of their number was undoubtedly Stephen Gosson. His plays have not survived, but his own description of their fortunes in the public playhouses has. In *The Schoole of Abuse* (1579) he repents of having soiled his hands with them.[19]

'Now if any man aske me why my selfe have penned Comedyes in time paste, and inveigh so egerly against them here, let him knowe that *Semel insanihimus omne*: I have sinned, and am sorry for my fault: hee runnes farre that never turnes, better late than never. I gave my self to that exercise in hope to thrive but I burnt one candle to seek another, and lost bothe my time and my travell [i.e. work], when I had done.'

It is a sad confession of failure; but I regard it also as indicative of that more general failure of nerve which, for some reason, overtook the early efforts of liberal-minded, Calvinist churchmen to reach a compromise with the theatre. I suspect the reason to be that by 1560 it was already too late for the Church, in any of its branches, to regain that control over the form and content of play-texts demanded by Martin Bucer in his *De Honestis Ludis* of 1551,* already in part surrendered to and in part seized by the professional actors during the preceding twenty years of religious and political strife. Substance is given to this belief by the anonymous author of *The Pedlar's Prophecy* (printed 1595) in his scathing attacks on the rapid growth of sectarianism in England and his fears for the future of Christianity and government quoted in Chapter VIII (pp. 215–16 below); the cynicism of Christopher Marlowe reinforces the point, as does the Archbishop of Canterbury's failure to prevent the Master of the Revels from reducing the Licensing Commission of 1589 to insignificance and abrogating its powers into his own hands within a few years of its establishment.†

These considerations, however, take us outside the chronological bounds of this book and into those of the final volume. All that needs to be noted here is that the Calvinist effort of the first two decades of Elizabeth's reign was not wasted. Indeed, more than any other influence on the theatre it induced play-makers to consider tragedy as a possible dramatic genre and led authors like Woodes and Marlowe actually to write it‡ Thereafter, Calvinist opposition to dramatic activity of any kind supplied professional acting companies and their play-makers with the opposite polarity to their own determination to thrive commercially by pleasing the public; and thereby they created an aura of moral tension inside and outside the theatre by questioning the whole purpose of plays and play-acting such as had never before been experienced in England. To this tension William Shakespeare and his contemporaries were the direct heirs.

*See *EES*.ii(1), Appendix C.
†See *EES*.ii(1). 87 f.
‡See pp. 235–9 below.

BOOK THREE

Play-makers and Play Texts

VIII

ENGLISH COMEDY FROM ITS
ORIGINS TO 1576

---

1 Christian attitudes and assumptions

I T is difficult to speak meaningfully about 'comedy' and 'tragedy' in the Middle Ages in any of the senses that these words have come to possess for Western society since the sixteenth century.

Neither comedy nor tragedy was recognized formally as a dramatic genre in the senses that Sir Philip Sidney, Ben Jonson and their successors defined them;[1] they were not recognized theatrically as something different in kind from each other or from pastoral in the sense that Italian scenic designers from Serlio onwards distinguished them visually;[2] yet they were recognized as early as the fourteenth century—at least by Dante, Boccaccio, Chaucer and Lydgate—as possessing distinctive qualities in terms of literary narrative. John Lydgate is succinct:

> My maistir Chaucer, with his fresh comedies,
> Is ded, allas, cheeff poete off Breteyne,
> That whilom made ful pitous tragedies;
> The fall of pryncis he dede also compleyne.
> *(Fall of Princes*, ll. 246–9)

In his *Troy Book* he elects to define his own understanding of both terms.

> And to declare, schortly in sentence,
> Of bo(th)e two (th)e final difference:
> A comedie hath in his gynnyng,
> At prime face, a manner compleynyng,
> And afterward endeth in gladnes;
> And it (th)e dedis only doth expres
> Of swiche as ben in povert plounged lowe;
> But tragidie, who so list to knowe,
> It begynneth in prosperite,
> And endeth ever in adversite;
> And it also doth (th)e conquest trete

173

Of riche kynges and of lordys grete,
Of my(gh)ty men and olde conquerou(ri)s,
Whiche by fraude of Fortunys schowris
Ben overcast & whelmed from her glorie.

(Troy Book, II, ll. 845–59)

Both the shape of the story and the persons appropriate to it are thus sharply and clearly distinguished in each case; nor do Lydgate's distinctions depart far from those respected by Terence, Plautus, Seneca and Horace in what, for them, was a dramatic rather than a literary context. Yet there is a difference, and an important one at that; for Lydgate, Chaucer and Dante were all writing as Christians in a Christian ordered society; and in Christian society comedy found its source along with tragedy in the Fall of Lucifer and the Fall of Adam. In both cases an error of judgment brings about a catastrophic reversal of fortune that corresponds with Aristotle's description of the tragic hero.

Where tragedy is concerned, Chaucer states the case eloquently in the opening stanzas of his Prologue to 'The Monkes Tale'. There, the narrator says he will 'biwayle in maner of Tragedie' tales of those illustrious men of high degree whose prosperity was suddenly shaken, and who were overtaken by calamity.

At Lucifer, though he an angel were,
And nat a man, at him I wol biginne;
For, thogh fortune may non angel dere,
From heigh degree yet fel he for his sinne
Doun into helle, wher he yet is inne.
O Lucifer! brightest of angels alle,
Now artow Sathanas, that maist nat twinne
Out of miserie, in which that thou art falle.

Lo Adam, in the feld of Damassene,
With goddes owene finger wroght was he,
And nat bigeten of mannes sperme unclene,
And welte al Paradys, saving o tree.
Had never wordly man so heigh degree
As Adam, til he for misgovernaunce
Was drive out of his hye prosperitee
To labour, and to helle, and to meschaunce.

The conduct of both Lucifer and Adam, tragic as its consequences were for them, was regarded by the Christian fathers as absurd, ludicrous, almost laughable because it was so unnecessary: both of them had rebelled by *choosing* to disobey the protective instructions supplied by God. All other men would follow them; but after Christ's Crucifixion and Harrowing of Hell this 'adversity' could at least be

translated into the 'prosperity' of ultimate salvation based on remembrance of Christ's sacrifice and personal repentance for past
misdeeds.

This polarization between the good and serious on the one hand,
and the bad and ridiculous on the other, establishes a contrast in
behaviour, once biblical characters start to appear on the stage,
which any actor must necessarily copy and embroider in the manner
that best befits the character he is required to represent. Thus in the
earliest Christian liturgical music-drama of the tenth and eleventh
centuries, the behaviour demanded of the actors in the dialogue
(which was chanted) and in the rubrics of the service books (which
served as stage-directions) is uniformly serious, since all the characters
are themselves serious and devout believers: the three Maries and the
angel at Christ's sepulchre, and the shepherds and the Magi at
Christ's crib. It is only when the narrative content of this lyrical
drama is extended to include Old Testament characters like the
prophets and their enemies, or New Testament characters whose
purpose is to frustrate God's will, that trouble begins;* for their
behaviour patterns must be the opposite of devout and instantly
recognizable as inspired and guided by Lucifer.[3] Bad characters,
moreover, and those about whom the Bible has very little to say (like
Mrs Noah) positively invited imaginative attention: and while no one
in his senses would have tried to invent anything about God for fear
of dire and immediate consequences, anyone could blacken the Devil
and his allies to his heart's content and still not make them wicked,
stupid or absurd enough. Two of the earliest examples of such imaginative treatment of character in liturgical music-drama are Belshazzar
and the evil counsellors in *The Play of Daniel*, and King Herod and his
soldiers in *The Massacre of the Innocents*;[4] all of these characters are
diabolic in their intentions and are required to behave in an appropriately indecorous and barbaric manner; vanity informs their
actions, and in their tyrannical boastfulness they earn—and are
intended to earn—their audience's contempt. Malignity is here
balanced against absurdity, and the result, as far as the spectator
is concerned, is fear, counter-balanced by mirth. In short, we are
invited to reject these characters, and such thoughts as motivate
their actions, by laughing at them.

Thus believers are made to triumph through their faith, courage and
good works: unbelievers are overthrown and dismissed in ridicule.
This technique is fully explicit in the *Anti-Christus* from Tegernsee of
the late twelfth century.[5]

The balance between the malign and the comic in theatrical

*See Ch. II, pp. 32–4 above.

characterization was at best a precarious one and likely in a liturgical environment to open dramatic representation to question—at least as an integral part of a particular 'order of service'. The danger lay in the threat to the gravity of the occasion being celebrated by recourse to re-enactment of the original, sacred event, since no obvious frontiers existed to limit the degree of indecorousness in which non-Christian characters might indulge. Thus the Abbess of Hohenburg, near Strasbourg, between 1167 and 1195 can lament the sad contamination of the *Officium Stellae* by unruly priests, which, she says,[6] has become an act of

'irreligion and extravagance conducted with all the licence of youth. The priests, having changed their clothes, go forth as a troop of warriors; there is no distinction between priest and warrior to be marked. At an unfitting gathering of priests and laymen the church is desecrated by feasting and drinking, buffoonery, unbecoming jokes, play, the clang of weapons, the presence of shameless wenches, the vanities of the world and all sorts of disorder. Rarely does such a gathering break up without quarrelling.'

Devils provide the extreme example, eclipsed only by Anti-Christ himself: yet on more than one calendar holiday the Church was itself prepared to tolerate complete inversion of hierarchy and order in the liturgical celebration of the Feast of the Ass, and the Feasts of Fools and of the Boy Bishop, a paradox that could only encourage trouble in other areas of liturgical music-drama.*

Another paradoxical feature of liturgical music-drama was that it owed its existence to the major feasts of joy, praise and thanksgiving in the Christian calendar, and was thus festive and celebratory in essence—a factor more nearly aligned with the comic than the tragic spirit, and of itself likely to lead to some measure of detraction from the 'seriousness' of the occasion. Re-enactment of the central events of Christian faith—Christ's miraculous birth and Resurrection—was intended to enhance and explain their abiding significance; and this was the 'earnest' that the 'plays' were required to reflect. Yet *the shape* of the narrative relating these events—a movement from adversity towards prosperity, from sorrow (through God's redeeming love for mankind) to joy—conformed to that of comedy, as articulated in classical antiquity, not tragedy.† Consciousness of this dichotomy between the gravity of the 'earnest' of a liturgy proper to the worship of the Deity and the relative levity of the 'game' of mimetic re-enactment is apparent in the shift of nomenclature in the service books,

*See pp. 182–4 below.
†See *EES*.i.314–19.

first from *ordo* and *officium* to *representatio*, and then to *ludus*. These changes, moreover, are accompanied not only by a shift in the placement accorded to liturgical music-drama away from the centre towards the periphery of the services proper to the feast, but also by the intrusion of a recognizably didactic element in the rubrics and texts. This is particularly noticeable in the case of the Anglo-Norman *Jeu d'Adam* of the late twelfth century which is scripted largely in the vernacular and not in Latin, and has been moved out of the Church to the porch, and also in quasi-liturgical plays on eschatological subjects.* Yet despite these changes of attitude on the part of monastic establishments implicit in the changes of title, in liturgical and physical location, and in increasing didacticism, when Christ's Passion finally came to be dramatized at the close of the thirteenth century it was normal to frame it—invariably in the Corpus Christi plays of the fourteenth and fifteenth centuries—with the Fall of Lucifer and Adam on one side and with Christ's Resurrection and Ascension on the other, and thus, once again, to place it within a 'comic' rather than a 'tragic' narrative structure as defined by Chaucer and Lydgate. Indeed it became the whole purpose of Gothic religious drama to prove that man's 'adversity' occasioned by Adam's Fall was no longer an everlasting impediment to final 'prosperity', thanks to Christ's redemptive atonement and His gifts of contrition and repentance through grace and penance; only those who wilfully declined these gifts and ignored these signs should anticipate the full tragic fate of everlasting separation from the Godhead—the fate of Dr Faustus. Reconcilement through love, mercy and forgiveness thus supplied a new and specifically Christian reason for the change of fortune from adversity to prosperity stipulated within the inherited, classical formula as the structural basis of 'comic' narrative: wilful disobedience, followed by an equally wilful refusal to repent, provided a new and no less specifically Christian reason for the parallel change of fortune from prosperity to adversity stipulated as the structural basis of tragic narrative.† It also generated a third possibility, stipulated neither by the medieval Latin grammarians nor by the classical authors from whom they derived their own pronouncements, tragi-comedy. A pattern thus develops, particular to medieval religious drama and repeated in miracles, moralities and saint plays alike, of innocence (prosperity), falling from grace followed by life in sin (adversity), and finally a return through contrition, repentance and penance to grace (prosperity). This was inevitable since the pattern reflected the shape of ultimate reality—earnest—as perceived in Roman Catholic philo-

*See Ch. II, pp. 36–8 above.
†See p. 174 above.

sophy and theology, and since drama conceived as *ludus*, 'game' or 'play' existed in order to mirror that 'earnest' in the mimetic, microcosmic world of theatre. Even martyrdom was safely embraced within this pattern, since death itself was eclipsed by receipt of the martyr's crown to be worn throughout eternity in heaven, with Christ's Crucifixion, Harrowing of Hell, and Resurrection providing the archetype.

In England, therefore, comedy and tragedy, as distinct dramatic genres, developed alongside of and out of religious tragi-comedy: they were thus supplements to rather than the basic or natural forms of medieval and Renaissance dramatic structure. Ever since English was first established as a university discipline it has been normal for teachers to inform their pupils that comedy arrived in England in the 1550s with *Gammer Gurton's Needle* and *Ralph Roister Doister*, and that tragedy followed it a decade later with *Gorboduc*. I use the word 'arrived' because, again, it has habitually been argued that neither 'comedy' nor 'tragedy' were native products since both were products of the Renaissance imported from Italy. On that basis, it was possible to justify, in framing the curriculum, getting quickly to grips with Marlowe, Shakespeare and other 'interesting' playwrights while leaving the 'tiresomely didactic' and predominantly religious drama of an earlier epoch to look after itself as handled by philologists, or simply to gather dust on stackroom shelves. Yet scholarly research of the past thirty years has been shaking our faith in this all-too-convenient hypothesis; and enough evidence has emerged by now to make it seem probable to scholars today that the Reformation played a far more important role in giving English drama of the Elizabethan and Jacobean era its distinctive shape and particular quality than did the examples of classical antiquity and Renaissance Italy. The time has thus now come to claim that any careful reading of the evidence relating to English religious drama between the late tenth and the early sixteenth centuries reveals unmistakably that as drama existed to postulate and propagate Roman Catholic doctrine, so that drama inevitably drew its structure from doctrine; and granted a doctrine of redemption obtainable through repentance, this drama was thus, inescapably, tragi-comic. And later comedy and tragedy must thus be regarded as grafts upon this native root-stock, imposed somewhat awkwardly, by a relatively small but very articulate and influential group of bookmen.

2 *From* ordo *to* ludus: *'earnest'*, *'game' and 'play'*

If, as I have just postulated, tragi-comedy was the basic or natural dramatic form for English play-makers of the Middle Ages—and not only Sir Philip Sidney's attack on the ubiquity of 'mongrel tragi-comedy' in the professional theatre of his own day, but the large proportion of surviving plays cast in that form between Chaucer's time and Sidney's leaves little doubt that it was—it is important for historians and critics alike to understand why this should have been so.

The primary reason, as it seems to me, lies in the relationship discerned and defined by the early Christian fathers between the mortal and the spiritual world, between mankind's transitory bodily environment on earth and the soul's future in the eternal worlds of heaven and hell. It was an axiom of belief that all three worlds were coequal in their actuality, even if those of heaven and hell could only be glimpsed fleetingly by the imagination, aided by such signs as the Holy Trinity had granted to man, partly in the form of the Gospels, partly in the gift of reason, and partly in experience of life itself, to assist him in his efforts to define them. Monastic Neoplatonism insisted that all such signs could never provide more than imperfect and deceptive images of spiritual actuality and urged fellow Christians at all times to preserve a clear distinction between 'the idea' and 'the sign'; as St Augustine had postulated, 'signs' (the facts and figures of daily life) had their uses, and as pointers that might lead men in their thinking towards 'the idea' or vision of spiritual truth, they were to be commended. The dramatic and mimetic arts, however, depending as they did for their fulfilment upon exhibition, impersonation and re-enactment, dealt directly and almost exclusively in signs, and were, on that account alone, especially untrustworthy. If the idea of Christ's Resurrection could be explained and made memorable by recourse to signs and symbols, whether visual, musical or mimetic, or by a combination of all three as in the case of the *Officium Visitationis Sepulchri*, employment of such signs could be authorized and encouraged. But if the signs themselves were to become ambiguous, as is clearly the case when a serious liturgy becomes confused in the minds of those celebrating it with an entertainment, their value, as promoters of the idea, is at once open to question.

It is this problem which accounts for the shifting of the more explicitly dramatic liturgical music-dramas to the outer edges of liturgical practice; and it is in these hazier areas that we find such plays located as the Anglo-Norman *Ordo Representacionis Adae* (or *Jeu d'Adam*), *Ad Representandum Conversionem Beati Pauli Apostoli* from Fleury, the *Ludus Danielis* of Beauvais and the *Anti-Christus* from Tegernsee, all of the twelfth century.

All these plays are more remarkable for the significant departures from normal liturgical practice which they display than for their similarities to the Easter and Christmas offices. The Fleury 'St Paul'

179

extends the connection between liturgy and occasion from Easter Sunday (*Visitatio*), Christmas Day (*Pastores*) and Epiphany (*Stella*) to a saint's day in late January (28th).[7] The Beauvais 'Daniel' admits some French vernacular phrases and is loosely attached to the Advent or Christmas season, rather than to one specific calendar feast.[*8] The Tegernsee *Anti-Christus* appears to have been presented at Christmas, *c.* 1160; it contains battles (four of them) and abstract personifications, and it is certainly politically orientated, probably as propaganda for Frederick Barbarossa's concept of the status and function of the Holy Roman Emperor and in support of the third crusade.[9] The 'Adam' is the most radical of them all. Not only is it almost wholly in the vernacular (and probably of English provenance), but it was almost as surely intended for performance in a churchyard as was the Beverley Resurrection Play (*c.* 1220). The play itself concerns Adam's Fall, Cain's murder of Abel and a sequence of specifically Jewish prophets—*not* the prophets of Christ, but prophets of Doomsday—and adds up to a didactic dramatic sermon on sin and punishment.[†] It is in no way linked organically either to Christmas or Easter liturgical plays, but it is particular to the spirit of Lent, and was probably presented at Shrovetide.[10]

Collectively these plays prove beyond doubt that the original spiritual purity of liturgical dramatic composition was being sharply assaulted in the twelfth century by interests external to those of simple, monastic culture.

Significantly, Robert Mannyng of Brunne in his *Handlyng Synne* (1303) goes well beyond merely recognizing this problem; for while commending the Easter and Christmas dramatic offices as aids to establishing faith, he roundly condemns other dramatic re-enactments of Scripture 'in streets and churchyards' as 'a sight of sin'.[11]

> A clerk of order þat haþ þe name,
> Ȝyf he iuste.[‡] he ys to blame
>   [4 lines omitted]
>   hyt ys forbode hym, yn þe decre,[§]
> Myrácles for to make or se;
> For, myrácles Ȝyf þou bygynne,
> Hyt ys a gaderyng, a syght of synne.
>   He may yn þe cherche, þurgh þys resun,
> Pley þe resurreecyun,—
> þat ys to seyë, how God ros,

*On the *Historia de Daniel Representanda* of Hilarius see p. 181 below.
†For fuller discussion see Ch. II, pp. 36–9 above.
‡ *iuste*: joust.
§Pope Innocent III's decretal of 1207.

God and man yn myȝt and los,—
To make men be yn beluë gode
þat he ros with flesshe and blode;
And he may playe, withoutyn plyght
howe God was bore yn ȝolë nyght,
To make men to beleve stedfastly
þat he lyght yn þe vyrgyne Mary.

ȝif þou do hyt yn weyys or greuys,
A syght of synne truly hyt semys.
Seynt Ysodre, y take to wyttnes,
For he hyt seyþ, þat soþe hyt es;[12]

What this uncompromising statement suggests is that a clear distinction must be preserved between devotional offices initiated and controlled by responsible ecclesiastics, and those corruptions of liturgy which through contact with life outside the cloister owed much of their form, music, language and style of acting to the histrionic practices of *trouvères* and jongleurs; such plays were thus more fittingly described as *ludi* because of what they were manifestly borrowing from the mimes and entertainers of Provence.*

Further substance is given to this interpretation of the situation at the close of the twelfth century by the three surviving texts of Abelard's pupil, Hilarius, whom Sir Edmund Chambers regarded as a goliard,[13] and about whose surviving work even the cautious Karl Young declared,

'This little volume of some sixteen leaves exhibits astonishing literary variety. Here are two student songs, a versified *vita*, a poem in praise of a resort of learning, eight verse-letters to women and boys, and three highly significant plays. In this agreeable *mélange* are expressed sly merriment, outspoken anger, equivocal amorousness, pious laudation, and dramatic tension.'

The plays are *Suscitacio Lazarus*, *Historia de Daniel Representanda* and *Ludus super Iconia Sancti Nicolai*. The first two were probably intended to be associated with festivities in the Advent or Christmas season since both have a rubric appended inviting the singing of the *Te Deum* if presented at Matins, or the *Magnificat* if presented at Vespers; his St Nicholas play appears to lack any liturgical justification whatsoever.[14] Indeed, all three plays, together with the Fleury *Versus de Resuscitacione Lazari* and *Ad Representandum Conversionem Beati Pauli Apostoli*, and with other eschatological successors, can be much more readily accommodated within the extant evidence as symptomatic of the intrusion of, and contamination by, a parallel goliardic and

*See *EES*.i. 179–90.

courtly tradition of entertainment, than as organic and evolutionary developments of strictly liturgical antecedents.[15]

Another clear pointer in this same direction is the existence in the late twelfth century and after of the seemingly liturgical *Festum Stultorum* or *Festum Asinorum* for which no formal provision is made at all in any service book of the period in Western Christendom, and that of the *Festum Archiepiscopum Puerorum* for which some evidence of formal sanction does exist.[16] This is a case of the left hand permitting what the right hand refused to recognize; in other words of a ritual composed for and executed by novices, lay servants and schoolboys celebrated on a day in the annual calendar devoted to children, 28 December (Holy Innocents) or 1 January (Circumcision), or sometimes on adjacent days depending on local convenience and practice.* Justified by the senior clergy who loaned their choirs, their sanctuaries, their refectories, and often their vestments, to their juniors, pupils and servants as an appropriate acknowledgment of those qualities of innocence and humility required of all Christians, these ceremonies were nevertheless regarded as 'permissible' rather than mandatory. For the most part the senior clergy refrained from participating themselves and never accorded the actual rites the formal recognition of an official place in liturgical use.[17] Admitted but not regularized, these 'liturgies' that were not liturgies and took the form of a religious drama that was not performed by ecclesiastics, thus invited the intrusion of external entertainers and the consequent subjection of their original purpose to such extraneous musical, verbal and mimetic variants as this abnormal liberty prompted; and so vigorously was this invitation accepted that historians and critics today are now confronted with more complaints about them, and even prohibitions, than actual descriptions.[18]

As always in school and collegiate circles on occasions of licensed revelry, parody of normal routines informs both the choice of much of the subject-matter and the manner of treatment accorded to it, while mimicry of particular local administrators and mentors holds the balance between realism and absurdity, extravaganza and normality. Both of these aspects of revelry are apparent in surviving descriptions of the Feast of Fools and the Feast of the Boy Bishop; but, as might be expected, the schoolboys, being more amenable to discipline, maintained greater decorum in the conduct of their festivities than the subdeacons and their associates did in theirs. It is thus the latter group, many of whom were frequently more closely associated with the

*26 December (St Stephen), 27 December (St John the Evangelist), 6 January (Epiphany), 13 January (octave of Epiphany) and, occasionally, 6 December (St Nicholas). See Ch. I, pp. 12–15 above, and Appendix B below.

faculties of theology in the newly established universities than with their own chapters, who formed the prime targets of the decretals and injunctions levelled against these quasi-liturgical ceremonies.[19]

In England, celebration of the *Festum Puerorum* spans a period of some 300 years. Evidence of its existence is established by 1222 at Salisbury where we learn that the cathedral then owned 'one gold ring for the Feast of the Boys',* and at St Paul's Cathedral in London by 1225 when a certain John de Belemains offered 'a white mitre fringed with gold for the boy bishop'.† By the end of the century we have notices of its existence at York, Canterbury, Lincoln, Hereford and probably at Exeter; thereafter it is traceable all over the country until, in 1541, a royal proclamation launches the official suppression of the feast and all ceremonies associated with it in the name of the Reformation.[20]

'And whereas heretofore dyverse and many superstitious and childysshe observations have been usid, and yet to this day are observed and kept in many and sondry parties of this realm, as upon sainte Nicholas, sainte Catheryne, saint Clement, the holye Innocentes, and such like; children be strangelye decked and apparelid to counterfaite priestes, bysshopps, and women; and so ledde with songes and daunces from house to house, bleassing the people, and gatherynge of monye; and boyes doo singe masse, and preache in the pulpitt, with suche other unfittinge and inconvenyent usages, rather to the derision than to any true glory of God, or honour of his saints; the kyng's majestie therefore mynding nothing so moche, as to avaunce the true glory of God without vayne superstition, willith and commaundeth, that from henceforth all suche superstitions be loste and clyerlye [*clearly*] extinguisshed throughowte all this his realmes and dominions, forasmoche as the same doo resemble rather the unlawful superstition of the gentilitie [i.e. *gentiles, pagans*] than the pure and sincere religion of Christe.'
(*A decree for observing the feasts of S. Luke, S. Mark, and S. Mary Magdalene, etc.*, 1541).

The *Festum Stultorum* was likewise established in England in the early years of the thirteenth century. In 1225 it is coupled with the *Festum Puerorum* in London in the inventory from St Paul's Cathedral already quoted, and in 1238 Robert Grosseteste, as Bishop of Lincoln, banned its observance in the *Constitutions* for his diocese:[21]

'Execrabilem etiam consuetudinem, quae consuevit in quibusdam ecclesiis observari de faciendo festum stultorum....'.

* 'annulus unus aureus ad Festum Puerorum'.
† 'mitra alia alba addubbata aurifrigio, plana est; quam dedit J. Belemains episcope innocentum'.

That it reappeared sporadically both at Lincoln and elsewhere is certain, but in general the superior clergy in England succeeded in imposing far more effective control over the rowdier and more blasphemous and licentious aspects of both feasts than their continental counterparts. Lack of firm evidence makes it impossible to adduce particular reasons for this, but I suspect myself that the principal reason may lie in a determination on the part of English bishops to give priority within the Churches to the more easily controllable *Festum Puerorum*, and an equally firm resolve to shift the *Festum Stultorum* into the more appropriate, secular environment of the halls and refectories in universities, law schools and baronial palaces.[22]

It is easy to overestimate the importance of these feasts of inversion and irreverence in their influence upon the drama, for when all is said and done they consisted of ceremonies, processions, levies or collections, potations and banquets rather than plays, and were more nearly analogous, in an ecclesiastical context, to civic pageantry and tournaments than to stage-plays. What they do contain, however, is an undeniable theatricality and element of parody that is far removed from the austere, contemplative quality of early liturgical music-drama; and this theatricality, moreover, stems unquestionably from sources in reaction against monastic culture. Starting from a generalized attack on hierarchy and the spirit of order itself—in other words, an assertion of man's natural condition in the face of society's attempts to regulate and tame it—these quasi-liturgical ceremonies rapidly developed into expressions of what, at an unselfconscious or natural level, we may term 'release', and of what at a more self-conscious and sophisticated level we may term 'rebellion' or 'assault', incorporating satire and complaint directed against abuses of power in Church and State alike, winning instant popular favour by occasioning mirth, merriment and laughter.[23]

Under these pressures the superior clergy were forced into making a clear-cut distinction between *honestus* and *inhonestus*, or 'seemly' and 'unseemly' uses of dramatic art.[24] They did so in terms of changes of name and location, substituting *ludus* for *officium* and churchyard and refectory for the choir and nave of the church itself, and by acknowledging the contribution that a *ludus* could make to promoting Christian faith and belief if deliberately employed as a teaching instrument. There was never any question of letting chanted Latin liturgical offices evolve by gradual accretion and coalescence into spoken vernacular cycles as postulated by Charles Magnin and Marius Sepet in the nineteenth century;[25] nor was there any question of the Church itself being short of an adequate number of clerics in the twelfth and thirteenth centuries from whose ranks to cast their plays, as postulated by Sir Edmund Chambers in *The Mediaeval Stage* and by all who have followed him since then;[26] nor was there any physical need to shift plays from inside churches to exterior locations because of inadequate space to perform them, which seems to have been assumed by all historians who accepted Sepet's and Chambers's hypotheses relating to coalescence of plays and insufficient actors to perform them without laymen to assist.[27]

On the contrary, there is no play composed before the close of the thirteenth century that survives to us that could not be presented in an average size cathedral, church, minster or priory; there is no play that could not be cast several times over by the normal establishment of any monastery or collegiate church; and there is ample evidence that dramatic activity originating among professional minstrels and their student associates was making deep enough inroads into the routine observances of major calendar festivals during the thirteenth century for cardinals, bishops and abbots throughout Europe to feel challenged by a sense of impropriety, and to issue instructions to all clergy under their jurisdiction to regulate this situation. They did so by protecting and preserving the sacred dramatic offices particular to the liturgies for Christmas, Epiphany and Easter; by attempting to suppress or control the excesses of the unofficial and quasi-liturgical ceremonies of deliberately inverted hierarchy between St Stephen's Day and the octave of Epiphany; and by encouraging the development of *honesti ludi*, calculated to teach Christian history and doctrine and to urge laymen to amend their sinful lives, a process within which laymen could be invited to apply their talents and which would fulfil the purposes of such plays if presented in halls, market squares or at appointed preaching places. It is this situation, coupled with the growth of the mendicant orders of preaching friars and the rise of the cities and their bourgeois citizens, which marks the advent of the moralities, the saint plays and *The Play Called Corpus Christi.**

In this transitional period the overriding contrast between idea and sign, earnest and game, is still paramount, but ideas and signs are self-evidently parting company, with the signs coming to acquire a life of their own: instead of merely pointing a way towards comprehension of those abstract ideas summed up in the word 'earnest', they are beginning—especially when used for satirical purposes—to assert their ability to supply a realistic mirror image of earnest in themselves. In other words, play-makers are acquiring a self-conscious control over their medium made explicit in the new concepts of *representatio* and *ludus*, *gomen* and *plega*, *spiel*, *jeu* and *gioco*.† In future the deviser, or

*See pp. 191–2 below.
†See pp. 193–4 below.

'maker', of the 'game' or 'play' will himself select the device, or combination of active visual images reinforced by verbal *exempla* or *figura*, that will serve to mirror the shape of ultimate reality, or at least those portions of it that he perceives for himself and wishes to communicate to audiences through the actions and dialogue of his actors; but in doing so he will be licensed by the Church to draw far more heavily upon the sights and language of daily life around him than he was within the stricter confines of liturgical offices.

In this transition I do not find any contradiction between religious and secular motive and expression since what is secular is the mode; and a secular mode can be as useful in expressing religious moods and doctrines as liturgical ones; indeed, more useful if the play-maker wishes to criticize betrayals of religious ideals and abuses of privilege in a hierarchically ordered society. Moreover, it only needs a measure of flexibility on the part of senior ecclesiastics for them to adapt their own approach to Christian philosophy and to its expression in dramatic form for the Church to maintain its control over the directions in which the new drama should develop, including criticism of the establishment in the interests of reform.*[28]

Continued observance of the traditional calendar festivals, patronal feasts and, above all, the institution of the new Feast of Corpus Christi at the start of the fourteenth century, gave them ample opportunity to forge a new relationship with the laity and thus to remodel religious drama into a popular teaching instrument for evangelical purposes.[29] Rejecting the introverted monasticism of the tenth and eleventh centuries in favour of a more militant crusading spirit, spearheaded by the new orders of preaching friars and blessed by the papacy itself, cathedral chapters, parochial clergy and private chaplains alike seized this opportunity, and in doing so were able to provide their congregations in convent courtyard, market squares, traditional game-places and baronial halls with a rich and varied repertoire of plays embracing both tragic and farcical aspects of human life.

These new requirements, however, still carried no obligation to respect dramatic genre as particularized in classical antiquity— comic, tragic, or tragi-comic; what they did oblige was a close enough observation of life as actually lived to embrace images of vice contrasted with virtue, honest labour with luxury and corruption, mirth with sorrow, and persons of high degree with low within the ultimate boundaries of birth and death, heaven and hell.† And since these constituent materials of the new drama were themselves a mixture of the grave and serious with the comic and grotesque, the images selected by the

*See *EES*.i.112 ff.
†See *EES*.i.150–9 and 316–22.

play-makers to represent them 'in game' could be easily and comfortably aligned with the tragi-comic form of narrative structure already supplied by the tenets of Christian philosophy to contain it, and which I have discussed in the preceding section of this chapter.

This approach to the dramatist's art and craft was particular to the Middle Ages and owed very little to classical precedents; indeed, it rejected (or ignored) the classical assumption that a play was a form of argument—'tragic' if serious, 'comic' if witty or farcical. This kind of dialectical approach to the creative act of scripting a scenario did not appeal to medieval play-makers: not only was it artificial and arbitrary, involving the division of people into the exclusive groupings of 'men of high degree' (particular to tragedy) and those 'in povert plounged low' (required for comedy)—the groupings commended by Aristotle and Horace although quite alien to the actual circumstances of everyday life—but it was at best tangential, if not altogether irrelevant, to the depiction in stage terms of God's purposes for man. Neither heaven nor hell was accorded any firmly defined position within either its philosophy or its structure; the concepts of original sin and the possibility of redemption from it failed to find a place in any such approach to comedy or tragedy. By striking contrast the concept of *ludus* as the medieval Church came to define it—of 'game' or 'play' as a mirror image of earnest—permitted the mixing of kings and commoners, the passage of time, travel in this world, life after death, and the juxtaposition of comic with serious character and incident. *Ludus*, therefore, when interpreted as the microcosmic mirror of macrocosmos—despite its inevitable dependence on signs, make-believe action and pretence—offered Christian society of the Middle Ages a more suitable approach to the play-maker's art (as viewed from the standpoint of its clerical creators) than that of classical antiquity.

In no way did this approach deny argument a place in the play-maker's armoury of dramatic techniques;* but neither did it forbid the inclusion of both improvised incident and epic narrative, nor the depiction of confrontations between God himself and men and women of all degrees within a frame of universal time and place.

There was nothing inevitable about the outcome of a *ludus*. Predetermined as man's state of being may have been by Lucifer's and Adam's falls, his future rested in his own hands in his deeds, in his respect for the sacraments, and in his will-power under divine Grace. If Judgment Day would bring with it a happy or a tragic ending to his story, the determining factor lay unequivocally within his own control; and if,

*See pp. 134ff. above *sub* 'Disputatio'.

for 400 years, these basic assumptions remained unquestioned—notwithstanding the early years of the Reformation—it should not surprise us that the regular form of play-making that Sir Philip Sidney found in the public playhouses of Elizabethan England was mongrel tragi-comedy: for such was the fabric of life itself, which, time out of mind, it had been the entire purpose of actor and play-maker alike to capture, order and distil within the overriding image of *theatrum mundi*.

3 The genesis of English comedy

While, theoretically, there is no reason for comedy to have begun life in England with a flying start over tragedy in any sequence of developments serving to push tragi-comedy towards an exclusive concern with the comic or the tragic, there were in fact four strong reasons for this to have been the case in the event.

The first of these is grounded in human nature itself. All human beings possess a sense of the incongruous and inconsistent in life around them, and on recognizing it they react by laughing. Happily for all of us, the number of people altogether lacking a sense of humour is small. Comedy rests on the fundamental assumption that life, for all its stresses and strains in this world, makes sense; and that, consequently, there is a practical solution (often hard to find, but nevertheless there) to any difficulty. Tragedy, by contrast, arises from the fear that things do not make sense, and that there is no practical solution to many of life's troubles; and while a sense of tragic possibility may affect everyone, it is normally only a matter of studied concern to a well-educated, intellectual minority—as the manager of any theatre company will readily confirm. In short, comedy, when it exists as a dramatic genre, perennially commands a far wider audience than tragedy. The Middle Ages, under the all-pervasive guidance of the Roman Catholic Church, was the period *par excellence* when life did make sense; and so it was always likely that the sense of tragic possibility made explicit in the Fall of Lucifer and the Fall of Adam would be subsumed in Christian philosophy within a comic, reconciliatory solution.

The second reason promoting the rapid advance of comedy in medieval Europe was the existence of those hierarchical divisions and barriers within a feudally structured society that invited assault and demolition by those born on the wrong side of them and condemned to remain there. While no vassal in such a society could expect to defy or deny his overlord with impunity and thus alter his own allotted place within it, the long tradition of mimicry and parody preserved by the minstrels did focus attention upon its inequities and provide some release from them by puncturing their pretensions wherever occasion offered an opportunity to do so. Festivals of inverted status, like those discussed in the preceding section of this chapter, provided one such occasion; the contrast in behaviour required of actors to distinguish Christian from non-Christian characters in liturgical music-drama discussed in the first section provided another; folk-games and sophisticated revels customary at calendar and patronal festivals provided yet another.

A fourth, and perhaps the most dynamic of all reasons for the advance of comic modes and methods existed in the growth of a third class of person in thirteenth-century society whose status was vested in merchandise or professional expertise and in money rather than in land or birth or manual labour, and of large groups of clerics with sufficient education and freedom of movement in society—notably Dominicans and Franciscans—to observe and satirize social injustice in their sermons and poems.[30] Allied with the latter were the students of the newly founded universities at Paris, Oxford, Padua, Bologna and Cracow whose arts faculties in particular were a byword for rebellious and undisciplined behaviour, and many of whose number—like Chaucer's 'clerk of Oxenford' a century later with his songs and his 'sautrie'—joined the ranks of other entertainers to supplement meagre financial resources.[31]

> And thus this sweete clerk his time spente
> After his freendes finding and his rente.
> ('Miller's Tale', ll. 111–12)

The perennial concern of youth with sexual prowess and opportunity, and youth's irritation with the irksome controls of authority inevitably became the principal subjects of the ballads, dialogued debates and mimetic games in the repertoires of these goliards: but the satirical sermons of fellow mendicants offered models for a wide variety of other 'truffe' or jokes, directed against the aristocracy and professional classes. Contrasts in life-style and, above all, in ethics and moral values, where incongruity in the guise of blatant hypocrisy and inconsistency in the form of rank injustice contradicted official pronouncements, gave rise to a form of comedy in the Middle Ages that relied far more heavily upon incident, improvisation and anecdote which carried caricature to the point of the grotesque, than upon any particular form, style or structure postulated by the Latin grammarians and their monastic successors.

One of the earliest of these entertainments in English is *The Interlude of the Student and the Maiden* (*Interludium de Clerico et Puella*), *c.* 1300.

Only two brief scenes of this play written in East Midland dialect survive in a manuscript now in the British Museum (MS. Add. 23986). In the first, the student pleads with the girl to accept him as a lover which she, contemptuously, refuses.

> 'By Christ in Heaven and St John
> I don't care for any student,
> For many a good woman have they brought to shame!
> By Christ, you should have stayed at home!'

In the second scene the student visits an old procuress whose help he hopes to secure in return for lavish promises of cash.[32]

Of approximately the same date—probably earlier—is *The Dialogue of the Blind Man and the Boy (Garçon et l'Aveugle)* from Tournai in northeastern France. An old, lecherous and far from penniless blind man appears before an audience begging for alms. Help is offered by a feckless youth who joins him and then sets about stripping his shameless but helpless victim of his wench, his wealth and his clothes.[33]

In both of these short trifles, command of dramatic action and of comic mood and method is so deft as to make it well-nigh unbelievable to the modern reader that either play could have been the first of its kind in either French or English. Moreover, it must be remembered that French at this time was still widely spoken in England: this makes the group of four plays from Arras in Picardy, of even earlier date, just as relevant in this context.[34] Of these Richard Axton writes as follows:

'Arras, a manufacturing town with a thirteenth-century population in the region of twenty thousand inhabitants, had enough prosperous and educated burgher-patrons to support a group of resident poets and *jongleurs*. Some of these entertainers were practitioners of traditional mimic skills; many had clerical schooling; some had acquired a knowledge of ecclesiastical drama as well as of the epic and love-poetry of the feudal courts in northern France. Their own dramatic compositions were... suited to the practical interests of their business-minded audiences and usually had a firmly 'realistic' basis in the mimic style.'

(*European Drama of the Early Middle Ages*, p. 131)

All four plays are moralistic in intention, but by recourse to farcical situation, irony, wit and festive ritual, each makes its point by distinctively comic methods. In two of them—Jean Bodel's *Play of St Nicholas* and the anonymous '*Courtois' of Arras*—a tavern is used as a setting to exemplify vicious aspects of life:* the evils attendant upon drinking and gambling, and the fate that boastful and pretentious

*See Ch. V, pp. 94–9 above.

youths are likely to meet at the hands of sophisticated and unscrupulous prostitutes. Another, Adam de la Halle's *Robin and Marion*, is a pastoral which, idealized as its shepherds and shepherdesses may be, succeeds in contrasting, by comic irony, the social differences between leisured and labouring classes. The fourth, *The Play of the Green Canopy (Jeu de la Feuillée)*, is sharply anticlerical and more farcical in its use of incident: it also relies heavily upon both local and topical targets for its humorous effects.[35]

What then are we to make of this varied and vigorous secular comic tradition in the thirteenth and fourteenth centuries, literary as well as mimetic and separate from, if not wholly independent of, the religious drama of the early Middle Ages?

First we must recognize the combination of caustic realism, ribaldry that often verges upon the obscene, and the predominance of characters 'in povert plounged lowe' that gives the surviving texts their special quality and sets them apart from the more stylized 'laughable' conduct and 'ridiculous' language that attaches to non-Christian characters and their actions in the liturgical music-dramas of Christian worship.

Next, we must remark the singular conjunction of physical dramatic techniques and conventions of professional mimes and minstrels with the advent during the thirteenth century of university students as authors and performers of dramatic texts that rely heavily upon irony, satire and verbal wit for their effect; and that just such satire was being legitimized by the authority of the Church itself in the sermons of the preaching friars.[36]

Third, we must note that both of these changes were occurring at a point in time when medieval society was having to accommodate itself to the rapid growth of a third class of individuals—the merchant burghers and professional men of the wealthier cities—who occupied the middle ground between the landed aristocracy (baronial and ecclesiastical) and the illiterate peasantry.

By the close of the fourteenth century these men and their wives had become the regular patrons of this secularly oriented comic drama, able to commission it and to reward its executants, even to devise it. Some of them, moreover, had already become the butts of its satire as may be judged from a reading of *Piers Plowman* and *The Canterbury Tales*. A specific example of this survives from Exeter where, on 9 August 1352, the Bishop felt worried enough to address a mandate to the Archdeacon forbidding a proposed performance of a play satirizing the exorbitant profits being made by the leatherworkers in the city under pain of excommunication. A court of inquiry is to be set up instead.* It was these same men who founded the *compagnie* in Italy, the

*See Appendix C, pp. 264–6 below.

confradias in Spain, the *confréries* and *puys* in France, the chambers of rhetoric in Flanders and the guilds in England:[37] and when a new feast in the Christian calendar came to be instituted in the fourteenth century—the Feast of Corpus Christi—these men with their trade associations, their charitable brotherhoods, and their quasi-religious guilds were already firmly enough established to be able to offer the Church their assistance both in organizing and in funding the new feast, or to make them the most obvious source of help to which the Church itself might turn.[38] When, therefore, a new style of drama, still religious and thus controlled by doctrine in its tragi-comic structure, but scripted and spoken in the vernacular, was initiated *specifically to celebrate this feast—The Play Called Corpus Christi*—its 'makers' were likely to have to make some further moves to accommodate the tastes of this new bourgeois class and thus to incorporate comic forms and techniques of goliardic origin if their 'plays' were to hold their audiences' attention over several days of performance.

These moves included satire drawn from a tradition already formulated and exploited by generations of preachers who now attacked the particular vices of knights, lawyers, merchants and clerics with the same accuracy of observation and fearless fervour that they had meted out in the previous century to feudal lords and their ladies, and to their less than faithful servants.* To this end they employed analogue, thus characterizing Caiaphas and Annas as cardinals or bishops, Pilate as an English magistrate and Pharisees as lawyers; and the representatives of these classes therefore come to loom as large in the Doomsday plays of the cycles as the wicked popes, emperors, kings and queens.[39]

The point at issue is that a keen sense of contrast and incongruity between the poor man's expectancies of the rich man in whatever walk of life and the treatment actually received at his hands thus comes to inform both the continental passion plays and the English cycles, moralities and saint plays of the fourteenth and fifteenth centuries with a realism that is at times grimly ironic and at others farcically comic. The extreme polarities of these behaviour patterns become apparent in the conduct of God and true believers on the one hand and that of Lucifer and his disciples on the other; while in between are placed those contrasts in daily life between rich and poor, man and beast, natural function and artificial pretension which were to be recognized in the incongruity of the one usurping the manner of the other. The chance to give expression to both, especially in dramatic

---

* The earliest example of this forthright style of criticism to appear within an English play is to be found in the *Episcopus*'s stern admonition of Rex Vivus in *The Pride of Life*: see *Non-Cycle Plays and Fragments*, ed. Norman Davis for EETS, 1970, pp. 100–2.

form, occurred at all calendar festivals when holy days and holidays were one and indivisible. The sense of occasion promoted the drama, and the drama sought, if not always to explain, at least to hold the occasion up to public view and to comment on its significance. Whenever and wherever this awareness of contrast was sharpened and formulated in images that defined and pointed up incongruity of situation, conduct and language, comedy resulted. It could be crude and farcical with slapstick predominant; it could be subtle with wit and irony as the principal instruments of mirth. Either way, the sense of the comic grew and fed upon itself, borrowing, stretching, parodying and classifying until a stock of examples, types and formulae became the common property of actors, authors and audiences alike: the old man with a young wife, the priest who is both greedy and lecherous (made all the more conspicuous by the preaching of Wyclif and his Lollards);[40] lawyers who take bribes and merchants or farmers who cheat their clients by buying cheap and selling dear, or by giving short-change; pastoral innocence contrasted with courtly corruption; tyrannical barons outwitted by timorous bumpkins; the braggart who is a coward; puns, double-meanings and burlesque.

It was out of this material in real life that the monologues, debates, farces and other comic games of social recreation were fashioned; and it was from this storehouse of typed character, familiar situation, comic tale of the biter bit or the poseur exposed that the clerical authors of vernacular religious drama derived the materials with which to characterize biblical and allegorical persons, histories and debates—anachronistically but realistically—for audiences representing the entire spectrum of society, the medieval *communitas*.

Yet however much these rebellious explosions of natural man may have contributed through the twelfth, thirteenth and fourteenth centuries to the repertoire of comic ideas—'routines' as today's professional comedians would call them—especially in the realm of knock-about farce, it is to be doubted whether they could ever have contributed much on their own to the development of the more intellectual and serious notion of comic narrative with its emphasis upon story-line, a balanced structure and appropriate characterization, as received from classical antiquity and transfigured by Christian philosophy. At least Dante's justification for his choice of the word 'comedy' to describe his philosophical epic poem makes no concessions to such theatrical irreverence and irresponsibility. For him the word 'comedy' is appropriate because his story begins in adversity, *Infernus*, and 'in the end it is happy, pleasing and to be desired, being, *Paradisus*'; moreover, his words and images are signs—allegory—chosen to lead readers of the poem towards an understanding of the shape of ultimate reality.[41] Comedy in this serious, narrative and philosophical sense must somehow itself be restored from the pages of a book or the rhetorician's oration to the stage as action before those other forms of comic incident and jocularity can begin to affect its nature and quality in any vital way. All the evidence surviving to us and presented thus far in this chapter suggests that sufficient self-consciousness of both forms existed late in the fourteenth century for attempts at fusion to begin; and we are at least possessed of clearly documented testimony contemporary with the event that it was in this twin-headed condition—sublime, reconciliatory and romantic narrative viewed from one standpoint, or rebellious, corrective and grotesque incident viewed from another—that notions of comedy, and what that word described, reached Chaucer, Lydgate and the anonymous authors of the great English cycles, moralities and saint plays.* In short, by the start of the fifteenth century it had become possible, from an artist's viewpoint, not only to choose between 'high' or serious tragi-comedy and 'low' or farcical comedy, but to opt, however tentatively, to bring the one into conjunction with the other in the service of romance or play. By then the 'signs', in the Neoplatonist sense of the word, had come to rival the 'ideas'; and having acquired a life of their own, a much more modern interpretation of the distinction between 'the sublime' and 'the profane' was beginning to emerge in consequence, the former directed to provoking a contemplative delight, the latter to the more vulgar and simpler pleasures of merriment and laughter.

Thus in drama, as in sculpture and painting, the calm reflective statements of the Romanesque era came steadily to be replaced by more forceful, demonstrative and individualistic forms of expression, emotional, theatrical and often deliberately shocking. This shift of emphasis and technique is visible in the gargoyles, corbels and roof-bosses of Gothic churches, in the fanciful marginalia of illuminated manuscripts, in wood-carvings on pew-ends and choir-stalls; it is also strikingly apparent in the proliferation of comic ideas incorporated into sermons, romances, *fabliaux* and plays to sharpen and define their moralistic purpose.[42] This spirit informs Langland's *Piers Plowman*, Chaucer's 'Miller's Tale' and 'Franklyn's Tale'; it informs *The Castle of Perseverance* (*c*. 1410–25)—and it is the very life-blood of Lydgate's *Mumming at Hertford*.

Lydgate, it is important to remark, was himself a Benedictine monk; yet his *Mumming at Hertford* is a light-hearted and sophisticated entertainment devised for the young King Henry VI, *c*. 1425, to celebrate New Year's Eve in the banquet hall of Hertford Castle.[43]

*See pp. 173–5 above.

The poet-presenter introduces a group of six actors: they are described as 'hynes, here stonding oon by oon' (1. 25), i.e. as humble working-
men. They have come to complain to the King 'Upon the mescheef
of great adversytee' in which they find themselves. So we know
immediately where we are: we are about to witness a comedy. Quickly
we learn why these 'sweyne', who look 'ful froward of ther chere' are
so wretched: they all have the misfortune to be married to shrews,
and beg the King to restore them the right of mastery in their own
homes. The comedy arises from this inversion of normality: the so-
called fair and gentle sex having turned into viragos rougher than
proverbial Turks and Amazons, while the visibly tough, bearded
bread-winners are subjected to every kind of physical indignity and
mental cruelty.

Lydgate then advances us to the second movement of his 'play',
a meeting with these shrewish wives. One of them speaks for all six.
She starts by citing Chaucer's wife of Bath, and challenges the very
idea of mastery belonging to men as of right, and goes on to substitute
customary usage as justification for their own claims to mastery.
And so, in their turn, they ask the King to give judgment for them.

The third movement of the comedy—the reconciliatory one—is
advanced through a spokesman for the King himself, probably a
herald. The question raised, he says, is so important and of such
universal application that it would be most imprudent to deliver a
snap judgment. Time is needed to sift all the evidence in order to
arrive at the right answer. Judgment is thus postponed for a year.
In the meantime wives will not be denied what they claim to be their
customary rights; but single men are warned to weigh up the likely
price of getting married while they are still free to do so.

Thus the comedy ends on a jocular note appropriate to the festive
occasion. The King, we should remark, was still a bachelor.

Here, then, the formula for the construction of comedy, as a type of
literary narrative, is faithfully followed and then transferred bodily
to the stage. There it is reinforced with the comic realism of everyday
life, each married couple depicted being vividly re-created with details
particular to their way of life, yet all of them exaggerated and so
inverted as to produce grotesque effects that are comic in themselves.
Pictorially this is especially so of Bartholomew the 'bochier stoute and
bolde/ þat killed haþe bulles and boores olde', who 'for al his brode
knyff' and 'his bely rounded lyche an ooke' is nevertheless routed by
his even tougher wife, Pernelle.

In English literature it is not until the end of the century, when we
reach Henry Medwall's *Fulgens and Lucres* (1497) that we will again
find this same command of secular, romantic comedy both in overall

shape and in particular incident. That this is due to loss and destruction of scripts rather than to lack of them is virtually certain since these intervening decades mark the advent and rapid numerical growth of professional acting companies—the 'players of enterludes'—in so many noble households; and such companies could not have satisfied their masters if they lacked a suitable repertoire of interludes to play.[44]

Some clues, at least, to the likely nature and quality of these missing scripts can be gauged from study of the *farces*, *sotties* and *entremets* which proliferated rapidly during this same period in France and the Low Countries, many of which have survived.[45] What these reveal, above all else, is the extension of comic method to pillory in words and deeds the sanctimonious self-righteousness, hypocrisy and greed of the professional classes in society—doctors, merchants, lawyers and civil servants—as well as the habitual targets of peasant ignorance, marital and extra-marital relationships, disobedient children and disrespectful servants.

In England, the Wyclifite preacher John Balle and Henry Medwall show themselves to be of the same mind when the former asks his famous question—

> When Adam delved and Eve span,
> Who was then the gentleman?

—and when, a century later, Medwall makes his Lucres decide to marry the man whose claim to merit lay in his own achievements rather than in inherited wealth and titles. However, even if we lack the rich treasury of scripts that has survived in France, the same tendencies can still be charted with ease in the treatment accorded during the fifteenth century to biblical and homiletic narrative in the miracle cycles, moralities and saint plays. All of these must be regarded as tragi-comedies in point of structure for the reasons I have already advanced:* all of them, however, contain passages, even whole scenes, of sustained comic incident and characterization borrowed from recognizably secular sources where an armoury of realistic comic moods and methods is deployed to define and demonstrate the doctrinal points at issue. Here it must suffice to glance briefly at the most famous medieval group of comic figures, Lucifer and his diablerie, and one or two other specific uses of comic treatment of character and situation in religious plays.

In all four surviving English cycles Lucifer owes his fall to pride and vanity. Once he has fallen it is dramatically necessary for him to be regarded as a figure of pity and ridicule: it is also theatrically necessary

---

*See pp. 176–7 above.

for the audience to see this change clearly reflected in his costume and person. He is thus made to retain the outline of his former angelic shape, including his wings, but all the details have become grotesque parodies of the original image; feet are translated into cloven hooves, hands into vultures' claws, the smooth gilded skin into tangled fur, the teeth into fangs, the gorgeous wings garnished with peacock feathers collected from the castle-keep into a tattered assortment of goose and hen feathers gleaned from the byre and the midden. The former archangel has become a gross parody of his earlier self, at once pathetic and awesome, but also comic. The antithesis in this juxtaposition of images is thus complete, and Christ's antagonist in the latter half of the cycles has accordingly already been reduced to a figure of ridicule before battle is ever joined.

In the temptation of Eve two more techniques—disguise and analogy —are drawn upon by the Norwich and Chester playwrights to the same end. Satan thus appears in Paradise having again changed his costume. Equipped with a woman's face-mask, a pair of false breasts, gloves to hide his claws, and a snake-skin to hide his hooves, he assumes a falsetto voice when addressing Eve. By these means he is placed squarely before the audience as an equivocator, a fraud and a cheat. We are expected to laugh, but also to learn.[46] (See Plate X, No. 14.)

In the later scenes of the 'Temptation of Christ' and the 'Harrowing of Hell' greater stress is laid upon the language than the costume. In these scenes the dramatist is particularly concerned with establishing the ignorance and stupidity of all the devils resident in Hell-castle. They fail to recognize Christ for who He is and, squabbling among themselves, are outwitted by superior intelligence and verbal dexterity.[47] The Chester playwright refines this technique by using cynicism to undercut the boasts of Lucifer in the 'Temptation': indeed, he never loses control of the malign dimension in his Lucifer. In the 'Harrowing of Hell' the Wakefield dramatist goes further still, developing the comedy on two levels simultaneously—the romantic and the grotesque—by coupling the idea of Christ as bridegroom to the soul in the lyrical treatment of his principal theme with a diabolic burlesque of a council of war which parallels the parody of parliamentary procedures in Hell itself that precedes the Temptation in *Ludus Coventriae*. Both treatments are as striking and innovative as they are funny for the audience; rude mirth in both instances is brilliantly married to amused delight: the former forecasts Marlowe's self-pitying Mephostophilis, and the latter Falstaff's ribald parody of a royal audience at the 'Boar's Head' tavern in East Cheap, and the Porter in *Macbeth*.[48]

Other techniques warrant at least a passing glance: the use of comedy to prepare or stimulate spectators to receive a mystical statement, and direct application of low-life comic realism to Scripture. The most familiar example of comic anticipation is to be found in the Wakefield *Secunda Pastorum* where the farcical tale of the stolen sheep concealed in the crib directly parallels the inexplicable mystery of Christ's Nativity that follows immediately upon it.[49] This technique was also to be used by Shakespeare in *1* and *2 Henry IV* where both Prince Hal and the audience are instructed in the qualities required of kingship and the responsibilities attendant upon it by the juxtaposition of tavern (hellish) and palace (heavenly) scenes. In this way, too, Shakespeare teaches his audience how to take the measure of Parolles in Act II, scene iii of *All's Well* by first letting the clown, Lavache, in the preceding and otherwise almost pointless scene with the Countess, parody Parolles's manner of handling a Court conversation.

Fine examples of low-life realism are offered in *Ludus Coventriae* by the young man in 'The Woman Taken in Adultery' who flees from his mistress's bed in such haste as to have to leave the stage while still attempting to dress, and by the Wakefield master in the plays of the 'Scourging' and 'Crucifixion' where the warders and soldiers in charge of the proceedings are depicted as devoid of all pity and treat Christ as a mere object, regarding both activities as forms of sport; the children's game of blind-man's-buff, and the adult entertainments of bear- and bull-baiting (with gambling attached) provided the models in daily life for the use made of these images in both plays.[50]

The sport of bear-baiting also provides the anonymous author of *Mankind* (*c*. 1465) with an image to introduce the Vice, Mischief, and his companions Nought, Nowadays and New Guise,[51] while the whole of *The Castle of Perseverance* (*c*. 1410–25) is structured on the model of a particular form of tournament, the *pas d'armes*, or storming by challengers of a defended gate or castle. Indeed, time and again in the morality and saint plays, popular games provide the authors with a formula, that they can develop through the vices, for baiting traps to ensnare human kind.*

Satirical attacks directed against the professional classes are highlighted by the anonymous author of *Wisdom* (*c*. 1460) by recourse to the device of a sequence of three mummings: the knights, the lawyers and the courtiers associated respectively with Wrath, Avarice and Lechery.† Lawyers are again attacked, this time directly, in *Hick-Scorner*.

Imagination In Westminster Hall every terme I am;
To me is kynne many a grete gentyll-man;
I am knowen in every countre.

*See pp. 94–9 above.
†See pp. 110–11 above, and Plate VII, No. 11.

'And I were deed, the lawyers' thryfte were lost,
For this wyll I do yf men wolde do cost:
   Prove ryght wronge, and all by reason,
And make men lese* both hous and londe;
   For all that they can do in a lytell season.
Peche men of treason prevyly I can,
And, whan me lyst, to hange a trewe man.'†
(Manly I, ll. 217–26)

A little later Pity takes up the same story in a lament.[52]

'Loo, vertue is vanysshed for ever and aye;
   Worse was hyt never!
We have plente of grete othes
And clothe ynoughe in our clothes,
But charyte many men lothes:
   Worse was hyt never!
Alas! now is lechery called love, indeede,
And murdure named manhode in every nede;
Extorsyon is called lawe, so God me spede;
   Worse was hyt never!'
(ibid., ll. 551–60)

On other occasions realism is achieved by recourse to familiar detail. Thus, in II *Nature*, Worldly Affection, left on his own while Pride takes Man to try on his new clothes, makes use of the fireplace in the banquet hall and calls on the audience to provide him with a seat.

'thys good fyre and I wyll not depart(;)
For very cold myne handys dó smart(:)
It maketh me wo(-)bygon.
Get me a stole(!) Here(!) may ye not se(?)
Or ellys a chayr(!)Wyll yt not be—
thou pyld knave! I speke to the(;)
How long shall I stande(?)'
(Rastell's ed., sig. G)

Theatrically this trick works splendidly, as Worldly Affection momentarily comes 'out of character' and addresses some wretched individual singled out on the spur of the moment as if he were a character in the play: it is assured of laughter. No less entertaining in its vividly realistic detail is Imagination's description in *Hick-Scorner* of his encounter with the owner of the horse he had stolen (*ed. cit.*, p. 395)

---

lese: lose.
†Folly in *Mundus et Infans* is no less scathing:
      'For I am a servaunt of the lawe;
      Covetous is myne owne felowe.'
(Manly I, ll. 576–7)

and of the rude interruption of his casual affair with a girl picked up off the streets:

> 'I wote not what we dyde togyder,
> But a knave catchpoll nyghed us nere,
> And so dyde us aspye.
> A strype he gave me; I fled my touche;
> And frome my gyrdle he plucked my pouche,—
> By your leve, he lefte me never a peny.'
>
> *(ed. cit.,* ll. 208–13)

Thus each and every vice, or deadly sin (and many of the virtues), notwithstanding the abstract idea that he or she personifies, comes to be endowed with a realistic identity through the localized settings in which they operate, and the particular way in which, by comic contrasts, they promote their own fraudulent or serious ends. For instance, as Mankind capitulates to the Vice and decides to abandon work and church-going in favour of dicing, drinking and wenching in the tavern, the steady deterioration in his character is faithfully reflected by the play-maker in his speech. The contrast between true virtue and viciousness is thus exhibited theatrically by incongruity of action and language.[53] When therefore we reach the interludes of the early sixteenth century, the foundations had already been laid of a solid tradition of comic modes and methods within a tragi-comic frame: for not only *Mankind*, but the anonymous *Wisdom, The World and the Child, Everyman, Hick-Scorner*, Medwall's *Nature* and Skelton's *Magnyficence* all follow this pattern.

I thus find myself bound by the weight of the evidence to regard the debt that English play-makers of the later sixteenth century undoubtedly owed to their much closer familiarity with the rediscovered comedies of Plautus and Terence, and to the revival of interest in Horace's views on dramatic theory, as one that served rather to extend and refine existing comic possibilities in drama than to initiate them. In other words Tudor 'makers of enterludes' became heirs to two traditions—the one Gothic-English, Roman Catholic and satirically tragi-comic; the other Graeco-Roman, free of doctrinal controls, festive if specifically corrective, and wholly comic—and could draw on both as they pleased. Skelton, while genuflecting to Horace and Plautus, preferred the former: John Heywood, while still working within the boundaries of orthodox Roman Catholicism inclined towards the latter. And so things might have continued, as they were to do in Spain, had it not been for the English Reformation. Striking in the 1530s, translating the ethical morality into the play of political polemic, and bringing government censorship in its wake, the

Reformation in England served to shatter five centuries of Roman Catholic doctrinal control over English dramatic structure and to force play-makers into considering moves away from tragi-comic form towards exclusively comic or tragic alternatives.*

4 *The rationalizing of English comedy*

Plautine influence obtained a toe-hold in England, at least at the universities and at some schools (notably St Paul's under the successive High Masterships of Dean Colet and William Lyly) during the reign of Henry VII, and a much firmer footing following Henry VIII's accession.[54] In the 1520s, Cardinal Wolsey and King Henry himself arranged for choir-boys to present plays by Plautus at Court, and in 1534–5 Nicholas Udall, as Headmaster of Eton, published his *Floures for Latine speaking* culled from the plays of Terence. The plays associated with Sir Thomas More's charmed circle from the pens of John Heywood, John Redford and the Rastells were clearly written under this influence;* but nothing appears (or survives) in England in this period to approach that freedom of treatment *in stilo imitativo* achieved in Italy by Machiavelli in his *La Mandragola, c.* 1515.[55] Gone is any attempt to mirror 'earnest' in the microcosmic world of the medieval stage-play: instead, we are confronted with artifice of an altogether different kind—a simple situation that provokes a witty argument among bourgeois characters, a sequence of farcical misunderstandings that result in the final cuckolding of a jealous old man by a young rival, all accomplished within strict limits of time and place. The play exists only to ridicule folly, to warn others by example, and to amuse. Morally it can claim to be corrective and punitive, but it is in no way redemptive or reconciliatory. In other words its mode is purely comic, verging on the farcical and diverting; but not tragi-comic. Subject-matter and characters are recognizably Italian and contemporary, but the playwright's approach to it, the setting, and the structure chosen to express it in action and dialogue are just as clearly faithful copies of Roman example with no concessions made to the intervening 1,500 years of Christian play-making.

At almost the same time that Machiavelli was writing *La Mandragola*, John Skelton in England was writing *Magnyficence*. In *The Garland of Laurel* (1523) Skelton proudly includes

> Horace also with his new poetry
> Master Terence, that famous comicar,
> With Plautus, that wrote full many a comedy

*See *EES*.ii(1), Ch. I.

among his own predecessors as laureated poets.[56] Skelton had described his earlier *Magnyficence* on its title-page as 'A Goodly Interlude and a Merry': that sub-title could properly be construed as meaning 'a moral play, but an amusing one' which is at least compatible with Horace's precept in *The Art of Poetry* about the need to mix profit with pleasure in comedy, and resembles the stock French label, 'Farce nouvelle, très bonne, et forte joyeuse'. Yet in its construction *Magnyficence* conforms strictly to Chaucer's and Lydgate's understanding of comic form, and not with that used by Terence, Plautus or Machiavelli; for not only does it mix characters of high and low degree, but its story-line is tragi-comic.

The character of the title-role is quickly reduced from the highest position in the State to a condition of suicidal wretchedness, in part by evil counsellors who persuade him to abandon moderation (personified as Measure) and in part by his own inability to resist 'Despair'; only at the last minute do the cardinal virtues come to his rescue: redemption is then achieved through a dawning consciousness of his own folly, reinforced by a subsequent determination to use greater discretion in future. It thus ends happily with Magnyficence reconciled with his Maker.[57]

While this comedy therefore contains recognizably classical features in the punishment meted out to folly and in its corrective moral intention, it is firmly structured on Roman Catholic, tragi-comic principles, following the example of English moralities in its treatment of the title-role and of the cycles in failing to concern itself exclusively with characters 'in povert plounged lowe': the protagonist is the spirit of kingship incarnate, and his antagonists are all courtiers. Most of these courtiers are, of course, counterfeits—vices whose clothes, manners and language conceal their vulgar origins and malign intentions—and are equivocators. Yet abstractions as these vices may be—Counterfeit Countenance, Crafty Conveyance, Cloaked Collusion, and the other 'seemers' who, like Lucifer tempting Eve,* deploy every known form of disguise to cheat their employer and master— they are also satirical portraits (however generalized) of the cynical tribe of new-rich, Tudor civil servants on the make. Each is equipped with a verse metre of his own, an original technical device through which Skelton both achieves variety and individualizes these characters. As I have demonstrated in my discussion of 'device' (see pp. 100–9 above), this technique was bold and effective enough to hold the stage for the rest of the century, assumed names, borrowed clothes, feigned voices and racy language combining to contrast the

*See p. 197 above.

outer with the inner man, and to bring about an endless sequence of deceptions followed by unmaskings. A century later this method still had enough life left in it to supply Ben Jonson with the central device for the construction of *Volpone* and *The Alchemist*, and Shakespeare with a convenient instrument for the discomfiting of both Lucio and Angelo in *Measure for Measure*. In the latter, Shakespeare explicitly acknow-ledges his debt when making the Duke remark, on deciding to use the bed trick,

> 'Craft against vice I must apply:
> With Angelo to-night shall lie
> His old betrothéd but despiséd,
> So disguise shall, by th' disguiséd,
> Pay with falsehood false exacting,
> And perform an old contracting.'
>
> (III.ii.247–52)

If Skelton used abstract personifications, where Machiavelli did not, it was not because in some barbarous, Gothic way he knew no better; for, as we have just remarked, he was among the first English authors to acknowledge acquaintance with the work of classical 'comicars', or makers of comedy, and was himself provided by Medwall in *Fulgens and Lucres* with precedent for the direct portrayal of living men and women. What we thus have to recognize is that the shift of emphasis within English moral interludes, more especially in 'merry' or satirical ones, from theological to social or political issues which occurred during the early Tudor period created special dangers for both playwrights and actors of a kind that did not arise in Italy at this time; and these dangers could best be deflected by oblique rather than direct methods of characterization. Disguise thus comes to acquire a double signi-ficance: protection for both the character and the dramatist.[58] Vices habitually disguised themselves to conceal their true identity and intentions from their victims; but by the same token no play-maker who wished to discuss doctrine, kingship, or government of the Commonwealth on the stage, particularly at Court, could afford to jettison abstract virtues and vices as vehicles for such debate since the very anonymity of such characters provided the play-maker with just that shield of ambiguity that he needed to protect himself and his players.*

John Bale, some twenty years after the production of *Magnyficence*, would still opt for the retention of abstract persons in both *Three Lawes* and *Kyng Johan*, as would Sir David Lyndsay in *Ane Satyre of the Thrie Estaities* and the anonymous author of *Respublica* (1553): indeed, Bale

*See pp. 76–8 and 103–4 above.

himself found it necessary to turn history into allegory before he could dramatize it at all—a fact which in itself provides a glowing tribute (if an unconscious one) both to the strength of the inherited, medieval tradition and to its reinforcement by the Reformation. In Elizabethan England the device would, on frequent occasions, still be retained; but, much more importantly, it would be transmuted by Chapman and others to form the basis of 'humours' comedy where variety of incident and situation serves to illuminate a dominant characteristic like 'hypocrisy' or 'irritability' from as many angles as possible.

The point at issue is that the retention of abstract personifications in Tudor drama was a matter of choice. For most of the century this device served, as much on grounds of common prudence as of aesthetic principle, positively to help play-makers in their efforts to exhibit the discrepancies between outward semblance and actuality in the conduct of affairs of State, an incongruity best suited to stage treatment in terms of satiric comedy. Comic incident, and other comic techniques besides this one, thus continue to be interpolated into serious plays of the Tudor era along lines familiar to audiences, and to give these plays that distinctive quality of 'mongrel tragi-comedy' so disliked by Sir Philip Sidney.*

One very important aspect of this question in Henry VIII's England was the swelling tide of anticlericalism that burst its banks when Cardinal Wolsey was appointed Papal Legate. Even Skelton threw discretion to the winds and wrote satire bordering upon plain invective, pillorying the opulence of Hampton Court and York House together with the vanity of their builder-owner who dared, notwithstanding 'his base progeny/And his greasy genealogy' to outface his sovereign. Wolsey was outraged and clapped Skelton into prison.[59] The same fate attended Sir John Roo (or Rowe) following performance of his play about 'Lord Governaunce' and 'Lady Publicke Wele' in 1527, notwithstanding his use of the protective device of abstract personi-fications and allegory.[60] As this tide of long pent-up anticlerical feeling grew in intensity, so it was inevitable that actors and play-makers would point their satire at the clergy and direct audiences' attention to their flagrant forgetfulness of their vows, their constant concern with money and possessions, and their ruthless gulling of their superstitious flocks.

It was John Heywood who, in drama, first seized upon this new opportunity for comic invention. Here there was no longer any need for the distancing effects of abstract personification in characterization or use of the historical past. Avoiding kings and courts, Heywood sets his plays in town or country parishes and then peoples them with

*See Ch. VIII, p. 173 above, and nn. 1 and 2, p. 291 below.

humbler folk—the priests, doctors, merchants, and the husbands and wives familiar to us in French farce. Daily life, the weather, food, confidence-tricks and tricksters, the inversion of norms, double-meanings and witty conversational games provide him with his subject-matter. Heywood's comedy is almost wholly corrective, and often flavoured with the niceties of the law courts; it is grounded in the discrepancies between outward appearance and inner man, between words and deeds, as was the case with Skelton's courtly vices; but it possesses another dimension, the discrepancies between man's physical desires and social opportunities, coupled with his wish to control his environment and his inability to do so.

Thus Heywood's disreputable Pedlar in *The Four PP* outwits the three professional men who are his social and intellectual superiors; John John is not only cuckolded by the parish priest in *John, Tyb and Sir John*, but is made the instrument of his own discomfiture by his wanton wife; and in *The Play of the Weather*, Jupiter is dethroned and humanized to arbitrate between the conflicting desires of a merchant, a huntsman, a game-keeper, a water-miller, a wind-miller, a lady and a laundress. Neither the game-keeper nor the laundress are above criticizing their employers.

> 'Small is our profit [says the former] and great is our blame.
> Alas! For our wages, what be we the near?
> What is forty shillings, or five mark, a year?'

Charged with envy by the lady, the laundress retorts tartly,[61]

> 'It is not thy beauty that I disdain,
> But thine idle life that thou has rehearsed,
> Which any good woman's heart would have pierced.
> For I perceive in dancing and singing,
> In eating and drinking and thine apparelling,
> Is all the joy, wherein thy heart is set.
> But nought of all this doth thine own labour get;
> For, hadest thou nothing but of thine own travail,
> Thou mightest go as naked as my nail.'

Heywood can thus mix satire with humour, and play the moralist predominantly as he does in *Witty and Witless* and *The Play of Love*; but he is at his best when he assumes the role of empirical humanist, and matches correction with tolerance and a gentle mixture of cynicism and faith. By constantly pitting authority, whether derived from rank or books, against experience, he signposts a road towards *Love's Labour's Lost* and *A Midsummer Night's Dream* where the way of the world is to be read in women's eyes, in men's manners, and in the phases of the moon.

With the Reformation, drama in England reverted sharply towards moralist techniques in the service of propaganda and polemic. This did not inhibit invention—indeed, it encouraged satire of an outrageously outspoken kind—but it frosted the gentler forms of comic release: these appear to have died with Sir Thomas More or to have sought sanctuary in schools and universities disguised as agents of education within Greek and Latin texts.[62] Satire, however, eventually outreached itself, as it has a habit of doing when given its head: governments whose interests it at first aspired to serve, later took fright and legislated against it both on the stage and in print.[63] When calmer times returned satire was itself the major casualty: into the vacuum thus created the gentler forms of comedy emerged cautiously from their academic hiding places, led by a bevy of dons, no longer necessarily churchmen.[64] Nicholas Udall, Thomas Ingelend, Richard Edwards, Mr Stevenson and Francis Merbury are the names we have to reckon with. All of them genuflect to classical precedent; but was this any more genuine than Skelton's graceful obeisance?

Martin Bucer, Regius Professor of Divinity at Cambridge and author of the first serious treatise on dramatic theory in England, stated in his *De Honestis Ludis* (presented to Edward VI in 1551) that the principal purpose of 'acting comedies and tragedies [is to] provide their public with wholesome entertainment which is not without value in increasing piety'.* He goes on to say that 'it is more important to modify the poetic style than to subtract anything from the duty of edifying the audience'. As if that were not enough, he adds,

'So that Christ's people ... may profit from religious comedies and tragedies, men will have to be appointed to the task of preventing the performance of any comedy or tragedy which they have not seen beforehand and decided should be acted.'

In this discourse Bucer shows himself to be aware not only of Aristotle's *Poetics*, but also 'that wit, that charm and grace of language ... in the plays of Aristophanes, Terence and Plautus', together with 'the dignity, the subtlety and polished style of Sophocles, Euripides and Seneca': yet he has no hesitation in advising the young king in his conclusion that[65]

'those to whom God has granted it to excel in these matters should choose to employ their gift to his glory rather than to hinder the good desires of others by untimely criticisms; and that they should prefer moreover to present comedies and tragedies in which knowledge of eternal life is manifestly clear (even if some literary niceties are lacking),

*For the full text see *EES*.ii (1). 329–31, Appendix C. See also Plate IX, No. 17.

rather than plays in which both spirit and character are defiled by impious and disgusting interchanges of buffoonery, even if some pleasure is given by refinements of wit and language.'

Bucer's advice was either taken seriously, or his views were shared by his academic contemporaries and successors. Why?

The answer emerges, I think, quite clearly from his own writings. Bucer had actually read Terence's and Plautus' plays as he claims to have done and had disliked what he found, at least in Plautus, because of what he understood to be the ridicule accorded to those very moral values that Protestant churchmen cherished most highly—wifely decorum, filial obedience, diligent study; thrift, and above all respect for fathers and religion—in a word, *pietas*. Comedy which pilloried these virtues *must* be regarded by such men as at best ambiguous and at worst offensive, even seditious: hence his demand for censors. What Bucer failed to recognize (as Stephen Gosson was also to do when writing *The Schoole of Abuse*) was that the levity of festive Plautine comedy had been designed to serve the same purpose in Augustan Rome by releasing audiences from the oppressive restraints of *gravitas* in daily life as the Feast of Fools and Carnival had served in the Middle Ages.* What Romans had wanted was a momentary escape from *pater Aeneas*, heroic virtue and the concealing folds of the toga; and Plautus had given them exactly that by taking them, on licensed holidays, to Athens for an imaginative spree, just as Victorians would later go 'bunburying', or cross the Channel to 'gay Paree'. To Bucer and his fellow reformers, such licence was only equatable with a return to the superstitious and reprehensible excesses of Roman Catholicism and therefore inadmissible.[66]

What, then, we find in most of the plays written under Edward VI and early in the reign of Elizabeth I is an uneasy state of flux between an evident awareness, even admiration, of Roman comic method and a zealous determination to uphold the seriousness of Protestant ideals. 'Sport' or 'merriment' thus still tends to be firmly confined within an homiletic frame and the objects of *incidental* merriment to be the ignorance and hypocrisy of Roman Catholics, and the castigation of disobedient children, idleness and prodigality which, paradoxically, were almost the opposites of the objects of Plautine ridicule.[67] In other words, Martin Bucer, along with most of his academic contemporaries, took himself and his cause much too seriously to admit of any need for festivals of inversion and release: both were abominations in the sight of the Lord, and that was that. Catholics and Catholic

---

*See pp, 182–5 above. On the performance of Plautus' *Aulularia* before Elizabeth I in the chapel of King's College, Cambridge, see *EES*.i. 248–9.

sympathizers found it much easier to escape from this dilemma concerning Roman comedy than did their Protestant fellow-play-makers, but at the risk of exposing themselves to accusations of heresy and worse: only under Mary I could they afford to jettison this caution and, significantly, it is within this five-year period (1553-8) that the central government's attempts to regulate performance of plays by censorship was also extended to cover the printing of them.*

It is in this light that we must view the re-emergence of Lydgate's and Heywood's homely world of village japes and jealousies in Udall's *Ralph Roister Doister* (*c.* 1550), Mr S.'s *Gammer Gurton's Needle* (*c.* 1553), and in *July and Julian* (*c.* 1560), all of which have now been thrust into a firmly Latinized plot-structure and unquestionably reveal more respect for Plautine example than any previous English comedy with the exception of *Thersytes* (1537) and *Calisto and Melibea* (*c.* 1525).[68] But in all other plays surviving from between 1550 and 1570 of a comic character—*Wealth and Health, Jack Juggler, The Disobedient Child, The Longer Thou Livest the More Fool Thou Art, Impatient Poverty, Damon and Pithias, The Trial of Treasure* and *The Pedlar's Prophecy*—the homiletic strain, however jocularly treated, predominates, and authors cling to a tragi-comic structure and to dramaturgical techniques lifted from Bale, Skelton, Medwall and the earlier cycles, moralities and saint plays rather than Plautus. In every case Christian doctrine overtly controls the shape of the plot, but the doctrinal patterns are now Protestant and directly derived from William Tyndale's *Obedience of a Christian Man*, Bucer's *De Honestis Ludis*, and Foxe's *Book of Martyrs*;[69] the satire, now muted in a political sense, is anti-Catholic with corresponding changes of emphasis in the moral values respectively supported and attacked through the personified virtues and vices. Much of the criticism behind the satire, however, has become social, and most of the comedy seems, to today's reader or director, to fall far short of being festive.

One play that is genuinely festive, *Tom Tyler and his Wife* (*c.* 1560) interestingly tries to combine classical, corrective comedy with a reconciliatory conclusion.[70] The subject-matter links Lydgate's *Mumming at Hertford* with Shakespeare's *The Taming of the Shrew*; but Tom's shrew is only temporarily tamed, and then by her husband's friend, Tom Taylor, not her husband. When she discovers the trick that has been played on her, she revenges herself by placing her husband in greater fear of her than he was before. A personification of Patience intervenes to secure concord at the end, but the reconciliation is not one that carries much conviction. Figured in terms of a conflict

*See *EES*.ii(1). 66-75.

between 'Desire' and 'Destiny', the moral is simple and free of religious doctrine: having chosen your bed you must lie on it.

By contrast, although the same moral informs Thomas Ingelend's *The Disobedient Child* of the same date, the obtrusive hand of doctrine once again controls the play's shape. Ingelend follows the story of the prodigal son up to the point where the son, having abandoned school against his father's wishes in order to take a wife, and found that he has married a shrew, returns home. This father, however, does not kill the fatted calf: he simply tells his son that it's now too late to repent his headstrong folly, gives him some cash to help him on his way, and insists that he keep his marriage vows. That is his punishment.

> *Father* If that at the first thou wouldest have been ordered,
>   And done as thy father counselled thee,
>   So wretched a life had never chanced,
>   Whereof at this present thou complainest to me;
>   But yet come on, to my house we will be going,
>   And there thou shalt see what I will give:-
>   A little to help thy need living,
>   Since that in such penury thou dost live;
>   And that once done, thou must hence again,
>   For I am not he that will thee retain.
>   (H-D II, pp. 315–16; Farmer, p. 88)

Parents are warned also that to spare the rod is to spoil the child.[71] The same moral is pointed in Richard Wever's *Lusty Juventus*, but within a theological frame of glaring Protestant concern. The parents blamed in this interlude are those who persuade or permit their children to grow up in the old, superstitious world of Roman Catholicism thinking that they will be saved by their good deeds. Led by 'Good Council' to 'Knowledge', Juventus is told succinctly:

> 'By these wordes which unto you he [*i.e. Knowledge*] doth expresse
> He teacheth that you ought to have a stedfast faith,
> Without the which it is impossible doutlesse,
> To please god, as Saint Paul sayth:
> Where faith is not, godly livyng decayeth,
> For whatsoever is not of faith, saith S. Paul, is sinne:
> But where perfite faith is, there is good workyng.'
>   (*MSR*, 1971, ll. 211–17)

Thus catechized, Juventus nevertheless succumbs swiftly to the blandishments of the vices who urge him to pay lip-service only to the new religion while indulging his true inclinations to the full behind this protective but hypocritical screen. In this instance the tragi-comic structural frame is preserved because Juventus is willing to admit error, to repent and to recover faith in God's promises.[72] This frame, however, cannot hold once a play-maker has advanced within Protestant theology to a Calvinist position; for there the reprobate will be predestinately damned, and will have to acknowledge that in his heart he has either never possessed true faith, or has lost it, and thus cannot repent; and once this has happened, the drama has crossed the frontiers of Christian redemptive tragi-comedy and stepped into a new realm of Christian tragedy.* Yet within the tragi-comic mode there was still room for experiment and expansion, notably in social criticism and romantic narrative.

Under the growing pressures of Protestant free-enterprise capitalism and galloping Elizabethan inflation, opportunities for travel and adventure grew larger, but social injustice and change became ever more glaringly apparent, particularly among those with 'small Latin and less Greek' whose support the professional player had to command if he was to earn a living from acting.† *Impatient Poverty* (*c.* 1560) speaks in its title for itself and, as in other plays of the time, usury is a prime target of its comic satire, together with corruption in ecclesiastical courts. Although ostensibly cast as a warning against the sin of envy, this play projects the message that in Elizabethan England this is inevitable (if not forgivable) when there is one law operating for the rich and another for the poor. Impatient Poverty himself, having acquired a comfortable sufficiency, desires more, capitulates to Envy and is reduced to penury for his pains. In that state he is called to Court by the Summoner and accused of envy and slander. Lacking funds now with which to bribe the Summoner to secure a verdict of 'not guilty', he is forced to do public penance. By contrast, Abundance, after boasting that 'with my purse I can both save and hang', is accused of keeping another man's wife in his house as his mistress; yet he is able to reach an accommodation with the Summoner.[73]

Abundance	What is the best for me to do?
	Rather than I to the Court will go,
	I had liever spend twenty pound.
Summoner	Sir! Of such a way may be found
	To excuse you; what will ye then say?
Abundance	Now hereof heartily I thee pray!
Summoner	Ye shall come home to my master's place
	And say that ye be put up of malice;
	Thrust money in his hand apace;
	And so shall ye go quit away.
Abundance	For thy counsel, gramercy! Hold! here is forty pence!
Summoner	Come on, sir! I will do my dilligence.

Exeunt ambo.

*See pp. 231–9 below.
† See pp. 169–70 above.

The next visual image presented by the play-maker to his audience is that of Poverty 'with a Candle in his hand doing penance about the place'.

Another common target is the influx of foreigners, most of them refugees from war and religious persecution in France and the Netherlands, but many of whom, being skilled craftsmen and successful merchants, appear to be more prosperous than their English neighbours. This xenophobia figures largely in *Wealth and Health* (printed *c.* 1559) as a subject of comic satire, and again, if less glaringly, in *The Tyde Taryeth no Man* (printed 1576) and *The Pedlar's Prophecy* (not printed till 1595).[74] In *The Tyde*, Hurting Helpe tells No-good Neighbours that a London landlord will be only too glad to dispossess 'a longer dweller of good name and fame' even if he is English,

> 'For among us now, such is our countrey zeale,
> That we love best with straungers to deale,
> To sell a lease deare, whosoever that will,
> At the french, or dutch Church let him set up his bill.
> And he shall have chapmen, I warrant you good store,
> Looke what an English man bids, they will give as much more.'
>
> (ll. 496–501)

In *The Pedlar's Prophecy* an artisan remarks,

> 'such a number of Alians,
> And that of all nations are come hither to dwell,
> As he said, even Jewes and Barbarians,
> So that the Realme is like to be made another hell.'
>
> (ll. 832–5)

and protests,

> 'I would gladly get my living by mine Art,
> But Aliants chop up houses so in the Citie,
> That we poore crafts men must needs depart,
> And beg if they will, the more is the pittie.'
>
> (ll. 877–80)

The Pedlar is an unsympathetic listener, saying that if he had houses to let,

> 'I would let them all to Alians and straungers,
> Before in any of them an English man I would set:
> For why (?) a straunger will give me what I will require,
> And at his day he will keep touch and pay:
> An English man in London cannot an house hyre,
> Except he be undone for ever and a day.'
>
> (ll. 883–8)

211

In other words he will have to go to a money-lender to raise a loan, and the rate of interest will first cripple and finally bankrupt him, as it does the young Courtier in *The Tyde Taryeth no Man*. The Pedlar lays the blame instead on the Mariner who, he says,

> 'bring them in daily,
> So you may have pence,
> You make your selves rich and go gaily,
> I would you were as readie to carry them hence(!)
> You would bring in the divell for pence and groates:
> Ye shall see them one day play their parts gaily,
> When we thinke least, they shall cut our throates.'
>
> (ll. 893-9)

The picture of a society that has elected to place monetary gain before any morality, Protestant or Catholic, that emerges from these and other plays of the period is reminiscent in its bitter humour of the satire and complaint of the preaching friars of the fifteenth century.* It is employed fleetingly in Ulpian Fulwell's *Like Will to Like* (printed 1568), powerfully in George Walpull's *The Tyde Taryeth no Man* (printed 1576) and in William Wager's *Enough is as Good as a Feast* (printed 1565–70), and, as the title proclaims, overwhelmingly in Thomas Lupton's *All for Money* (printed 1578).[75]

Wager's concern in *Enough is as Good as a Feast* is not so much with avarice *per se*, as with the fear that the power that accompanies office and wealth in conjunction will destroy the Reformation from within. This is evident from the plot-structure where the perennial 'Humanum Genus' figure has had to be split into two separate entities—heavenly Man who is 'elect' in the Calvinist sense, and Worldly Man who is predestinately 'reprobate'—and where the usual tragi-comic pattern has had to be altered in order to deny the possibility of repentance to the latter. He dies of 'God's Plague', actually in debt, thus losing both his wealth and his soul: Heavenly Man, however, being content with 'enough' is shown to live and die well.†

The Prologue to *The Tyde Taryeth no Man* leaves the audience in no doubt that the play's central concern is Avarice.[76] London has become a veritable Rialto of greed and viciousness.

> But where such people are, small love there doth rest,
> But greedy desyre supplieth the place:
> The symple ones commonly, by such are opprest,
> For they nothing way‡ any needy mans case.

*See pp. 191–3 above.
† See pp. 232–4 below.
‡ *nothing way;* i.e. they are so selfish that they never consider.

This moral is then illustrated in turn by the shameless dispossession of a 'long-dweller', a loan to a young courtier at extortionate rates of interest, and finally by the arrest of a modest debtor while he is attending church on Sunday.[77] Faithful sums up this state of affairs to Christian.

> 'Covetousnesse is accoumpted no sinne,
> Usury is a science and art:
> All wayes are good, whereby we may win,
> Although it be to our neighbours smart.'
>
> (ll. 1645–8)

It is to be doubted whether any more concise condemnation of the aims and methods of the world of banking and commerce than that contained in these four lines was uttered from any English stage before those which, thirty years later, Shakespeare gave to Cloten in *Cymbeline*:

> ' 'Tis gold
> Which buys admittance: oft it doth; yea, and makes
> Diana's rangers false themselves, yield up
> Their deer to th' stand o'th' stealer; and 'tis gold
> Which makes the true man kill'd and saves the thief;
> Nay, sometime hangs both thief and true man. What
> Can it not do and undo?'
>
> (II.iii.65–71)

Yet it is obvious that Elizabethan entrepreneurs, and more especially their Jacobean successors, were sensitive to these strictures and did their best to compensate through charitable enterprises and donations as is readily apparent from the texts of civic pageants praising the liberality of founders and donors; even the theatres earmarked a proportion of their profits for the churchwardens of their local parishes to dispose of in assisting the indigent and infirm.* Yet the suspicion remains that for the majority of these commercial brigands the Protestant ideals of thrift and family interest proved to be far more agreeable than the outmoded Roman Catholic virtue of charity. Thomas Lupton takes up this point in *All for Money* from where George Walpull left off. Theology, Science and Arts introduce the play, by lamenting that their respective disciplines are no longer followed in the interest of either the subject or the community, but only for private gain. Money is cast in the role of the father of Satan (old Snottienose) and the grandfather of Sin.[78]

*On pageant texts see pp. 55–8; on the motivation behind such gifts see pp. 48–50 above, and *EES*.ii(2). 22.

'I am worshipped and honoured, and as a god am esteemed:
Yea manie loves me better then God.'

> (1st ed., sig. Aiv; ed. Vogel, ll.223–4)

Prest for Pleasure adds,

'It is a hard thing that I would not do for money.
I would cut my father's throte if I might get money thereby.'

> (*ibid.*, sig. Bii and ll. 356–7)

Money himself proves the point.

'Since I was here last, I swere by this light,
I have made manie a crooked matter straight:
The theefe that all night was robbing and stealing,
If I beare him witnes was all night in his bed sleeping.
A mans wife that was taken in bed with an other,
Could have no harme when I did excuse her:
When I spake she was taken to be of good behaviour,
And they that found her were set by the heeles* for their labour.
There was a man killed and twentie witnesses by,
But I sayd he killd him selfe with his owne dagger truely:
And when I had spoken everie one helde his peace,
And then the officers the murtherer did release.'

> (*ibid.*, sig. Biv and ll. 914–25)

It is Sin who comments ironically on the predicament of Moneyless who cannot get justice, charity or redress precisely because he is who he is.

'Is not my grandfather Money thinke ye of great power
That could save from hanging such abomi[n]able whoore,
That against all nature her owne childe did kill?
Thus you may do for money what mischiefe you will.
And yonder poore knave that did steale for his neede
A fewe sorte of ragges, and not all worth a crowne,
Because he lackes money shalbe hanged for that deede,
You may see my Grandsyre is a man of renowne:'

He then attacks the audience.

'It were meete when I named him that you all kneeled downe.
Nay, make it not so strange, for the best of you all,
Do love him so well, you will come at his call.'

> (*ibid.*, sig. Dii and ll. 1120–30)

The only vestiges of charity displayed throughout this fiercely satiric comedy are the meal offered by Learning-with-Money to Learning-

---

*set by the heeles; i.e. put in the stocks.

without-Money and All-for-Money's offer to give house-room to Sir Laurence, the priest who has been stripped of his living because of his ignorance of the Gospels, on the grounds that he is a good drinker and gambler.[79]

Another feature of this astringent social criticism within a still pervading tragi-comic, doctrinal frame—and perhaps the most significant of all in terms of the future of English comedy—is a cautious but explicit element of cynicism about the rapid escalation in the number of religious sects whose representatives all claim to be possessed of the only true religion, yet behave as rapaciously as any merchant, landlord or lawyer. No less conducive to cynicism was the conduct of many men, clerical and lay, with estates and official positions who had trimmed their religious allegiance over some thirty years to match each turn of the tide. An example is that of Lord Rich, in Essex, who 'having accommodated himself to the religious views of Henry VIII, became a Protestant under Edward VI and a persecutor of Protestants under Mary'.*

Elizabeth I's accession brought with it the return of the English Protestant exiles most of whom had become disciples of Calvin; but it also encouraged foreign Protestants of many sects to seek asylum in England from persecution at home. In *The Pedlar's Prophecy* the Pedlar accuses the Mariner of importing into England 'Fortie thousand enemies to the Crowne The deadly poyson of hell', and then enumerates them satirically as

> 'Jewes, Russians, Moores, Turkes, and Tartarians,
> With these you have mixed the virgins people
> Anabaptists, Lybertines, Epicurians and Arians
> Infinit of these, your country to infeeble.'
>
> (ll. 824–7)

Gone in these plays is the innocent simplicity of a feud between Roman Catholics and Reformers that characterizes *Respublica* or *New Custom*, for that has been superseded in real life by a modern Tower of Babel. Thus when the Mariner defends himself and his fellows by claiming naïvely that their actions are prompted not by greed, but by Christian charity, the Pedlar greets this riposte with sardonic mirth.

> *Mariner* But whereas thou laiest to the charge of Mariners,
> That we have filled the land full of Alians,
> Thou beliest us, we bring in none but Gospellers,
> And such as we know to be very good Christians.

*This case can be paralleled by the career of Bishop Bonner.

Pedlar   Oh holy Ghospell, ô tydings of health most pure,
Thou art made a cloake to all abhomination!

(ll. 904 ff.)

At the close of *The Pedlar's Prophecy* the Interpreter, on entering, warns the audience of the likely consequences.

> 'It greeveth me at the heart, God I take to record,
> To see the varietie, and chiefly in religion,
> That it may be soone amended, I beseech Christ our Lord,
> Or else let us looke shortly for a greevous destruction?'

(ll. 1203–6)

It is not a far cry from this plea to the all-pervading self-interest that saturates Marlowe's *The Jew of Malta*, even if Marlowe's satire, as in *The Massacre at Paris*, is consistently anti-Catholic rather than anti-Christian.[80] Yet this was the world in which actors and their play-makers opened the doors of the first, regular public and private playhouses in England in 1576—James Burbage's Theater in the precincts of the dissolved Holywell Priory in Shoreditch, and Richard Farrant's playhouse in the former refectory of the dissolved Dominican priory of Blackfriars, near St Paul's Cathedral; and on their stages they did not shrink from trying to reflect this world for their audiences, 'earnest' still mirrored in 'game' and 'play'.

It was within this same decade that Queen Elizabeth I was excommunicated and that the government decided to tighten up its censorship procedures by reforming the Revels Office and by suppressing overtly religious plays.* However, just as the ancient morality play, reliant as it was on the academic art of disputation, had proved capable of easy transformation into plays of political satire and then into plays of social criticism, so the episodic saint play, which had been no less reliant upon exotic settings and sensational (not to say miraculous) incident, was to prove equally adaptable in the service of romantic narrative.†

The idea of man's journey through life—an image which Henry Medwall used to open I *Nature*—conjoined with the idea of love as redemptive offering and reconciling agent—an image central to the Corpus Christi cycles and no less explicit in the second part of Medwall's *Nature*—retain their old power to move audiences when spliced to tales drawn from chivalry, romance, and even history, legend and myth, like Richard Edwards's adaptation of Chaucer's 'Knight's Tale' under the new title of *Palamon and Arcite* (1565); John Phillip's *Patient and Meek Grisell* (c. 1566) adapted from the last novel of the

*See *EES.* ii(1). 75–90.
†See p. 217 below.

Decameron; Robert Greene's *James the Fourth* (1590), the source of which was Giraldi Cinthio's *Hecatommithi* rather than Scottish history; or *King Leir* of the same year.[81]

The best English examples of these ingredients as mixed within their original, overtly religious frame are *The Conversion of St Paul* and *St Mary Magdalene* among the so-called Digby plays of the early sixteenth century (Bodl. MS. Digby 133), and the somewhat earlier *Play of the Sacrament* from Croxton in Norfolk (Trin. Coll. Dublin, MS. F.4.20); an even more sensational example is *The Life of St Meriasek*, written in Cornish and dated 1504 (Hengarth MSS.). *St Paul* is scripted in three parts; *Mary Magdalene* and *St Meriasek* in two parts.[82] What is common to all three texts is biographical narrative presented in chronological sequence as a series of incidents, tableaux, or scenes. In each play tyrants, torturers and devils provide rhetorical excitement, and in each, scenic spectacle figures prominently as an accompaniment to the abrupt changes of luck that characterize the fortunes of the title-role. St Paul, as Saul, is struck by lightning and thrown from his horse; Mary Magdalene sails by ship from Judea to Marseilles via Turkey and Sicily inside ten lines of text and causes Mahomet's Temple to be set on fire and its priests to sink from view; Meriasek heals cripples and causes outlaws to flee on horseback from impending destruction in a forest fire. Yet it is the earlier Croxton play which contains perhaps the most spectacular stage-directions, well worthy of John Webster. 'Here the owyn [*oven*] must ryve [*split, burst*] asunder, and blede owt at the cranys, and an image appere owt with woundis bledyng' (1. 632).

Invariably, for doctrinal reasons, these plays end happily, however near to tragedy their heroes may have been brought; so their form is always tragi-comic.

Following the Reformation, and as the attack on images of saints and martyrs grew in intensity as a matter of government policy under Cranmer and Cromwell—encouraged, let it be said, by play-makers like John Bale—the days of the saint play were numbered; nevertheless, it was not difficult to retain for the theatre the essential components of both form and content, provided that new figures of indisputably secular origin could take over the title-roles.[83] With the accession of Elizabeth I, and as professional actors strove to overcome the obstacles that the censorship placed in the way of their own survival, this possibility—combining, as it did, chronicle with biography—was offered with increasing regularity on public stages, creating a new vogue for romantic tragi-comedies like *Misogonus* (? 1565), *Clyomon and Clamydes* (*c.* 1570), *July and Julian* (*c.* 1570), *Common Conditions* (*c.* 1576) and *Promos and Cassandra* (1578).[84]

Safely distanced though these romantic tales might appear to be from local and contemporary events by being set in foreign parts and earlier times, it remained as easy for play-makers as it had ever been to inject topicality into them, if they so wished, either by specific allusions in the dialogue, or by allegorizing the original source material, as John Bale had done in *Kyng Johan* (first performed in the 1530s, but revived in the 1560s), to invite comparison with parallels in the contemporary political or social scene. Thus the 'mirror image', first supplied by Bale in his epilogue to the first part of *Kyng Johan*, survives in comedies like *The Pedlar's Prophecy*, Lyly's *Endimion*, or Greene's *A Looking Glass for London* to be transmitted to the young Shakespeare as a device whereby to parody, in comparative safety, not only the chivalric pretensions of his social superiors led by Sir Philip Sidney and Sir Fulke Greville when storming 'The Fortress of Perfect Beauty' in the tiltyard at Whitehall to impress the Queen, but also the literary and dramatic posturing of these sophisticated amateurs in respect of 'mongrel tragi-comedy'.[85] And as the old century gave place to the new with George Chapman, Ben Jonson and John Marston pushing these newfangled neo-classical views into the ascendant, English comedy in its old Roman Catholic, tragi-comic form could still reassert itself unambiguously in both its romantic, narrative style as in *The Merchant of Venice* and its more demanding, debating style as in *Measure for Measure*, thereby creating problems which have worried actors, directors and critics ever since.

IX

ENGLISH TRAGEDY FROM ITS ORIGINS TO 1576

---

1 The genesis of English tragedy

T RAGEDY, as a dramatic genre in England, is generally held to date from the performance in 1561 and publication in 1565 of Thomas Sackville's and Thomas Norton's *Gorboduc: or The Tragedy of Ferrex and Porrex*;* and in one sense at least there is some substance behind this belief, for it is in this same decade that English translations of Seneca's plays start to appear in print, that tragedies written in Latin begin to appear on university stages, and that these academic interests acquire a foothold in London at the Inns of Court and the Palace of Whitehall.[1] Yet in another sense this belief is an illusion for, as remarked in the preceding chapter, English ideas about tragedy have a common origin with ideas about comedy in the Fall of Lucifer and the Fall of Adam:† they therefore stretch back to Lydgate and Chaucer, and behind them to Boccaccio and the *trouveres* of Provence. Nevertheless ideas about tragedy and plays that can be described as tragedies are not the same thing; and so, when we come to examine the surviving repertoire of plays up to 1550 we find ourselves forced back (as we were in surveying the growth of comedy) to what Englishmen of the Middle Ages evidently regarded as the natural or basic dramatic form, tragicomedy. This idea lingers still within Webster's *The White Devil* when the Duke of Florence, planning Brachiano's murder, observes,

> 'My tragedy must have some idle mirth in't,
> Else it will never serve.'
>
> (IV.i.119–20)

---

*Entered in the Stationers' Register in 1565 as *A Tragedie of Gorboduc*, the play was printed in that year by William Griffith under the title of *The Tragedie of Gorboduc;* and then, without a date (*c.* 1571) by John Day under the title of *The Tragedie of Ferrex and Porrex*. Editors have thus come to combine all three titles into *Gorboduc: or The Tragedy of Ferrex and Porrex* and then to abbreviate this into *Gorboduc*.

†See pp. 173–5 above.

It was the manifest concern with the presence of evil in the world, and the inevitability of death and decay, displayed by the writers of the miracle cycles and moralities that led J. M. R. Margeson in *The Origins of English Tragedy* (1967) to examine in the context of medieval and Tudor drama what he calls 'examples of conflict between individual will and divine will', or 'conflict between human will and a superior law which is either antagonistic to human will or remote and difficult to comprehend'.[2] G. R. Owst in *Literature and Pulpit in Mediaeval England* (1933) delved still deeper into time-past seeing 'the great Judgement theme of revenge taking shape, as it were, in England, as far back as the thirteenth century' in the dire warnings of the wayside preachers which were to find theatrical expression in the morality and saint plays of the fifteenth century; while Willard Farnham in *The Mediaeval Heritage of Elizabethan Tragedy* (1936) viewed Boccaccio's *De Casibus Virorum Illustrium*, transmitted to Englishmen through Lydgate's *Fall of Princes*, as the dominant influence on the shaping of English tragedy. Writing myself on 'Genesis and the Tragic Hero' in 1969, I observed that the recurring threnody of Lydgate's *Fall of Princes* is that men reap what they sow.[3] His adaptation of his source was prepared for a special audience, the Court, and as such it is conservative in outlook; but, very importantly, Lydgate, as a Benedictine monk himself, follows the preachers in recognizing that 'nobility is by the grace of God and not by blood, and poverty is no bar to royalty: nor can anything good ever come out of an evil stock'; and in these precepts he foreshadows certain aspects of Calvin's thinking.[4]

In this work we meet most of the notable figures in past history from Adam to King Arthur; and in *l'Envoie* attaching to each tale Lydgate defines the particular vice that occasioned each prince to fall from 'the prosperity' he once was in into 'hell and to meschaunce' in terms of sin, singling out murder, slander, covetousness, ingratitude, pride and tyranny for special attention.* Lydgate, moreover, reinforces his puritanical insistence that moral weakness of character is the primary reason for a tragic decline of fortune by dismissing the notion that chance or fate might be held responsible, as expressed in the popular medieval image of Dame Fortune and her ever-turning wheel, as a mere excuse to deflect attention away from personal culpability:

> But such as list(e) nat correctid be
> Bexaumple off othre fro vicious governaunce,
> And fro ther vices list nat for to fle:
> Yiff thei be troubled in ther hih puissaunce,

*See Dr Bergen's introduction to his edition for EETS.

Thei arette* it Fortunys variaunce,
Touchyng the giltes that thei deden use,
Ther demerites ful falsli to excuse.
(EETS, ed. Bergen, Vol. I, p. 201)

Many Elizabethan and Jacobean writers of tragedy would question this dogmatically orthodox Christian position, but writers of domestic tragedies like *Arden of Faversham* and *A Woman Killed with Kindness* still found it acceptable enough for their purposes.

Viewed from this standpoint, many tragi-comedies of the fifteenth century and of the early sixteenth tremble on the brink of tragedy and could well be concluded in a manner fitting Chaucer's and Lydgate's definitions of tragic narrative structure had it not been for the play-makers' overriding, evangelistic concern with repentance.† *Mankind* and *Magnyficence* provide two particularly striking examples; for in both cases the concentration of dramatic action in the career of the title-role provides a very strong story-line with the road to suicide (and consequent damnation) being sharply and poignantly charted. The subsequent intervention of the virtues has an almost mechanical air about it, and the hero's salvation appears to owe more to doctrinal requirement than to natural and genuine inclination. Yet these plays are not as similar as their parallel story-lines might suggest; for where, in *Magnyficence*, Skelton unquestionably follows the *de casibus* principle in demonstrating the fall of a prince, the anonymous author of *Mankind* takes a representative man of low degree who, in classical terms of reference, is a character only fitted for inclusion in comedy, and translates him into the hero of his play. In other words, if Skelton's play signposts a way forward to Marlowvian and Shakespearean tragedy of kings and princes, *Mankind* just as clearly signals the Elizabethan and Jacobean alternative of domestic, homiletic tragedy.

What both plays share is a concern with rebellion and retribution; but in pursuing this theme dramatically the two authors part company. Skelton is prepared to admit that Fortune and her wheel play some part in the downfall of his prince, even if that lady is here operating under God's orders. The author of *Mankind* subscribes to a more single-mindedly Christian viewpoint. Stage 4, scene 26 of *Magnyficence* starts as follows:

Enter Adversity
Magnyficence Alas, who is yonder, that grimly lookés?
Fancy   Adew, for I will not come in his clutches.
                    (*Exit* Fancy)

---

*arette: i.e. they attribute it to...
†See pp. 41ff. and 186–7 above.

Magnyficence   Lord, so my fleshé trembleth now for dread!
              Here Magnyficence *is beaten down, and*
              spoiled from all his goods and raiment.
Adversity   I am Adversity, that for thy misdeed
              From God am sent to 'quite* thee thy meed.
              Vile vilyard, thou must now my dint withstand,
              Thou must abide the dint of my hand.
              Lie there, losel,† for all thy pomp and pride;
              Thy pleasure now with pain and trouble shall be tried.
              The stroke of God, Adversity I hight;
              I pluck down king, prince, lord and knight.
                                    (ed. Henderson, p. 223)

There is no suggestion here that Adversity has come to pluck down artisans and farmers as well. Magnyficence is his target, who survives the assault by learning that Fortitude is the virtue above all others that princes need to ward off such blows.

The author of *Mankind*, by contrast, makes his peasant hero embark upon the road that will bring him to ruin fully aware of what the consequences will be and at his own choice.

    'My name is Mankind. I have my composition
    Of a body and a soul, of condition contrary.
    Betwixt the twain is a great division:
    He that should be subject, now he hath the victory.
    This is to me a lamentable story:
    To see my flesh, of my soul to have governance;
    Where the goodwife is master, the goodman may be sorry.'
                              (EMI, ll. 193–9)

Where Skelton and the author of *Mankind* converge again is in returning their respective prodigals to the paths of righteousness. In both cases, therefore, the reader or spectator is confronted with a question raised by Dr Margeson about all morality plays: 'Was it necessary for the didactic to be eliminated before tragedy could emerge?' My own answer to that question is 'no'.‡ Dr Margeson answers it by saying: 'When the nature and intensity of the human experience became a matter of greater concern in the drama than the moral idea, then tragedy became possible.'[5] If we can agree with him at least in regarding 'the nature and intensity of the human experience' to be a prime requisite of tragedy as we understand the word today, then why did it take so long (more than half a century in fact) for play-makers to move

'quite; require.
†*losel;* wretch, villain.
‡ See pp. 251–2 below.

beyond what had already been achieved in *Mankind* and *Magnyfycence*?

In my view the reason is three-fold. First, play-makers had still to learn how to handle the virtuous man (as opposed to the wilful sinner) who nevertheless falls from prosperity into adversity as a seeming victim of circumstance. Next, the multiplicity of vices operating in the world as agents of Lucifer in the respective liveries of the seven deadly sins had to be concentrated, by play-makers and actors working in conjunction, into a single, malign and irredeemable disseminator of evil, able to carry the plot of a play on his own shoulders (as in the case of Shakespeare's Iago) or into a single but impersonal evil force (as in *Hamlet*). Third, audiences had to learn to prefer plays structured in a genuinely tragic mould rather than in a tragi-comic one; and not surprisingly, university and Court audiences were ready to explore this possibility in their halls long before popular audiences in public theatres; and I think, moreover, that the moving spirits in any such amateur and academic experiments, then as now, would have found schoolboy and student actors far more co-operative partners than sceptical professionals. Professionals in any case had strong reason to appear orthodox.*

The surviving evidence from the early years of the sixteenth century reveals that the conditions necessary for the fulfilment of these three requirements already existed, albeit in embryo. If the doctrinal format of the cycles and moralities militated against the development of the tragic hero, that of the saint plays did not: for there, not only was the hero virtuous by definition and martyred by cruel and unheeding persecutors, but as a named character of early Christian history who lived and worked in a world of equally real human beings, his or her sufferings pointed directly to the dramatic exploitation of 'the nature and intensity of the human experience'. Second, the steady growth in the popularity of the professional players of interludes with their need for a rapidly expanding repertoire of plays for small casts exerted its own pressure on play-makers to scale down the numbers of virtues and vices appearing simultaneously on the stage to correspond with the number of actors available to sustain the roles; and this practical requirement sufficed of itself to drive them to concentrate the forces tempting, deceiving and abusing their hero into a single, dominant vicious character, the Vice.[6] Third, the spread of both Greek and Latin studies in English universities and schools under Henry VII and Henry VIII generated an interest in classical plays and dramatic theory in a small but influential group of men with ready access both to halls in which to perform plays, and to boys and undergraduates eager to

*See pp. 167–70 above.

present them as a temporary escape from less congenial studies, at no higher cost to themselves than the time thus deflected from those studies: this group was also in close touch with printers who were only allowed to operate in Oxford, Cambridge and London.

One of these desiderata, the concentration of vices into Vice, as David Bevington convincingly demonstrated in *From Mankind to Marlowe*, was already well advanced when John English and his successor, Richard Gibson, were leading the King's Players of Interludes, and has already been discussed;* but the other two had to wait for their advancement until the Reformation. This, when it came, involved a root-and-branch attack on those same Roman Catholic doctrines that had given English tragi-comedy its distinctive shape. John Bale, as one of the leaders of this protest action within the theatre, is succinct in directing ridicule at what he terms 'popetly plays'.†

One relatively swift result of this volte-face was for actors and play-makers to lose their former control over the theological basis of their plays: this passed by statute in 1543 to the State in the person of the monarch speaking through his Privy Council in his new capacity of Defender of the Faith in England, and was followed by the abolition in 1548 of the Feast of Corpus Christi itself.‡ After the death of Henry VIII, this statute was repealed by the Parliament of Edward VI on the instructions of Protector Somerset, and a fresh flood of anti-Catholic polemic was released onto public stages for the next four years, much of it doctrinally orientated towards a Calvinist viewpoint. When Mary I acceded to the throne in 1553, this process was put sharply into reverse; the Feast of Corpus Christi was restored and the staging of the cycles was again legitimized; plays of anti-Protestant polemic were encouraged and anti-Catholic plays suppressed.§ Another reversal followed Elizabeth I's accession in 1558, but this time a new and harsher voice was heard in the land—that of extremists among the returning Protestant exiles (notably the Anabaptists) who had come to believe that *all* theatrical exhibition of no matter what theological persuasion was unworthy of a place in any well ordered Commonwealth. Not all Puritans adopted this extreme viewpoint, but many did: even some Anglicans were forced into it.[7]

After some twenty years, therefore, of constant religious turmoil no play-maker could have been left in any doubt that if any religious, didactic element was to figure in his plays, it must conform with the

*See Ch. VII, pp. 162–6 above.
†See pp. 103–4 above and pp. 228–9 below.
‡See *EES*.ii(1). 69–70.
§See pp. 225–7 below.

doctrine approved by the government and be formally licensed through the newly constituted Revels Office.* Thus any discussion today of a shift from tragi-comic patterns of play construction in Tudor England towards wholly tragic ones must take theological considerations into account along with literary and practical ones. Protestantism, for all its excesses in the early years of the revolution, broke many of the doctrinal barriers that had formerly shackled play-makers to tragi-comic dramatic structure. With its initial emphasis upon direct inspiration, on personal acquaintance with the Old and New Testament, and on the subject's prime duty of obedience to a divinely appointed sovereign, Protestantism gave both the theme of retributive justice and that of martyred innocence new dimensions of terrestrial immediacy and national urgency; and this change could only be hastened and reinforced as the more extreme doctrine of predestination began to take root in England.[8]

Tragedy, however, as interpreted by Horace and Aristotle, and as exemplified in the plays of the classical authors, possessed another and quite different attraction, at least for those academics who were acquainted with their works: it appeared to release them altogether, as did classical precept on comedy, from any overt concern with the contentious and dangerous religious issues of the time. This exemption was in fact illusory, since the Fates that at first seemed to be exclusively responsible for a hero's destiny in classical drama were soon to become associated with Calvinist theology and thus with the inscrutable workings of Divine Providence. Nevertheless, between 1543—the year of Henry VIII's statute forbidding any actor or play-maker to meddle with 'interpretations of scripture or matters of doctrine now in question'—and 1569–70—the years of the Northern Rebellion and the excommunication of Elizabeth I—experiments in the writing and performance of plays constructed on classical lines had obvious attractions for those sufficiently literate in Greek and Latin to pursue them; and these are the years that lead up to Sackville's and Norton's *Gorboduc* and the staging of pseudo-classical tragedies both in the universities and at Court.

However, some Protestant academics adopted a sternly different and disapproving view. One such was Martin Bucer, Regius Professor of Divinity at Cambridge from 1549 to 1551 and the author of *De Honestis Ludis* already cited on p. 206 above in the context of comedy; † another was Peter Martyr (Pietro Martire Vermiglio), an Italian Protestant who was appointed Regius Professor of Divinity at Oxford in 1548. Both came to England at the invitation of Archbishop Cranmer

*See *EES*. ii(1). 49–52.
†See Plate XI, No. 17.

as refugees from persecution on the Continent where both had been active associates of Zwingli and Calvin. Bucer, like John Bale, had started his career as a Roman Catholic (as a Dominican), but in 1518 he joined Luther, married, and founded a Protestant community in Strasbourg in 1523. As a theologian Bucer became accepted as Zwingli's successor in Zurich and helped Calvin to revise the 1539 edition of *The Institutes of Christian Religion*. On leaving Strasbourg for Cambridge, Bucer assisted Cranmer with the preparation of the Edwardian Book of Common Prayer and published his own *De Regno Christi*. In the section devoted to the writing and performance of tragedies and comedies Bucer reveals his knowledge of the works of Aristotle, Sophocles, Euripides and Seneca, but he clearly places his loyalty to his Puritan beliefs above that to his literary and aesthetic conscience. He never forgets that the classical authors, for all their virtues, were pagan authors born in ignorance of Christ; that the Bible is much to be preferred to any other source for plot material; and that stylistic pleasantries are matters of inferior worth when rated against moral truth. Tragedy, in short, if it is to be good tragedy, must be thorough-going Christian tragedy.* If it is not, then it should have no place in the new Protestant State, and censors must be appointed, men who are 'both outstanding in their knowledge of this kind of literature and also of established and constant zeal for Christ's Kingdom'.[9] Nothing could be less equivocal. By 'established and constant zeal for Christ's Kingdom' Bucer meant 'acceptance of the total sovereignty of God, the total corruption of man, Justification by Faith Alone, together with their corollary of each man's predestination to bliss or damnation by the sovereign will of God'.[10] Like Calvin, moreover, he accepted the ideas of greater equity for the oppressed poor and of participation by civil magistrates in the government of the Church; he was thus able to encourage those radicals in the universities who recognized the social pressures activating the Reformation in England and were anxious to appease those honest, educated and devout laymen who were no longer willing to accept either royal or episcopal in-fallibility in matters of religion. This demand extended directly to the drama and was met by Bucer in the type of person whom he indicated to be suitable as censors. In fact the licensing powers newly vested in the Revels Office represent a shift in this direction; but I do not think one can claim that the power of the Church was finally broken in this

---

*The same view is expressed by Robert Beaumont, Vice-Chancellor of Cambridge, who says, when writing to Archbishop Parker in 1565, that while the religious situation is reasonably satisfactory 'two or three in Trinity College think it very unseeming that Christians should play or be present at any profane comedies or tragedies'.

respect until the establishment of the Licensing Commission in 1589.*

One may fairly conclude therefore that the Reformation, while it both released play-makers early in its progress from many of the sacramental restraints formerly imposed upon dramatic structure by the old religion, and encouraged the academics amongst their number to experiment with classical forms, nevertheless succeeded in imposing new restraints of a specifically Puritan character upon the general directions in which tragedy might develop out of tragi-comedy. One of these was 'zeal', or that passionate determination to prove to oneself and to the world that one was numbered among God's elect, and not among the reprobate, and thus assured of bliss; another was 'patience', the armour of endurance in the faith in times of provocation and persecution. At the same time, the case of the individual who lacked faith and recognized himself as reprobate, rejected and damned had to be taken into account; so too, and more especially after the bonfires of the Marian persecution, did the spiritual situation of an individual when judged by his conduct in the face of death by burning. Historically it is beyond doubt that the Marian persecution left an indelible mark on the Protestant conscience, two characteristics of which were relevant to the drama. The first of these was the heroism of the martyrs whose steadfastness through torture and a frightful form of death inspired those who witnessed it, and could easily be translated into patriotism if the threat to faith were to shift to an external source as it did under Elizabeth I. The second was the enormity of the cruelty, not to say barbarism, which those officials from Mary I and Philip II of Spain to Cardinal Pole and Bishop Bonner downwards could bring themselves to inflict upon pious and honest men and women in all walks of life.[11]

An examination of some of the plays written between 1530 and 1576 will, I think, confirm that it was such real-life factors as these, particular to the Reformation in England, rather than interest in classical tragedy *per se*, that broke the old tragi-comic frame of English drama and encouraged play-makers to consider the theatrical possibilities of separating recognizably tragic situations and individuals from comic ones, and of according them separate treatment in a manner akin to certain classical precedents first exploited by George Buchanan and John Christopherson in their respective Latin and Greek tragedies devoted to the subject of Jephthah and his rash vow.†

---

*See *EES*.ii(1).87–9.
†See p. 239 and nn. 25 and 26 below.

2 *The rationalizing of English tragedy*

Two key plays in this context, although of a slightly earlier date, are John Bale's *Kyng Johan* (1536) and the anonymous *Godly Queen Hester* (*c.* 1527); others are *Jacob and Esau* (*c.* 1553), *Enough is as Good as a Feast* (*c.* 1564), *Apius and Virginia* (*c.* 1564), *Gorboduc* (1561–2), *Horestes* (*c.* 1566) and *The Conflict of Conscience* (*c.* 1580).* None of these plays can be described as a regular tragedy in the Aristotelian sense; but all of them make at least one radical departure from past tradition and thus helped subsequent play-makers to consider experimenting themselves with predominantly and even exclusively tragic characters and situations.

Bale's *Kyng Johan*, besides being both the first attempt to construct a play around a central character, or title-role, taken from 'modern' English history, and containing the most savagely satiric political comedy so far achieved in England, was revolutionary in yet a third sense; for it sought to present a virtuous character 'overwhelmed by Fortune's showers' and translated from a state of prosperity into one of adversity by circumstances rather than by sin. Today, when King John is only remembered for Magna Carta and his connection with Robin Hood, it might be thought that these would have been the topics that would have interested a Tudor play-maker; but Bale ignores both since what attracted him in the story of John's reign was the stand John made against papal interference in the nation's affairs. In this context John acquires an heroic stature comparable to that of Moses and John the Baptist, as Bale indicates uncompromisingly in his epilogue to Part I of the play.

> In thys present acte we have to yow declared,
> As in a myrrour, the begynnynge of kynge Johan,
> How he was of God a magistrate appoynted
> To the governaunce of thys same noble regyon,
> To see maynteyned the true faythe and relygyon.
> But Satan the Devyll, whych that tyme was at large,
> Had so great a swaye that he coulde it not discharge.
>
> Upon a goode zele he attempted very farre
> For welthe of thys realme to provyde reformacyon
> In the churche therof. But they ded hym debarre
> Of that good purpose, for by excommunycacyon
> The space of vii yeares they interdyct thys nacyon.

---

*The dates given here are those for likely date of composition, not first printing. For the first printed edition see each title *sub* Plays, pp. 323–35.

These bloudsuppers* thus, of crueltie and spyght,
Subdued thys good kynge for executynge ryght.
(ll. 1086–99)

When editing the play, Barry B. Adams remarked in his critical introduction that from the outset John's will is unchanging. 'At his first appearance he reveals himself as a noble ruler concerned above all for the welfare of his subjects.'[12] Even when John is required to yield the crown to Cardinal Pandalphus, Bale excuses him.

'O Englande, Englande, shewe now thyselfe a mother;
Thy people wyll els be slayne here without nomber.
As God shall judge me, I do not thys of cowardnesse
But of compassyon, in thys extreme heavynesse.'
(ll. 1717–20)

When John dies at the poisoner's hand, it is as a martyr-king.

'I have sore hungred and thirsted ryghteousnesse
For the offyce sake that God hath me appoynted;
But now I perceyve that synne and wyckednesse
In thys wretched worlde, lyke as Christe prophecyed,
Have the overhande; in me it is verefyed.
Praye for me, good people, I besych you hartely,
That the lorde above on my poore sowle have mercy.
(ll. 2167–73)

Given a competent actor in the title-role, the anguish below the surface of these lines and those surrounding them, born of a sense of defeat coupled with exemplary Christian fortitude and acceptance, suffices, even today, to move an audience, if not to tears, at least to a sympathetic understanding of both John's and Widow England's grief.

If the play had ended there, no dispute would arise about its predominant characteristic, and it could fairly be entitled *The Tragedy of King John*; but Bale's overriding purpose disallowed this, for in terms of his extended dramatic metaphor, King John is intended to prefigure Henry VIII by whom Anti-Christ (the Pope) and his agents will be successfully chased out of England. Thus both the 'A' and the 'B' texts make provision for a final messianic scene that promises the advent of the New Jerusalem in England under a Protestant sovereign; and this of itself returns the play as a whole into the normal tragi-comic structural pattern.[13]

By striking contrast *Godly Queen Hester* goes to the opposite extreme in depicting at its centre, a character, Aman, whose swift rise to fame and fortune followed by overthrow and execution are brought about almost exclusively by his own villainy.[14] Here the play-maker's

*A clear and provocative reference to transubstantiation.

central theme is retributive justice. The biblical account of the Queen's plea to Ahasuerus to show mercy to the Jews provides him with his frame, and within it he depicts Aman, a man whose ambition (like Cardinal Wolsey's) carries him by flattery and graft from 'very base parage and poor estate' to the Office of Lord Chancellor.* He is thereupon warned by the King,

> 'take hede to this lesson.
> See ye doe justice and trueth ever approve[,]
> Or[,] to your destruction[,] we shall you soone remove[.]'
> (ed. Greg, *Materialien*, V, pp. 6–7, ll. 110–12)

Once in office, Aman's pride increases to the point where he aims, by bending the law to suit his own purposes, and by the rapacious seizure of his victims' estates to his own use, to outface his sovereign.

> *Ahasuerus* We favored hym that he was called
> Our father, and all men dyd to him honoure[.]
> But his harte[,] wyth pryde, so strongly was walled
> That[,] by his slyght and crafty demeanoure[,]
> Had we not espyed his subtyle behavioure[,]
> He wolde have dystroyd quene Hester[,] our wife[,]
> And from us[,] at lengthe[,] have taken our lyfe[.]
> (*ibid.*, p. 44, ll. 1131–7)

As one of Aman's intended victims remarks of him,

> 'He woulde be glorified above creatures all,
> And yet I trust(,) as Lucifer depe he shal fal.'†
> (*ibid.*, p. 33, ll. 832–3)

With everything thus ordered for the writing of a tragedy taking the same narrative form as, later, will Shakespeare's *Richard III* and *Macbeth*, the play-maker then wastes his opportunity by avoiding *direct depiction* of any of Aman's motives or methods: these are handled descriptively by the vices Pride, Adulation and Ambition (who wittily claim that they have been destituted by Aman) by the licensed fool, Hardydardy, and by Queen Hester.[15] There is good reason to believe that the play-maker intended his play to reflect Wolsey's behaviour, and this in itself suffices to explain the oblique, self-protective technique used;‡ it also explains why this text, as it actually stands, remains a satiric morality in biblical dress; but it does mark a notable advance towards tragedy by bringing to the stage, as Bale does with his Johan, a named individual rather than an abstraction whose

---

*See p. 204 above.

†Thus Shakespeare will speak of Wolsey; *Henry VIII* (III.ii. 371–2).

‡See p. 203 above.

career follows an unmistakably tragic pattern. Aman admits his guilt, but does not repent; he pleads for his life, but is promptly 'hoist with his own petard' by being hung from the same monstrous gibbet 'fifty cubits high' that he had prepared for the disposal of his intended victims. It should also be remarked that both these early experiments in tragic situations derive the form in which they are actually cast from the nature of topical events which they sought to reflect for their audiences while protecting their devisers.

No less radical, despite its biblical camouflage, is the anonymous *Jacob and Esau*, as the Prologue makes plain at the outset.[16] We are informed that Isaac and Rebecca had two sons, of whom Esau was the elder.

> But before Jacob and Esau yet borne were,
> Or had eyther done good, or yll perpetrate:
> As the prophete Malachie and Paule witnesse beare,
> Jacob was chosen, and Esau reprobate.

In other words, the former's seizure of the latter's birthright was predestined.

> Jacob I love (sayde God) and Esau I hate.
> For it is not (sayth Paule) in mans renuing or will,
> But in Gods mercy who choseth whome he will.

This is fine for Jacob who might well regard the play as 'A New, Merry and Witty Comedy'; but it is no less evidently a tragedy from Esau's standpoint for whom there is no comfort to be derived from the Epilogue's exclamation,

> 'Oh the deepnesse of the riches of Gods wisedome,
> How unsearcheable are his wayes to mans reason:
>   Our parte therefore is first to beleve Gods worde,
> Not doubtyng but that he wil his elected save:
> Then to put full trust in the goodnesse of the Lorde,
> That we be of the number which shall mercy have:
> Thirdly so to live as we may his promise crave.
> Thus if we do, we shall Abrahams chyldren be:
> And come with Jacob to endlesse felicitie.'

This stark statement of Calvinist belief colours the play-maker's entire handling of this unpleasant story of shameless opportunism and deceit.[17] Esau is depicted as a caricature of the hunting squirearchy who even threatens to turn cannibal! Jacob is a prig manipulated by his mother. Yet when Esau finally learns how he has been cheated by this scheming pair, the play-maker shies away from the tragic potential of the scene and is content to let Esau rant against his brother like

Herod against the Innocents, and then to grant his mother's request to forgive Jacob simply because she is his mother. Even so, Esau's lines in this scene, given as an aside, are his best in the play and the most ominous.

> 'It must nowe be thus, but when I shall Jacob fynde,
> I shall then do, as God shall put into my minde.'

This comment (*MSR*, ll. 1755–6) is presumptuous coming from Esau who is 'reprobate', and borders upon blasphemy. It is a remark worthy of Shakespeare's Richard III.

Doctrine thus again imposes a tragi-comic shape upon this play which closes with Esau apparently reconciled and ready to join in a family hymn of praise and thanksgiving; the allegorical objective is to justify Protestants in claiming both England as their birthright and sanctification in their theft of it by virtue of being the elect—the chosen people—while Catholics of the old régime, as reprobates, must learn to come to terms with what now appears to be a *fait accompli*.[18] Yet in Esau's baleful defiance of his mother the play-maker has cracked the old, reconciliatory frame of his tragi-comedy; and in doing so, like Bale and the author of *Godly Queen Hester*, he has signposted yet another route towards a new and genuinely tragic 'conflict between human will and a superior law that is antagonistic to human will or remote and difficult to comprehend'.* Other play-makers will follow this lead and so bring it to its fulfilment in Nathaniel Woodes's *The Conflict of Conscience* (c. 1580), Marlowe's *Dr Faustus* and Shakespeare's *Macbeth*.

The first play that survives in which the tragi-comic frame has patently been broken rather than fractured by the emergence of a tragic central figure is William Wager's *Enough is as Good as a Feast* (c. 1564). Although described as a 'Comedie or Interlude' on its title-page and said to be 'very fruteful, godly and ful of mirth', it focuses attention upon Worldly Man, a character whose name, in a Puritan context, signifies that whatever style of Christianity he may profess to embrace, he has deliberately chosen to place more trust in earthly pleasures than in spiritual ones.[19] In one sense this character is only 'Everyman', 'Mankind' or 'Humanum Genus' under a new name; but in another sense he is a new creation since this sinner, while he recognizes the error of his ways and repents early in the play, at length wilfully relapses into his former avaricious pursuit of office and wealth, and dies unconfessed and unshriven. As a 'device' through which to figure his predicament, the play-maker opts to create a counter-

*See pp. 220 and 222–3 above.

weight character—elect as opposed to reprobate—called, appropriately, Heavenly Man, who is content with 'enough', and who lives and dies well in consequence.

Thus the old 'Humanum Genus' figure has been split into two figures, one of whom, Heavenly Man, is as dull as he is good, and the other of whom acquires a tragic dimension because of an overriding passion that he can recognize and acknowledge, but cannot control.* Warned by Heavenly Man and Contentation that avarice breeds anxiety and distress, not contentment, Worldly Man agrees to seek heavenly treasure instead (ed. de Ricci, sigs B to Biv); but he is quickly seduced by the vices, Inconsideration (alias Reason), Temeritie (alias Agility), Precipitation (alias Ready Wit) and Covetousness (alias Policy) into seeking material wealth and status by rapacious and corrupt means that cause others to suffer acute distress. The moral is drawn by two of Worldly Man's dependents, a tenant whom he has dispossessed of his home and a workman whom he has failed to reward adequately for his labour.

Hireling	he is no better than a theef:
	For so that he may have it, he cares not who suffers greef.
Tenant	Nay, by the masse, that woords is but to true:
	So that his riches encreaseth he careth not who rue.

(sigs Eii–Eiib)†

In such conduct Wager is figuring in concrete terms, visual and verbal, that flat contradiction of Puritan determination to secure a more equitable distribution of wealth and opportunity in society which Worldly Man's ambitions and behaviour are serving to effect. Wager thus arranges for Worldly Man's heedless pursuit of private gain to be sharply interrupted, first by a Prophet (the ghost of Jeremiah) and then by the direct affliction of God's Plague. Doctors fail to cure him.

Ignorance	Passion of me he is dead, how shall we do now.
Covetousness	Can't thou not tel? no more can I, I make God avow.
	Sira heer was a trim end that he did make:
	Thou never heardst him the name of God in his mouth take.

(sig. G)

This, of course, is precisely the state of mind in which Hamlet will later hope to take Claudius. Ignorance proceeds:

---

*For discussion of Thomas Ingelend's handling of this issue in *Nice Wanton* see pp. 234–5 below.

†For other treatments of this theme, see Ch. VIII, pp. 210–16 above.

'Tush, God: a strawe, his minde was other waies occupyed:
All his study was who should have his goods when he dyed.'

(ibid.)

The complete reversal of Worldly Man's dreams and the waste of his
efforts is then hammered home to the audience by Covetousness as he
delivers the lifeless corpse to Satan.

> Come, let us go hence, heer is no more to be said:
> Farewell my masters, our partes we have played.
>
> Enter heer Sathan
>
> *Satan* Oh, oh, oh, oh, all is mine, all is mine,
>   My kingdome increaseth every houre and day.
>
> (ibid.)

As Satan hoists the corpse of Worldly Man over his shoulder and exits,
the virtues bring the play to its end with a moral reprise and the
customary prayer for the Queen and council.

Once again then, as in *Godly Queen Hester*, we are confronted with a
tragedy of retributive justice, but this time at the expense of the old
tragi-comic frame. Worldly Man has lost out altogether; materially
he dies in debt, and spiritually he is damned. It is damnation that has
been dramatized; salvation is left in the wings as a speculative possibility assumed as the birthright of Heavenly Man.* As in *Jacob and Esau*,
Calvinist belief in predestination has obliged Wager to modify the
traditional dramatic structure of the play, since it is the 'reprobates'
within the reformed Church that have come to wield power through a
combination of wealth with office and who now threaten its future by
standing between the 'elect' Reformers and their Christian-socialist
ideals.

Where Wager fails to advance on *Jacob and Esau* is in his treatment of
Worldly Man's recognition of the fate awaiting him. This, however, is
more fully exploited by Thomas Ingelend in *Nice Wanton* where, once
again, the good brother, Barnabas (who can do no wrong) is saved, and
the reprobates—mother Xantippe, brother Ismael and sister Dalilah—
are all given time and opportunity to recognize and lament the price
required of them for their wilfully antisocial conduct.

---

*Precedent, it should be remarked, has here been set for that juxtaposition of
similarly contrasted characters so frequently adopted by later dramatists. Banquo and
Macbeth offer the most obvious and interesting example since Banquo is treated as
'elect' in a double sense; the good man who recognizes temptation but resists it and is
rewarded, via Fleance, by the begetting of the line of kings that will bring James VI of
Scotland to the throne of England as James I; Macbeth, being 'reprobate', does not
resist temptation and dies childless and damned.

Xantippe My fair daughter Dalilah is dead of the pox:
My dear son Ismael hanged up in chains—
Alas, the wind waveth his yellow locks—
It slayeth my heart, and breaketh my brains!
   Why should God punish and plague me so sore?
To see my children die so shamefully!
I will never eat bread in this world more!
With this knife will I slay myself by and by.*

(ll. 481–8)

At this point the good son, Barnabas, enters and stops her. He tells her that both children only got their just deserts, and that their behaviour was the result of her own unwillingness to check or punish them. He then directs her attention to himself.

'In that God preserved me, small thank(s) to you!
If God had not given me special grace,
To avoid evil and do good, this is true,
I had lived and died in as wretched case
As they did, for I had both sufferance and space.'

(ll. 503–7)

Finally he urges her to repent and beg for Grace. We do not learn whether she finds herself able to do this since she exits without reply.[20]

It is in Nathaniel Woodes's *The Conflict of Conscience*, however, that the tragic implications opened up in these Calvinist-orientated dramas become fully explicit. Although Woodes uses the word comedy to describe his play on its title-page—'An Excellent new Comedy'—he is doing so in the Latin sense, meaning a play rather than a novel or a poem, and is not speaking about the play's narrative pattern or its hero's destiny: the true description of the play in those terms of reference follows immediately.

'A most lamentable example, of the dolefull desperation of a miserable worldlinge, termed, by the name of Philologus, who forsooke the trueth of God's Gospel for feare of the losse of lyfe & worldly goods.'

There is no hint here, nor in the subsequent Prologue, of any 'sport' or 'merriment' to alleviate this 'lamentable example'. The play is founded on fact, Philologus being pseudonym for Francisco Spira, an Italian Protestant, who recanted under torture at the hands of the Inquisition.†

by and by: immediately.

† The first edition, printed 1581, survives in two states; the first gives Francisco's name on the title-page, describes the story as a 'hystorie' instead of as an 'example', and concludes with his suicide; the second omits the name but adds an announcement of a deathbed repentance to the final scene. The Cardinal who conducts the examination in the Consistory Court may well be a portrait of Cardinal Pole or Bishop Bonner.[21]

Woodes regarded Spira as a reprobate and says so in his Prologue: 'the grace and love of God' have been deflected from him because he let 'the flesh' take precedence over his conscience. 'Then (wretch accurst) no power hath, repentence to beginne.' The question of why God should trouble his elect is then taken up in the opening debate between Philologus and his friend Mathetes, and summarized by the latter.

> 'This is the summe of all your talke, if that I gesse a right,
> That God doth punnish his electt to keepe their faith in ure,
> Or least that if continual ease, and rest enjoy they might:
> God to forget through hautinesse, fraile nature should procure:
> Or els by feeling punishment, our sinnes for to abjure:
> Or els to prove our constancy, or lastly that we may,
> Be instruments in whom his might, God may abroad display.'
>
> (sig. Bii)

The moral exposition is completed with the entry of the vices who, after quarrelling among themselves in the approved manner,* change their names and costumes.† Only Hypocrisy does not because he has already deceived the other two successfully.

The action then begins with the announcement that the Papal Legate 'hath come into our coastes'. Philologus expresses fear that he will lack stability in his Protestant faith if exposed to persecution, more especially as the Legate has ordered the reinstitution of Roman Catholic observances, just as Cardinal Pole had done on his arrival in that capacity under Mary I in 1554. Woodes then introduces a Scottish Catholic priest, Caconux, who betrays Philologus; and so, with the opening of Act IV, the action shifts to the Consistory Court with the Legate presiding and with Philologus required to clear himself of the charges of heresy brought against him. This examination is presented with lively realism. Sent to prison, Philologus is bribed by Hypocrisy to recant, but refuses on grounds of conscience. He is then told that his house will be seized and his goods confiscated before his wife has time to disperse them among friends for safekeeping. Avarice (alias Careful Provision) is next to try to bribe him to recant, but when this also fails Tyranny (alias Zeale) secures the assistance of Sensual Suggestion who then describes to Philologus the effects that seizure of his house and goods is having on his wife and children. As the pressure mounts upon him, a tragedy of personal choice develops. The Legate states it boldly.

> 'I promise thee *Philologus*, by my vowed chastitie,
> If thou wilt be ruled by thy friendes that be heere,

*See pp. 154–5 above.
†See pp. 100–9 above.

Thou shalt abound in wealth and prosperitie:
And in the Countrie chiefe rule thou shalt beare,
And a hundred pounds more thou shalt have in the yeere:
If thou will this curtesie refuse,
Thou shalt die incontinent, the one of these chuse.'

(sig. Fivb)*

At this juncture Sensual Suggestion plays a trick on Philologus in offering him a hand-mirror that reflects every form of worldly pleasure: this suffices to break his resistance, and he recants. Having signed his declaration, he is released on bail. Yet at this seemingly joyous moment when Philologus is returning home, not only a free man but materially much better off than he was before, Woodes introduces a character called Spirit (voice of conscience) who warns him that he is now doomed. After a lengthy debate with Sensual Suggestion (akin to that between the Good and Bad Angels in *Dr Faustus*) Philologus capitulates.

'Hap, what hap wyll, I will not loose these pleasures manyfolde
Wherefore conduct mee once againe, heere take mee by the hande.'

(sig. Giib)

Reunited with his children, Philologus is congratulating himself on his good fortune when Horror, alias Confusion of the Mind, arrives and gives him another mirror in which he can see only his sins and the penalties due. Recognizing that he can temporize no longer, he twists and turns to free himself from the anguish that now consumes him.

'My sinne is unto death, I feele Christes death doth me no good,
Neither for my behoofe, did Christ shed his moste precious bloud.
. . . .
I am condemned into hell, these torments to sustaine.'

(sig. Hiib)

'My name within the Booke of lyfe, had never residence,
Christ prayed not, Christ suffered not, my sinnes to recompence:
But only for the Lordes elect, of which sort I am none,
I feele his justice towardes mee, his mercy all is gone.'

(sig. Hiii)

'I have no fayth, the wordes you speake my heart doth not beléeve
I must confesse that I for sinne, am justly throwne to hell.'

(sig. Hiiib)

*The handling of this scene closely resembles Foxe's account of the treatment accorded to William Hunter, a nineteen-year-old apprentice silk-weaver of Brentwood in Essex, by Edmund Bonner, Bishop of London, who promised to make him a Freeman of the City of London, and an option on £40 in cash or a job as his personal steward if he would recant. He did not and was burned a month later. See Foxe, *Book of Martyrs*, VI, pp. 722–7.

'To pray with lips, unto your God, you shall mee soone intreate,
My spirit, to Sathan is in thrall, I can it not hence get.'

(sig. Hiv)

'I am secluded cleane from grace, my heart is hardened quight,
Wherefore you do your labour loose, and spend your breth in vayne.'

(sig. Hivb)

'Tush sirs, you doo your labours loose, see where Belzabub doth come,
And doth invite mee to a feast, you therefore speake in vaine.'

(sig. Iiiib)

Although Woodes's verse never approaches a level that could invite comparison with Marlowe's, he nevertheless anticipates Marlowe by at least a decade in depicting the nature and quality of the experience of rejection and isolation that overtakes Philologus following his recantation: for this is vividly portrayed in the final disputation with his family and friends, and in language that is at least adequate to the extremity of feeling that afflicts him. Woodes thus opens the way to a poet of Shakespeare's stature and experience as a professional play-maker to refine and distil the vacancy and terror of this predicament: for when Macbeth is forced to revisit the bloody and lifeless body of the king whom he has murdered he, like Philologus, will recognize that he has placed himself among the damned, and will likewise speak prophetically of his own future:

> 'Had I but died an hour before this chance,
> I had lived a blessèd time; for from this instant
> There's nothing serious in mortality.
> All is but toys: renown and grace is dead;
> The wine of life is drawn, and the mere lees
> Is left this vault to brag of . . . '
>
> (II.iii. 84–9)

The sight of Duncan's gory corpse and his murder of the innocent grooms has done for Macbeth what the reflections in Horror's mirror did for Philologus:* so, too, will these prophecies be fulfilled, for just as Philologus comes to recognize that having given his soul to Satan he 'can it not hence get', Macbeth will come to admit that time has for him lost all meaning, moving only at an idiotic, petty pace to its last syllable.[22]

Unlike *Macbeth*, Woodes's play is neither epic nor heroic, but

---

*Macbeth now sees the dead Duncan in the likeness of an icon of Christ crucified, 'His silver skin lac'd with his golden blood'; the grooms as workmen 'Steeped in the colours of their trade, their daggers/Unmannerly breech'd with gore' (II.iii. 105–10).

238

bourgeois and domestic; yet it is tragic, at least in its first printed state before the Messenger was added (for what reason it is impossible to tell) with the announcement of an off-stage deathbed repentance; and singularly, *The Conflict of Conscience* would itself make as appropriate a sub-title for *Macbeth* as any that could be devised.

If the line of descent of this form of Christian tragedy is thus apparent and explicable in terms of the replacement of Roman Catholic by Protestant doctrinal considerations, the filling of the no less self-evident stylistic gap, achieved in the three decades between the opening of public and private playhouses in 1576 and James I's adoption of the Lord Chamberlain's company of players as his own in 1603 may best be accounted for in terms of external factors grafted onto Protestant-orientated, Christian tragedy by play-makers who were themselves aware of the new possibilities that were being explored at the universities in Greek and Latin, and at the Inns of Court in English adaptation.[23]

The first indications of the presence of such factors in England survive from the 1540s when a small group of university dons started writing tragedies in Latin and Greek. Whether this activity was motivated by theatrical rather than linguistic and literary interests must remain an open question; in the present state of knowledge one may only guess that, as in Italy, the latter took precedence.[24] What the known facts do record is that this activity encouraged a closer acquaintance with classical precept in respect of tragedy derived from Aristotle and with classical practice as exemplified by the plays of Euripides, Sophocles and Seneca than had been the case before.

Two of the first plays to be written under these auspices have the subject of Jephthah and his daughter in common, the one in Latin by George Buchanan and the other in Greek by John Christopherson.[25] Both respect Aristotle in taking as protagonist a virtuous man of more than ordinary ability and achievement; both follow the received classical tradition of a story-line that translates him from a state of prosperity into one of adversity as a result of circumstance coupled with an error of personal judgment—in this case Jephthah's vow to offer as a sacrifice to Jehovah 'whatsoever first/shall come to meet me from my threshold forth'.[26] This results in a tragedy of choice—to sacrifice his daughter or his vow—akin to that which confronts Bale's Johan, Worldly Man in *Enough is as Good as a Feast* and Philologus in *The Conflict of Conscience*. Buchanan's play is the more lively of the two since he chooses to exploit the mother's right to express an opinion as well as father and daughter. Both plays sink, however, from a theatrical standpoint because of their authors' inability to engage the chorus in the action. Familiarity, nevertheless, with the principles of constructing this kind of tragedy, even within so small an academic circle, and notwithstanding the cautionary admonitions against uncritical enthusiasm for classical precedent issued by Martin Bucer, Peter Martyr and others, was bound to have some impact on friends and pupils;* and it was not long before similar experiments were being undertaken in schools, and at the Inns of Court in London.[27]

Few of these plays survive. What must surprise us about those that do is the superficiality of the resemblances which they bear to the models which provoked their composition. Most of these similarities are formal and external: five-act structure, a chorus, particular rhetorical figures and *sententiae*, the stress placed on Fortune's part in the catastrophe, and a concentration of action upon named individuals whose lives have already reached a point of crisis. Yet these are qualities which any play-maker who is aware of them can borrow, adapt or ignore as best suits his own purpose; and in the pragmatic world of the popular theatre their use was at best sporadic and peripheral. Nevertheless this vogue among the intelligentsia for classical tragedy clearly had important consequences of a more intangible character for English drama by arousing interest, as it did, in both the expression of violent human passions and those melodramatic situations that served to whip those passions into action, and to project them forcefully into public view. If certain scenes in the mystery cycles and moralities could offer precedent for the dramatic treatment of cruelty, terror and pity—Abraham's sacrifice of Isaac, Herod's massacre of the children, the Crucifixion, Everyman's loss of all his friends—nothing in existing English literature could offer examples of such sustained treatment of them as became available with translation of the plays of Euripides and Seneca;[28] and it is these emotional qualities which make their stage-début as dominant factors in such plays as *Cambises* (*c.* 1561), *Apius and Virginia* (*c.* 1564), *Gorboduc* (1561–2),† *Jocasta* (1566), *Gismond of Salerne* (1566–7) and *Horestes* (*c.* 1566).‡

It should not surprise us therefore if, on public stages, figures like Lucifer, Cain, Herod, and Judas should have retained their hold upon the popular imagination as emblems of varied forms of villainy to whom even Jacobean play-makers, some thirty years after the suppression of the cycles, could safely refer; but other figures were needed if

*See pp. 206–7 above.

†On the circumstances surrounding the performance and publication of this play see p. 219 above and pp. 242–8 below.

‡The dates given here are those of composition, not publication. For the first printed edition, see each title *sub* Plays, pp. 323–34. *Tancred and Gismond* is also known as *Gismond of Salerne*.

full justice was to be done to the range and complexity of human passions, and if sufficient pressure was to be brought to bear upon the major characters through intrigue, shock, fear and other melodramatic devices to make them react and release these extremities of feeling in tirades and counter-action. Here the dons and students of the universities and law schools rendered the public stage a singular service by opening up to them not only in classical plays, but in other Latin and Italian literature a treasure-trove of just such biography and situation. Medea's frenzied jealousy, Oedipus' shame and grief, Orestes' rage and remorse, Dido's inconsolable tears and many other vivid examples of emotion drowning reason added much, if not to the repertoire of tragic possibilities, at least to the range and intensity of emotional response in Elizabethan playhouses. Yet borrow or imitate these foreign models as they might, the play-makers clung tenaciously to the didactic controlling concepts inherited from Bale, Bucer, Ingelend and others, of martyred innocence, shameless reprobate and retributive justice governed inscrutably but surely by Divine Providence: nor would they willingly abandon a reflection of society itself in the mixing of characters of high and low degree and mirth with sadness. In *Apius and Virginia* (*c.* 1564) Virginius and Virginia, like Jephthah and his daughter, suffer extremities of grief and anguish; but Apius, whose untameable lust brought Virginius to the point of killing his daughter, is unmasked and punished (just as Promos will be in *Promos and Cassandra* and Angelo in *Measure for Measure*); the play-maker oscillates between these two tragic themes unable to focus attention on the one rather than the other and then adds to the confusion by providing Apius with a comic servant-come-vice called Haphazard whose function is also ambiguous since he is neither genuinely evil nor very funny.[29]

As a play, John Pickering's *Horestes* (*c.* 1566) is better organized.[30] The difficulty implicit in discussing regicide at all is overcome by presenting Clytemnestra's murder of Agamemnon as so heinous a crime that it justifies Orestes in his determination to avenge it.* After a near-farcical interlude provided by the still obtrusive vices, Haultersyke and Hemstringe, the serious moral argument is resumed, this time in the form of a disputation between Orestes and Nature on his prospective crime of matricide. With this disposed of, Orestes and his army proceed to capture Aegisthus who is then brutally hanged on stage.[31] Following Clytemnestra's death (off-stage) Menelaus returns and clamours for vengeance on Orestes. However, he is finally per-

---

*The implication is that as the gods cannot let such a crime go unpunished Orestes, as their instrument of retribution, has their support. See p. 246 and n. 37, and p. 307 below on this same problem in *Gorboduc*.

suaded that Orestes had no alternative, and so agrees to let him marry his daughter Hermione. The play thus becomes a tragi-comedy despite its title.

Another play that might be thought by its title to be a translation or adaptation of a classical tragedy is George Gascoigne's and Francis Kinwelmershe's *Jocasta*.[32] In fact it is no such thing, being a translation of the Venetian poet, Lodovico Dolce's *Giócasta* written in Italian and based on a Latin version of the Euripidean original; this was undertaken for performance at Gray's Inn in 1566. Nevertheless, Gascoigne and Kinwelmershe must be given credit for achieving a play which approximates both in its construction and content to the spirit of classical tragedy more closely than any other play of its time written and performed in English. As J. W. Cunliffe remarked in his introduction to *Early English Classical Tragedies* (1912, p. lxxxv), it was

'the philosophical reflections and the dignity of the dialogue that impressed a public eager for the introduction of these classical virtues into English literature. The stir and movement of the action, the sensational situations, and the romantic sacrifice of Meneceus appealed to dramatic tastes already firmly established. These qualities are, of course, due to Euripides, and not to Dolce and his translators.'

To advance either this play, however, or *Horestes* as evidence of direct Senecan influence on English drama is clearly incorrect. I myself suspect that the choice of subject was deliberately intended to reflect Elizabeth I's first speech to Parliament in which she presented herself as married by her coronation ring to the realm (alias her subjects), and that the authors intended the tragic outcome of their tragedy of incest to be regarded as both a warning against such metaphoric thinking and as an exhortation to the Queen to marry and give her subjects a recognizable heir.

Of all these quasi-classical tragedies by far the most interesting is *Gorboduc: or Ferrex and Porrex* which conforms much more successfully to the external appearances of classical precedent than any of its predecessors; yet beneath this façade it remains stubbornly within the English dramatic tradition received from Bale, Bucer and Ingelend: and in one respect at least, the pseudo-classicism of its form is merely one of several self-protective techniques adopted by its authors to soften the acerbity of its didacticism.[33] If the young lawyers at the Inner Temple recognized the affinities between Seneca's *Thebais* and Geoffrey of Monmouth's account of the reign of Gorboduc, King of Britain, and chose to dress the latter in the literary robes of the former, they were also fully aware of Richard Mulcaster's pageants for Queen Elizabeth's coronation three years earlier, and recognized the importance of 'device' in the play-maker's craft, as may be seen from the five dumb-shows which introduce each act and have no precedent in any Senecan drama.[34]

The play was written for performance at the Inner Temple during the Christmas Revels for 1561–2 and was promptly taken to Whitehall for performance before the Queen on 18 January 1562: its message is aimed directly at her and her council. This too is transparent, despite the protective devices of classical tragic form, historical primitivism and allegory used by the authors to distance the action and characters into a legendary land of remote antiquity; for this play is as explicitly topical as Bale's *Kyng Johan*.*

The keys to the cipher were provided not only in the mime of the dumb-shows and their choric explanations, but in the use made of Troy, the Brutus legend and the Duke of Albany within the text.[35] King Gorboduc, with his two sons, represents the last of Trojan Brutus' dynasty, just as Elizabeth I herself is the last direct heir of the house of Tudor, and the same afflictions will overtake the kingdom of Britain if she dies without an heir, or at least an agreed successor, as followed the deaths of Ferrex and Porrex and tore it apart in civil war. As the house of Tudor had been equated throughout the sixteenth century with the second Brutus whom Merlin had prophesied would return to reunite the kingdom (as, indeed, Henry VII had done in marrying Elizabeth of York, and as Richard Mulcaster, the author of the civic pageants marking Elizabeth's coronation, had reminded Londoners visually and verbally only three years previously in his. pageant of 'The Uniting of the two houses of Lancastre and Yorke'), † no member of the two privileged audiences watching this play could have had much difficulty in discerning the 'earnest' there set out 'in game'.[36] As a tragedy in the true, classical sense, *Gorboduc* does not end where it should with the death of the King; instead, like Bale's *Kyng Johan*, it begins again at the start of Act V with a new story, a new antagonist in the person of Fergus, Duke of Albany, and with King Gorboduc's Secretary of State, Eubolus, elevated to take his place as protagonist. Sackville and Norton arranged their plot to permit this for strictly political and topical reasons, just as Bale did; and these reasons have little or nothing to do with tragedy in any

---

*See pp. 228–9 above.

† This pageant depicted Henry VII within a red rose sitting beside Elizabeth of York within a white rose; two branches grow upwards and are gathered into one to support Henry VIII sitting beside Anne Boleyn, and so upwards to a third level with 'a seate royall, in the whiche was sette one representynge the Queenes most excellent majestie . . . '. See *EES*.i. 72 and 78. See also p. 51 above.

genuine Senecan or Euripidean sense; rather are they polemical and moralistic.

The first Act, in its dumb-show and choric exposition, declares in a general way that a united state under one ruler is a secure state, but that a state divided against itself invites destruction. The act itself is cast in the form of an academic disputation, and the Trojan theme that serves to associate this *sententia* with the house of Tudor is first articulated by Eubolus, Secretary of State to Gorboduc in scene 2 at line 269.

> 'Your grace remembreth how in passed yeres
> The mightie *Brute*, first prince of all this lande,
> Possessed the same and ruled it well in one,
> He thinking that the compasse did suffice,
> For his three sonnes three kingdoms eke to make,
> Cut it in three, as you would now in twaine.
> But how much Brittish bloud hath since bene split,
> To ioyne againe the sondred unitie?
> What princes slaine before their timely houre?
> What wast of townes and people in the lande?
> What treasons heaped on murders and on spoiles?
> Whose just revenge even yet is scarcely ceased,
> Ruthefull remembraunce is yet rawe in minde.
> The Gods forbyd the like to chaunce againe:
> And you (O king) geve not the cause thereof.'*

Gorboduc ignores this advice, and the chorus then narrows the play's moral focus from this broad analogy with the situation confronting the house of Tudor to Queen Elizabeth herself by prophesying that

> ' . . . this great king, that doth divide his land,
>
> . . . .
>
> A myrrour shall become to Princes all,
> To learne to shunne the cause of suche a fall.'
>
> (ll. 388–94)

The second act serves simply to implement Eubolus's warning of an impending civil war, and to reinforce a monarch's need to distinguish between flattery and sober, disinterested advice. Act III is shorter still (a mere 192 lines), but at its outset Gorboduc acknowledges that the disaster now overtaking Britain is a continuance of the same curse that doomed Troy itself; no citizen of New Troy, or Troynovant (alias London), could fail to spot the significance of this association, still less the sovereign who was herself the last of her line.

*The general tenor of this advice should be compared with that given by the Bishop of Carlisle to Henry Bolingbroke in *Richard II* (IV.i.14–19). Eubolus may have been associated with Secretary Cecil.

'O cruel fates, O mindful wrath of Goddes,
Whose vengeance neither *Simois* stayned streames
Flowing with bloud of *Troian* princes slaine,
Nor *Phrygian* fieldes made ranck with corpses dead
Of *Asian* kynges and lordes, can yet appease,
Ne slaughter of unhappie *Pryams* race,
Nor *Ilions* fall made levell with the soile
Can yet suffice: but still continued rage
Pursues our lyves, and from the farthest seas
Doth chase the issues of destroyed *Troye*.'

(ll. 1–10)

Told that Ferrex is about to attack Porrex, Gorboduc exclaims, '*Jove* slay them both, and end the curséd line!' and adds, seven lines later, 'Their death and myne must peaze the angrie Gods' (ll. 99–106). Plans to intervene to prevent this are then rudely interrupted by a messenger who announces that Porrex has already invaded Ferrex's half of the kingdom and killed his brother: civil war is now inevitable.

Act IV is introduced by a spectacular dumb-show presenting the furies rising through a stage-trap out of hell

'clad in black garmentes sprinkled with bloud and flames, their bodies girt with snakes, their heds spred with serpentes in stead of heare, the one bearing in her hand a Snake, the other a Whip, and the third a burning Firebrand: ech driving before them a king and a queene, which moved by furies unnaturally had slaine their owne children.'*

This vivid spectacle of retributive justice at work is followed immediately by the play's first Senecan outburst of passionate emotion when Videna, maddened by grief for the loss of her first-born, Ferrex, vows vengeance on his murderer, even though he is her younger son, Porrex.

'Murderer I thee renounce, thou art not mine.
Never, O wretch, this wombe conceived thee,
Nor never bode I painfull throwes for thee.
Changeling to me thou art, and not my childe,
Nor to no wight, that sparke of pitie knew.

. . . .

But canst thou hope to scape my just revenge?
Or that these handes will not be wrooke on thee?

*Is this the datum point for Marlowe's famous tableau of the 'pampered jades of Asia'? It is improved upon by Gascoigne in the opening dumb-show of *Jocasta* (also an Inns of Court play) in 1566 where a king 'sitting in a Chariotte very richely furnished' is drawne in by foure kinges in their Dublettes and Hosen, with Crownes also upon their heades'.

245

Doest thou not know that *Ferrex* mother lives
That loved him more dearly than her selfe?
And doth she live, and is not venged on thee?'

(ll. 66–81)

If this does not attain to Tourneur's and Webster's flights of vindictive poetry, it at least offers a route towards them.

Gorboduc himself, on meeting Porrex, behaves more humanely and banishes him, only to learn from another messenger, Marcella, that 'Porrex (alas) is by his mother slaine' (1. 187). Act V brings further disasters with the murders of both Gorboduc and Videna, an event impossible in the circumstances of Elizabethan performance to pass over without elaborate theological apology.[37]

With the whole royal family fallen as Fortune's victims and now dead, and with Brutus' line extinct, the tragedy is over from any genuinely classical standpoint: it only requires a final chorus to sum up and bring the play to an end. But *Gorboduc* is not a truly Senecan tragedy; and it is precisely at this point in the play that it reveals through its structure its native English root-stock by switching the audience's attention both to another major character, Fergus, and to a demand for action to avert a similar catastrophe in time-present.

Fergus makes his first appearance at a meeting of the Privy Council called by Eubolus to deal with the situation. When the others have departed, he turns to the audience and says,

'If ever time to gaine a kingdome here
Were offred man, now it is offred mee.'

(V. i. 124–5)

Who is this ambitious man with treasonous intentions? Swiftly comes the answer: he is the Duke of Albany and thus a collateral descendant of Brutus' son Albanact, King of Albion or Scotland.[38]

This reference to the pretender to the English throne across the border, Mary Stuart, recently welcomed to Edinburgh on her return from France, is far too obvious to have been missed by any spectator at the Inner Temple or at Whitehall. Fergus's closing lines spell out the double nature of the threat.*

'Forthwith therefore will I in post depart
To *Albanye*, and raise in armour there
All power I can: and here my secret friendes,
By secret practise shall sollicite still,
To seeke to wynne to me the peoples hartes.'

(V. i.158–62)

*Elizabeth did not have to die for this threat to materialize: it did so in 1569–70 in the form of the Northern Rebellion coupled with her excommunication.

In the next scene, just as Eubolus appears to be re-establishing order, a messenger arrives declaring that 'Fergus, the mighty Duke of Albany,/ Is now in arms', and adding,

> 'Dayly he gathereth strength, and spreads abrode
> That to this realme no certeine heire remaines,
> That Brittayne land is left without a guide,
> That he the scepter seekes, for nothing els
> But to preserve the people and the land,
> Which now remaine as ship without a sterne.'
> (V. ii. 80–5)

The implication is clear: these are the tactics that Mary Queen of Scots will use to win over the people to accept her claim to the succession, and with it a return of Catholic rule. This is the point of Duke Maudrud's reference to Fergus as 'This growing foe of all our liberties' (1. 104) and Duke Cloyton's reference to 'His deepe dissembling shewes of false pretence' (1. 91).

Duke Arostus then proposes that Parliament be called, that the crown be vested in it, and that it alone shall have the power to elect a successor.*

It is then left to Eubolus to point the moral and conclude the play. This he does under three major headings. First, he reiterates the analogy between Brutus' heirs and the house of Tudor, asking the audience to recognize in the 'mirror' of this tragedy the fate that will overtake the country if Elizabeth were to die without an heir.

> 'Loe here the end of *Brutus* royall line,
> And loe the entry to the wofull wracke,
> And utter ruine of this noble realme.
> The royall king, and eke his sonnes are slaine,
> No ruler restes within the regall seate,
> The heire, to whom the scepter longes, unknowen,
> That to eche force of forreine princes power,
> Whom vauntage of our wretched state may move
> By sodeine armes to gaine so rich a realme,
> And to the proud and gredie minde at home,
> Whom blinded lust to reigne leades to aspire,
> Loe Brittaine realme is left an open pray,
> A present spoyle by conquest to ensue.'
> (V. ii. 180–92)

---

*The authors were both members of Elizabeth's first Parliament, and Thomas Norton, two years after the production of the play, became Chairman of the House of Commons Committee which presented Elizabeth with a petition 'for the Limitation of the Succession'.

He dismisses Duke Arostus's suggestion of vesting the crown in Parliament as an idea that comes too late to be effective since no one will respect the decision once civil war has resumed its sway.

> 'Alas, in Parliament what hope can be,
> When is of Parliament no hope at all?
> Which, though it be assembled by consent,
> Yet is not likely with consent to end.'
>
> (V. ii. 253–6)

What should have been done was to have adopted this course of action while Gorboduc was still alive and in control of events.

> 'No, no: then Parliament should have bene holden,
> And certeine heires appointed to the crowne,
> To stay the title of established right,
> And in the people plant obedience,
> While yet the prince did live, whose name and power
> By lawfull sommons and authoritie
> Might make a Parliament to be of force,
> And might have set the state in quiet stay.'
>
> (*ibid.*, 264–71)

In the light of these sentiments can anyone doubt what the gentlemen of the Inns of Court in 1561 wanted the Queen and her council to do? If ever there were a case of 'earnest' being mirrored in 'game', and of drama being the handmaid of occasion, this is it. Seneca assists, but neither controls the play's form nor informs its fable. Nevertheless, the play does succeed in breaking out of the old tragi-comic frame. It does not mix characters of high and low degree; and it does not mix 'sport', 'merriment' or 'mirth' with its two serious concerns, the tragic story of King Gorboduc's lack of foresight and the no less tragic projection of an analogous disaster in the near future should Queen Elizabeth and her council ignore the play's historical moral. Sir Philip Sidney was thus correct to recognize *Gorboduc* as 'right tragedy'; but posterity is also correct to recognize in it a play that is as deeply indebted to Bale's *Kyng Johan* as it is to classical antiquity.

Some six years later, however, the young gentlemen of the Inns of Court bestowed their energies on mounting another play for presentation before the Queen, *The Tragedie of Tancred and Gismond*.[39] We are told in a letter from William Webbe to one of the co-authors, Robert Wilmot, that the play was[40]

'of her Majesty....as princely accepted, as of the whole honorable audience notably applauded: yea, and of al men generally desired, as a work, either in statelines of show, depth of conceit, or true ornaments of poeticall arte, inferior to none of the best in that kinde: no, were the Roman *Seneca* the censurer.'

We are also told in the same letter that the acting text had been revised for publication nearly twenty-five years after its original performance. Although Wilmot acknowledges a didactic purpose in 'commending vertue, detesting vice, and lively deciphering their overthrow that suppresse not their unruely affections' (*MSR*, p. xxiii) his own concern and that of his earlier collaborators is not political polemic and historical analogue (as was the case with *Gorboduc*), but simply to provide his audience with 'a discourse of two lovers':

> 'Behold here for your gaine
> *Gismonds* unluckie love, her fault, her wo
> And death, at last her cruell Father slaine
> Through his mishap, and though you do not see,
> Yet reade and rew their wofull Tragedie.'

> (*MSR*, sig. A)

Appropriately, Cupid acts as prologue: his servant, Myrrha, concludes the spectacular induction with the line, 'Love rules the world, Love is a mightie Lord' (sig. A4). This, together with the Preface, suffices to explain why this tragedy is to be read as a doleful, if moral, romance, and not as an analogue, allegory or polemic; for, unlike *Gorboduc*, it was prepared specifically for the Queen's maids of honour rather than for the Queen herself: and it is they, in the persons of Gismond's four ladies-in-waiting, who are figured in the role of chorus. The stage-direction between lines 215 and 216 thus reads: 'Tan(*cred*) and Gis(*mond*) with the Gard, depart into the pallace, the four maydens stay behind, as Chorus to the Tragedie.' Each of the four speaks in turn, concluding the first Act with a reiterated threnody on the fickleness of Fortune.

> 'Not Euripus unquiet floud so oft
> Ebs in a daie, and floweth too and fro,
> As Fortunes change, pluckes downe that was aloft,
> And mingleth joy, with enterchange of wo.'

> (*MSR*, ll. 258–61)

While acknowledging a debt to Seneca in the letter to William Webbe already quoted, Wilmot also pays tribute in his Dedicatory Epistle to the Middle Temple to 'that rare Scot (the scholer of our age) *Buchanan*, his most pathetical Jephtha':* and, indeed, Wilmot's tragedy is similarly centred on a catastrophic relationship between father and daughter. However, where Buchanan, in choosing a biblical story, had found himself as much restricted by the need to respect theological con-

---

**MSR, p. xxiv; see also pp. 239–40 above.

siderations of a specifically Protestant character as concerned with the vicissitudes of Fortune, Wilmot, in grounding his plot on a Boccaccian romance, freed himself wholly from the dictates of religious doctrine.* And as neither he nor his co-authors were addressing the Queen directly, they escaped no less successfully from all the restrictions of political polemic and so were free to concentrate, as the authors of *Gorboduc* were not, on strictly literary and aesthetic concerns.[41]

In terms of drama this effectively meant that with due deference paid to 'gaine' (alias moral profit) the audience's attention could be directly focused on emotional conflict—the feelings of a young widow torn between desire for a new lover and obedience to a royal father's refusal to permit a second marriage, and the feelings of a father torn between love of his daughter and his wish to revenge the shame he thinks she brings on both herself and him by taking a lover.

> *Tancred*   Oh what a conflict doth my mind endure?
> Now fight my thoughts against my passions:
> Now strive my passions against my thoughts.
> Now sweates my heart, now chil cold falles it dead.
> (*ed. cit.*, sig. E2b, ll. 1025–8)

The authors succeed in heightening these opposing conflicts still further by keeping virtually all the action off-stage. The audience sees nothing in the course of the five acts of either Count Palarin's clandestine visits via a subterranean passage to Gismond's bedchamber or the consummation of this illicit love; instead it is asked to listen to the mental anguish that results in consequence for both lovers and the King. The eye is catered for by the scenic dumb-shows which introduce each act, the fourth of which does supply a single glimpse of the two lovers in each other's company and a stage-picture of them caught *in flagrante* by the jealous Tancred.

The moral aspect of the conflict is consigned to the Furies.

> 'Furies must aide when men surcease to know
> Their gods: and hel sends forth revenging paine
> On those whom shame from sin cannot restraine.'
> (*ed. cit.*, sig. E, ll. 906–8)

The one word 'sin' thus still links this play vestigially to Lydgate's *Fall of Princes* within a tradition of Christian tragedy;[42] but almost everything else about it is conceived in literary and dramatic terms far removed from Lewis Wager's *The Life and Repentaunce of Marie Magdalene* (*c.* 1558) where the word 'tragedie' is unequivocally equated with 'damnation', as was again to be the case with Nathaniel Woodes's

*Decameron, IV.i.

The Conflict of Conscience written some fourteen years after the first performance of *Gismond of Salerne*.[43]

What then *Gismond of Salerne*, *c.* 1566–7 (*Tancred and Gismond*, 1591), represents is a bookman's drama of occasion, prepared by the intellectual *avant-garde* for a particular audience consisting of the Queen's maids of honour accompanied by their mistress and other sophisticated representatives of her government and judiciary. Self-consciously neo-classical in form and content, the play carefully eschews both political and religious issues; but it asserts no less didactically that the disasters which overtake Gismond, her father and her lover are all directly attributable to an error of judgment on her part, figured in the person of Cupid as the passion of love, and to her father's misguided decision to use his royal authority to obtain personal revenge, figured by the fury, Megaera.[44]

As in *Gorboduc* there are no characters of 'low degree', and there is no 'mirth' or 'merriment' to vary the serious tone of the dialogue. Yet *Gismond of Salerne* was as near as Elizabethan tragedy was to get to those classical precedents in this dramatic genre which these young lawyers sought to imitate. Thus 'accepted' though it may have been by Queen Elizabeth I, and 'applauded' as Wilmot claims it was by its first and only audience, it manifestly failed to win the approval or acceptance of professional actors and their public audiences. If reason is required to explain this, I find it myself—as I have tried to demonstrate throughout these volumes—in the Reformation; for this was an event that proved to be as radical and pervasive in the changes which it forced upon the English theatre as it was in religious, political and social life. The Reformation served, in England, to precipitate a crisis of identity expressed as much in a subject's respective loyalty to God and to Caesar as in the monarch's responsibilities under God to his or her subjects: conflict and tension thus became an almost constant state of being in real life, rather than an exceptional and unfamiliar occurrence, as is attested not only by the grim recital of burnings, torture and other forms of suffering depicted in Foxe's *Book of Martyrs*, but in the savage sequence of threats and reprisals meted out by Protestants to Catholics.

Recalling J. M. R. Margeson's question, therefore, that I cited at the start of this chapter, 'Was it necessary for the didactic to be eliminated before tragedy could emerge?' I find that my own answer is plainly 'no'.* Rather does it appear that tragedy, as we understand the word today, emerged gradually in the Elizabethan theatre in two distinct forms, more or less simultaneously: the one overtly Christian,

*See p. 222 above.

with a strong Calvinist bias, and largely dependent for its effect on its story-line; the other focused more sharply on situation and paying lip-service at most to specifically Christian ethics, yet no less self-consciously moral in its didacticism. What is new and links the former to the latter is that in both cases the play-makers had discovered theatrical means to anatomize what I have called this crisis of identity; or, in other words, to depict a character or characters confronted with a dilemma provoking an extreme conflict of emotional responses. With this achieved, the responses could be manipulated in several directions, including physical suffering, mental anguish, pity, terror and remorse, so that the way in which a man or woman faced death and the here-after could be discussed in depth. Villains, within this new context, were intrinsically as interesting as injured innocents; timely repentance no less moving than condign punishment; and the recovery of order out of chaos an end devoutly to be prayed for, since therein, if anywhere, lay the answer to the crisis of identity. Indeed, it is this last idea that will later underpin all of Shakespeare's late romances following the reuni-fication of the British Isles under James VI and I.

Broadly speaking, coterie audiences at Court and in the schools, universities and Inns of Court (familiar as they were with academic disputations)* preferred to dwell on the debating points precipitated by such conflicts, suitably dressed in a self-consciously latinate, rhetorical style: audiences in public playhouses, by contrast, preferred action, with vivid pictorial tableaux to corroborate each step of the narrative as it advanced. Insufficient plays, however, in either kind survive from the 1570s to allow us to be more definite than that, and it is very important to recall that the universities, besides being the primary centres of Renaissance, classical studies, were also the hotbeds of advanced, Calvinist thought; even so it is fairly safe to assume that by the time James Burbage and his fellow-players in the Earl of Leicester's company received their patent from Elizabeth I in 1574 to act regularly on weekdays in London they were at least aware that a conflict of conscience could be handled *either* melodramatically in the manner of the traditional saint play *or* oratorically as a dramatic disputation ornamented by appropriate, if occasional, dumb-shows, and were content to label both as tragedies on their playbills.

The tension that resulted from consciousness of these two, alternative approaches, itself the product of divergent standards of taste and expectancy among audiences, could only have been reinforced by the fact that the acting companies were themselves required to serve two masters. As household servants of the noble patrons whose liveries they

*See pp. 134–41 above.

wore, and on whose goodwill depended their right to act in public, they could not ignore the tastes of the more sophisticated courtiers and bookmen when their services were called upon to celebrate some special occasion.* Yet as fathers of families attempting to earn a living from acting, they were obliged to respect the wishes of their regular weekday customers in London and the provinces. Inevitably the lessons learned from experience—applause and boos are strict taskmasters—cross-fertilized the two types of play bracketed under the label of tragedy. As this occurred, so it became desirable for these actors to acquire the services, as play-makers, of men already acquainted with Graeco-Roman literature (even if only in translation) who were nevertheless willing (if only in their own self-interest) to acquire the less bookish and more practical crafts of the popular theatre, most of which were more visual than literary.† This was the challenge that faced the generation of poets newly graduating from the universities and anxious to make a mark as men of letters in the besieged, Protestant citadel of Europe in the 1580s.

George Gascoigne provides the most fitting final comment on this situation in the sub-title he appended to *The Glasse of Government* of 1575: 'A tragicall Comedie so entituled, bycause therein are handled aswell the rewardes for Vertue, as also the punishment for Vices.'[45] Although, as Sir Edmund Chambers supposed, Gascoigne's play is 'perhaps only a closet drama' (*ES*.iv.321), this descriptive title aligns it with Thomas Preston's more familiar *Cambises* which entered the repertoire of a professional company *c.* 1570. This is subtitled, 'A Lamentable Tragedie, mixed full of pleasant mirth, containing the life of Cambises, King of Percia, ... '.‡ If, twenty years later, Shakespeare could still mock such titles in *A Midsummer Night's Dream* with 'A tedious brief scene of young Pyramus/And his love Thisbe; very tragical mirth' (V.i.156–7), it must be remembered that he himself never elected to eliminate either mirth or 'persons of low degree' from his own tragedies.

*See *EES*.ii(1). 106–21.
†See pp. 216–18 above.
‡See *EES*.i. 353, Appendix G.

APPENDIX A

Y<small>ULE IN</small> Y<small>ORK</small>
A printed broadside, *c.* 1570; formerly MS. Bodl. Top. Yorks. *c.* 18
(ff. 81–2), now Vet. A l a. 5(1) Reprinted from *Records of Early English
Drama*, 1976, no. 1, pp. 6–8

Our Sauiour is come.
MAns teares and wofull plaint, hath pierst the lofty
skies,
with gladsom newes in glittring robe, from heauen an
Angell flies,
the clouds now open wide, & grace sends downe it
shewers,
Which watereth natures barren soyle, with euerlasting
flowers.
The ayre therefore resounds, Yule, Yule, *a Babe is borne,*
O bright and blazing day, to saue mankind that was
forlorne.

Our God from mercies throne, beheld old Adams ragge,
And how proude Sathan hath displaid abroad his
flaunting flagge,
His robes imbrude with bloud, his signes of conquest
braue,
Haue caused God, from heauen to send his sonne, mans
soule to saue.
The ayre etc.

When mercy on her knees, gusht out a wayling floude,
Our Father sent his Sonne for vs, to spend his precious
bloud,
He sent no Angell bright, he sent the Lambe of God,
Our Iesus sweete, to shrowde vs from Sin and Sathans
rod.
The ayre etc.

The old Lawe which was writt in tables faire of stone,
Could not redeeme vs from the deuill, nor yet deliuer
one,
When shaddowes would not serue, the Lambe of God is
sent,

An offering sweete for vs, on crosse his Cristiall bloud
was spent.
The ayre therefore etc.

When sathan did outrage and Sin did most abound,
And cruell death man trodden downe, with dinting
dart did wound
Then God from heauen did shew, the riches of his
grace,
The Lyon then of Iuda came, the Dragon to displace.
The ayre therefore etc.

O Deuill, O Death, O Sinne, disgorge your bitter gall,
A babe is borne, the which wilbe, the ruine of you all.
O Deuill where is they rage, O Death where is thy
sting,
O Sinne where be thy chaines, a child, your force to
ground will bring
The ayre therefore resounds, Yule, Yule, *a Babe is borne,*
O bright and blazing day, to saue mankind that was forlorne.

The meaning of Yule, *in Yorke.*

Yule com(*m*)eth
of Yulath that
is to say, A
babe is borne
for vs.

O famous Yorke reioyce, and thinke of this no shame,
To dubble *Yule* with sounding voice, to the honour of
Gods name.
For *Yulath* Hebrew word, expresseth very well,
That babe the which was borne to saue our soules from
damned hell.
True Isralites resound, Yule, Yule, *a babe is borne,*
O bright and blazing day, to saue mankind that was forlorne.

No Cittie but
Yorke was euer
hearde to
welcome our
Sauiour, with
this ioyfull
word, Yule.

It was not without cause, that God gaue the grace,
With *Yule* to welcome his deare sonne, who Sathan did
deface,
Triumph O Yorke, reioyce, this priueledge is thine,
In this all other townes, thou doest, and Citties ore'shine.
Therefore eftsoones resound, yule yule, *etc.*

Christ is our
Pascall Lambe
offered vpon
the Crosse for
vs.I.Cor.5.
I am the bread
of Life.Io.6.
True Isralites.

The shoulder of the Lambe the man in hand doth
beare,
Doth represent the lambe of God which Iewes on crosse
did reare.
The Cake of purest meale, betokeneth very well,
The bread of life which came from heauen in earth with
vs to dwell.
True Isralites resound, Yulath *a babe is borne,*
(*O bright and blazing day*) *to saue mankind that was*
forlorne.

255

The Angels Trumpe doth blowe, the childrens cries
resounde
The ioyfull noyse in earth belowe, to heauen aboue
rebounde
Because faire *Iessies* branch, brought forth that noble
Nut,
Which being crackt vpon the crosse, did sinne and
Sathan gut.
Therefore we will resound etc.

All haile renowned king, we thanke thee for thy loue,
Through which for vs, thou lefts thy throne, in haughty
heauen aboue
Be thou our Iesus sweete, grant grace to follow thee,
To keepe thy lawe and sacred word, that saued we may
be.
And we will still resound, Yule, Yule, *a Babe is borne,*
(O bright and blissfull day) to saue mankind that was forlorne.

True Isralites.

The man wrongfully called *Yule*, and his wife, resemble true Isralites crying *yule*, and reioycing for their deliuerance from Sathan, through Iesus Christ.

Children.

The children crying after them, do signifie our Children and Successors, who shall celebrate this Feast to the worlds end, with ioyfull & triumphall clamours.

Shalmes.

The Shalme and musicke, resemble the mirth and melody of Angels.

Nuts.

Nuts casten abroad, puts vs in rememberance of that most noble Nut our sauiours blessed body, springing miraculously from that beautifull branch of *Iesse*, the most pure and imaculate virgin. As it was possible (according to Saint Austen) for the rod of Aaron, to bring forth Nuts, against the common course of nature. So was it possible for the blessed virgin, to bring forth that most excellent nut our sweete Sauiour, contrary to the lawe of nature, whose sacred body (according to the same Saint Austen) is aptlie compared to a nut. For the Nut hath in it body a triple vnion, that is to wit, *Testam* the shell, signifying the bones; and *Corium et nucteum*, the skinne, and kirnell signifying the flesh & inward soule of our Sauiour. The nut destroyeth poyson, Our sauiour crushed vpon the crosse, imbraced with a liuely faith, destroyeth the poyson, of sinne and Sathan.

Sergeants.

The officers, resemble the noble spreaders & publishers of this Mysticall and miraculous Nut.

Reiected Draffe.

The reiected draffe, doth signifie the shaddowes and carnall ceremonies of the old law, Which being weake and vnable to iustifie or saue vs, are (according to S. Paule) to be reiected and esteemed as dung and dirt, in comparison of the light of truth it selfe, which hath now shined vpon vs.

Distaffe or Rocke.

The very Rocke, sheweth that women laying aside their seruile workes, must make good preparation for this solemne feast.

Thus you haue the meaning of this notable and antient spectacle, of *Yule* in Yorke, conteyning a briefe sum of verity in it.

Soli Deo, sit honor et gloria.
FINIS.

Ian Lancashire has subsequently noted (*Records of Early English Drama*, 1976, n. 2, pp. 9–10) that the broadside quoted above was noticed in *Notes & Queries*, 8th series, no. 10, 26 December 1896, but erroneously dated and only partially transcribed.

APPENDIX B

A table of Christian calendar festivals and their relationship to seasonal dramatic entertainments during the Middle Ages and early Renaissance.

Principal associated gods and festivals of the pre-Christian calendar	*Christian calendar*		*General nature and purpose of holy days*
WINTER SOLSTICE (*21 December*) **Roman** Sol Invictus Kalends Rex Saturnalitius	ADVENT SUNDAY 30 November 6 December 21 December	(last in November) St Andrew St Nicholas St Thomas	FEASTS OF PREPARATION
Teutonic Totenfest	25 December 26 December 27 December	Christ's Nativity St Stephen St John the Evangelist	FEASTS OF CELEBRATION
Celtic Wassail Yule	28 December 1 January	Holy Innocents Circumcision	*Feasts of humility and inversion*
	6 January	Epiphany	
	25 January	Conversion of St Paul	
	2 February	Purification of the Virgin (*Candlemas*)	
	(25 March	Annunciation of the Virgin)	

pecial character of celebrations	*Specific dramatic features in the early Middle Ages*		*Specific English examples from the later Middle Ages and Tudor period*
t Nicholas—patron saint of ildren, scholars, prisoners, agrants		*Ordo Prophetarum* St Nicholas plays *Ludus Danielis*	Yule at York (21 December)
welve day holiday 6 December—6 January -Banquets -Gift-giving -Inversion of social norms *Children and folly* -Epiphany: *Twelfth Night*	M I S R U L E	*Ordo Visitationis Praesepe* Mummings & disguisings Songs & dances Acrobatic & mimetic games Athletic games 'Boy Bishop' 'Feast of Fools' Prince of Misrule *Ordo Stellae*	*Mankind* (Christmas) *Fulgens & Lucres* (Christmas) *Respublica* (Christmas) *Jack Juggler* (SS Stephen & John) Lydgate's *Mumming at Hertford* (Twelfth Night)
-Women and children		Plough Play (Monday after Epiphany)	Digby *Conversion of St Paul*

Principal associated gods and festivals of the pre-Christian calendar	Christian calendar (1) Variable feasts*	(2) Fixed feasts	
VERNAL EQUINOX (*21 March*) **Graeco-Roman** Dionysus/Bacchus Artemis/Diana Demeter/Ceres	SHROVETIDE CARNIVAL. Sunday, Monday, Tuesday *before* the start of the 40 days of Lent. Late February to late March depending on the date of Easter Sunday		
Teutonic/Nordic Eostre Erce Freya	ASH WEDNESDAY. The start of LENT PALM SUNDAY. One week before EASTER MAUNDY THURSDAY (Last Supper) GOOD FRIDAY (Crucifixion) EASTER DAY (Resurrection; latest 25 April)	23 April	St George
Celtic Beltane (May Day)	ASCENSION WHITSUNTIDE (Pentecost) (7th Sunday, Monday & Tuesday after Easter)	25 April 1 May	St Mark SS. Philip & James
	TRINITY SUNDAY (8th after Easter)	11 June	St Barnabas
SUMMER SOLSTICE (*21 June*) **Graeco-Roman** Mithras	CORPUS CHRISTI (instituted 1313) (First Thursday after Trinity Sunday: late May to late June)	24 June 29 June	St John the Baptist St Peter
Teutonic/Nordic Baldur Fire festivals Hlafmaesse (Hlammaesse)		22 July 25 July 1 August	St Mary Magdalene St James Lammas (loafmass)

*Dates fixed annually, with Easter Day itself to fall on the Sunday following the first full moon after 21 March, the vernal equinox.

General nature and purpose of Christian holy days	Special character of celebrations	Specific dramatic examples from the Middle Ages and early Renaissance
Shrovetide: Repentance	Penitential sermons, processions and plays	*Le Jeu d' Adam* (?) *Wisdom*
Carnival: Licence, youth, Folly (comparable with 28 December to 1 January)	Feasting, mummings, farces and inversion	Mummings, farces, masques
LENT: Contrition & penance (preparation for baptism)	ABSTINENCE, physical & aesthetic	NO PLAYS
EASTER: Joy & thanksgiving	CELEBRATIONS devoted to the life-force and fertility	*Ordo Visitationis Sepulchri* Lydgate's *Mumming at Bishopswood* May-Games, King-Games, Robin Hood Games and Plays Hocking Church ales
CORPUS CHRISTI: Eucharistic redemption	Midsummer vigils and bonfires Harvesting begins	Corpus Christi procession and plays Croxton *Play of the Sacrament* Midsummer Watches Digby *St Mary Magdalene* Progress entertainments Commercial play season in London ended
No Christian equivalent	Bread offerings and first fruits	Referred to by Nurse in *Romeo and Juliet*, I.iii.16–18 to recall and establish calendar date of Juliet's birthday

	Principal associated gods and festivals of the pre-Christian calendar	Christian calendar		Special characteristics
AUTUM-NAL EQUINOX (*21 September*)	**Roman** Demeter Persephone	15 August 24 August 1 September	Assumption of the Virgin St Bartholomew St Giles	HARVEST FAIRS and BONFIRES
	Teutonic Walpurgis Night (31 October)	21 September 29 September	St Matthew St Michael and All Angels	Torchlight processions Thanksgiving
	Celtic Samhain (Samhagan)	18 October 28 October 30 October 1 November	St Luke SS. Simon and Jude Hallowe'en Hallowmas (All Souls; All Saints)	VENERATION OF THE DEAD
		11 November	St Martin (Martle-mas)	

pecific dramatic examples from the
1iddle Ages and early Renaissance

---

ishing-village   carnivals and plays

ex et Regina Autumnatis

arvest-home, Church Ales and games

eer and grape festivals: licence and inversion

tart of commercial theatre season in London

ord Mayor's Show in London

lizabethan Accession Day Tilt (17 November)

263

APPENDIX C

An injunction against performance of a satirical play aimed at the leatherworkers of Exeter for alleged profiteering, and directed to the Archdeacon for action, 9 August 1352

This injunction is abstracted from Vol. I of the *Registrum Communae* of John de Grandisson, Bishop of Exeter, 'Anno Domini, M° CCC^mo lj°, et Consecracionis Domini XXV°', folio 172b; edited in 3 vols by F. C. Hingeston-Randolf, London, 1894, Vol. II, p. 1120.

Johannes, etc., dilecto in Christo filio, Archidiacono Exonie, vel ejus Officiali, salutem, graciam, et benediccionem,—Invidus hostis antiquus malorum omnium insensator, qui agit assidue ut tranquillitatis humane delicie extra mundi terminos exularent, ibi sue venena nequicie lacius nititur diffundere ubi se severius estimat obfuturum. Sane, licet artes mechanicas, ut rerum experiencia continue nos informat, mutuo, necessitate quadam, oporteat se juvare; pridem, tamen, intelleximus quod nonnulli nostre Civitatis Exonie inprudentes filii, inordinate lascivie dediti, fatue contempnentes que ad ipsorum et universalis populi indigenciam fuerunt utiliter adinventa, quendam Ludum noxium qui culpa non caret, immo verius ludubrium, in contumeliam et opprobrium allutariorum,*necnon eorum artificii, hac instanti Die Dominica, in Theatro nostre Civitatis predicte publice peragere proponunt, ut inter se statuerant et intendunt; ex quo, ut didicimus, inter prefatos artifices et dicti Ludi participes, auctores pariter et fautores, graves discordie, rancores, et rixe, cooperante satore tam execrabilis ire et invidie, vehementer pululant et insurgunt; adeo quod, nisi ab illorum illicito proposito, spiritu ducti consilii sanioris, se abstineant totaliter et desistant, insultus et aggressus terribiles, pacis Regis et Regni turbacio, verbera et sediciones, ac eciam ex consequenti animarum amarius deploranda pericula, prochdolor, insequentur. Considerantes, igitur, quanta mala corporum et animarum, sub velamine et colore Ludi eciam liciti, stimulante diabolo, eveniunt et contingunt, ad resistendum, in quantum possumus, talium fluctuum et procellarum principiis, ne deterius inde sequatur, non inmerito provocamur. Quocirca vobis injungimus firmiter et mandamus quatinus, ne aliqui, quocumque nomine censeantur, dictum Ludum, tam acerbis periculis indicia ministrantem in nostra Diocesi, et presertim in nostra Civitate predicta, inchoare, vel inchoatum perficere presumant quomodolibet vel attemptent, primo, secundo, tercio et peremptorie inhibeatis publice et expresse, sicuti ipsi tenore Presencium inhibemus, sub pena Excommunicacionis Majoris, quam in ipsos, et ipsorum quemlibet, si Monicionibus et Inhibicionibus hujusmodi non paruerint cum effectu, exnunc prout extunc ferimus in hiis Scriptis. Ad hec, quia memorati artifices, qui, ut clamosa insinuacione vulgi recepimus, in mercibus suis distrahendis plus justo precio, modernis temporibus, a contrahentibus cum eisdem adeo excessive recipiunt et extorquent quod ipsorum inmoderancia talibus operacionibus materiam subministrat, ac ipsi, per hoc, justo lucro absque rapina non contenti, in promptum suarum periculum incidunt animarum; vobis, ut supra, injungimus et mandamus quatinus artifices predictos, omnes et singulos, publice et sollempniter moneatis et efficaciter inducatis, ipsosque moneri et induci per Ecclesiarum dicte Civitatis nostre Curatos, modo simili, faciatis ac eciam inhiberi, sicuti ipsis tenore Presencium inhibemus, ne exnunc, in vendendo que ad eos pertinent, precium per Excellentissimum Principem et Dominum nostrum, Anglie et Francie Regem illustrem, et Consilium suum, pro utilitate publica limitatum, exigant quovis modo, set Statutum in hac parte salubriter editum striccius teneant et observent. De die, vero, recepcionis Presencium, modo et forma execucionis presentis Mandati nostri, ac eciam nominibus et personis premissis contraveniencium, et de fautoribus eorund- em, nos, citra Octabas Assumpcionis Beate Marie (22 August), reddatis debite cerciores per Literas vestras patentes, harum seriem dilucide conti- nentes.—Datum apud Chuddeleghe, ix^a die mensis Augusti, Anno Domini Millesimo CCC^{ma} quinquagesimo secundo, et Consecracionis nostre vicesimo quinto.

TRANSLATION

John, to the beloved son in Christ, the Archdeacon of Exeter, or to his officer, sends greetings, grace and benediction: The envious enemy of old and instigat- or of all evil, who assiduously strives to remove from the world the pleasures of human tranquillity, is labouring to pour forth the poison of his viciousness more widely in those places where he detects the best hope of trouble-making. Although the mechanized arts, as experience continually reveals to us, should of necessity help each other, yet we were led to understand some time ago that certain imprudent sons of the City of Exeter, addicted to brawling and wantonness, and foolishly scorning that which had been profitably ordered for their needs and those of the whole community, have banded themselves together and now intend to perform publicly a certain harmful and reprehen- sible play, or rather a scurrilous piece of mockery to abuse and dishonour the leatherworkers* and their craft on this coming Sunday in the theatre of our aforesaid City of Exeter; as a result of which as we are informed, grave discord, rancour and strife breed and grow between the afore-mentioned artisans and the makers of this same play and their supporters with the assistance of the author [i.e. the devil] of such hateful wrath and envy; so that unless persuaded

*E.K. Chambers refers to this document in the text of *The Mediaeval Stage* (ii. 190) describing the artisans (the *allutarum* of his quotation from the Latin in footnote 4) mistakenly as clothworkers.

by saner counsels wholly to abstain and desist from their unlawful purpose there must follow terrible brawls and riots, breaches of the peace of the King and of his Realm, fighting and uprisings, and even, in their outcome, dangers still more deplorable, alas, for men's immortal souls. Considering, therefore, how much harm of body and soul—delightful to the devil—is likely to occur and grow under cover and colour of a play, supposing that it is accorded licence to proceed, we feel obliged to restrain, so far as it lies in our power to do so, the root cause for such upheaval and tumult lest worse ensue therefrom. Wherefore we firmly enjoin and command you that you should on three separate occasions forbid, with all the authority vested in these our Orders, peremptorily and publicly, any persons under whatever name they may be known to presume or attempt in any way to begin, or having begun to complete the said play, so fraught with dangers within our diocese and especially in our said City: and this under penalty of the Greater Excommunication, which we authorize in this letter, as from now, and in the future, against those, or any of those, on whom these warnings and injunctions shall have had no effect. Further, the artisans named [i.e. in this play], as we hear from the loud protestations of the public, charge more than a fair price in these times for their goods, and receive excessive and extortionate amounts from those who deal with them; and it is their want of moderation in such affairs that has provided the subject-matter [i.e. for this play]; not content with a fair price, free of extortion, they go [i.e. in their trading] in immediate peril of their souls; and so, as before, we enjoin and straightly command you, effectively to warn and persuade the aforesaid artisans, all and singular, publicly and solemnly; and both they and our Church Wardens are to be warned and persuaded from the pulpits of the said City, in similar fashion, to be forbidden—with all the authority vested in these Orders—when selling what belongs to them from exceeding in any way the price fixed by our Excellent Prince and Lord, illustrious King of France and England, and his Council, in the public interest; instead, they must follow and observe more strictly the Statute which, in this provision, has been prudently promulgated. Now you are duly to inform us before the Octave of the Assumption of the Blessed Mary (22 August) under the authority of your Letters Patent, containing clearly the order of these matters: of the day of receipt of these Presents; of the manner and form of execution of this present Command of ours; and also of the names and persons contravening the aforesaid [commands]; and of their supporters.

Given at Chudleigh, on the 9th day of the month of August, in the year of Our Lord 1352, and in the 25th [year] of our Consecration.

APPENDIX D

Plot summaries and emblematic devices for masques on three successive nights in Sir William Cecil's handwriting among the papers which, at his death in August 1598, passed to his secretary, Sir Michael Hicks, transcribed from BM MS. Lansdowne 5, Art. 38, folios 126–7, with contractions expanded and punctuation modernized

fo. 126   'Devices to be shewed before the quenes Ma(jes)tie by waye of maskinge, at Nottingham castell, after the meteinge of the quene of Scott(e)s.'

The firste night

ffirste a pryson to be made in the haule, the name whereof, is Extreme Oblyvion, and the kepers name thereof, Argus otherwise called Circumspection, then a maske of Ladyes to come in after this sorte.

ffirst Pallas rydinge uppon an unycorne, havinge in her hande a Standarde, in w(hi)ch is to be painted ij Ladyes hand(e)s, knitt one faste w(i)thin thother, and over thand(e)s written in letters of golde—ffides.

Then ij Ladyes rydinge togethers thone uppon a golden Lyon, w(i)th a crowne of gold on his heade, thother uppon a redd Lyon w(i)th the like crowne of gold, signifyinge ij vertues; that is to saye, the Lady on the golden Lyon, is to be called Prudentia; and the Ladye on the redd Lyon—Temperantia.

After this to followe vj, or viij, Ladyes maskers, bringinge in captive Discorde, and false Reporte, with ropes of gold about there neck(e)s. When theis have marched about the haule, Then Pallas to declare before the quenes Ma(jes)tie in verse, that the goddes understandinge the noble meteinge of those ij quenes, hathe willed her to declare unto them, that those ij vertues Prudentia and Temperantia have made greate and longe sute unto Jupiter that it wold please hym to gyve unto them false Reporte and discorde to be punisshed as they thinke good; and that those Ladyes

267

have nowe in there presence determyned* to committ
them faste bounde unto thafforesayde pryson of Extreme
Oblyvion, there to be kept by thafforesayde gaylor
Argus, otherwise Circumspection(,) for ever(;) unto whome
Prudentia shall delyver a locke whereuppon shalbe
wrytten ineternum. Then Temperantia shall likewise
delyver unto Argus a key whose name shalbe
nunqua(m); Signifyinge that when false Reporte and
Discorde are committed to the pryson of Extreme
Oblyvion, and locked there everlastinglie, he should put
in the key to lett them out nunqua(m), and when he
hathe so done then the Trompett(e)s to blowe, and
thinglishe Ladies to take the nobilite of the straunger
and daunce.

The seconde night

fo. 126b
    ffirst a Castell to be made in the haule called the
Courte of plentye; then the maske after this sorte(.)

ffirste Peace rydinge uppon a Chariott drawen w(i)th
an Oliphant uppon whome shall ryde ffryndeshippe,
and after them vj, or viij, Ladyes maskers, and when
they have marched rounde aboute the haule
ffryndshippe shall declare before the quenes highnes in
verse, that the goddes Pallas hath latelie made a
declarac(i)on before all the godd(e)s, howe wo(r)thilie
the night precedent theis ij vertues, Prudentia, and
Temperantia, behaved them selves in Judginge, and
condempninge, false Reporte, and Discorde, to the
prison of Extreme Oblyvion; And understandinge that
those ij vertues do remaine in that cowrte of plentye,
they have by there mightie power, sent this vertu
peace there to dwell with those ij Ladyes, for ever. To
this Castell p(er)teyneth ij porters, thone to prudentia
called Ardent desyer and thother porter to Temperantia,
named p(er) petuitie; Signifyinge that by ardent desyer,
and p(er)petuitie, perpetuall peace and tranquillitie
may be hadd & kept throughe the hole worlde. Then
shall springe out of the cowrte of plentie Conditt(e)s
[i.e. conduits, fountains] of all sort(e)s, of wynes,
duringe w(hi)ch tyme, thinglishe Lord(e)s shall maske
w(i)th the Scottishe Ladyes.

*determyned: stuck out.

The thyrde night

ffirste shall come in Disdaine rydinge uppon a wilde
bore,* w(i)th hym prepencyd Malyce, in the similitude
of a greate serpent. These ij shall drawe an Orcharde
havinge golden Apples in w(hi)ch Orchard shall sitt vj,
or viij, Ladyes maskers. Then Dysdaine shall declare
before the quenes Ma(je)stie in verse, that his M(aste)r
Pluto the greate god of hell takith no little displeasure
w(i)th Jupiter the god of heaven, for that he in the ij
other night(e)s precedent hath firste by Pallas sent
Discorde and false Reporte(,) being ij of his chefe
servant(e)s, unto Prudentia, and Temp(er)antia, to be
punisshed at there pleasure, and not content w(i)th
this, but hathe the laste night, sent unto those ij Ladyes,
his moste mortall enymye Peace, to be onlie betwene
them ij imbraced; Wherefore Jupiter shall well under-
stande that in dispite of his doing(e)s, he hath sent his
chefeste Capitayne(,) prepencyd Mallyce(,) and wyllithe
ether Argus, otherwise Circumspection, to delyver unto
to hym Discorde and false Reporte, his saide master(')s
servaunt(e)s, or ells thafforsaid ij porters Ardent Desyer,
and perpetuitie, to delyver hym there master(')s
enymie, peace; chuse them whether.

Then shall come in Discretion, after hym Valyant
courage, otherwise Hercules, rydinge uppon a horse
whose name is boldnes, Discretyon leadynge hym by
the raynes of the brydell; after hym vj or viij Lord(e)s
maskers. Then Discretion shall declare before the
quenes highnes in verse, that Jupiter dothe well foresee
the mischev(i)ous intent of pluto, and therefore to
confounde his pollyc(e)s, hathe sente from heaven this
vertu Valyant courage, w(hi)ch shalbe suffycient to
confounde all plutos devic(e)s. Neverthelesse thos ij
dyvells dysdaine, and prepencyd Malyce, are mervailous
warryours, Yea such as unlesse theis vertues Prudentia,
and Temp(er)antia, will of them selves by some signe(s)
or token(s) conclude to imbrace peace, in such sorte as
Jupiter hathe sent hym unto them, itt wilbe to harde for
Valyant courage, to overcome those vyces, but if they
once speake but one worde the battail is overcome as a
trifle; And therefore Jupiter hathe willed Discretion, in
the presence of thos ij (s) quene [sic: final 's' cut off at
end of line] to repaier unto the cowrte, of plentie, and

*I.e. the Pope an Anti-Christ: see n. 22, pp. 282–3 below.

there firste to demaunde of Prudentia, how longe her
plesure is of her hono(u)r, that peace shall dwell
betwene her, and Temperantia. Then Prudentia shall
let downe unto Discretion, w(i)th a bande of gold, A
grandgarde of Assure, whereuppon shalbe wrytten, in
letters of gold. Ever. Then discretion shall humblie
demaunde of Temperantia uppon her honor, when
peace shall dep(ar)te from Prudentia, and her grace.
Then Temperantia shall lett downe unto Discretyon a
girdell of Assure, studded w(i)th gold, and a Sworde of
stele, whereuppon shalbe written—Never—w(hi)ch
grandgarde, and sworde, Discretion shall bringe, and
laye at the fete of the ij quenes. Then Discretion (after
a fewe word(e)s spoken) shall before the quenes
highnes, arme Valyant courage, otherwise Hercules,
w(i)th the grandgard of Ever, and gyrte hym w(i)th the
sworde, of Never; Signifyinge that those ij Ladies have
p(ro)fessed that peace shall ever dwell w(i)th them, and
Never dep(ar)te from them; and Signifyinge also that
there Valyant courage shalbe ever at defyance, w(i)th
disdaine, and prepencyd mallice and never leave until
he have overcome them; and then shall valyant courage
alone go and fight w(i)th those ij, in the myddeste of
w(hi)ch fight, disdaine shall run(n)e his wayes and
escape w(i)th life, but the monster pr(e)penced mallyce
shalbe slaine for ever; Signifyinge that some ungodlie
men maye still disdaine the p(er)petuall peace made
betwene thos ij vertues, but as for there prepenced
Mallice, it is easye troden under theis Ladyes fete.
After this shall come out of the garden (ie the
'Orchard'), the vj, or viij, Ladies maskers, w(i)th a
songe; that shalbe made hereuppon, as full of Armoney
as maye be devised.

fo. 127b

May, 1562

This MS. was previously transcribed and printed with contractions and the punctuation of the original by Sir Edmund Chambers and W. W. Greg in *MSC* I.2 (1909),
with a short introduction, pp. 143–8.

NOTES AND SOURCES

Chapter I, pages 3–22. Drama and Festival

1. See Charles Lamb, *Essays of Elia*, 'My First Play', ed. William MacDonald, 1903, 195–200.
2. The primary authority for these associations in Athens is Aristotle's comments on comedy, tragedy and the satyr play in *The Poetics*, sketchy as these are, coupled with the surviving texts of plays by Aeschylus, Aristophanes, Sophocles and Euripides. They are however substantially reinforced by many objects found by archaeologists including masks and vase-paintings.
3. William Crawshaw, *The Sermon preached at the Crosse, Feb. xiiij, 1607*. This derivation stems largely from the reversion of interest among English Protestants, notably Calvinists, to the patristic writings and thus to the denunciations contained in them of degenerate, Roman *spectacula* and heathen religious rites encountered by the early missionaries within the Empire. See pp. 11–20 above and Ch. VIII, n. 66, p. 299 below.
4. On sympathetic magic see Sir James Gordon Frazer, *The Golden Bough*, abridged ed., 1922, Chs III–V, pp. 11–82. I have deliberately refrained from joining in the controversy over 'survivalist' and 'structuralist' approaches to this subject since this would occupy far too much space if justice is to be done to it, and since in any case this debate is not germane to the drama of Christian Europe that is unequivocally related to both religion and occasion. Readers who wish to pursue this matter for themselves are referred to C. Lévi-Strauss, *The Savage Mind*, 1966; *Introduction to a Science of Mythology*, I and II, trans. John and Doreen Weightman, 1969–73; also E. E. Evans-Pritchard, *Social Anthropology*, 1951, and J. Huizinga, *Homo Ludens: A Study of the Play-element in Culture*, trans. R. F. C. Hull, 1949. See also Peter Burke, *Popular Culture in Early Modern Europe*, London, 1978.
5. It should be remarked that most animals are endowed by nature with special devices to protect themselves whenever they regard themselves as threatened by predators. Some secrete foul odours, others blinding substances; others utilize special camouflage effects, or display their teeth. Men lack such devices: instead, however, in primitive societies, they gave warning in warlike dances that frequently imitate animals that are so equipped. See E. E. Cawte, *Ritual Animal Disguise*, Cambridge, 1977.
6. This attitude is reflected in dance movements indicative of submission and supplication which include genuflection, prostration and self-immolation and can lead to the choosing of a scapegoat and sacrifice.
7. See H. D. F. Kitto, *The Greeks* (paperback ed.), pp. 173–6, and H. A. Harris, *Sport in Greece and Rome*, 1972, and *Greek Athletes and Athletics*, 1964.
8. See W. Warde Fowler, *Social Life at Rome in the Age of Cicero*, 1908, pp. 285–318, and John Ferguson, *The Religions of the Roman Empire*, 1970.
9. It is for this reason that corn, fruit, meat, water and wine occupy so prominent a place in all religions known to social anthropologists. See pp. 12, 13, 16 and 17 above, and Plate IV, No. 6, also Appendix A.
10. A particular characteristic of this phase of a festive occasion is the inversion of

271

normal social status and a removal of normal taboos, extending to licensed blasphemy, obscenity, parody and ridicule. All of these characteristics figure in Greek Old Comedy as practised by Aristophanes. In Christian Europe these characteristics apply to the Feast of Fools and that of the Boy Bishop, as also to the name and function of the Lord of Misrule. Nor is it altogether absent from the conduct of victorious rowing or football teams today, and among their supporters, after the game.

11. 'Concilio de Lazaro I' in J. P. Migne, *Patrologiae Cursus Completus: Patrologia Latina*, Paris, 1844–64, vol. xlviii, p. 963, a sermon preached the day after that at Antioch, 'Oratio Kalendis Habita' (in Migne, Series Graeca, Paris, 1857–66, vol. xlviii, p. 953). Both are cited by Chambers in *Med. Stage*. ii. 291–2. I owe this translation of the extract from the 'Concilio de Lazaro' to my colleague, John Northam. See also *Med. Stage*. i. 13–18.

12. On 'round tables' see *EES*.i.16 f. The Romans also left theatres and amphitheatres behind them, and it is inconceivable that they should have gone to the trouble and expenditure of erecting these large stone buildings and never to have used them for mimetic and athletic games. What memories of these games lingered in Christian Britain and in how debased a form it is impossible to tell. See *EES*.ii.(2), Plates I–VII and IX, and pp. 48 ff.

13. See *Med. Stage*. i. 234–42.

14. *Contra Symmachum*, i. 237 in Migne, *Patrologia Latina*, lx. 139 cited in *Med. Stage*. ii. 291. 'Iano etiam celebri de mense litatur auspiciis epulisque sacris, quas inveterato heu! miseri sub honore agitant, et gaudia ducunt festa Kalendarum.'

15. *Comm. in Ephes*. vi. 4 in Migne, *Patrologia Latina*, xxvi.540. I owe the translation of this passage with its highly elliptical syntax to my colleague, Michael Anderson, who has added the verb in brackets to clarify the sense.

> Legant episcopi atque presbyteri, qui filios suos saecularibus litteris erudiunt, et faciunt comoedias legere, et mimorum turpia scripta cantare, de ecclesiasticis forsitan sumptibus eruditos; et quod in corbonam pro peccato virgo aut vidua, vel totam substantiam suam effundens quilibet pauper obtulerat, hoc kalendariam strenam, et Saturnalitiam sportulam et Minervale munus grammaticus, et orator, aut in sumptus domesticos, aut in templi stipes, aut in sordida scorta convertit.

See also *Med. Stage*. i. 17–18, and ii. 292–3.

16. *Iudicia*, c. 23 (Migne, *Patrologia Latina*, lxxxix.594) cited in *Med. Stage*.ii.303. 'Si quis ... ut frater in honore Iovis vel Beli aut Iani, secundum paganam consuetudinem, honorare praesumpserit, placuit secundum antiquam constitutionem sex annos poeniteant. Humanius tres annos ivdicaverunt.' Recourse to formal penalties does suggest that by then pagan observances were becoming less of a problem.

17. See *Med. Stage*. i. 95 ff. Tradition claims that St Paul's Cathedral in London replaced a temple and grove dedicated to Diana. See E. C. Cawte, Alex Helm and Norman Peacock, *A geographical index of English Ritual Drama*, London (Folk-Lore Society), 1967.

18. 'Oratio Edgari Regis (969) pro monachatu propaganda', ed. David Wilkins, *Concilia Magnae Britanniae et Hiberniae*, 4 vols, 1737, i, p. 246.
Cf. the Decree of the Council of Clovesho, 747 (*Med. Stage*. i.31): 'ut monasteria ... non sint ludicrarum artium receptacula, hoc est, poetarum, citharistarum, musicorum, scurrorum'. The fear is that not only will they corrupt the morals of the brethren but also the liturgy itself.

19. Hugh Latimer, *Seven Sermons before Edward VI ...* , ed. E. Arber, 1869, pp. 173–4. The actual language used in this passage, it should be noted, provides a ready base for parody of the kind given by Jonson to Zeal-of-the-Land Busy in *Bartholomew Fair.*

20. *Med. Stage.* i.99.

21. On the collection, or *quête*, of folk-drama see E. K. Chambers, *The English Folk-Play*, 1933 (reprinted 1969), pp. 63–71; Alan Brody, *The English Mummers and Their Plays*, 1971, pp. 59 and 67; and G. Wickham, *The Medieval Theatre*, 1974, pp. 146–50.

22. See Ian Lancashire and Alexandra Johnston, 'Yule in York' in *Records of Early English Drama*, Newsletter 1, 1976, pp. 3–10. See also Henry VIII's Proclamation of 1541 which I have printed in Ch. VIII, p. 183 above, and which supplies the original grounds for the belated action of the Ecclesiastical Commission in the North in suppressing the Yule Riding in York.

23. For other derivations see *Med. Stage.* i.230 and 132 ff.

24. The following passage from Honorius of Autun's *Gemma animae* (*c.* 1100) cited by Hardison in *Christian Rite*, pp. 39–40, tells the same story, but at the other end of the time-scale, since it is Honorius's purpose to allegorize the physical actions of the Mass, including the eating of bread, the drinking of wine and Christ himself as sacrificial lamb.

> 'It is known that those who recited tragedies in theaters presented the actions of opponents by gestures before the people. In the same way our tragic author (i.e. the celebrant) represents by his gestures in the theater of the Church before the Christian people the struggle of Christ and teaches to them the victory of His redemption. Thus when the celebrant [*presbyter*] says the *Orate* [*fratres*] he expresses Christ placed for us in agony, when he commanded His apostles to pray. By the silence of the *Secreta* he expresses Christ as a lamb without voice being led to the sacrifice ... '

The original text is given in J. P. Migne's *Patrologiae Cursus Completus: Patrologia Latina*, clxxii.570; the translation is Hardison's own.

25. The original text is given in Hist. MSS., 1. 107, *Convocation Book*, cited by Chambers *Med. Stage.*i.176; the translation is mine. For the following quotation from the 'Reynes Extract' see *Non-Cycle Plays and Fragments*, ed. Norman Davis for EETS, 1970, pp. cxx–cxxiv and 123.

26. On 'Midsummer Watches' see *Med. Stage.*i.188 f. and ii.165–6; R. Withington, *English Pageantry*, Vol. 1; and *MSC*, III, Introduction.

27. John Stow, *A Survey of London*, ed. C. L. Kingsford, Vol. I, pp. 101–2.

28. See F. M. Salter, *Mediaeval Drama in Chester*, pp. 22 and 27–8.

29. See *Med. Stage.*i.116 ff; on the East Harling games see *EES*.ii(2).32–3.

30. Bodl. MS. Ashmole. 59; it has been reprinted in *The Minor Poems of John Lydgate*, ed. H. N. MacCracken for EETS, 1911 (reprinted 1934), and again by me with a critical introduction in the Appendix to *English Moral Interludes*, hardback 1976, paperback 1977.

31. On the Roman *feriae* see W. Warde Fowler, *Social Life at Rome in the Age of Cicero*, 1908, pp. 287 ff. It should be remarked that when acting was licensed again after the Restoration in 1660 regular performances were restricted to London; and had it not been for the annual fairs, race-meetings and so on that provided strolling players with an audience, the provinces would have lacked any form of dramatic entertainment: see Sybil Rosenfeld, *Strolling Players and Drama in the Provinces, 1660–1795*, 1939.

32. For an example of a Royal Charter authorizing and establishing an annual fair, see *Winchester Cathedral Records*, ed. C. W. Kitchin, 1886, which contains that for St Giles Fair at Winchester dated 1392: Latin text, pp. 26–42; English translation, pp. 43–57; Kitchin's own Introduction (pp. 5–26) provides an excellent account of the early history of English fairs. On St Werburgh's Fair, Chester, see *EES*. i. 138–9.

Chapter II, pages 23–47. Drama of the Christian Calendar

1. See *Med. Stage*.i.108–9.
2. See *Bedae Opera de Temporibus*, ed. Charles W. Jones, Cambridge, Mass. Medieval Academy of America, 1943. This editor, in his long introduction, discusses medieval and earlier methods of computing time as well as giving detailed references to all writers who participated in the Easter controversy.
3. See *Med. Stage*. i.228 ff.
4. See O. B. Hardison, Jnr, *Christian Rite and Christian Drama in the Middle Ages*, 1965, pp. 80–138. A feast of consequence, however, that can fall just inside Lent, if rarely, is that of the recently discredited St George (23 April): St Mark's Day (25 April) will always fall outside Lent, but can coincide with Easter Day itself when Easter is at its latest. See n.6 below and note to Plate VI, No. 9 regarding the Resurrection and Corpus Christi plays at Beverley, Yorkshire.
5. Henry VIII issued his first decree abolishing the majority of annual festival days in 1536 on the grounds that their number had become so excessive as to prejudice agriculture and to promote idleness and riotous behaviour. Four principal feast days were to be observed—Christmas Day, Easter Day, St John the Baptist and St Michael—which correspond still with the solstices and the equinoxes. St George's Day, the Feasts of the Apostles and the Virgin were also excepted from the ban. A further decree, in the form of a proclamation, was issued in 1541, making it clear that the earlier Act was not being fully observed: this is quoted in Ch. VIII, p. 183 above. See also Ch. I, pp. 13–14 and 18–19 above.
6. The Latin text is to be found in *DMC*.i.587: see also *DMC*. 1. 201 ff., and J. Q. Adams, *Chief Pre-Shakespearean Dramas*, Cambridge, Mass., 1924, pp. 9–10. Also William L. Smoldon, 'The Origins of the *Quem Quaeritis* and the Easter Sepulchre Music-Drama as Demonstrated by their Musical Settings' in *The Medieval Drama*, ed. Sandro Sticca, Binghamton, 1972, pp. 121–54.
7. For the Latin text see *Med. Stage*.ii.306–9, and *DMC*.i, Plate VII. For an English translation see G. Wickham, *The Medieval Theatre*, pp. 39–40; A. M. Nagler, *A Source Book in Theatrical History*, New York, 1952, pp. 39–41. See also Plate I, Nos 1 and 2, and *DMC*.i, Frontispiece and Plates III, VIII and IX.
8. For the Klosterneuburg text see *DMC*.i.421–32, and for the Benediktbeuren text, *ibid.*, 432–8. On anti-masque see G. Wickham, 'Masque and Anti-Masque in *The Tempest*', *Essays and Studies*, 1975, p. 4.
9. For the Tours text see *DMC*.i.438–50.
10. See *DMC*.i.451–83; also Adams, *op. cit.*, pp. 21–4.
11. See Axton, 'Popular Modes in the Earliest Drama', Stratford-upon-Avon Studies 16: *Medieval Drama*, ed. Neville Denny, p. 28; *Med. Stage*.ii.36; *Non-Cycle Plays and Fragments*, ed. Norman Davis for EETS, pp. xiv-xxii, 1–4 and 124–33: also *DMC*.ii.514–23.
12. Text in *DMC*.i.484–9; also *Med. Stage*.ii.66, n. 1.
13. See *Med. Stage*.ii.11, 65, 129 and 395; also *DMC*, Plate XI (facing p. 488).

14. W. Lambarde, *Alphabetical Description of the Chief Places in England and Wales*, ed. 1730 from a sixteenth-century MS., p. 459.

15. See *DMC*.ii.4–5; *Med. Stage*.ii.41–4.

16. See *DMC*.ii.12–20; Adams, *op.cit.*, pp. 25–7.

17. Karl Young traces this play's development in *DMC*.ii.59–101: the quotation is from the end of the Fleury version, the complete text of which is to be found between pp. 84 and 89. Adams gives the Rouen text, *op.cit.*, pp. 28–31.

18. 'Popular Modes in the Earliest Drama', Stratford-upon-Avon Studies 16: *Medieval Drama*, p. 20. The creation of the character of Herod, however, serves to undermine this approach to a point where it becomes untenable. Writing of the Compiègne version, Young (*DMC*.ii.58) notes that

    'the play is no longer a compilation of liturgical and Biblical passages, but an independent literary composition. Through this freedom and inventiveness, moreover, is achieved a highly acceptable gain in characterization. Herod himself begins to disclose those traits of pomposity, impetuousness and violence which promise well both for dramatic conflict and for comedy.'

    See also David Staines, 'To Out-Herod Herod: The Development of a Dramatic Character', *Comparative Drama*, X. (spring 1976), no. 1, pp. 29–53. Discussing Herod's progress from a Latin liturgical to a popular vernacular character, he says (p. 29):

    'From the wretched villain of biblical and apocryphal accounts, Herod grows in liturgical drama to a figure of potential comedy, potential tragedy and increasingly less villainy. In the mystery cycles he reaches the apex of his dramatic career as he becomes at times the comic braggart, at times the tragic ruler, at times a combination of comic and tragic hero.'

19. On the *Ordo Prophetarum* see *DMC*.ii.125–71, and *Med. Stage*.ii.52–62. A *Ludus de Sancta Katherina* was performed at Dunstable, *c.* 1100, the author of which was a schoolmaster, but the text of which has not survived: see Catherine B. C. Thomas, 'The Miracle Play at Dunstable', in *MLN*, XXXII (1917), pp. 337–44; and Hardin Craig, *English Religious Drama*, pp. 97–9 and 321. On early saint plays in London as recorded by William Fitzstephen (*c.* 1170–82) see *Med. Stage*.ii.379–80.

20. For the texts of surviving liturgical plays of St Nicholas see *DMC*.ii.311–60. See also Carleton Brown, 'An Early Mention of a St Nicholas Play in England', *Studies in Philology*, XXXVIII (1931), pp. 594–601. An English translation of *Le Jeu de Saint Nicholas* (*c.* 1200) is given by Richard Axton and John Stevens in *Medieval French Plays*, 1971, pp. 71–135.

21. For the text see *DMC*.ii.219–24.

22. For the Anglo-Norman text see Paul Aebischer, ed., *Le Mystère d'Adam*, Paris, 1963; for English translations see Axton and Stevens, *op.cit.*, pp. 1–44; and Lynette R. Muir, 'Adam', *Proceedings of the Leeds Philosophical and Literary Society: Literary and Historical Section*, Vol. XIII, Part V, January 1970, pp. 149–204. For comment see Grace Frank, *MFD*, pp. 76–87; R. Axton, *European Drama of the Early Middle Ages*, 1974, pp. 112–30; and Lynette R. Muir, *op.cit.*, pp. 155–65.

23. Axton, *op.cit.*, p. 114.

24. Muir, *op.cit.*, p. 156. She then proceeds to explain the omission of Noah.

25. Muir, *op.cit.*, interestingly suggests that the play may be associated with the Lent Ember Days (p. 163).

26. Muir, *op.cit.*, p. 192. Another play presented was a Resurrection play at Beverley Minster, Yorkshire, *c.* 1220. Axton ('Popular Modes', pp. 27–8) says, 'The play

was of the resurrection and it was played in summer; it was *therefore* [my italics] unconnected with its appropriate liturgical feast.' I cannot agree, since it is quite possible that this play may have been performed at either Whitsun or Ascension, both of which are summer festivals, and covered biblical events starting with the Resurrection and concluding respectively with the descent of the Holy Ghost or Christ's ascent into heaven, as does the Anglo-Norman *La Seinte Resureccion* (see n. 33 below). It should also be noted that the subsequent Corpus Christi plays at Beverley were held annually on St Mark's Day, 25 April. It is thus quite possible that this exceptional practice derived from an earlier tradition of presenting a Resurrection play on that day. See *Med. Stage*.ii.338–41; *DMC*.ii.539–40; and A. F. Leach, *Beverley Town Documents*, Selden Society, XIV. At present, therefore, the case for presuming the Beverley Resurrection play to have been connected with an appropriate liturgical feast appears to be a better one than that for regarding it as unconnected.

27. Text in *DMC*.ii.361–9: see also *Sponsus: An Eleventh Century Mystere* transcribed, edited and translated by W. L. Smoldon, Oxford, n.d. (reprinted 1972).

28. Text in *DMC*.ii.266–76.

29. *DMC*.ii.199–219.

30. *DMC*.ii.258–66.

31. *DMC*.ii.167–70.

32. For these two subjects depicted in conjunction see the stained-glass windows of Fairford church in Gloucestershire.

33. The Anglo-Norman text was edited for the Anglo-Norman Text Society, Oxford, 1943, by T. A. Jenkins, J. M. Manly, M. K. Pope, J. G. Wright; an English translation appears in *Medieval French Plays* translated by Richard Axton and John Stevens, 1971, pp. 45–69. I have suggested in n. 26 above that it may well have been a play of this kind, covering events from the Deposition to the Ascension, that was performed in the churchyard at Beverley, *c*. 1220. The play is important in its own right as being the first to provide a substantial part for a narrator or expositor who comments throughout the action as well as supplies the prologue: there is no epilogue as the MS. breaks off at the arrest of Joseph of Arimathea, but the list of *loca* supplied in the prologue provides for the extension of the text to the Ascension. For comment see *MFD*, pp. 85–92. This play, like the *Jeu d'Adam* and the *Sponsus*, makes provision for a hell and devils (Prologue, ll. 25–6); see Ch. VI, p. 154 above.

34. On the promulgation of the dogma of transubstantiation in 1215 and its relationship to the promulgation and institution of the Feast of Corpus Christi respectively in 1264 and 1311 see V. A. Kolve, *The Play Called Corpus Christi*, Stanford, Calif., 1966, pp. 44–9.

35. On this controversy see O. B. Hardison, Jnr, *op. cit.*, pp. 1–34, and G. Wickham, *Shakespeare's Dramatic Heritage*, pp. 3–23.

36. See Edwin Norris, *The Ancient Cornish Drama*, 2 vols, 1859: reprinted by Benjamin Blom, 1968.

37. See Kenneth Cameron and Stanley J. Kahrl, 'The N-Town Plays at Lincoln', *Theatre Notebook*, XX (winter 1965–6), no. 2, pp. 61–9; F. M. Salter, *Medieval Drama in Chester*; and *Med. Stage*.ii.379–82.

38. On the suppression of the plays see H. C. Gardiner, *Mysteries' End*, New Haven, Conn., 1946; reprinted 1967.

39. See G. Wickham, 'The Staging of Saint Plays in England', in *The Medieval Drama*, ed. S. Sticca, New York, 1972, pp. 99–119; David L. Jeffrey, 'English Saints' Plays', in Stratford-upon-Avon Studies 16: *Medieval Drama*, ed. N. Denny, 1973, pp. 68–89.

40. See *MSC*, V, ed. F. P. Wilson, 1959, pp. 43–62.
41. See *MSC*, II (Pt 2), ed. W. W. Greg, 1923 ('The Academic Drama at Cambridge: Extracts from College Records', ed. G. C. Moore Smith), pp. 150–230.
42. See G. Wickham, *English Moral Interludes*, 1976, 'General Introduction', pp. v-xv, and R. Potter, *The English Morality Play*, 1975.
43. See *DMC*.ii.369–96. An English translation is provided by J. Wright, *The Play of Anti-Christ*, Toronto, 1967. For comment see Axton, *European Drama of the Early Middle Ages*, pp. 88–94; Peter Munz, *Frederick Barbarossa: A Study in Medieval Politics*, Ithaca, N.Y., and London, 1969; and Frederick Heer, *The Holy Roman Empire*, trans. Janet Sondheimer, 1968, pp. 73–6.
44. See Richard Barber, *The Knight and Chivalry*, 1970, Ch. 3, 'The Heroic Age and Chivalry: the *Chanson de Geste*', pp. 37–55, and Ch. 11, 'The Tournament and Politics', pp. 178–88. Axton provides strong grounds for adopting this approach in his chapter on combat as one of the four major components of popular modes in the earliest drama in *European Drama of the Early Middle Ages* (pp. 33–46); but, strangely, he ignores the tournament almost entirely.

Chapter III, pages 48–61. Non-recurrent Court and Civic Festivals

1. *The Kings Maiesties Speech*, 19 March 1603, printed by Robert Barker, 1604, sig. B2b.
2. Four MS. accounts of the entry survive, all of which are in the British Museum: MS. Harl. 53, fo. 157b; MS. Harl. 565, fo. iiib; MS. Cotton Jul. E. iv, fo. 113; and MS. Sloane 1776 which is a poor copy of the Cotton MS. The best is MS. Harl. 53 and this was printed by J. Strutt in *Manners and Customs*, Vol. II, pp. 50 ff.
3. Much the fullest and best account of these festivities is given by S. Anglo, in *Spectacle, Pageantry and Early Tudor Policy*, 1969, pp. 137–69.
4. For the full text see *The Minor Poems of John Lydgate*, ed. for EETS by H. N. Mac-Cracken (2 vols), Vol. II, pp. 695–8; and *EES*.i.201–2 for comment.
5. For the text see MacCracken, *op.cit.*, Vol. II, pp. 672–4; and for comment *EES*.i.200.
6. The text is given by MacCracken, *op.cit.*, Vol. II, pp. 668–71, and by me in *English Moral Interludes*, pp. 210–12; for comment see *EES*.i.199–200. It also anticipates Sir Philip Sidney's *The Lady of May* by 150 years: see pp. 54–5 above.
7. For the texts see MacCracken, *op.cit.*, Vol. II, pp. 682–91 and 698–701; for comment see *EES*.i.200–1 and 204–5.
8. L. H. Loomis, 'Secular Dramatics in the Royal Palace, Paris, 1378, 1389, and Chaucer's "Tregetoures"', *Speculum*, XXXIII (1958), pp. 242–55; reprinted in *Medieval English Drama: Essays Critical and Contextual*, ed. J. Taylor and A. H. Nelson, 1972, pp. 98–115; see also *EES*.i.212–16.
9. See *EES*.i.213–14, and Loomis, *op.cit.*
10. See D. L. Jeffrey, 'English Saints' Plays' in Stratford-upon-Avon Studies 16: *Medieval Drama*, ed. N. Denny, 1973, 68–89; especially pp. 72–3. See also pp. 168–9 above.
11. The text is given by MacCracken, *op. cit.*, Vol. II, pp. 630–48. See also R. Withington, *English Pageantry*, Vol. I, pp. 141 f.
12. The best text is given by Carleton Brown in *MLR*, VII, pp. 225–34; the best commentary by Brian Crow, 'The Development of the Presentation of Human Actions in Medieval and Renaissance Drama', Ph.D. thesis, University of Bristol, pp. 57–61. See also Robert Fabyan, *The New Chronicles of England and France*, ed. Henry Ellis (from Pynson's 1516 ed.), 1811, p. 617.

13. See *Coventry Leet-Book* ed. for EETS by Mary D. Harris, 1907–9, Vol. II, pp. 285 ff; also Withington, *op.cit.*, Vol. I, pp. 149–50.

14. On this entry see Withington, *op.cit.*, Vol. I, pp. 138–41.

15. On this entry see David Bergeron, *English Civic Pageantry, 1558–1642*, pp. 11 ff.

16. See S. Anglo, *Spectacle, Pageantry and Early Tudor Policy*, pp. 170–206; also Withington, *op. cit.*, Vol. I, pp. 174–9.

17. BM MS. Harl. 41 and MS. Harl. 6148, fo. 26 ff.: see also S. Anglo, *op.cit.*, pp. 243–61 and Withington, *op.cit.*, pp. 180–4.

18. *Op. cit.*, Vol. I, p. 180.

19. The full text is given in *The Complete Works of George Gascoigne*, ed. for Cambridge English Classics by J. W. Cunliffe, Vol. II, 1910, pp. 91–131, from *The Whole Workes of George Gascoigne*, 1578. See also *ES*.i. 122–3 and iv. 61; and Withington, *op. cit.*, Vol. I, pp. 207–9.

20. The text is given by Cunliffe, *op. cit.*, Vol. II, pp. 473–510, edited from BM MS. Royal 18 A xlviii. See also *ES*.iii.400. The quotation is from Laurence Humphrey's *Oratio* delivered at Woodstock, 11 September 1575, given in Nichols, *PQE*.i.590.

21. First published in 1598, *The Countesse of Pembroke's Arcadia* was reprinted in 1599 and ten times thereafter between 1605 and 1662. See *ES*.iii.491–2 and modern editions of Sidney's works.

22. On the history of the entertainments authorized and paid for by the livery companies of London, see *MSC*, III, ed. Jean Robertson and Donald Gordon, 1954, 'Introduction', pp. xiii-xlix. For additional items see *MSC*, V, 1959, 'A Calendar of Dramatic Records in the Books of the London Clothworkers' Company', ed. Jean Robertson, pp. 3–16.

23. *MSC*, III, p. 136.

24. The Merchant Taylors banned the further use of their hall for plays in March 1573. Their court book injunction reveals that the admission charge levied was normally one penny. The immediate cause of the ban was the unruly behaviour of the younger members of the audience. See *MSC*, III, p. 140.

25. A possible exception is the play by 'the Children (of) poules scole after dynnar' presented to the Mercers' Company in February 1583–4; this complained about the lack of scholarships to the universities which gave offence enough for the text to have been copied and preserved. It has been edited and printed in *MSC*, III, pp. 142–64.

26. See *MSC*, III, pp. 41–7; also Bergeron, *op. cit.*, pp. 126–30.

27. See *MSC*, III, pp. xxiv ff.

28. It was during the 1580s that the number of pageants both on the river and in the city began to multiply, and that descriptive pamphlets began to be printed and sold.

29. In this context see especially Thomas Nashe's *Summer's Last Will and Testament* (1592).

30. *Venetian Papers*, Vol. VII, p. 11: Il Schifanoya to Castellan of Mantua. He also provides a brief description of one of the Shrovetide masques and states: 'Then at the dance the Queen performed her part, the Duke of Norfolk being her partner, in superb array' (*ibid.*, p. 27).

31. Chambers, *ES*.i.155–70 catalogues all the Elizabethan masques; and on p. 158, n. 1, he collates the costume items listed by Feuillerat, *RO* (*E&M*) and *RO* (*Eliz*), with the masques known to have been presented in 1558–60.

32. 'Gascoigne's devise of a maske for the right honourable Viscount Montacute' ed. J. W. Cunliffe, *Works*, Vol. I, 1907, pp. 75 ff., edited from *A Hundreth Sundrie Flowres*

bounde up in one small Poesie, 1573. For comment, see C. T. Prouty, *George Gascoigne: Elizabethan Courtier, Soldier and Poet*, New York, 1942, pp. 173–7. Gascoigne, in his own introduction to the reader, explains that the amateur masquers had already chosen a Venetian subject as their device for this masque, but were in a quandary which they asked him to resolve:

> Nowe then they began to imagine that (without some speciall demonstration) it would seeme somewhat obscure to have Venetians presented rather than other countrey men. Whereupon they entreated the Aucthour to devise some verses to bee uttered by an Actor wherein might be some discourse convenient to render a good cause of the Venetians presence.

Gascoigne did as he was asked (at great length) and commissioned 'a Boye of the age of twelve or xiiij yeeres' to learn and recite this speech. The boy made his entry with four torchbearers, and spoke his lines concluding,

> Behold, lo nowe I see them here, in order howe they come,
> Receive them well my lord, so shall I praye all wayes,
> That God vouchsafe to blesse this house with many happie days.

The masquers then entered with their drumme and chose their partners from the spectators for the dances. That they did not speak is made clear in the epilogue, given to a local worthy, who promises that the masquers will return.

> Then will they speake them selves, such english as they can,
> I feare much better then I speake, that am an english man.
> Lo nowe they take their leaves of you and of your dames,
> Here after shal you see their face and knowe them by their nam(e)s.

After the departure of the masquers the Presenter made his own exit with a graceful flourish.

33. See n. 30 above.
34. See *MSC*, VII, ed. Giles Dawson (Kent); *MSC*, VIII, ed. Stanley Kahrl (Lincolnshire); and *MSC*, IX, ed. G. R. Proudfoot (Dorset and Suffolk).
35. On the visit to Bristol (1574) see *PQE*.i.396 ff.; Bristol Archives (Audits 1570–4) and Bergeron, *op. cit.*, pp. 26–30. On those to Worcester (1575) and Norwich (1578) see *PQE*.ii.136 ff.; seq: also Withington, *op.cit.*, Vol. I, pp. 210–12, and Bergeron, *op. cit.*, pp. 37–44.

Chapter IV, pages 65–82. Play-makers and Device

1. On Lyly's authorship of this entertainment, and for an edition of the full text, see Leslie Hotson, *Queen Elizabeth's Entertainment at Mitcham*, New Haven, Conn., 1953.
2. Hamlet's version of it is 'pressure': see I.v. 100 and III.ii.24, ed. Dover Wilson. Drummond of Hawthornden stated, 'In an impresa, the figures express and illustrate one part of the author's intention, and the words the other.' See Plate XII.
3. See Roy Strong, *The Cult of Elizabeth*, 1977.
4. See Ch. III, p. 55 above.
5. See *Emblematum Flumen Abundans* (Lyons ed., 1551), reprinted and edited by Henry Green for Holbein Society, 1871.
6. For editions see Ch. VIII, nn. 56 and 57, p. 298 below.
7. *MSR* (3rd ed.), sig. Biv, 1. 407, and sig. Ciii, ll. 615–16. The play was first printed

by William Coplande, *c.* 1562, and again shortly after. It was edited and reprinted by J. S. Farmer, *Anonymous Plays*, series 3, 1906, and again in 1912 for *Tudor Facsimile Texts*, and then in 1914, ed. W. H. Williams. The Malone Society's Reprint was edited by E. L. Smart and W. W. Greg, 1933. A third Elizabethan edition, again without a date, was discovered in 1936 and reprinted by B. I for Evans and W. W. Greg for the Malone Society in 1937. Skelton, of course, is not being original in his earlier use of these words. Nearly a century earlier still Lydgate had exploited them to the full in his *Mumming at Hertford*: 'Hit is no game but an hernest play' (l. 72).

8. See Ch. VIII, n. 1, p. 291 below.

9. For editions of these two plays see Ch. VIII, nn. 74 and 75, pp. 300–1 below.

10. This play was first printed in 1566 by J. Charlewood, and again in 1567. It has since been edited and reprinted by F. I. Carpenter, Chicago, 1904, and again for *Tudor Facsimile Texts*, 1908; quotation ed. Carpenter, ll. 80–3.

11. Ed. de Ricci, sig. A iii. On this play see Ch. VIII, n. 75, p. 300 below.

12. *Respublica* was first edited by A Brandl in *Quellen des weltlichen Dramas in England vor Shakespeare*, 1898, and then for EETS by L. Z. Magnus, 1905, and again by W. W. Greg, 1952. Quotation from Greg's ed., ll. 5–6, punctuation modernized.

13. *MSR*, ed. W. W. Greg, 1933, ll. 59–64. See n. 7 above.

14. This play was first printed by J. Tyndale, n. d., *c.* 1560. It was reprinted by J. S. Farmer in *Six Anonymous Plays*, 1905, and again for *Tudor Facsimile Texts*, 1912. The best modern edition is in A. W. Pollard's *English Miracle Plays, Moralities and Interludes* (1965 ed.), pp. 126–45.

15. *Ed. cit.*, ll. 33–40; see n. 10 above.

16. Ed. for EETS by Norman Davis, *Non-Cycle Plays and Fragments*, 1970.

17. This play has been edited from BM MS. Add. 15233 by F. P. Wilson for *MSR*, 1951.

18. For editions see n. 7 above.

19. See A. G. Dickens, *The English Reformation*, 1964, p. 260, and J. H. Graham, 'St Ignatius and Cardinal Pole', *Archivum Historicum Societatis Iesu*, XXV (1956), pp. 72–98.

20. *MSR*, 1933 ed., ll. 108–11 (punctuation modernized). Farmer misread *moull* for *nowl* in his edition, and glosses *nowl* as meaning 'head' or 'skull'.

21. *Ibid.*, ll. 1150–6. In l. 1156 where 3rd ed. reads 'life', 1st ed. reads 'lfie', an obvious printer's mistake.

22. *King Darius* was first printed by T. Colwell, 1565, and again in 1577. It was reprinted by J. S. Farmer, *Anonymous Plays*, series 3, 1906, and again for *Tudor Facsimile Texts*, 1907 and 1909.

23. See Inga-Stina Ewbank, 'What words, what looks, what wonders?: Language and Spectacle in the Theatre of George Peele', *Elizabethan Theatre*, Vol. V, ed. George Hibbard, 1975, pp. 124–54.

24. See D. H. Zucker, *Stage and Image in the Plays of Christopher Marlowe*, Salzburg Studies in English Literature, VII, 1972, p. 7.

25. See *PQE* (ed. 1823); also James M. Osborn, *The Queenes Majesties Passage*, New Haven, Conn., 1960, and David Bergeron, *English Civic Pageantry, 1558–1642*, 1971, pp. 13–23.

26. This was also Mary I's personal device. Interestingly, the author of *Respublica* weaves it neatly into his text on several occasions, most strikingly in the prologue:

> ... tyme trieth all and tyme bringeth truth to lyght
> that wronge may not ever still reigne in place of right.

(ed. EETS ll. 27–8)

and again,
Veritee, the daughter of sage old Father Tyme
Shewith all as yt ys, bee yt vertue or Cryme.
(*ibid.*, ll. 33–4)

Cf. Shakespeare's use of this device in *The Winter's Tale;* see pp. 86–7 above.

27. BM MS. Lansdowne 5, Art. 38, fo. 126. This MS. was edited and printed by E. K. Chambers and W. W. Greg in *MSC*, I. 2 (1909), pp. 144–8 and commented upon by the former in *ES*.i.159–60. Many details survive of other Court entertainments, especially those relating to costume materials and costs in the Revels Office accounts; but these do not extend to texts and descriptions: see *ES*. i, Chs V and VI; also Feuillerat, *RO (E&M)* and *RO (Eliz)*.

28. Negotiations for this meeting began in May 1562, but were finally broken off in July. It is interesting to compare what is said in the last act of *Gorboduc* (1561) about Anglo-Scottish relations and what, a year later, is being proposed in this masque; on the former see pp. 243–8 above. On the Secretary's interest in entertainments see *EES*.i.240, 277–8 and 284–5.

Chapter V, pages 83–123. Device and Visual Figuration

1. For this text (BM MS. Egerton 2615) see *DMC*.ii.290–306 and *The Play of Daniel*, ed. Noah Greenberg, 1959. See also Ch. II, pp. 39–40 above on its typological relationship to the *Peregrini*.

2. See, for all three stages of development, *DMC*.i.239–410. The Dublin text is also given in *Med. Stage*.ii.315–18, ed. from Bodl. MS. 15846.

3. The Noah play of *Ludus Coventriae* is unique in this respect in omitting this quarrel. There, however, the play-maker's purpose is to figure Christ's marriage with his Church in the marital harmony between Noah and his wife that serves to pluck salvation out of disaster.

4. For the full Cornish text with English translation alongside, see Edwin Norris, *The Ancient Cornish Drama*, 2 vols, 1859: reprinted by Benjamin Blom, 1968.

5. For a discussion of a similar treatment of historical event within *The Tempest*, see G. Wickham, 'Masque and Anti-Masque in *The Tempest*', *Essays and Studies*, 1975, pp. 1–14. See also Ch. IV, n. 26 above.

6. This play was first printed by John Rastell, n. d., *c.* 1516–25. It has been reprinted four times since then, ed. A Brandl, *Quellen*, 1898; W. Bang, *Materialien*, XII, 1905; J. S. Farmer, *'Lost' Tudor Plays*, series 3, 1907; and for *Tudor Facsimile Texts*, 1908. The passages quoted occur in Reason's opening speech in Part II, sig. e iii.

7. *Towneley Plays*, ed. for EETS, George England and A. W. Pollard, 1897: 'Crucifixion', ll. 89–94 and 107–12. See also A. C. Cawley, *The Wakefield Pageants in the Towneley Cycle*, 1958, and Ch. IV, p. 74 above.

8. I *Fulgens and Lucres*, ed. G. Wickham in *English Moral Interludes*, ll. 1145–1234. See also n. 36 below.

9. For editions of Udall's *Ralph Roister Doister* see n. 18 below; *Thersytes* was first printed, n. d., *c.* 1560 by J. Tyndale and then reprinted by J. S. Farmer, *Six Anonymous Plays*, 1905, and for *Tudor Facsimile Texts* in 1912; the best modern edition is in A. W. Pollard's *English Miracle Plays, Moralities and Interludes* (1965 ed.); *Gammer Gurton's Needle* was first printed by T. Colwell, 1575, and is available in many modern editions and collections.

10. First printed for H. Jackson, 1576, George Walpull's play was reprinted in *Shakespeare Jahrbuch*, XLIII, ed. E. Rühl, 1907, and again for *Tudor Facsimile Texts*, 1910. For a modernized edition see *EMP*.

11. Preston's *Cambises* was entered in the Stationers' Register for printing 1569: see *EES*.i,Appendix G, for title-page and cast-list. For Peele's and Greene's plays, see MSR, 1906 and 1907 respectively.

12. These quotations and the sequel are from Rastell's edition, *c*. 1516–25, sigs Aiib, Biii and Gii. For other editions see n. 6 above.

13. The play was first printed by J. Rastell, n. d., *c*. 1525, and not again until 1848 when it was edited by J. O. Halliwell for the Percy Society, Vol. XXII; it was then reprinted by J. S. Farmer, *Six Anonymous Plays*, 1905, and again for *Tudor Facsimile Texts*, 1908. As the archaic spelling together with the lack of any punctuation in Rastell's edition makes the sense of the text very difficult to follow, I have modernized both the spelling and punctuation in this and the following quotations from the play, starting at sig. Bivb.

14. Ed. F. J. Furnivall, *The Digby Plays* for EETS, 1896, pp. 72–6.

15. This play exists in three Tudor editions printed between 1528 at the earliest and 1560: W. Copeland's based on J. Waley's, based on Wynkyn de Worde's. It was edited and reprinted by W. Bang in *Materialien*, XII, and by J. S. Farmer, *Six Anonymous Plays*, series 2, 1906: also for *Tudor Facsimile Texts*, 1909. A modernized edition of this play exists in H-D II, and another in *EMP*; also in P. Happé's *Tudor Interludes*, Penguin, 1972.

16. This play was first printed by Wynkyn de Worde, n. d., *c*. 1513. It has since been reprinted by J. S. Farmer, *Six Anonymous Plays*, 1905, and again for *Tudor Facsimile Texts*, 1908. The edition used here is J. Manly's in *Specimens of the Pre-Shakespearean Drama*, Vol. I.

17. Printed 1560 for J. King. It was reprinted by J. S. Farmer in *'Lost' Tudor Plays*, 1907, and for *Tudor Facsimile Texts* the same year; then by W. Bang, *Materialien*, XXXIII,1911. The quotations are from Bang's edition with the spelling and punctuation modernized.

18. Udall's *Ralph Roister Doister* was first printed by H. Denham for T. Hackett, *c*. 1566. It was reprinted for *MSR*, ed. W. W. Greg, 1934 (1935), and appears in many collections of Tudor plays.

19. See n. 9 above.

20. First printed by W. How for A. Veale, 1573, this play was reprinted by J. S. Farmer, *Anonymous Plays*, series 3, 1906, and again for *Tudor Facsimile Texts*, 1908: also in H-D III.

21. Thomas Ingelend's *Nice Wanton* was first printed by J. King, 1560, and has since been reprinted for *Tudor Facsimile Texts*, 1909; by J. Manly, *Specimens of the Pre-Shakespearean Drama*, Vol. I, and by me in *English Moral Interludes*. It also appears in *The Dramatic Writings of Richard Wever and Thomas Ingelend*, ed.J. S. Farmer,1905.

22. I suspect myself that Shakespeare had a specific purpose in mind in choosing to give his Eastcheap tavern that particular name. The key is supplied by John Bale in *Kyng Johan*. The play opens with King John in debate with Widow England and Sedition. England is blaming clergy for her widowhood: when John rebukes her at line 68 she replies,

> 'Nay, bastards they are, unnatural, by the rood!
> Since their beginning they were never good to me.
> The wild boar of Rome—God let him never to thee—
> Like pigs they follow, in fantasies, dreams and lies,
> And ever are fed with his vile ceremonies.' (Spelling modernized)

The king is puzzled and questions her.

John   By the boar of Rome I trow thou meanest the pope?
England   I mean none other but him. God give him a rope!
John   And why dost thou thus compare him to a swine?
England   For that he and his to such beastliness incline.
           They forsake God's word, which is most pure and clean,
           And unto the laws of sinful men they lean.
           Like as the vile swine the most vile meats desire
           And hath great pleasure to wallow themselves in mire,
           So hath this wild boar, with his church universal—
           His sow with her pigs and monsters bestial—
           Delight in men's draff and covetous lucre all.
           Yea, *aper de sylua** the prophet did him call.†

If readers regard this argument as tenuous, they still have to reckon with those lines in *Mundus et Infans* where the vice, Folly, a graduate of the Inns of Court who knows his London pubs very well, persuades Manhood to accompany him there.

Manhood   Peace, but it is hence a great way.
Folly   Pardee sir, we may be there on a day,
           Yea, and we shall be right welcome, I dare well say,
           In Eastcheap for to dine,
           And then we will with Lombards‡ at Passage play,
           And at the Pope's Head sweet wine assay.
           We shall be lodged well *à-fin*.
              (*EMP*, ll. 667–73; ed. Manly, ll. 669–75.)

Manhood accepts the invitation. Folly, however, has already spoken to the audience and revealed to them his true intentions:

           'Ah ha, sirs, let the cat wink,
           For all ye wot not what I think,
           I shall draw him such a draught of drink
           That Conscience he shall away cast.'
           (*ibid.*, ll. 647–50; ed. Manly, ll. 648–52)

When we meet Manhood next, he appears as Age, ruined and on the brink of despair. In a Protestant world we should therefore expect to find the 'Pope's Head' transformed into the 'Boar's Head' in this context.

23. This play was first printed by T. Colwell, n. d., *c.* 1566, but is likely to have been written at least thirty years earlier. The fragment that survives was reprinted in *MSC*, I. 3, ed. W. W. Greg, 1909, pp. 229–42.

24. First printed by Wynkyn de Worde, 1522; since reprinted for *Tudor Facsimile Texts*, 1909, and by J. Manly, *Specimens of the Pre-Shakespearean Drama*, Vol. I, pp. 353–85. Also (modernized) in *EMP*.

25. Ed. R. L. Ramsay for EETS, 1908 (reprinted, 1958), pp. 27–8. On this play see Ch. VIII, nn. 56 and 57, p. 298 below. The same degree of pleasure in new clothes is displayed by Infans in *Mundus et Infans* (if more briefly) on being dubbed a knight:

*Psalm 80 : 13.
†See *EES*. ii(2), Plate VIII, No. 10, and G. Wickham, *The Medieval Theatre*, Plate 30.
‡ I.e. Italian craftsmen.

'I am ryall arayde to reven [dream] under the ryse [tree],
I am proudely aparelde in purpure and byse [grey],
As golde I glyster in gere.'

(ed. Manly, 11. 268–70)

26. On editions of this play see n. 16 above.
27. *The Tudor Interlude*, 1958, p. 75.
28. First printed 1538, it was reprinted and edited by A. Schroeer in *Anglia*, V (1882), and again for *Tudor Facsimile Texts*, 1908. See also J. S. Farmer, *The Dramatic Writings of John Bale*, 1907, pp. 1–82 (reprinted 1966), and Thora Blatt, *The Plays of John Bale*, Copenhagen, 1968.
29. Ed. G. Wickham, *English Moral Interludes*, 1976, pp. 127–42, ll. 73–5.
30. EETS (1952), p. 5, 11. 68–86, with punctuation modernized. On editions see Ch. IV, n. 12, p. 280 above.
31. For editions see n. 17 above.
32. This play survives in BM MS. Add. 26782. The most recent editions are Trevor Lennam's for *MSR*, 1971, and my own in *English Moral Interludes*, 1976, pp. 163–93.
33. Geoffrey Whitney, *Choice of Emblemes*, Leyden, 1586. For *Gismond of Salerne* see *MSR*, III, 2. 842; also pp. 248–51 above.
34. The play was first printed by S. Stafford, 1602, and was reprinted for *Tudor Facsimile Texts* in 1912 and for *MSR*, ed. W. W. Greg, 1913.
35. Sometimes known as *Mind, Will and Understanding*, the play survives in MS. among the Macro Plays, now in the Folger Library, Washington, D.C. This MS. was first edited and printed for EETS by F. J. Furnivall and A. W. Pollard, 1904, and re-edited by Mark Eccles and reissued in 1969. *Wisdom* is discussed in the latter, pp. xxvii-xxxvii, and the text is given on pp. 113–52; the excerpts quoted are taken from this edition.
36. First printed by J. Rastell, n. d., it was edited and reprinted by S. de Ricci for Huntington Facsimile Reprints, New York, 1920, in an edition restricted to 200 copies. It was also reprinted with a critical introduction by F. S. Boas and A. W. Reed in 1926, and by me in *English Moral Interludes*, 1976, pp. 37–101.
37. The play survives in MS. among the Macro Plays now in the Folger Library, Washington, D.C. The most recent editions are to be found in *The Macro Plays*, ed. Mark Eccles for EETS, pp. 153–84; *Folger Facsimiles: The Macro Plays*, 1972; and G. Wickham, *English Moral Interludes*, 1976, pp. 1–35.
38. For editions see n. 13 above.
39. This play survives in MS. (now in the Huntington Library, California) and is itself a copy, dated 20 November 1557. It was edited and printed by J. S. Farmer in *Six Anonymous Plays*, series 2, 1906, and again by R. W. Bond in *Early Plays from the Italian*, 1911; reprinted Benjamin Blom, New York, n.d.
40. *Damon and Pithias* was first printed by Richard Jones, 1571. The best modern edition is *MSR*, ed. F. P. Wilson, 1957.
41. *The Trial of Treasure* was first printed by Thomas Purfoot, 1567, and was reprinted by J.O. Halliwell, Percy Soc., 1842; by J. S. Farmer, *Anonymous Plays*, series 3, 1906, and again for *Tudor Facsimile Texts*, 1908. See also H-D III.
42. On the emblematic qualities of this play see Margot Heinemann, 'Middleton's *A Game at Chess*: Parliamentary-Puritans and Opposition Drama', *English Literary Renaissance*, V (no. 2), spring 1975, pp. 232–50.
43. The earliest use of this device of disfigurement known to me is that in *Wisdom* where Anima's appearance is described as 'fowlere þan a fende' (s. d. at l. 902, EETS ed.). There the cause, so Wisdom observes to Anima, is attributed directly to original sin.

'For ʒe be dysvyguryde by hys [i.e. Adam's] synne,
Ande dammyde to derknes from Godys syghte.'

(ll. 117–18)

44. This and the following quotations are given in my own text in *English Moral Interludes*, 1976, pp. 143–62. The play was first printed by J. King, 1560. It was reprinted in 1905 by J. S. Farmer in *The Dramatic Writings of Richard Wever and Thomas Ingelend*, and again for *Tudor Facsimile Texts*, 1909. It also appears in J. Manly, *Specimens of the Pre-Shakespearean Drama*, Vol. I, pp. 457–80.

45. First printed by R. Warde, 1584, and again in 1592. It was reprinted in 1911 for *Tudor Facsimile Texts*. The only other editions are that in Vol. VI of Hazlitt's *Dodsley* and J. P. Collier's in *Five Old Plays*, 1851.

46. The play was first printed by J. Rastell, n. d., *c.* 1527. It was reprinted for *MSR*, ed. Frank Sidgwick and W. W. Greg, 1908, and again for *Tudor Facsimile Texts*, 1909. The quotatious in the text are from *MSR* at ll. 399, 425–6, 612, 792 and 205–7 with spelling modernized.

47. In the Wakefield 'Buffeting', Primus Tortor observes:

'All men hym prase/both master and knave
Such wychcraft he mase'.

(EETS, ll. 102–3)

In the Chester 'Resurrection' Annas explains the soldiers' account of what transpired at the tomb to the angry Caiaphas and Pilate:

'this foolishe prophett, that we all to-rent,
through his witchcraft is stolen away.'

(EETS, ll. 296–7)

48. *Dives and Pauper*, ed. for EETS by Priscilla Heath Barnum, 1976, I, i, pp. 167 ff.; *Ludus Coventriae*, ed. for EETS by K. S. Block 1922 (reprinted 1960), 'The Council of the Jews', pp. 232–3. In 'Passion Play II' Jesus is charged both by Annas before Pilate and by the Second Jew before Herod with 'nygramancye' (*ed. cit.*, ll. 251 and 383, pp. 280 and 284).

49. For editions of this play see n. 16 above.

50. For editions of this play see n. 15 above.

51. For editions of *Apius and Virginia* see Ch. IX, n. 29, p. 306 below; for editions of *Nice Wanton* see n. 44 above.

52. For editions of *Liberality and Prodigality* see n. 34 above. Another play that assists in elevating the device of the trial scene to this degree of seriousness is George Peele's *The Arraignment of Paris, c.* 1581–3.

Chapter VI, pages 124–55. Device and Verbal Figuration

1. Strictly speaking blank verse was 'invented' by Surrey, late in the reign of Henry VIII, for epic, not dramatic, purposes, as an English equivalent to the Latin hexameter in his translation of the *Aeneid*, ii. and iv; but once available it could be borrowed and used to assist with declamatory rhetoric in the theatre.

2. See J. A. Mosher, *The Exemplum in the Early Religious and Didactic Literature of England*, New York, 1966.

3. See H. C. Maxwell Lyte, *A History of the University of Oxford*, 1886, pp. 23–30.

4. Letter 58, cited by F. S. Stevenson, *Robert Grosseteste, Bishop of Lincoln: A Contribution . . .*, 1899, p. 79.

5. *Handlyng Synne*, ed. F. J. Furnivall for EETS, 1901, p. 3, ll. 46–8.

6. *The English Works of Wycliffe*, ed. F. D. Matthews, 1888, Ch. 5, p. 16.
7. *Mirk's Festial*, ed. Theodor Erbe for EETS, 1905, pp. 7 and 67.
8. For Hick-Scorner's tale see Manly, *Specimens of the Pre-Shakespearean Drama*, Vol. I, pp. 386–420; for Thomas Lupton's *All for Money* see E. Vogel's edition in *Shakespeare Jahrbuch*, XI, 1904, pp. 177–9, and *EMP*, pp. 462–4.
9. *Jacob's Well*, ed. A. Brandeis for EETS, 1900.
10. See *LPME*, pp. 485–6:

> 'In England, indeed, where the golden age of vernacular religious drama coincides, so far as existing records suggest, with the golden age of vernacular preaching, the parallels between them are far too numerous and arresting to be mistaken for mere coincidences. Even when due allowance is made for the fact that both drew inevitably upon a common store of theological doctrine, there remain overwhelming similarities in the actual handling of the matter, the details of certain characters and topics, the very texture and language of the two classes of composition. The generic varieties of 'Miracle' and 'Morality' themselves suggest to us at the outset two general types of sacred discourse. On the one hand, we have the *Sermones super Evangelia* and *Sermones de Sanctis* concerned like the former with episodes in the lives of Christ and His Saints; on the other hand, moral discourses devoted like the latter to *Credo, Paternoster,* or Commandments, along with special emphasis upon the character of Vices and Virtues.'

> More recently Richard Axton has postulated that sermons must be regarded not only as a means to 'sterilize or consecrate a popular "play" form by giving it a religious significance', but also both as a means of allegorizing dance and game forms and as a prelude to a play: see 'Popular Modes in the Earliest Plays' in Stratford-upon-Avon Studies 16: *Medieval Drama*, ed. N. Denny, pp. 29–30.

11. See H. C. Maxwell Lyte, *op. cit.*, pp. 205–12.
12. Disputations did not end with the award of the bachelor's degree but played their part also in the skills required at more advanced level for the award of the master's and doctor's degrees at both Oxford and Cambridge: *ibid.*, pp. 211–25.
13. The text of *The Longer Thou Livest the More Fool Thou Art* was reprinted and edited by A. Brandl in *Shakespeare Jahrbuch*, XXXVI, 1900, and again for *Tudor Facsimile Texts* in 1910: also by R. M. Benbow, Lincoln, Nebr., 1967. At line 177 Discipline, despairing of Moros's childish ways, rounds on the audience and says:

> 'Let this ungracious and foolish person
> Bee as an Image of such bringing up,
> Like to be as unhappie a patron
> As ever dranke of any mans cup.'
>
> (ed. Brandl)

14. A particularly interesting play in this context is John Rastell's *The Four Elements* which centres on the author's interest in natural philosophy and cosmology. On this play see Bevington, *From Mankind to Marlowe*, pp. 45–7: for editions see Ch. V, n. 13, p. 282 above.
15. Ed. W. H. Fairholt as *Wit and Folly* for Percy Soc., 1846. Three of Heywood's plays have recently been issued as *Malone Society Reprints*, ed. G. R. Proudfoot: *Johan Johan*, 1972; *The Play of the Weather*, 1977; *A Play of Love*, 1978. The best version of *The Four PP* is to be found in Manly, *op. cit.*, Vol. I, pp. 488–522. For the texts of Heywood's plays see *The Dramatic Writings of John Heywood*, ed. J. S. Farmer, 1905; also *Tudor Facsimile Texts*, 1909. For comment see Ian Maxwell, *French Farce and John Heywood*, Melbourne and London, 1946.

16. For editions see Ch. VIII, n. 78, p. 301 below.
17. Although this early Elizabethan disputation is executed in Heywood's manner, the characterization is weak and the situations lack both wit and subtlety. Printed anonymously and without date, it was reprinted in 1907 by J. S. Farmer in '*Lost*' *Tudor Plays*, and also for *MSR*, ed. W. W. Greg and Percy Simpson.
18. First printed by J. King, 1560, *Impatient Poverty* was reprinted in 1907 by J. S. Farmer in '*Lost*' *Tudor Plays* and for *Tudor Facsimile Texts*, and by W. Bang, *Materialien*, XXXIII, 1911. See Ch. V, n. 17, p. 282 above.
19. For an extended discussion of these plays see pp. 76–8 and 97–8 above.
20. See Ch. VII, 'Practical Considerations', pp. 161–2 above. The quotation is given from my own edition in *English Moral Interludes*, pp. 78–9.
21. For the texts of *Gentleness and Nobility* see *The Writings of John Heywood*, ed. J. S. Farmer, 1908 (reprinted 1966), and *Tudor Facsimile Texts*, 1908. A modern edition was supplied by K. W. Cameron in *The Authorship and Sources of Gentleness and Nobility*, 1941. It was reprinted again for *MSR*, ed. A. C. Partridge and F. P. Wilson, 1950, with a critical commentary on the authorship controversy.
22. See n. 14 above, also Ch. V, n. 13, p. 282 above.
23. *Jocus* provides the root for the word 'joculator', and thus for 'jongleur' in medieval literature, by which time it had come to incorporate almost any form of entertainment that an individual performer could present on his own.
24. Ed. for EETS by Priscilla Heath Barnum, 1976, Comm. I, xxxix, pp. 167 ff. For an extended discussion of witchcraft in early English drama see pp. 118–19 above.
25. See Bernard Spivack, *Shakespeare and the Allegory of Evil*, New York, 1958; T. W. Craik, *The Tudor Interlude*, 1958; David Bevington, *From Mankind to Marlowe*, 1962. Also L. W. Cushman, *The Devil and the Vice in English Dramatic Literature before Shakespeare*, Halle, 1900.
26. For editions see n. 15 above. The quotations are given in Farmer's edition for ease of immediate comprehension.
27. For the full context of this phrase see *EES*.i.82–3, ad Sidney, *op. cit.*, ed. Arber, p. 33.
28. Ed. Manly, ll. 296–9; for other editions, see n. 8 above.
29. Wager expresses this danger in a memorable image of the Chariot of Adversity, depicting in words the pageant-wagon of a Petrarchian triumph:

> The Chariot of Covetouse as Barnard dooth write,
> On foure wheeles of vices is caried away:
> And these be the foure vices that he dooth resite,
> Contempt of God, forgetfulnes of death each day.
> Faint courage, and ungentlenes he dooth say.
> These be the wheeles that to adversityes cart dooth belong:
> These have persuasions to begile men many and strong.
> The same Chariot hath two horses which dooth it draw,
> The one named Raveny and the other nigardship:
> Their Carter is Desire to have, who alwaies dooth claw,
> By fraude or guile one an other to nip,
> This Carter hath two cordes to his Whip.
> The one Appitite and felicite for to get:
> The other is called Dread and fear to forlet.
>   (ed. S. de Ricci, sig. Civ)

See also Plates VIII and IX.
30. This play was edited and reprinted three times in 1907: by J. S. Farmer for *Tudor*

Facsimile Texts and in '*Lost*' *Tudor Plays*; and by W. W. Greg for *MSR*. The passage quoted is from *MSR*, sigs AiijB and Aiv, ll. 102–33. The image was still lively enough a hundred years later for Bunyan to use in *The Pilgrim's Progress*.

31. Ed. F. I. Carpenter, Decennial Publications, Second Series, Vol. I, Chicago, 1904. Cf. Discipline's lament in William Wager's *The Longer thou Livest* at line 1011:

> Two thinges destroye youth at this day:
> *Indulgentia parentum*, the fondness of parents
> Which will not correct there noughty way,
> But rather enbolden them in there entents;
> Idleness, alas, Idleness is an other.
>
> (ed. A. Brandl, *Shakespeare Jahrbuch*, XXXVI, 1900)

32. In both plays the moral, 'spare the rod and spoil the child', is conveyed in the epilogue.

33. Ed. Ernst Rühl, *Shakespeare Jahrbuch*, XLIII, 1906–7; also in *EMP*.

34. The actual revenge is no less carefully balanced in terms of visual figuration, the device employed (the arbour) being the reverse of that used in the Digby *Play of St Mary Magdalene* to contrast her corruption with her redemption: see p. 85 above.

35. *MSR*, ed. Arthur Brown, W. W. Greg and F. P. Wilson, 1951, pp. 18–22. In this instance I have modernized the spelling and punctuation for the sake of clarity.

36. Ed. W. W. Greg for EETS, 1952, I. iv, pp. 12–15.

37. *MSR*, ed. Trevor N. S. Lennam, 1966 (1971), pp. 40–2. Again I have here modernized the spelling and punctuation for the sake of greater clarity. For editions of *The Trial of Treasure*, see Ch. V, n. 41 above.

38. In the former play the Vice, Infidelity, seduces Mary verbally before leading her to Jerusalem.

> *Inf.* Mistresse Mary, can you not play on *the* virginals?
> *Mary* Yes, swete heart, that I can, and also on the regals,
>   There is no instrument but that I handle can,
>   I thynke as well as any gentlewoman.
> *Inf.* If that you can play upon the recorder,
>   I have as fayre a one as any in this border.
>   Truely, you have not sene a more goodlie pipe;
>   It is so bigge that your hand can it not gripe.
>
> (Ist ed., sig. Diii; ed. Carpenter, ll. 734–41)

In *Mother Bombie* Lyly's device is to wring humour out of the precociousness of his boy-actors' bland statements about the art of love which, in terms of their age, they can neither have experienced nor fully understood. It is clear from Wager's *Marie Magdalene* (1. 719) that 'Mother bee' was itself a colloquial name for a bawd or brothel-keeper.

39. See William L. Smoldon, 'The Melodies of the Medieval Church Dramas and their Significance' in *Medieval English Drama: Essays Critical and Contextual*, ed. Jerome Taylor and Alan H. Nelson, Chicago, 1972, pp. 64–80. Discussing Karl Young's work, he says (pp. 64–5):

> 'What has been forgotten by the 'literary' writers on the subject is that the works that they are considering are not just dramas (relying on text and *spoken* delivery alone to bring about their effects), but *music*-dramas, in which every word is sung, and where the effects of the dramatic texts are often enough considerably enhanced by the vocal melodies given to them. The techniques of this vocal music are far subtler than is commonly supposed.'

40. Ed. K. S. Block for EETS, 1922 (reprinted 1960), p. 17.
41. *DMC*.i.350.
42. *The Chester Play of Antichrist*, ed. W. W. Greg, 1935, p. 69 (Devonshire MS. at l. 726). The Peniarth MS. Stage direction differs slightly: 'Tunc ibit angelus adducans ennock et helyam ad celum cantans Gaudete iusti in domino' (p. 68).
43. *DMC*.i.503 ff.
44. See Howard Mayer Brown, 'Musicians in the Mystères and Miracles' in *Medieval English Drama*, pp. 81–97; also 'Notes on the Music in the Shrewsbury Liturgical Plays' in *Non-Cycle Plays and Fragments*, ed. Norman Davis for EETS, 1970, pp. 124–33; and J. Stevens, 'Music in Medieval Drama', in *Proceedings of the Musical Association*, 84th Session, 1957–8, and 'Music in Some Early Medieval Plays' in *Studies in the Arts*, ed. Francis Warner, 1958.
45. Ed. Mark Eccles for EETS, *Macro Plays*, 1969, pp. 113–52. The music prescribed throughout this play is so elaborate as to suggest a sophisticated, collegiate provenance.
46. *Ibid.*, pp. 153–84, ll. 331–43.
47. See G. Wickham, *English Moral Interludes*, p. 88.
48. *Ed. cit.*, p. 156, l. 72.
49. For editions see Ch. V, n. 13 above; for this stage direction see Farmer, *Six Anonymous Plays*, p. 41: 1st ed., sig. Eivb
50. See Happé, p. 328 at l. 176; H-D III, p. 315; Farmer, p. 10.
51. See T. W. Craik, *The Tudor Interlude*, pp. 42 and 45–8.
52. *John Philip's Patient Grisell*, ed. W. W. Greg and R. B. Mckerrow for *MSR*, 1909.
53. See Lynette R. Muir, 'Adam', *Proceedings of the Leeds Philosophical and Literary Society: Literary and Historical Section*, Vol. XIII, Part V, January 1970, p. 183.
54. For this and the following quotations see *The Digby Plays*, ed. F. J. Furnivall for EETS, 1896, pp. 43–6. On the staging of this play, however, see the introduction to my edition in *English Moral Interludes*, pp. 103–6.
55. Ed. K. S. Block for EETS, 1922 (reprinted 1960), p. 176, ll. 231–2.

Chapter VII, pages 156–70. Practical Considerations

1. See *European Drama of the Early Middle Ages*, 1974, and 'Popular Modes in the Earliest Plays' in Stratford-upon-Avon Studies 16: *Medieval Drama*, ed. Neville Denny, 1973, pp. 13–39.
2. As far as I am aware no serious study has yet been made of these shifts in Christian outlook as they affected the drama. Various aspects of the subject have been tackled from time to time starting with G. R. Owst's *Literature and Pulpit in Mediaeval England*, 1933. H. C. Gardiner's *Mysteries' End*, 1946, was no less influential in establishing the effects of the Lutheran Reformation on drama of Roman Catholic origin than Owst's work has been in evaluating the influence of the Dominican and Franciscan preachers on the development of vernacular drama. Rainer Pineas's *Tudor and Early Stuart Anti-Catholic Drama*, 1972, has advanced the work begun by Gardiner still further. As yet, however, no one has tackled the specifically Calvinist influences at work on the drama in the latter half of the sixteenth century in any systematic way. My own attempts in the course of this book—notably in this chapter and its two sequels—are those of an amateur, and in any case do not pretend to take the matter at all thoroughly beyond the end of the reign of Elizabeth I.
3. See *Med. Stage*.ii.102–3: see also n. 4 below.

4. Ed. W. C. Hazlitt, *The English Drama and Stage under the Tudor and Stuart Princes, 1543–1664*, 1869 (reprinted, n. d.), pp. 73–95. Arguing that Christ's miracles were actual and effective, the author goes on to complain that re-enactment merely brings them into contempt (p. 74):

> He errith in the bileve, for in that he takith the most precious werkis of God in pley and bourde, and so takith his name in idil, and so mysusith oure bileve. A! Lord! Syther an erthely servaunt dar not taken in pley and in bourde that that her erthely lord takith in ernest, myche more we shulden not maken oure pleye and bourde of the myraclis and werkis that God so ernestfully wrouȝt to us; for sothely whan we so done, drede to synne is taken away, as a servaunt when he bourdith with his mayster leesith his drede to offendyn hym, namely, whanne he bourdith with his mayster in that and that his mayster takith in earnest.

5. A company of four actors and a boy did not exclude the employment of super-numeraries, whether local amateurs or paid 'hirelings'. Medwall's minstrels and mummers in II *Fulgens and Lucres* offer an example. They make one appearance only; it is not critical to the argument, and is treated farcically. If it cannot be cut, it can easily be tailored to suit the talent and resources available. *The Four Elements* states on its title-page that a disguising may be added 'yf ye list'.

6. See R. L. Ramsay's long introduction to his edition of *Magnyfycence* for EETS, 1908, pp. ix–cxcvii, an astonishingly original and perceptive piece of criticism for its date, not only of that play, but of Tudor interludes in general.

7. The best modern reprint is in Manly, *Specimens of the Pre-Shakespearean Drama*, 1897, Vol. I, pp. 353–85; it was also reprinted by J. S. Farmer in *Six Anonymous Plays*, series 1, 1905 (reprinted 1966), and for *Tudor Facsimile Texts*, 1909. The play was first printed by Wynkyn de Worde, 1522. It is also included in *EMP*.

8. Gayley, *Representative English Comedies*, Introduction, p. lvii: Bevington, *From Mankind to Marlowe*, p. 117. See also Ramsay, *op. cit.*, pp. clxxiii ff., and T. W. Craik, *The Tudor Interlude*, pp. 80–3.

9. For editions other than Ramsay's see Ch. VIII, nn. 56–7 below.

10. Ramsay, *op.cit.*, pp. xlviii–xlix.

11. On *Three Lawes* see T. W. Craik, *op. cit.*, pp. 73–5; Thora Blatt, *The Plays of John Bale*, pp. 65–86 and 133–48; and Brian Crow, 'The Development of the Presentation of Human Actions . . . ', pp. 117–225.

12. See L. B. Campbell, *Scenes and Machines on the English Stage*, pp. 73–115; also G. Wickham, *Shakespeare's Dramatic Heritage*, pp. 67–83, and *EES*.ii(1). 83–6.

13. This technique is akin to that of 'N-Town' in respect of the *Ludus Coventriae* pro-clamation. The actors can simply switch the named localities to those most appropriate in any other city in which they wish to present the play. *Mankind*, as a play of provincial origin, can be similarly handled where the names of villages and local worthies are concerned. By contrast, *Everyman* is wholly generalized and can be played anywhere without altering a word of the text; but, what it gains on that account, it loses in terms of the sense of proximity and topicality supplied by the device of name-dropping.

14. On hall screens and their uses see Richard Hosley, 'The Origins of the Shake-spearean Playhouse', *Shakespeare Quarterly*, XV, no. 2 (spring 1964), pp. 29–39. On Hans Holbein's contributions to the revels at Court under Henry VIII see S. Anglo, *Spectacle, Pageantry and Early Tudor Policy*, pp. 215, 218–19, and 250; also *EES*.ii(2), Appendix B.

15. On the use of musician-actors in *Wit and Science* see T. W. Craik, *op. cit.*, pp. 47–8.

16. Ramsay (*op. cit.*, p. cxxviii), citing Chambers, *Med. Stage*.ii.201, notes that Henry VIII is reputed to have been so bored by Medwall's *Finding of Truth* at Christmas, 1513, that he rose and 'departyd to hys chambre'. As Chambers's source is Collier (i. 69), and as no text survives, this statement must be viewed with some suspicion, more especially since Medwall shows himself to be so sensitive in II *Fulgens and Lucres* to this very danger: this passage is quoted on pp. 139–40 above.

17. See 'English Saints' Plays', pp. 72–3; see also Stanley J. Kahrl, *Traditions of Medieval English Drama*, 1975, 'Of History and Time', pp. 121–35.

18. On Bale's 'cycle' see Thora Blatt, *op. cit.*, pp. 86–99 and 149–52: on other Protestant interludes see Rainer Pineas, *op. cit.*, pp. 6–8.

19. Ed. Arber, English Reprints, 1868, p. 41. On Gosson's retreat from the position of an active professional play-maker, first to that of a doubter, and finally to that of an outright opponent, see Arthur F. Kinney, *Markets of Bawdrie: The Dramatic Criticism of Stephen Gosson*, 1974 (Salzburg Studies in English, IV).

Chapter VIII, pages 173–218. Comedy

1. Sidney's comments on the true nature of comedy and tragedy—provoked by those which Stephen Gosson had printed in *The Schoole of Abuse* (Stationers' Register, July 1579), and dedicated to Sidney without first obtaining his permission, and then carried further in his *Apology* (Stationers' Register, November 1579)—first appeared in print in 1595 in *The Defense of Poesie* nine years after his death, although probably circulated in MS. in 1583. Ben Jonson included his comments in the prologues and dedicatory epistles to *Everyman In His Humour*, *Volpone* and *Catiline*, all of which appeared in print for the first time in the first folio of 1616.

    Writing of comedy, Sidney observed:

    'Perchance it is the Comick, whom naughtie Play-makers and Stage-keepers, have justly made odious. To the argument of abuse, I will answer after. Onely thus much now is to be said, that the Comedy is an imitation of the common errors of our life, which he representeth, in the most ridiculous and scornefull sort that may be ... So that the right use of Comedy will (I thinke) by no body be blamed.'

    Later he adds, 'Our Comedians thinke there is no delight without laughter .... Delight hath a joy in it, either permanent, or present. Laughter, hath onely a scorneful tickling' (pp. 44–5 and 65–6).

2. Serlio's comments on scenography were first published in 1545 in the second book of his *Architettura*, an English translation of which appeared in 1611. This book was devoted to the art of perspective and contained his three prototype drawings of 'Comicall', 'Tragicall' and 'Satiricall' scenes. Speaking of the first he says that 'the Houses must be made as if they were for common or ordinarie people'. They must be suitable for citizens, 'but specially there must not want a brawthall or bawdy house, and a great Inn, and a Church; such things of necessity to be therein'. For reproductions of these illustrations see L. B. Campbell, *Scenes and Machines on the English Stage during the Renaissance*, 1923, pp. 36–8 (reprinted 1961); and *ES*.iv. 359–62; also *EES*.ii(1), Plate XXX, No. 44.

3. See G. Wickham, 'The Romanesque Style in Medieval Drama', *Tenth Century Studies*, ed. D. Parsons, 1976, pp. 115–22, and *The Medieval Theatre*, 1974, pp. 35–43. Lydgate confirms this attribution and its lineage in his 'Order of Fools' (1460):

Chyffe of folis, men yn bokys redythe,
Able yn hys foly to holde residence,
Ys he that nowther god lovethe nor dredethe.

Ed. F. J. Furnivall for EETS, 1869, pp. 79–84, ll. 9–11, in *Queene Elizabethes Achademy* (Sir Humphrey Gilbert).

4. For Gerhoh of Reichersberg's scathing comments on Herod as handled by the monks of Augsburg, *c.* 1120, see *Med. Stage*.ii.98, n. 4; for Belshazzar and the Evil Counsellors in *Ludus Danielis* see *DMC*.ii.290–303, and *The Play of Daniel*, ed. Noah Greenberg for OUP, 1959, pp. 20–7, 60–8 and 79–85; see also n. 6 below.

5. The text is given in *DMC*.ii.371–87. For comment see *Med. Stage*.ii.64; also Richard Axton, *European Drama of the Early Middle Ages*, 1974, pp. 88–94. A complete translation was published by J. Wright, *The Play of Anti-Christ*, Toronto, 1967. See also Ch. II, pp. 46–7 above.

6. Christian M. Engelhardt, *Herrad von Landsperg*, Stuttgart and Tübingen, 1818, p. 104:

> Wohl mögen [sagt sie], die alten Väter der kirche, um die Gläubigen in ihrem Glauben zu stärken, und die Ungläubigen durch die Art des Gottesdienstes anzulocken, auf den Drei-Königstag oder die Octave, jene Art religioser Vorstellungen, wie der Stern die Magier zum Christuskinde leitet, von Herodes Grausamkeit, der Absendung seiner Kriegsleute, von dem Wochenbette der heiligen Jungfrau, von der Ermahnung des Engels an die Magier, nicht zu Herodes zurück zu kehren, und andere Begebenheiten der Geburt Christi angeordnet haben. Was geschieht aber heute in manchen Kirchen? Nicht eine hergebrachte Religionsform (*non religiosa formula*), nicht eine Handlung der Verehrung, sondern der Irreligion und Ausschweifung wird mit jugendlicher Zügellosigkeit vollbracht. Die Geistlichen, mit umgetauschten Kleidern, ziehen als ein Trupp Krieger heran. Zwischen den Priestern und den Kriegsleuten ist kein Unterschied zu sehen. In unordentlicher Zusammenkunft Geistlicher und Weltlicher wird das Gotteshaus durch Fressen und Saufen, Possenreissen, unziemlichen Scherz, offenes Spiel, durch Waffengeklirr, durch die Gegenwart frecher Dirnen, durch der Welt Eitelkeit und Unordnung jeder Art entweiht. Nie geht die Versammlung ohne Streit auseinander, und hätte sie auch noch so friedlich begonnen...

See also n. 5 above. No less ambiguous are some of the stage-directions in the Benediktbeuren Christmas play where, for example, Archisynagogus becomes, in Karl Young's words, 'aggressively obstreperous, striking his companions, shaking his head, stamping his feet, acting like a Jew generally [imitando gestus Judaei in omnibus] and ridiculing the prophecies concerning the birth of a child from a virgin.' Augustine, by contrast, is required in the rubric to speak 'voce sobria et discreta' [in a self possessed and controlled tone of voice]. *DMC*.ii.175ff.

7. For the text see *DMC*.ii.219–24.

8. *Ibid.*, ii.290–306.

9. *Ibid.*, ii.371–96. See also n. 5 above and Peter Munz, *Frederick Barbarossa: A Study in Medieval Politics*, Ithaca, N.Y., and London, 1969, and Frederick Heer, *The Holy Roman Empire*, trans. Janet Sondheimer, London, 1968. See also Ch. II, pp. 46–7 above, and Plate III, No. 5.

10. For the text itself see Paul Studer, *Le Mystére d' Adam, an Anglo-Norman Drama of the Twelfth Century*, Manchester, 1928; also Lynette R. Muir, 'Adam: A Twelfth-century Play Translated from the Norman-French with an Introduction and Notes', *Proceedings of the Leeds Philosophical and Literary Society; Literary and Historical Section*, Vol. XIII, Pt V, January 1970, 149–204. For comment see

Med. Stage.ii.70–1 and 80–2; Axton, *op. cit.*, pp. 112–30; Grace Frank, *MFD*, pp. 76–87 and 90–2; also the neglected but important chapter devoted to this play by Oscar Cargill in *Drama and Liturgy*, New York, 1930, pp. 93–104: and Karl Young's comments on it, *DMC*.i. 542. See also Ch. II, pp. 36–9 above.

11. This view was not original. It had been formulated as early as 1263 by Bernard de Bettone in his *glossa ordinaria* to the decretal of Pope Innocent III of 1207 in which he credits that pope with commending genuine liturgical plays. See *Med. Stage*.ii. 100, n. 2; also the Abbess of Hohenburg's remarks quoted in the text, p. 176 above.

12. Ed. for EETS by F. J. Furnivall, 1901. The parallel Anglo-Norman text of William of Wadington's *Manuel de Péché* is given opposite. This supplies some specific and significant histrionic details of a supplementary character. These include the use of face-masks: 'Lur faces unt la deguise/Par visers, li forsené', and notice that plays in streets and churchyards are presented 'apres mangers/Quant venent led fols volunters'. See pp. 154–5.

13. 'As might be expected, this author is a *scholaris vagans*, by name Hilarius. It would even be doing him no great injustice to call him a goliard.' *Med. Stage*.ii.57–8.

14. See *DMC*.ii.211. Another Latin play of about the same date, but of Austrian provenance, is the *Ordo de Ysaac et Rebecca et Filius Eorum Recitandus*: this too provides substantial realistic detail in its rubrics but, as Young observes, 'bears no evidence of attachment to the liturgy'. See *DMC*.ii.264. For comment see Cargill, *op. cit.*, pp. 72–92; Axton, *op. cit.*, pp. 77–83; Frank, *MFD*, pp. 37–9; and *Med. Stage*. i, Chs XIII-XV. Also Ch. II, pp. 35ff. above.

15. For these texts see *DMC*.ii.199–208 and 219–22. A parallel example to that of Hilarius in drama is provided in music by Guillaume de Machaut who was both priest and poet as well as composer. Born in Champagne *c*. 1300, Machaut was ordained in 1323 and died as a canon of Rheims in 1377. Besides composing a Mass and a number of sacred motets he was the author of a large repertory of love-songs and secular, instrumental pieces.

16. On dates and associated customs see *DMC*.i.104 ff. and *Med. Stage*.i.274 ff. Young, with the benefit of Chambers's exhaustive, hundred-page discussion of both feasts, and in the light of his own researches, summed up his own conclusions tersely: 'The Feast of Fools, then, can scarcely be said to occupy a very significant place in dramatic history. Its activities have to do with licensed mis-behaviour rather than with theatrical representation' (*DMC*.i.105). I agree with him; but the point I think he missed is that the facts surrounding its celebration and popularity indicate more clearly than anything else whence the pressures to develop drama in directions other than liturgical offices were arising. See pp. 180–1 and n. 15 above.

17. One strong reason for the lack of formal, liturgical sanction is the fact that the greater part of both feasts took the form of processions, visitations and banquets *outside* of both church precincts and the times prescribed for the normal liturgical offices.

18. The first surviving complaints and demands for reforms are those from the Cardinal of Capua, Papal Legate in France, to the Bishop of Paris (1199) and from Pope Innocent III (1207) to the archbishops and bishops of Poland. The latter was to become a datum point for subsequent critics and reformers (see n. 11 above) and is quoted by Chambers in *Med. Stage*.i.279, n. 1, in Latin: I give it in translation here.

Sometimes stage-plays are presented inside churches, and not only are horrible masks paraded there in spectacles of coarse buffoonery, but also in the three Calendar Festivals which follow immediately after that of Christ's Nativity, deacons, presbyters and sub-deacons in turn practise their grotesque mockeries and, by the obscene exhibitions of their gestures in the sight of the people, degrade the high standing of the clergy . . .

We command your brotherhood to make every effort to root out the afore-mentioned practice—or rather corruption—of coarse shows from your churches.

In England, Bishop Grosseteste of Lincoln was particularly active in the thirteenth century in his efforts to maintain discipline. The special object of his concern was the Feast of Fools which figures both in his *Statutes* and (twice) in his diocesan letters.

1. *Statutes*: Whereas in the same visitation it was reported in our presence by certain persons worthy of belief that vicars and clerks of the church itself dress up in lay clothing on the day of the Circumcision of Our Lord, and by their rowdiness, general tom-foolery, chatter and jokes (a custom which is widely and generally known as the Feast of Fools) in various ways frequently delay the celebration of the Divine Office, by the authority of these presents, we forbid unequivocally both present and future vicars from presuming to do such things; we also forbid the same vicars or any other ministers whatsoever of the church from engaging in public drinkings or any other indignities whatsoever in the church, which is the house of prayer, against the honour of the same.

(ii.247)

2. *Letters*: We command and strongly enjoin you by virtue of your obedience that as regards the Feast of Fools which is replete with vanity and soiled with sensuality, hateful to God yet acceptable to devils, you absolutely forbid it to be held in future on the Feastday of the Holy Circumcision of Our Lord in the Church (? Cathedral) at Lincoln. (translated from *Letters and Treatises*, ed. H. R. Luard, 1861, pp. 118–19)

We forbid completely, in virtue of the specific authority of an Apostolic Rescript that execrable practice which it is customary to observe in several churches of celebrating a Feast of Fools lest the house of prayer become a house of wanton games and the anguish of the Circumcision of Our Lord be derided by mockeries and lasciviousness.

(*ibid.*, p. 161)

19. See *Med. Stage*.i.292–4; also Helen Waddell, *The Wandering Scholars*, Ch. VI. As the latter observes (pp. 128–9),

the typical scholar of mid-century Paris is not John of Salisbury, grave, sardonic, remote, nor yet young Peter of Denmark, studying theology in St Geneviève, who falls ill of a quartan ague, and is sent home in the hope that his native air may restore him . . . but the Englishman, Serlon of Witton, whose brilliant and dissolute figure was as famous in his own generation as his spectacular conversion in the University sermons of the next.

20. See *Concilia Magnae Britanniae et Hiberniae, 446–1717*, ed. David Wilkins, 4 vols, 1737, Vol. III, p. 860. This decree arose out of the 'Act made for the abrogation of certain holy days' of 1536 (*op. cit.*, Vol. III, pp. 823–4) and the letter from the King to the bishops drawing their attention to the Act (*ibid.*, p. 824). The decree

purports to restore three of the cancelled holidays, but serves also to take away many more.

21. For translation and reference see n. 18 above.
22. See 17 above. It is in these locations from the fifteenth century onwards that we encounter the Lord of Misrule, or Christmas Lord. Henry VII and Henry VIII paid theirs substantial sums; see S. Anglo, 'The Court of Entertainments of Henry VII', *Bulletin of the John Rylands Library, Manchester*, XXXXIII (September 1960), no. 1, and *EES*.i.216–17. At the Inns of Court a *magister jocorum* was appointed from 1505 onwards, and probably earlier; see A. Wigfall Green, *The Inns of Court and Early English Drama*, New Haven, Conn., 1931, pp. 11–12.
23. G. R. Owst insists that the attack on feudal pride and avarice was generated by the preachers. Summing up his argument he says:

> At all events it is reasonable to believe that, without this age-long exposure and scorn from the pulpits, fomenting a general spirit of hatred and distrust, accustoming men's ears to unrestrained criticism of the privileged orders, the Tudor monarchs would never have accomplished so easily what they did in both Church and State.
>
> (*LPME*, pp. 289–90).

24. It is to be noted that this word *honestus* which is coupled so frequently with *inhonestus* in complaints about the Feast of Fools is that chosen by Martin Bucer to describe legitimate drama in a Protestant society, *c.* 1550. See *EES*.ii(1), Appendix C, and pp. 206–7 above.
25. C. Magnin, *Les Origines du théâtre moderne*, Paris, 1838, and M. Sepet, *Origines catholiques du théâtre moderne*, Paris, 1901.
26. *Med. Stage*.ii.78–88.
27. See Hardin Craig, *English Religious Drama*, 1955, pp. 88–114, and A. P. Rossiter, *English Drama from Early Times to the Elizabethans*, 1950, pp. 53–9.
28. See V. A. Kolve, *The Play Called Corpus Christi*, Stanford, Calif., 1966, pp. 33–56, and G. Wickham, *The Medieval Theatre*, 1974, pp. 43–94.
29. See *LPME*, pp. 480–2 and 488.
30. *Ibid.*, pp. 292–3 and 308 ff.
31. See Helen Waddell, *The Wandering Scholars*, 1927 and H. C. Maxwell Lyte, *A History of the University of Oxford*, 1886, pp. 97–8 and 132–3; see also G. M. Trevelyan, *English Social History*, pp. 48–55.
32. By Crist of heuene and Sant Jone!
    Clerc of scole ne kep I none,
    For many god wymman haf þai don scam.
    By Crist, þu michtis haf be at hame!
    (ll. 27–30)

See G. Wickham, *English Moral Interludes*, 1976, pp. 195–203 for full text with translation and critical commentary. See also Richard Axton's analysis of this fragment in 'Popular Modes in the Earliest Plays' in Stratford-upon-Avon Studies 16: *Medieval Drama*, ed. N. Denny, pp. 16–19.
33. *Garçon et l' Aveugle*, ed. Mario Roques, CFMA, 5, Paris, 1921.
34. See Georges Lecoq, *Histoire du théâtre en Picardie*, Paris, 1880 (reprinted by Slatkine, Geneva, 1971), 2nd part, 'Allégories—Farces et Moralités—Spectacles Populaires', pp. 125–61; also Grace Frank, *MFD*, pp. 95–105, 211–16, and 225–36.
35. *Courtois d'Arras*, ed. Edmond Faral, CFMA, 3, Paris, 1922; *Jeu de la Feuillée*, ed. Ernest Langlois, CFMA, 6, Paris, 1923; *Jeu de Robin et Marion*, ed. Ernest Langlois.

CFMA, 36, Paris, 1924. On early anticlerical and anti-bourgeois satire see *Med. Stage* and Appendix C, pp. 264–6 above.

36. On the ridicule which Bromyard poured in his sermons on feudal pride in noble birth and parentage see Owst, *LPME*, pp. 292–3; on his attitude to kings, judges and merchants see pp. 300–8 and 311. See also J. A. Mosher, *The Exemplum in the Early Religious and Didactic Literature of England*, New York, 1966.

37. See L. Toulmin-Smith, *English Guilds*, ed. for EETS, 1870; G. Cohen, *Histoire de la mise en scène dans le théâtre religieux français du Moyen Age*, Paris, 1926, pp. 164–205; G. R. Kernodle, *From Art to Theatre*, 1943, pp. 111–29; and N. D. Shergold, *A History of the Spanish Stage*, 1967, pp. 113–76. For an English play specifically attacking the leatherworkers at Exeter in 1352 see Appendix C, above.

38. See G. Unwin, *The Guilds and Companies of London*, 1908; J. Klein, *The Mesta: A Study of Spanish Economic History, 1273–1836*, Cambridge Mass., 1920; C. Gross, *The Gild Merchant*, 1890; H. Pirenne, *Mediaeval Cities, their Origin and the Revival of Trade*, trans. H. P. Halsey, 1925; F. A. Gasquet, *Parish Life in Medieval England*, 1906; and Alice S. Green, *Town Life in the 15th Century*, 2 vols, 1894.

39. The satire in the sermons, as Owst has demonstrated, was directed at the professional classes who exploited the poor and needy. 'The lower orders of society are entirely at the mercy of a class of trained and educated specialists who take full advantage of their superior equipment in a highly technical field' (*LPME*, p. 341). One way of retaliating against these foxes in society was to liken their behaviour and motives to those of Christ's enemies in his own lifetime. As Bromyard observes of knights: 'they rise up against their fellow Christians, rage violently against the Patrimony of Christians, plunder and spoil the poor subject to them, afflict the wretched pitiably and pitilessly, and fulfil their extravagant wills and lusts'; or, as Langland observes of lawyers, 'Lawe is to lorlich, and loth to maken eende withouten presentes or pous' (*Piers Plowman*, A Text, pass. iii. ll. 156 f.). Indeed, so widespread is the sin of avarice among the professional classes that money may be said to make 'the deaf hear, the dumb speak and the blind see'. See also *Ayenbite of Inwyt*, ed. Rev. R. Morris for EETS, 1866, pp. 34–46, 'þet vifte Heaved of þe Beste' (i.e. avarice), and *Old English Homilies*, ed. Rev. R. Morris for EETS, 1873, from Trin. Coll. Camb. MS. B. 14. 52. The familiar Wyclifite 'Tretise of miraclis pleyinge' denouncing both plays and actors of them (EM. MS. Add. 24202, fo. 14) is printed in W. C. Hazlitt's *The English Drama and Stage under the Tudor and Stuart Princes, 1543–1664*, Roxburghe Library, 1869; reprinted, n. d. Burt Franklin, New York; a less familiar denunciation is that of an anonymous preacher who attacks audiences for supporting 'ydel pleyes and japes'; see n. 40 below.

40. A fifteenth-century preacher, indicting the lower orders of society, condemns them for their addiction to 'ydel pleyes and japes, carolinges, makynge of fool contynaunces, to ʒeve ʒiftes to iogeloures ... for þer ydel tales and japes ... in wrastlynge, in other dedes of strength doynge' BM MS. Harl. 45, fo. 58. Cf. *Jacob's Well*, ed. Arthur Brandeis for EETS, 1900, pp. 294–6, also Owst, *LPME*, p. 362.

41. See Nevill Coghill, 'The Basis of Shakespearean Comedy', *Essays and Studies*, ed. G. Rostrevor Hamilton, 1950.

42. See M. D. Anderson, *Drama and Imagery in English Medieval Churches*, 1963, and Clifford Davidson, *Drama and Art*, Kalamazoo, Mich., 1977. Irena Janicka provides some particularly apt illustrations of the way in which the visual arts parallel literary treatment of devils and vice versa in *The Comic Elements in the English Mystery Plays Against the Cultural Background (Particularly Art)*, Poznan, 1962; see also Robert Hughes, *Heaven and Hell in Western Art*, 1968.

43. For the complete text with a critical introduction see G. Wickham, *English Moral Interludes*, 1976, pp. 196–8 and 204–9.

44. *Ibid.*, pp. v-xvi.
45. For a full list of titles, editions, and approximate dates, see Ian Maxwell, *French Farce and John Heywood*, 1946, pp. 123–34; see also Grace Frank, *MFD*, pp. 243–64.
46. *The Chester Plays*, ed. H. Deimling for EETS, 1893, p. 28, ll. 189–208:

> *Serpens* Disguise me I will anon tyte
> and profer her of that ilke fruit:
> so shall they both for ther delight
> be banished from the blisse.
>
> A manner of an Adder is in this place,
> that wynges like a byrd she hase,
> feete as an Adder, a maydens face;
> her kinde will I take.
>
> And of that tree of Paradice
> she shall eate through my coyntice;
> for women are full liccoris,
> that she will not forsake.
>
> And eate she of it full witterly,
> they shall fare bothe, as did I,
> be banished bouth of that vallye
> and their offspring for aye.
>
> Therefore, as brocke I my pane,
> my adders coate I will put on,
> and into paradice will I gone,
> as fast as ever I may.
> (Versus: Spinx Volucris penna,
> serpens pede, fronte puella)

The Norwich Grocers' Play, B Text, *Non-Cycle Plays and Fragments*, ed. for EETS by Norman Davis, 1970, p. 14, ll. 41–3:

> 'With hyr [Eve] for to dyscemble, I fear yt nott at all,
> Butt that unto my haight some waye I shall hyr call.
> Oh lady of felicite, beholde my voyce so small!'

See also L. W. Cushman 'The Devil and the Vice in the English Dramatic Literature before Shakespeare', *Studien zur Englischen Philologie*, ed. L. Morsbach, Vol. VI, Halle, 1900, pp. 1–5 and 23.
47. See John B. Moore, *The Comic and the Realistic in English Drama*, Chicago, 1925, and Cushman, *op. cit.*, pp. 5–6 and 29: also Mark Pilkinton, 'The Antagonists of English Drama, 1370–1576', Ph.D. thesis, University of Bristol, 1974, pp. 24–57.
48. See *The Chester Plays*, *ed. cit.*, pp. 217–29 and 318–31; *Towneley Plays*, ed. George England and A. W. Pollard for EETS, 1897 (reprinted 1966), pp. 293–305; *Ludus Coventriae*, ed. K. S. Block for EETS, 1922 (reprinted 1960), pp. 193–200; see also Irena Janicka, *op. cit.*, pp. 59–70, and G. Wickham, 'Hell Castle and its Door Keeper' in *Shakespeare's Dramatic Heritage*, 1969, pp. 214–24. For visual depictions see R. Hughes, *Heaven and Hell in Western Art*; also *EES*.i, Plate XXXII, no. 52. See also Rosemary Woolf, 'The Theme of Christ the Lover-Knight in Medieval English Literature', *Review of English Studies*, n. s. XIII (1962), pp. 1–16; and Wilbur Gaffney, 'The Allegory of the Christ Knight in Piers Plowman', *PMLA*, XLVI (1931), pp. 155–68.
49. *Towneley ed. cit.*, pp. 116–40; see also John B. Moore, *op. cit.*, pp. 4–6 and 28 ff.;

and Arnold Williams, 'The Comic in the Cycles' in Stratford-upon-Avon Studies, 16: *Medieval Drama*, ed. N. Denny, pp. 109–23.

50. *Ludus Coventriae, ed. cit.*, pp. 200–9; *Towneley Plays, ed. cit.*, pp. 228–78.

51. See G. Wickham, *English Moral Interludes*, 1976, pp. 1–9. This interpretation was used with convincing results by Poculi Ludique Societas, Toronto, in their production of *Mankind* for the meeting of the Medieval Academy of America in Toronto in May 1977, and again by the Oxford Guisers at the Playhouse, Oxford, 1977.

52. This lament is strongly reminiscent of that given to Anima in *Wisdom* (ed. M. Eccles for EETS, 1969, p. 146, l. 996), and derives from the *planctus* of the *Visitatio Sepulchri*. See p. 152 above.

53. On foul language see *Ayenbite of Inwyt, ed. cit.*, p. 203. See also Paula Neuss, 'Active and Idle Language: Dramatic Images in *Mankind*', Stratford-upon-Avon Studies, 16: *Medieval Drama*, ed. Neville Denny, 1973, pp. 41–67; also J. E. Barnard, jnr, *The Prosody of the Tudor Interlude*, New Haven, Conn., 1939.

54. For more detailed studies of the spread of Italian ideas about Roman comedy in English universities and schools see L. B. Campbell, *Scenes and Machines on the English Stage during the Renaissance*, 1923 (reprinted 1961); T. H. Vail Motter, *The School Drama in England*, 1929; F. S. Boas, *University Drama in the Tudor Age*, 1914; and G. Wickham, 'Neo-classical Drama in England' in *Shakespeare's Dramatic Heritage*, 1969, pp. 67–83.

55. Edited and translated by J. R. Hale in *The Literary Works of Machiavelli*, 1961. The highly ambiguous morality of this play is saved from outright immorality by the *suggestions* (made twice) that Lucretzia has not consummated her marriage with her husband, and that this is the cause of her apparent sterility. The friar's conduct as an accomplice to the plot is indicative of the fact that anticlericalism was not confined to those countries about to become Protestant.

56. See Philip Henderson, *The Complete Poems of John Skelton*, 1931 (revised ed. 1948), pp. 347–97. In this poem he also refers to a now lost interlude entitled *Virtue* and 'His comedy, Achademios calléd by name', p. 386.

57. *Ibid.*, pp. 165–244; also *Magnyfycence*, ed. for EETS by R. L. Ramsay, 1908 (reprinted 1925 and 1958). On this play see also William O. Harris, *Skelton's 'Magnificence' and the Cardinal Virtue Tradition*, 1965.

58. See Rainer Pineas, *Tudor and Early Stuart Anti-Catholic Drama*, Nieuwkoop, 1972, especially pp. 7–8. This convention could only be reinforced by the advent of stage-censorship after 1543 and was, indeed, maintained as need occasioned until the Civil War; see *EES*.ii(1). 66 ff.

59. See Henderson, *op. cit.*, pp. 308–45, and Harris, *op. cit.*, pp. 3–45.

60. Even this protective device was not a guarantee of immunity. At Gray's Inn a play by John Rowe, sergeant at law, was presented at Christmas, 1526, when Wolsey's unpopularity was at its height; although the play, not unlike *Magnyfycence* in its general drift, had been written much earlier, Wolsey was convinced that it was a satire directed principally at him. Rowe himself and Thomas Hoyle, one of the leading players, were both committed to prison for a short while; see Sidney Anglo, *Spectacle, Pageantry and Early Tudor Policy*, 1969, pp. 238–9.

61. This and the earlier quotations from Heywood's plays are taken from *The Dramatic Writings of John Heywood*, ed. J. S. Farmer for the Early English Drama Society, 1905, pp. 107 and 123–4 (*MSR*, ll. 426–8 and 935–43); see also Farmer's edition of *Gentleness and Nobility*, an interlude attributed to Heywood, in *The Writings of John Heywood*, Early English Drama Society, 1908. The latter was printed again for *MSR*, ed. A. C. Partridge and F. P. Wilson, 1950. This

play takes the form of a disputation between a Merchant, a Knight and a Plough-
man 'with divers toys and jests added thereto to make merry pastime and
disport': see pp. 139 and 140 above. On the relationship between Heywood's
plays and earlier French models, see Ian Maxwell, *French Farce and John Heywood*,
Melbourne and London, 1946.

62. Aristophanes' *Pax* was performed at Trinity College, Cambridge, in 1546 when a
stir was created by the flying machine for Scarabaeus devised by Dr John Dee.
On the performance of Greek and Latin plays between 1540 and 1560 see n. 54
above; also A. Harbage and S. Schoenbaum, *Annals of English Drama, 975–1700*,
pp. 26–30.

63. See *EES*.ii(1). 54–119. The leading English anti-Catholic satirist was John Bale,
a sometime Carmelite friar, and Prior, first of Maldon, then of Doncaster, who was
converted at Cambridge, and served thereafter both Thomas Cromwell and
Archbishop Cranmer, writing many plays until he was forced to flee the country
after Cromwell's execution. From him play-makers learned to equate the Pope
with Anti-Christ, priests with devils and Protestant reformers with the prophets,
saints and martyrs. It was a technique that Roman Catholics could easily reverse
and apply to a Protestant sovereign and his ministers. Parliament felt sufficiently
concerned about this issue to take legislative action against it in 1543. See also
David Bevington, *Tudor Drama and Politics*, Cambridge Mass., 1968; also Plate XI,
No. 16 of this volume, and *EES*.ii(1), Plates II and III.

64. See Ch. VII, pp. 168–70 above.

65. Bucer's *De Honestis Ludis*, written in Latin, formed part of his *De Regno Christi*
presented to King Edward VI in 1551. On Bucer's career see pp. 225–6 above;
on the text see n. 69 below.

66. On Plautine comedy and the Roman audience see Erich Segal, *Roman Laughter*,
Cambridge, Mass., 1968, pp. 15–41; on the Feast of Fools see pp. 182–5 and nn.
17 and 18 above. In England, Stephen Gosson claimed to have discovered, as a
writer of plays for adult companies, that playhouses were little better than 'markets
of bawdrie', and sought to counter the aura of respectability that classical precedent
seemed to bestow on plays by attacking Plautus in particular; see *The Schoole of
Abuse*, 1579, sig. B5. When he came to write *Playes Confuted in Five Actions* three
years later, he had shifted his ground far beyond Bucer's, and had ceased to allow
that any play could serve a useful educative function: plays of the pre-Christian
era were to be dismissed as pagan idols, and those of the Christian era as works
of popish ignorance and superstition; see especially sigs B4b. and B6b. See also
Ch. I, p. 4, and Ch. VII, pp. 168–70 above.

67. The authors of *Lusty Juventus* (*c.* 1550) and *New Custom* (*c.* 1560) are particularly
sensitive to this danger, as is Thomas Ingelend in *The Disobedient Child* and *Nice
Wanton*. It is the older generation, placed in authority over their children by virtue
of their age, who are not to be trusted either as parents or teachers, and at whom the
satire of these plays is directed. See pp. 116–17 and 209–10 above.

68. *Ralph Roister Doister* was first printed by H. Denham for T. Hackett, *c.* 1566;
Gammer Gurton's Needle for T. Colwell, 1575; *July and Julian* was only found in MS.
in 1887 and is now in the Folger Library. *Roister Doister* was reprinted for *MSR*,
ed. W. W. Greg, 1934; *July and Julian* was printed for the first time, ed. Giles
Dawson and Arthur Brown, for *MSR*, 1955; *Gammer Gurton's Needle* was reprinted
in *Tudor Facsimile Texts*, 1910.

Thersytes was first printed by J. Tyndale, n. d. (*c.* 1560), and reprinted in *Tudor
Facsimile Texts*, 1912; also, ed. J. S. Farmer, in *Six Anonymous Plays* for the Early
English Drama Society, 1905. The best modern edition is in A. W. Pollard's
English Miracle Plays, pp. 126–45.

Calisto and Melibia was first printed by J. Rastell, n. d. (*c.* 1527), and reprinted for *MSR*, ed. F. Sidgwick and W. W. Greg, 1908, and again in 1909 for *Tudor Facsimile Texts*.

Plautus' Greek settings and names have been noted by the authors of *Roister Doister* and *Thersytes*, but have been ignored by the others.

69. William Tyndale, *The Obedience of a Christian Man, and how Christian Rulers Ought to Governe*, 1528, ed. Richard Lovett, n. d. Martin Bucer's *De Regno Christi* was dedicated to Edward VI, presented I January 1551, and printed posthumously in Latin at Basle in 1557, and in French at Geneva in 1558; see Constantin Hopf, *Martin Bucer and the English Reformation*, 1946, pp. 99–130. John Foxe, *Acts and Monuments of the . . . Ecclesiastical historie, contayning the actes and monuments of Martyrs*, 2 vols, 1570; see also William Haller, *Foxe's Book of Martyrs and the Elect Nation*, 1963, and *Foxe's Book of Martyrs*, ed. and abridged by G. A. Williamson, 1965.

70. First printed in 1661, possibly for Kirkman, it is described on the title-page 'As It was *Printed* and *Acted* about a hundred Years ago'. It was reprinted in 1906 by J. S. Farmer in *Six Anonymous Plays*, series 2, and again in 1910 for *MSR*, ed. G. C. Moore Smith and W. W. Greg; see also *Tudor Facsimile Texts*, 1912.

71. First printed by T. Colwell, n. d., and reprinted by J. S. Farmer, *The Dramatic Writings of Richard Wever and Thomas Ingelend*, 1905; see also *Tudor Facsimile Texts*, 1908. See pp. 97–8 of this volume; also *Nice Wanton*, *sub* 'Tragedy', pp. 234–5 above. Another play devoted to education is William Wager's *The Longer Thou Livest the More Fool Thou Art* of about the same date, where the Prologue informs the audience:

> 'In deede, to all man it is most evident
> That a pleasaunt Rose springeth a sharpe Thorne;
> But commonly of good seed procedeth good Corne;
> Good Parents in good manners do instruct their childe,
> Correcting him when he beginneth to grow wilde.'
> (ed. A. Brandl, *Shakespeare Jahrbuch*, XXXVI, 1900, ll. 23–7).

72. On the dating of the three Elizabethan editions of this play, see the edition prepared for *MSR* by J. M. Noseworthy, G. R. Proudfoot and Arthur Brown, and printed in 1971. Cf. *New Custom*, ed. J. S. Farmer, *Anonymous Plays*, series 3, 1906, where the vices, 'Perverse Doctrine, an old Popish Priest' and 'Ignorance, another, but elder' submit to the virtues 'New Custom, a minister' and 'Light of the Gospel, a minister', and acknowledge the error of their earlier ways.

73. First printed, J. King, 1560: reprinted by J. S. Farmer in *'Lost' Tudor Plays*, 1907; see also *Tudor Facsimile Texts*, 1907, and W. Bang, *Materialien*, XXXIII, 1911.
The passage quoted is from Farmer, pp. 343–4 (Bang, ll. 975–86). Scenes of this kind prepare the way for Ben Jonson's extended attack on lawyers in Act IV, scene 2 of *Volpone*.

74. *Wealth and Health* was reprinted both by W. W. Greg and Percy Simpson for *MSR* and by J. S. Farmer in *'Lost' Tudor Plays* in 1907. George Walpull's *The Tyde Taryeth no Man* was printed by E. Rühl in *Shakespeare Jahrbuch*, XLIII, 1907, and again in *Tudor Facsimile Texts*, 1910. See also *EMP*. *The Pedlar's Prophecy* was printed in *Tudor Facsimile Texts*, 1911, and again for *MSR*, ed. W. W. Greg, 1914.

75. Ulpian Fulwell's *Like Will to Like* was first printed by J. Allde, 1568, and again by E. Allde in 1587. It was reprinted for *Tudor Facsimile Texts* in 1909, and again by J. S. Farmer in *The Dramatic Writings of Ulpian Fulwell*, 1906; also in P. Happé's *Tudor Interludes*, Penguin, 1972.
William Wager's *Enough is as Good as a Feast* was first printed by J. Allde, n. d., and reprinted by S. de Ricci in a facsimile edition limited to 200 copies for Henry

E. Huntington Reprints (No. 2), New York, 1920. It has since been made more readily available, together with Wager's *The Longer Thou Livest the More Fool Thou Art* in a single volume, ed. R. M. Benbow, Lincoln, Nebr. 1967. Harbage and Schoenbaum, *Annals*, assign composition to 1560. Thomas Lupton's *All for Money* was first printed by Roger Warde and Richard Mundee, 1578. It was reprinted in 1904 in *Shakespeare Jahrbuch*, XL, ed. E. Vogel, and again in 1910 in *Tudor Facsimile Texts*. It is also in *EMP*.

76. Avarice, it should be noted, had already assumed a dominant role in *Respublica* some twenty years earlier, and finds its place in many plays reaching back to 'Covertise' in *The Castle of Perseverance* early in the fifteenth century. See n. 39 above. It also looks forward, of course, to such characters as Jonson's Sir Epicure Mammon and Massinger's Sir Giles Overreach.

77. Cf. Wager's *Enough is as Good as a Feast* (ed. S. de Ricci, n. 75 above) where Worldly Man in disclaiming the sin of sloth—

> 'It doth me good to tel the chinks in my hutch,
> More than at the Tavern or ale house to be.'
> (sig. Aiiib)

—unwittingly admits to that of avarice. It is this vice, since he can never be content with enough, which leads him to threaten to dispossess a tenant who has rented his house for £5 p. a. for thirty-six years unless he will agree to pay double that sum (sigs E and Eb).

78. 1st ed., Roger Warde and Richard Mundee, 1578; reprinted by E. Vogel in *Shakespeare Jahrbuch*, XL, 1904, pp. 145–86; also in *EMP*. Cf Wager's *Enough is as Good as a Feast* where Covetousness, as prime vice, concludes the play by handing Worldly Man's soul over to Satan, who enters exclaiming triumphantly,

> 'Oh, oh, oh, oh, all is mine, all is mine!
> My kingdom increaseth every houre and day...'
> (Sig. G)

See pp. 232–4 and 236–7 above.

79. A no less cynical view of lapsed Catholic priests is presented in the character of Sir Nicholas (alias the vice Devotion) in Wager's *Enough is as Good as a Feast*: together they provide a theatrical basis for Shakespeare's Sir Nathaniel in *Love's Labour's Lost*.

80. In *The Massacre at Paris*, Marlowe approaches the character of Navarre as Bale did that of King John fifty years earlier; both are presented to audiences as heroes at war with Catholicism. The Vice of Marlowe's play is the Duke of Guise whose very Catholicism is itself portrayed as merely a hypocritical disguise: Catholics are, in fact, atheists posing as Christians. An important aspect of this play, as also in Woodes's *Conflict of Conscience*, is Catholic cruelty—a feature that accurately reflects the change in English, Protestant sentiment following the Marian reaction, and which is carried forward faithfully and turned to tragic ends by Webster in *The Duchess of Malfi* and *The White Devil*. See Rainer Pineas, *Tudor and Early Stuart Anti-Catholic Drama*, 1972, pp. 9–10: also George T. Buckley, *Atheism in the English Renaissance*, New York, 1965.

81. Edwards's I and II *Palamon and Arcite* was presented to Queen Elizabeth I on her visit to Oxford in 1566; no text survives, but see J. S. Farmer, *The Dramatic Writings of Edwards, Norton and Sackville*, 1906, pp. 184–5, and *EES*.ii(1).250 ff. The Admiral's Men also possessed a play of that name in 1594. Philip's *Patient and Meek Grisell* was only discovered in 1907, but was reprinted for *MSR*, ed. W. W. Greg

and R. B. McKerrow, two years later. On Greene's play see *MSR*, ed. W. W. Greg and A. E. H. Swaen, 1921, and *The Scottish History of James the Fourth*, ed. Norman Sanders for The Revels Plays, 1970. *King Leir*, published in quarto in 1594, has since been reprinted for *MSR*, ed. R. Warwick Bond and W. W. Greg, 1908.

82. See Digby Plays, ed. F. J. Furnivall for EETS, 1896. On the staging of *The Conversion of St Paul* see G. Wickham, *English Moral Interludes*, 1976, pp. 103–7. On *Mary Magdalene* see D. L. Jeffrey, 'English Saints' Plays' in Stratford-upon-Avon Studies 16: *Medieval Drama*, ed. N. Denny, pp. 75–82. The full title of the Croxton play is *The Play of the Conversyon of Ser Jonathas the Jewe by Myracle of the Blyssed Sacrament*; it has been printed by J. Manly, *Specimens of the Pre-Shakespearean Drama*, Vol. I, pp. 239–76, and by N. Davies for EETS, in *Non-Cycle Plays and Fragments*, 1970, pp. 58–89. The MS. of *Beunans Meriasek*, signed Dom Hadton and dated 1504, was found in 1869 and edited and printed by Whitley Stokes, 1872.

83. In this context it should be recalled that under Mary I saint plays were revived both in London and the provinces; see *EES*.ii(1). 62, 66 and 70. It should also be noted that in his will, dated 15 March 1556, Sir Giles Capell directed that his tomb should be erected in the chancel of Rayne church, Essex, so that it might be used as the Easter Sepulchre. See James Oxley, *The Reformation in Essex to the Death of Mary*, p. 260. The switch to secular heroes is evident by 1559 in *Patient and Meek Grisell* (see n. 81 above) whose saintly conduct and near martyrdom are implicit in the play's title.

84. *Misogonus* exists in MS. dated 1577 and was first printed by R. W. Bond in *Early Plays from the Italian*, 1911. *Clyomon and Clamydes* was first printed in 1599 by Thomas Creede and belonged to the Queen's Players; it was reprinted for *MSR*, ed. W. W. Greg, 1913. For *July and Julian* see n. 68 above. *Common Conditions* was entered in the Stationers' Register, 1576, but printed without date; it was reprinted for Yale Elizabethan Club, ed. C. F. Tucker Brooke, 1915. George Whetstone's I and II *Promos and Cassandra* was first printed in 1578, and has been reprinted by Geoffrey Bullough in *Narrative and Dramatic Sources of Shakespeare*, Vol. II, 1958, pp. 442–513.

85. The 'Four Foster Children of Desire' who laid siege to the 'Fortress of Perfect Beauty', 15 and 16 May 1581, were Philip Sidney, Fulke Greville, Lord Windsor and the Earl of Arundel. The occasion was the arrival in London of the Marshal of France and other ambassadors to arrange a treaty of marriage between the Duke of Anjou and the Queen; see *ES*.iv.63–4, and Nichols, *PQE*.ii.310.

Chapter IX, pages 219–53. Tragedy

1. Of tragedies composed in Latin and Greek pride of place must go respectively to George Buchanan and John Christopherson both of whom chose the biblical story of Jephthah for their innovatory experiments, the former in 1542 and the latter in 1544. In 1543 Buchanan translated Euripides' *Alcestis* and *Medea* into Latin while Roger Ascham did the same for Sophocles' *Philoctetes*; but it is not until the accession of Elizabeth I that any serious efforts are made to translate Seneca's plays into English. On ideas circulating in England during the sixteenth century about 'greatness' (Latin *virtus;* Greek *arete*) see G. R. Hibbard, 'Goodness and Greatness', *Renaissance and Modern Studies* (Nottingham University), XI (1967), pp. 5–54. See nn. 25 and 26 below.

   The English word which I think best catches the meaning attached in the early sixteenth century to *virtus* and *arete* is 'fortitude'. This was regarded as the supreme princely virtue and sole protection against the immutability of Fortune, as Skelton demonstrates in *Magnyficence:* see pp. 201–3 above.

2. Margeson, *op. cit.*, pp. 6 and 2 respectively.

3. *Shakespeare's Dramatic Heritage*, pp. 42–63.

4. See Dr Bergen's Introduction to his edition for EETS, i, pp. x-xi.

5. Margeson, *op. cit.*, pp. 58–9.

6. See David Bevington, *From Mankind to Marlowe*, pp. 104–27, and Bernard Spivack, *Shakespeare and the Allegory of Evil*, New York, 1958; also pp. 162 ff. above.

7. The most notable case in the context of drama and theatre is that of Stephen Gosson who at first wrote plays in a professional capacity, then defended some while condemning others in *The Schoole of Abuse* (1579) and finally came to advocate the suppression of all play-acting in *Plays Confuted* (1582). See Ch. VIII, n. 66 above.

8. See A. G. Dickens, *The English Reformation*, 1964, pp. 59 ff.; H. C. Porter, *Reformation and Reaction in Tudor Cambridge*, 1958; and William P. Haugaard, *Elizabeth and the English Reformation*, 1968.

9. See Ch. VIII, pp. 206–8 and n. 65 regarding context and text. It is to be noted, moreover, that the Revels Office which had been constituted as a branch of the Royal Household by Henry VIII in 1545 was ready to accept the task of licensing plays, and in fact did so both for performance and, following the accession of Mary I, printing. See *EES*. i.275–6 and ii(1).49–52 and 71–5.

10 See Dickens, *ER*, pp. 199–200 and Porter, *op. cit.*, pp. 52–5 and 63–7. Bucer counted among his pupils at Cambridge Matthew Parker, Edmund Grindal and John Whitgift, all of whom were to serve Elizabeth I as Archbishops of Canterbury, and one of whom (Grindal) was to be Bishop of London during the theatre's most critical years of strife with the Guildhall. See *EES*.ii(1).77. See also Roger B. Manning, *Religion and Society in Elizabethan Sussex*, Leicester, 1969, pp. 188 ff., and Christopher Haigh, *Reformation and Resistance in Tudor Lancashire*, 1975, pp. 159 ff.

11. See Ch. VIII n. 80 above; also Dickens, *ER*, pp. 259–77, and J. E. Oxley, *The Reformation in Essex*, 1965, pp. 210–37. John Foxe's *Acts and Monuments* (better known as *The Book of Martyrs:* see Ch. VIII n. 69 above) with its horrifying engravings was published in 1563 and served to keep the memory of these Protestant martyrs alive long after the event, and to encourage Protestant bigotry in a later age (see 'Pre- and Post-Reformation Banns to the Chester Cycle', *EES*. i.Appendix D). Although rather fewer than 300 men and women were burned as heretics, a large majority of them met their deaths in or near London; many were quite young and, although simple craftsmen by trade, remarkably well read in the English Bible.

12. *John Bale's King Johan*, edited with an introduction and notes by Barry B. Adams, The Huntington Library, San Marino, Calif., 1969, p. 61. See also *Bale's King Johan*, ed. for *MSR* by J. H. P. Pafford and W. W. Greg, 1931; Thora Blatt, *The Plays of John Bale*, Copenhagen, 1968; J. W. Harris, 'John Bale; A Study in the Literature of the Reformation', *Illinois Studies in Language and Literature*, XXV, no. 4, Urbana, 1940; and T. W. Craik, *The Tudor Interlude*, 1958, *sub* King John.

13. The play was revived in a condensed version, edited and directed by Robert Potter, for the Drama Department of Bristol University in 1964. My comments are grounded on that experience.

14. *Godly Queen Hester* was first printed by W. Pickering and T. Hacket, 1561; it was reprinted by J. S. Farmer for the Early English Drama Society, *Six Anonymous Plays*, series 2, 1906. Yet if W. W. Greg's views attached to his edition of the play in *Materialien*, V, pp. iv-xvi, are accepted, the play was originally intended as a

satire on the conduct of Cardinal Wolsey and may thus be dated *c.* 1527. Cf. John Skelton's 'Why come ye not to Court?' and pp. 204–5 above.

15. If, as seems probable, the play was aimed at Wolsey, this in itself explains why the author should have elected to discuss Aman's motives and methods indirectly through the abstract personages of the vices, and place his moral in his epilogue.

> *Ahasuerus* My Lordes(!) by this fygure ye may well se,
> The multitude hurte by the heads necligence,
> If to his pleasure so geven is he,
> That he will no paine take nor dilligence,
> who careth not for his cure ofte loseth credence.
> (ed. Greg, *Materialien*, V, p. 45, ll. 1162–6)

The ambiguity of these remarks extends as much to Henry VIII as to Wolsey. It should also be noted that King Ahasuerus elects to withdraw from public view leaving Aman to govern in his place, as Duke Vincentio does with Angelo in *Measure for Measure*, and with the same end in mind: 'Hence shall we see,/If power change purpose, what our seemers be' (I.iii. 53–4). See also pp. 72–3 above.

16. *Jacob and Esau* was first printed by H Bynneman in 1568, and has since been reprinted by J. S. Farmer for the Early English Drama Society, *Six Anonymous Plays*, series 2, 1906, and again in *Tudor Facsimile Texts*, 1908. The most recent edition is John Crow's and F. P. Wilson's for *MSR*, 1956 from which my quotations are taken. The play was first licensed, 1557, to Henry Sutton for printing. Wilson is cautious about its authorship. Harbage and Schoenbaum, however, in *Annals of English Drama* allot the play confidently to 1554 (limits 1550–7) and go so far as to attribute its authorship (presumably following C. W. Wallace) to Nicholas Udall, or to William Hunnis (presumably following Mrs C. C. Stopes): yet they also attribute *Respublica* to Udall. What does not seem to have occurred to them is that the same man who wrote the latter with its scathing attack upon the Protestant reformers could not possibly have written a play like *Jacob and Esau* that is structured so firmly on uncompromising Calvinist principles. While the play may have been written during the reign of Mary I, I can see no possibility of its having been printed before the accession of Elizabeth I, unless clandestinely.

17. In this play it is to be noted that Esau, although keenly aware of the way in which he has been cheated, makes no attempt to try and bridge the gap between the doctrine of predestination and actual moral culpability. He thus side-steps the genuinely tragic dilemma with which, some thirty years later, Marlowe will confront Dr Faustus: 'What doctrine call you this? Che sera, sera!' (Qto 1604, 1. 73).

18. This bold claim emerges clearly enough in the epilogue where the poet urges the audience to recall that,

> 'Whan Adam for breakyng Gods commaundement
> Had sentence of death, and all his posteritiè:
> Yet the lorde our God who is omnipotent,
> Had in his owne selfe by his eternall decree,
> Appointed to restore man, and to make him free,
> He purposed to save mankynde by his mercie,
> Whome he once had created unto his glorie.
>   Yet not all fleshe did he then predestinate,
> But onely the adopted children of promise.'

But the radicalism of the play's implications does not stop there; for the poet goes on to claim that

> 'All must be referred to Gods election,
> And to his secret judgement' —

a statement that challenges even the monarch's supremacy. Tyndale's and Bale's insistence upon the total obedience owed by a Christian subject to his sovereign is thus overtaken by a philosophy that can justify deposition of the monarch, grounded on the Puritan assertion led by the Cambridge radicals under Martin Bucer and his pupils: see Porter, *op. cit.*, pp. 136–45. Once established, this view came to be regarded by Elizabethans as almost as extreme and seditious as Roman Catholic aspirations to recover England for Rome. Thus R. Bancroft in *Dangerous Positions* (1593) observed scornfully: 'They shall not need to expect either Prince or Parliament, but may throw down and set up, as great builders do, whatsoever shall be most agreeable to the mutability of their own affections.' It was against this background that Marlowe wrote *Edward II* and Shakespeare *Richard II*.

19. This play was first printed by J. Allde, n.d., *c.* 1565; see Ch. VIII, n. 75 above.
20. The quotations from *Nice Wanton* are given from my own edition of the play in *English Moral Interludes*, 1976, pp. 143–62.
21. *The Conflict of Conscience* by Nathaniel Woodes or Wood, a minister of Norwich, was first printed by Richard Bradocke in 1581. It was reprinted in *Tudor Facsimile Texts* in 1911, and again in 1952 for *MSR*, ed. Herbert Davis and F. P. Wilson. A modernized version exists in *EMP*. On the printing of the play and its sources, see the critical introduction to the Malone Society edition. On the possible portraiture of Cardinal Pole and Bishop Bonner within the play see Dickens, *ER*, pp. 265–6; and on Bonner's examination of William Hunter see Foxe, *op. cit.*, pp. 722–7; also p. 237 (footnote) above.
22. On the religious themes and imagery deployed within *Macbeth* see G. Wickham, *Shakespeare's Dramatic Heritage*, pp. 214–31; William Armstrong, *Shakespeare's Typology: Miracle and Morality Motifs in 'Macbeth'*, 1970; and Guy Butler, '*Macbeth*': *The Great Doom's Image*, Grahamstown, S.A., 1976.
23. See n. 1 above: also L. B. Campbell, *Scenes and Machines on the English Stage*, pp. 83–98, and the Introduction to J. W. Cunliffe's *Early English Classical Tragedies*, 1912.
24. See G. Wickham, 'Neo-Classical Drama in England' in *Shakespeare's Dramatic Heritage*, pp. 67–83, and Leo Schrade, *La Représentation d'Edipo Tiranno au Teatro Olimpico*, CNRS, Paris, 1960.
25. For English translations of these two plays see *The Sacred Dramas of George Buchanan*, translated into English verse by Archibald Brown, Edinburgh, 1906, and *John Christopherson's 'Jephthah'*, Greek text edited and translated by F. H. Forbes, Newark, Del., 1928.
26. Buchanan, *ed. cit.*, p. 31. Both authors strive to achieve as striking a reversal of fortune as can be managed. Thus Buchanan gives these lines to his chorus when Jephthah has decided that his vow must take precedence over pleas for mercy.

> 'O what a fall is here! Since time began
> No bliss endures unbroken unto man:
> The joys of earth are never undecayed;
> Fair as they bloom, only they bloom to fade.'
> (*ed. cit.*, p. 48)

Christopherson, likewise:

> 'It was but now,
> I was rejoiced by thoughts of victory,

When, of a sudden, fortune, by a shift,
Turned joy to grief.'
(ll. 1037–9 of Greek text)

Although Christopherson dedicated his play to Henry VIII, *c.* 1544, he was later to be numbered among those Cambridge dons who superintended the desecration of Martin Bucer's tomb.

27. See A. Wigfall Green, *The Inns of Court and Early English Drama*, New Haven, Conn., 1931, pp. 142 ff.

28. Thomas Newton's *Seneca, his tenne tragedies, translated into English* was published in 1581. See T. S. Eliot's edition in 2 vols, 1927; also n. 1 above on earlier translations of classical tragedies.

29. R. B.'s *Apius and Virginia* was first printed by W. How for R. Jhones, 1575, although mention of it occurs in the Stationers' Register in July 1567. It was reprinted for *Tudor Facsimile Texts*, 1908, and again for *MSR*, ed. R. B. McKerrow and W. W. Greg, 1911.

30. John Pickering's *Horestes*, which he described as 'A Newe Enterlude of Vice Conteyninge the History of Horestes with the cruel revengment of his Fathers death upon his natur(*a*)ll Mother', was first published by W. Griffith in 1567. Whether Pickering was or was not familiar with Aeschylus' *Oresteia*, or any other classical treatment of the story, is not material since he grounded the play on Caxton's *Recuyell of the Historyes of Troye*. See MSR, ed. D. Seltzer and A. Brown, 1961.

31. Granted a mere six actors, as claimed on the title-page, this 'army', with Idumeus and Orestes already on the stage, cannot have mustered more than four soldiers at most. On the division of parts, see Bevington, *op. cit.*, pp. 179–83: also 'Popular and Courtly Traditions on the Early Tudor Stage', in Stratford-upon-Avon Studies 16: *Medieval Drama*, ed. N. Denny, pp. 104–6. MSR, sigs Civb-Dii.

32. BM MS. Add. 34063. The play was first printed by Richard Smithe, 1573 (Q1), and then published under Gascoigne's name in 1575 (Q2), and again in 1587 (Q3). In editing the play for inclusion in *Early English Classical Tragedies*, 1912, J. W. Cunliffe used the text of 1575; on this see pp. 65–159.

33. The play exists in three quartos published respectively in 1565, 1570–1 and 1590. Q1 was published surreptitiously without the authors' consent; Q2 is the edition authorized by the authors as explained in the 'Preface to the Reader'. It was reprinted from Q2 by J. W. Cunliffe in *Early English Classical Tragedies*, 1912, pp. 1–64. On the staging of this play see Bevington, 'Popular and Courtly Traditions on the Early Tudor Stage' in Stratford-upon-Avon Studies 16: *Medieval Drama*, ed. N. Denny, p. 107.

34. On Mulcaster's coronation pageants see David Bergeron, *English Civic Pageantry, 1558–1642*, 1971, pp. 11–23; on the dumb-shows see Dieter Mehl, *The Elizabethan Dumb Show*, 1964, pp. 29–62.

35. On Tudor historical primitivism and the Troy story see E. A. Greenlaw, *Studies in Spenser's Historical Allegory*, Baltimore, 1932; also S. Anglo, *Spectacle, Pageantry and Early Tudor Policy*, 1969. On the Duke of Albany see G. Wickham, 'From Tragedy to Tragi-comedy: *King Lear* as Prologue', *Shakespeare Survey*, XXVI (1973), pp. 33–48, and Leo Kirschbaum, 'Albany', *Shakespeare Survey*, XIII (1960), pp. 20–9.

36. See n. 34 above; also James M. Osborn (ed.), *The Quenes Majesties Passage*, 1960.

37. The question of regicide is raised rhetorically by Gwenard, Duke of Cumberland in V.i, at line 17:

'Shall subjectes dare with force

To worke revenge upon their princes fact?
Admit the worst that may, as sure in this
The deede was fowle, the queene to slay her sonne,
Shall yet the subject seek to take the sworde,
Arise agaynst his lord, and slay his king?'

The Duke of Albany replies categorically,

'There can no punishment be thought to(o) great
For this so grevous cryme.'

The line of argument being adopted here stems directly from Tyndale's, *The Obedience of a Christian Man* of 1528 (see Ch. VIII, n. 69 above) and is clearly being used to counter Calvinist republican sentiment of the kind made explicit in *Jacob and Esau* (see pp. 231–2 above). Cf. the similarly elaborate discussion of the same topic in Act I of *Horestes* (see pp. 241–2 above).

38. See n. 35 above.
39. *Gismond of Salerne* (*c.* 1566–7) exists in two MSS.: BM MS. Lansdowne 786 and BM MS. Hargrave 205. Revised from these MSS. and probably two more (now missing) by Robert Wilmot, it was first published as *Tancred and Gismond* in 1591 and again in 1592. No authors' names appear on either MS., but five abbreviated names appear at the end of each Act in the printed editions. Act I. *Exegit Rod. Staf*(?ford): Act II. *Per Hen. No*(?el): Act III. *G. Al*: Act IV *Composuit Ch*(?ristopher) *Hat*(?ton): Act V and Epilogue. RW. It was reprinted by J. W. Cunliffe in *Early English Classical Tragedies*, 1912, pp. 161–216 with a critical introduction, pp. lxxxvi–xc, and again for *MSR*, ed. W. W. Greg, 1915. On Inns of Court plays see A. Wigfall Green, *The Inns of Court and Early English Drama*, New Haven, Conn., 1931, pp. 142–57.
40. All quotations are given in the *MSR* text; this one at p. xx.
41. The Queen's presence, however, is not neglected; for after the chorus has lamented, at the close of Act II, the loss of stoic virtue in modern women, an apology is tactfully appended:

'Yet let not us maydens condemne our kinde,
Because our vertues are not all so rare:
For we may freshly yet record in minde,
There lives a virgin, one without compare:
Who of all graces hath her heavenly share.
In whose renowme, and for whose happie daies,
Let us record this Paean of her praise.'
(*MSR*, ll. 578–84)

42. See pp. 220–1 above. What the authors could *not* do was to overlook the sexual morality of their own time; and so, on this account, they found themselves obliged to depart substantially from Boccaccio's original portraits of both Ghismonda and her lover. On these changes see Cunliffe, *op. cit.*, pp. lxxxvii–lxxxviii and 'Gismond of Salerne', *PMLA*, XXI, 1906, pp. 435–61.
43. For bibliographical details relating to these two plays see n. 21, and Ch. IV, n. 10.
44. See p. 250 above. Gismond's 'fault' lies as much in her failure to be faithful to her dead husband as in her failure to obey her father; thus filial impiety and what, in terms of orthodox, Elizabethan, Anglican opinion, amounted technically to adultery, are the joint and immediate causes of 'her wo and death'.
45. See J. W. Cunliffe, *George Gascoigne*, Vol. II, 1910, pp. 1–90.

NOTES TO ILLUSTRATIONS

PLATE I, No. 1

The Norman apsidal sanctuary of Copford Church, Essex. It was in the sanctuary, accommodating the high altar, that the earliest dramatic offices were presented. The apse at Copford, painted *c.* 1140, is one of the finest surviving from so early a date in England. Christ is here depicted as victor and king encircled by the rainbow and supported by angels. The arch over the entrance contains the signs of the zodiac. The glass is Victorian.

> Reproduced from *Medieval Essex Churches*, Essex Record Office Publications, no. 60, 1972, ed. J. R. Smith

PLATE II, No. 2

Romanesque Easter sepulchre. Constructed contemporaneously with the Norman conquest of England, this remarkable structure in the cathedral at Aquileia (between Venice and Trieste), with its own door and altar, stands nearly twelve feet high in the north aisle near the west end. As it is seven feet in diameter at the base, it could easily accommodate the three Maries.

On the building and siting of these 'sepulchres' see K. Lanckoronski, G. Nieman and H. Swoboda, *Der Dom von Aquileia*, Vienna, 1906; and Karl Young, *DMC*, ii.507–13. On Easter sepulchres provided in English churches as late as 1553–8, see p. 302, n. 83 in this book.

> Reproduced from Young, *Drama of the Medieval Church*, Clarendon Press, 1933, vol. 1.

PLATE II, No. 3

Adoration of the Magi (Officium Stellae). This magnificently austere rendering of the scene, carved on whale-bone and measuring only 14.5 by 6.5 inches, captures something of the purity of spirit of the liturgical drama prescribed for Epiphany. English eleventh or twelfth century. On the discordant element of Herod's behaviour when added to this sequence see pp. 32–3.

> Victoria and Albert Museum, London

PLATE III, No. 4

The Three Maries. A Polish version of the *Visitatio Sepulchri* painted, *c.* 1470, in oil on a panel surviving from a larger altar-piece now lost or destroyed.

> National Museum, Cracow

PLATE III, No. 5

Christ as Knight Crusader. In this Flemish tapestry (the seventh of a series commissioned and executed between 1377 and 1383 for Louis, Duc d'Anjou, to illustrate the Apocalypse) Christ is depicted brandishing his sword in pursuit of the Beast and the wicked, who are here seen dressed as Saracen soldiers.

The Orders of Knight Templars and Knight Hospitallers had come into being following Godfrey of Bouillon's successful recapture of Jerusalem in 1099 and played an important role in the Crusades that were mounted, following its loss to the Saracens, during the next three centuries. See pp. 46–7 and 50–1 above.

'Le Juste chasse la Bête et les mechants': Musée des Tapisseries, Angers, France Photograph: © Arch. Phot. Paris/ S.P.A.D.E.M.

PLATE IV, No. 6

Typological triptych of the Last Supper. This great altar-piece by an unknown German master of the late fifteenth century invites the viewer to consider the Last Supper from four different, but related, standpoints.

The right-hand panel presents 'The Gathering of Manna' by the Israelites in the wilderness during their forty-year return journey from Egypt to Canaan as related in Exodus 16: 13–36: 'And Moses said unto them, This is the bread which the Lord hath given you to eat.'

The left-hand panel presents Melchizedek, King and high priest of Salem, bringing bread and wine to Abraham as a thank-offering for the rescue of Lot and the treasure stolen from Sodom, and blessing him, as related in Genesis 14: 18–20. For this, Abraham gave Melchizedek one tenth of the recaptured treasure, thus providing the basis for the practice of tithes, as is explained in the Chester cycle play of Abraham and Isaac.

The central panel presents both the Last Supper itself and, above, an allegory of the Eucharist. Thus the two side panels prefigure the Last Supper, and all three biblical scenes are removed from historical time and carried forward into the present within ritual time in the Mass.

Musée Rolin, Autun, France: Photograph, Auguste Allemand

PLATE V, No. 7

Detail from a larger painting of the Seven Corporal Acts of Mercy above the arches of the nave in Pickering Church, near Scarborough, Yorkshire; fifteenth century.

The acts depicted here are (left to right) feeding the hungry, giving drink to the thirsty, visiting prisoners and visiting the sick.

The source is St Matthew's Gospel 25: 35–6. Another English version appears in the painted glass in All Saints' Church, North Street, York.

Photograph: Boak, Pickering

PLATE V, No. 8

A statue on the top of a fountain in Berne, depicting Justice wearing the armour of righteousness, blindfolded, carrying a sword and balances, and supported by the emblems of both civil and ecclesiastical courts; sixteenth century, Swiss.

Photograph: Bovey & Co., Geneva

PLATE VI, No. 9

Label-carvings of musicians, Beverley Minster, Yorkshire. Eight instrumentalist members of the medieval guild of musicians carved in the fourteenth century as label-stops for the blind arcading in the north aisle of the nave. The instruments depicted here are:

Top row (left to right)
1 Horn or oliphant; possibly a very early serpent.

2 Bagpipe.

3 Organistrum, or hurdy-gurdy.

4 Rebec held in the non-playing position. The lack of any tail-piece suggests that it is not a gittern.

Lower row (left to right)

1 Nackers; kettle drums.

2 Possibly a dulcimer; perhaps a Béarnais string-drum.

3 Psaltery.

4 Plucked fiddle (guitar).

A Corpus Christi play existed at Beverley at least as early as 1377, and was presented annually on St Mark's Day. The city waits were certainly employed to accompany the Riding of the Banns, and probably to assist with the performance. See *Med. Stage*.ii.338–41. The most recent and reliable commentary on the label-carvings of musicians is the article by Gwen and Jeremy Montagu, 'Beverley Minster Reconsidered', *Early Music* (The Early Music Gazette), London, Vol. 6, No. 3, July 1978, pp. 401–14.

Photographs by Simsons, Beverley

PLATE VII, No. 10

Heaven's musicians. Manuscript illumination from a choir psalter executed in Italy (probably Brescia or Padua) in the third quarter of the fifteenth century, now in the Bodleian Library, and illustrating the initial words of Psalm 80, 'Exultate Deo' (Book of Common Prayer, Psalm 81).

MS. Bodl. Lat. liturg. a.3, fo. 103

PLATE VII, No. 11

Hell's punishments. A detail from Taddeo di Bartolo's vividly realistic fresco of the fates awaiting sinners. This section depicts Lust which is here represented by a group of three adulteresses and a pair of male homosexuals. The former are being mauled and whipped by devils; the latter are impaled together on an iron stake, thrust by a devil through one of them into the mouth of the other, a vision that provides pictorial precedent for Lightborn's treatment of King Edward in Marlowe's *Edward II*. Fresco, north aisle, Collegiate Church, San Gimignano, near Siena.

Photograph: Anderson Girandon, Paris

PLATES VIII and IX, Nos 12 and 13

The Triumph of Love and *The Triumph of Death.* Two illustrations to Petrarch's *I Trionfi* of *c.* 1352 painted by an anonymous Florentine artist in the fifteenth century. Both are now in the Accademia at Siena.

Photographs: Anderson, Rome

PLATE X, No. 14

Adam, Eve and Satan. In this great east window, York Minster, painted by John Thornton *c.* 1405, Eve is shown handing the apple to Adam watched by Satan dressed in his adder's skin and woman's face-mask in the manner presented in the stage-directions in the Chester play. See pp. 197 and n. 46, 297 above.

York Minster Library; copyright Dean and Chapter of York

PLATE X, No. 15

Will Sommers. Court jester to Henry VIII and Edward VI; *fl.* 1525–60; depicted as 'Witless' in John Heywood's interlude of *Witty and Witless* (1533), and again as 'Presenter' in Thomas Nashe's *Summer's Last Will and Testament*. Engraving by Francis Delaram, n.d. (*c.* 1620).

The lines of verse in the lower margin read:

What though tho(u) thinkst mee clad in strange attire,
Knowe I am suted to my owne desire:
And yet the Characters describ'd upon mee
May shewe thee, that a King bestow'd them on mee.
This Horne I have betokens Sommers game;
Which sportive tyme will bid thee reade my name
All with my Nature well agreeing too
As both the Name, and Tyme, and Habit doe.

Guildhall Library, City of London

PLATE XI, No. 16

John Bale. Born 1495; sometime Carmelite prior; graduate of Cambridge; ardent Protestant convert, reformer, play maker, and for a short while Bishop of Ossory, near Dublin. He was exiled on the Continent in the last decade of Henry VIII's reign and again under Mary I, but was created a Canon of Canterbury on his return to England at the accession of Elizabeth I in 1558. He died in 1563. Copied from engraving by Wilhelm and Magdalena van de Posse for Henry Holland's *Herwologia*, 1620.

Guildhall Library, City of London

PLATE XI, No. 17

Martin Bucer. Born in 1491 in Alsace; sometime Dominican monk; graduate of Heidelberg; converted to Protestantism and ministered in Strasbourg until invited to England by Archbishop Cranmer in 1548 to avoid persecution; appointed Regius Professor of Divinity at Cambridge by Edward VI; died 1552. See pp. 206–7 and 225–6. Mezzotint by R. Houston printed in *The Lives of the Principal Reformers*, 1759, p. 86.

Reproduced from C. Hopf, *Martin Bucer and the English Reformation*, Oxford, 1945

PLATE XII, No. 18

Fame and Infamy. Personifications under the eye of Providence within a device, or emblem, of History. An explanatory poem by Ben Jonson is attached and reads:

From Death and dark Oblivion, ne'er the same,
    The Mistress of Man's life, grave History,
Raising the World to Good or Evil Fame
    Doth vindicate it to eternity.
Wise Providence would so: that nor the good
    Might be defrauded, nor the great secured,
But both might know their ways were understood,
    When Vice alike in time with Virtue dured.
Which makes that (lighted by the beamy hand
    Of Truth that searcheth the most hidden Springs
And guided by Experience, whose straight wand
    Doth mete, whose line doth sound, the depth of things),
She cheerfully supporteth what she rears,
    Assisted by no strengths, but are her own,

311

Some note of which each varied Pillar bears,
   By which, as proper titles, she is known
Time's witness, herald of Antiquity,
   The light of Truth, and life of Memory.

> Photographed from the frontispiece to
> Sir Walter Raleigh's *History of the World*
> ((1676 edition), engraved for the first
> edition of 1614) by Renold Elstrack,
> Arts Faculty Photographic Unit, University of Bristol.

LIST OF BOOKS

ADAMS, Barry B. *John Bale's King Johan*, Huntington Library, San Marino, Calif., 1960.

ADAMS, J. Q. *Chief Pre-Shakespearean Dramas*, Boston, 1924; reprinted Cambridge, Mass., 1952.

AEBISCHER, Paul (ed.). *Le Mystère d'Adam*, Paris, 1963.

ALCIATUS, Andreas. *Emblematum Flumen Abundans* (Lyons ed., 1551), reprinted and ed. by Henry Green for Holbein Society, 1871.

ANDERSON, M. D. *Drama and Imagery in English Medieval Churches*, Cambridge U.P., 1963.

ANGLO, S. *Spectacle, Pageantry and Early Tudor Policy*, O.U.P., 1969.

ARMSTRONG, William. *Shakespeare's Typology: Miracle and Morality Motifs in Macbeth*, London, 1970.

AXTON, R. 'Popular Modes in the Earliest Plays', Stratford-upon-Avon Studies, 16: *Medieval Drama*, ed. Neville Denny, 1973, pp. 13–39.

—— *European Drama of the Early Middle Ages*, London, 1974.

—— and STEVENS, J. (trans. and ed.). *Medieval French Plays*, O.U.P., 1971.

BANCROFT, R. *Dangerous Positions*, London, 1593.

BARBER, Richard. *The Knight and Chivalry*, London, 1970.

BARNARD, J. E., Jnr. *The Prosody of the Tudor Interlude*, New Haven, Conn., 1939.

BARNUM, Priscilla Heath. *Dives and Pauper*, ed. for EETS, 1976.

BEDE. See JONES, Charles W.

BERGERON, David. *English Civic Pageantry, 1558–1642*, London, 1971.

BEVINGTON, David. *From Mankind to Marlowe: Growth of Structure in the Popular Drama of Tudor England*, Harvard U.P., 1962.

—— *Tudor Drama and Politics: A Critical Approach to Topical Meaning*, Harvard U.P., 1968.

—— 'Popular and Courtly Traditions on the Early Tudor Stage', Stratford-upon-Avon Studies 16: *Medieval Drama*, ed. Neville Denny, 1973, pp. 90–107.

BLATT, Thora. *The Plays of John Bale*, Copenhagen, 1968.

BLOCK, K. S. *Ludus Coventriae: The Play Called Corpus Christi*, ed. for EETS, 1922; reprinted, O.U.P., 1960.

BOAS, F. S. *University Drama in the Tudor Age*, Clarendon Press, 1914.

BOND, R.W. *Early Plays from the Italian*, Clarendon Press, 1911; reprinted New York, n.d.

BRANDEIS, Arthur. *Jacob's Well*, ed. for EETS from Salisbury Cathedral MS. 103, 1900.

BRODY, Alan. *The English Mummers and Their Plays*, London, 1971.

BROWN, Archibald. *The Sacred Dramas of George Buchanan*, ed. and trans. into English verse, Edinburgh, 1906.

BROWN, Carleton. 'Lydgate's Verses on Queen Margaret's Entry into London', *Modern Language Review*, VII (1912), pp. 225–34.

—— 'An Early Mention of a St Nicholas Play in England', *Studies in Philology*, XXXVIII (1931), pp. 594–601.

BROWN, Howard Mayer. 'Musicians in the Mysteres and Miracles', *Medieval English Drama*, ed. Jerome Taylor and Alan H. Nelson, pp. 81–97.

BRUNNE, Robert Mannyng of. *Handlyng Synne*, ed. with William of Wadington's *Manuel des Pechiez* for EETS by F.J. Furnivall, 1901.

BUCER, Martin. *De Regno Christi*, ed. with Philip Melanchthon's *Loci communes theologici* by Wilhelm Pauck, London, 1969.

BUCKLEY, George T. *Atheism in the English Renaissance*, New York, 1965.

BURKE, Peter. *Popular Culture in Early Modern Europe*, London, 1978.

BUTLER, Guy. '*Macbeth*': *The Great Doom's Image*, Grahamstown, S. A., 1976.

CALVIN, John. *Institutes of the Christian Religion*, ed. John T. McNeil, trans. Ford Lewis Battles, 2 vols, London, 1961.

CAMERON, Kenneth, and KAHRL, Stanley J. 'The N-Town Plays at Lincoln', *Theatre Notebook*, XX, No. 2 (winter 1965–6), pp. 61–9.

CAMERON, K. W. *The Authorship and Sources of 'Gentleness and Nobility'*, New York, 1941.

CAMPBELL, L. B. *Scenes and Machines on the English Stage during the Renaissance: A Classical Revival*, 1923; reprinted 1961.

CARGILL, Oscar. *Drama and Liturgy*, New York, 1930.

CAWLEY, A. C. (ed.). *The Wakefield Pageants in the Towneley Cycle*, Manchester U.P., 1958.

CAWTE, E.C. *Ritual Animal Disguise*, Cambridge, 1977.

——, HELM, Alex and PEACOCK, Norman, *A Geographical Index of English Ritual Drama*, London (Folk-Lore Society), 1967.

CHAMBERS, E. K. *The Mediaeval Stage*, 2 vols, O.U.P., 1903.

—— *The Elizabethan Stage*, 4 vols, O.U.P., 1923.

—— *The English Folk-Play*, O.U.P, 1973; reprinted New York, 1969.

CHAUCER, Geoffrey. *The Complete Works*, ed. W. W. Skeat, 7 vols, reprinted, O.U.P., 1924.

COGHILL, Nevill. 'The Basis of the Shakespearean Comedy', *Essays and Studies*, ed. G. Rostrevor Hamilton, London, 1950, pp. 1–28.

COHEN, G. *Histoire de la mise en scene dans le Theatre religieux francais du Moyen Age*, Paris, 1926.

CRAIG, Hardin. *English Religious Drama*, O.U.P., 1955.

CRAIK, T. W. *The Tudor Interlude*, Leicester U.P., 1958.

CRAWSHAW, William. *The Sermon preached at the Crosse, Feb. xiiij. 1607*, London, 1608.

CREIZENACH, W. *Geschichte des neueren Dramas*, Vols I-III, Halle, 1893–1903.

CROW, Brian. 'The Development of the Presentation of Human Actions in Medieval and Renaissance Drama', Ph.D. thesis, University of Bristol, 1978.

314

CUNLIFFE, J. W. *The Complete Works of George Gascoigne*, 2 vols, Cambridge University Press, 1907, 1910.

—— *Early English Classical Tragedies*, Clarendon Press, 1912.

—— 'Gismond of Salerne', *PMLA*, XXI, 1906, pp. 435–61.

CUSHMAN, L. W. 'The Devil and the Vice in the English Dramatic Literature before Shakespeare', *Studien zur Englischen Philologie*, ed. Lorenz Morsbach, Vol. VI, Halle, 1900.

DAVIDSON, Clifford. *Drama and Art*, Kalamazoo, Mich., 1977.

DAVIS, Norman. *Non-Cycle Plays and Fragments*, ed. for EETS, 1970.

DEIMLING, H.W.E. *The Chester Plays*, ed. for EETS, 2 vols, 1893–1916; reprinted 1968.

DENNY, Neville. *Medieval Drama*, Stratford-upon-Avon Studies 16, London, 1973.

DICKENS, A. G. *The English Reformation*, London, 1964.

DUBY, Georges. *The Chivalrous Society*, trans. Cynthia Postan, London, 1977.

ENGELHARDT, Christian M. *Herrad von Landsperg*, Stuttgart and Tübingen, 1818.

EVANS-PRITCHARD, E. E. *Social Anthropology*, London, 1951.

EWBANK, Inga-Stina. 'What words, what looks, what wonders?: Language and Spectacle in the Theatre of George Peele', *Elizabethan Theatre*, Vol. V, ed. George Hibbard, London, 1975, pp. 124–54.

FABYAN, Robert. *The New Chronicles of England and France*, ed. Henry Ellis (from Pynson's 1516 ed.), 1811.

FARNHAM, Willard. *The Medieval Heritage of Elizabethan Tragedy*, Cambridge U.P. and U. California P., 1936.

FERGUSON, John. *The Religions of the Roman Empire*, Cornell U.P., 1970.

FEUILLERAT, A. 'Documents Relating to the Revels at Court in the Time of Queen Elizabeth' in *Materialien zur Kunde des älteren englischen Dramas*, ed. W. Bang, Vol. XXI, Louvain, 1908.

—— 'Documents Relating to the Revels at Court in the Time of King Edward VI and Queen Mary' in *Materialien zur Kunde des älteren englischen Dramas*, ed. W. Bang, Vol. XLIV, Louvain, 1914.

FORBES, F. H. *John Christopherson's 'Jephthah'*, Greek text and English translation, Newark, Del., 1928.

FOWLER, W. Warde. *Social Life at Rome in the Age of Cicero*, London, 1908.

FOXE, John. *Acts and Monuments of the ... Ecclesiastical historie, contayning the actes and monuments of Martyrs*, 2 vols, 1570. See also Foxe's *Book of Martyrs*, ed. and abridged by G. A. Williamson, London, 1965.

FRANK, Grace. *Medieval French Drama*, O.U.P., 1954.

FRAZER, Sir James Gordon. *The Golden Bough*, abridged ed., London, 1922.

FURNIVALL, E.J. *The Digby Plays*, ed. for EETS, 1896. See also *sub* Lydgate.

GAFFNEY, Wilbur. 'The Allegory of the Christ Knight in Piers Plowman', *PMLA*, XLVI (1931), pp. 155–68.

GARDINER, H. C. *Mysteries' End*, New Haven, Conn., 1946; reprinted, 1967.

GASQUET, F. A. *Parish Life in Medieval England*, London, 1906.

GAYLEY, C. M. (ed.). *Representative English Comedies*, London, 1903.

GOSSON, Stephen. *The Schoole of Abuse* (1579), ed. Edward Arber, English Reprints, London, 1868.

GRAHAM, J. H. 'St Ignatius and Cardinal Pole', *Archivum Historicum Societatis Iesu*, XXV (1956), pp. 72–98.

GREEN, Alice Stopford. *Town Life in the 15th Century*, 2 vols, London, 1894.

GREENBERG, Noah. *The Play of Daniel*, ed. with music for O.U.P., 1959.

GREENLAW, E. A. *Studies in Spenser's Historical Allegory*, Baltimore, 1932.

GROSS, C. *The Gild Merchant*, 2 vols, Oxford, 1890; reprinted, London, 1927.

GROSSETESTE, Robert. *Letters and Treatises*, ed. H. R. Luard, London, 1861. See also STEVENSON, F. S.

HAIGH, Christopher. *Reformation and Resistance in Tudor Lancashire*, Cambridge U.P., 1975.

HALLER, William. *Foxe's Book of Martyrs and the Elect Nation*, London, 1963.

HARBAGE, A., and SCHOENBAUM, S. *Annals of English Drama, 975–1700*, London, 1964.

HARDISON, O. B., jnr. *Christian Rite and Christian Drama in the Middle Ages*, Johns Hopkins Press, 1965.

HARRIS, H. A. *Greek Athletes and Athletics*. London, 1964.

—— *Sport in Greece and Rome*, London, 1972.

HARRIS, J. W. 'John Bale: A Study in the Literature of the Reformation', *Illinois Studies in Language and Literature*, XXV, no. 4 (1940).

HARRIS, Mary D. *Coventry Leet-Book*, ed. for EETS, 2 vols, 1907–9.

HARRIS, William O. *Skelton's 'Magnificence' and the Cardinal Virtue Tradition*, U. North Carolina Press, 1965.

HAUGAARD, William P. *Elizabeth and the English Reformation*, Cambridge U. P., 1968.

HAZLITT, W. C. *The English Drama and Stage under the Tudor and Stuart Princes, 1543–1664*, 1869; reprinted, n.d., Burt Franklin, New York.

HEER, Frederick. *The Holy Roman Empire*, trans. Janet Sondheimer, London, 1968.

HEINEMANN, Margot. 'Middleton's *A Game at Chess:* Parliamentary-Puritans and Opposition Drama', *English Literary Renaissance*, V, No. 2 (spring 1975), pp. 232–50.

HENDERSON, Philip (ed.). *The Complete Poems of John Skelton*, 1931; rev. ed., London, 1948.

HIBBARD, G. R. 'Goodness and Greatness: An Essay on the Tragedies of Ben Jonson and George Chapman', *Renaissance and Modern Studies* (University of Nottingham), XI (1967), pp. 5–54.

HILDBURGH, W. L. *English Alabaster Carvings as Records of the Medieval Religious Drama*, London, 1949.

HOLMES, David M. *The Art of Thomas Middleton: A Critical Study*, O.U.P., 1970.

HOPF, Constantin, *Martin Bucer and the English Reformation*, Clarendon Press, 1946.

HOSLEY, Richard. 'The Origins of the Shakespearean Playhouse', *Shakespeare Quarterly*, XV, no. 2 (spring 1964), pp. 29–39.

HOTSON, Leslie. *Queen Elizabeth's Entertainment at Mitcham*, New Haven, Conn., 1953.

HUGHES, Robert. *Heaven and Hell in Western Art*, London, 1968.

HUIZINGA, J. *Homo Ludens: A Study of the Play-element in Culture*, trans. R.F.C. Hull, London, 1949.

JAMES I. *The Kings Maiesties Speech, 19th March, 1603*, London, 1604.

JANICKA, Irena. *The Comic Elements in the English Mystery Plays Against the Cultural Background (Particularly Art)*, Poznan, 1962.

JEFFREY, D. L. 'English Saints' Plays', Stratford-upon-Avon Studies 16: *Medieval Drama*, ed. Neville Denny, 1973, pp. 68–89.

JONES, Charles W. (ed.). *Bedae Opera de Temporibus*, Cambridge, Mass., 1943.

KAHRL, Stanley J. *Traditions of Medieval English Drama*, U. Pittsburgh P., 1975. See also CAMERON, Kenneth, and KAHRL, Stanley J., and MALONE SOCIETY COLLECTIONS, VIII.

KENNARD, J. S. *The Italian Theatre from its Beginning to the Close of the Seventeenth Century*, 2 vols, 1932; reprinted, New York, 1964.

KERNODLE, G. R. *From Art to Theatre*, U. Chicago P., 1943.

KINDERMANN, H. *Theatergeschichte Europas*, 9 vols, Salzburg, 1957–70.

KINNEY, Arthur F. *Markets of Bawdrie: The Dramatic Criticism of Stephen Gosson*, 1974 (Salzburg Studies in English, IV).

KIRSCHBAUM, Leo. 'Albany', *Shakespeare Survey*, XIII (1960), pp. 20–9.

KITCHIN, G. W. (ed.). *Winchester Cathedral Records*, Hampshire Record Society, 1886.

KITTO, H. D. F. *The Greeks*, paperback ed., Harmondsworth 1951.

KLEIN, J. *The Mesta: A Study of Spanish Economic History, 1273–1836*, Harvard U.P., 1920.

KOLVE, V. A. *The Play Called Corpus Christi*, Stanford U.P., 1966.

LAMB, Charles. *Essays of Elia*, ed. William MacDonald, London, 1903.

LAMBARDE, William. *Alphabetical Description of the Chief Places in England and Wales*, ed. 1730 from a sixteenth-century MS.

LASCELLES, Mary. *Shakespeare's 'Measure for Measure'*, London, 1953.

LATIMER, Hugh. *Seven Sermons before Edward VI, on each Friday in Lent, 1549*, ed. E. Arber, London, 1869.

LEACH, A. F. *Beverley Town Documents*, Selden Society, Vol. XIV, 1900.

LECOQ, Georges. *Histoire du théâtre en Picardie*, Paris, 1880; reprinted, Geneva, 1971.

LÉVI-STRAUSS, C. *The Savage Mind*, London, 1966.

—— *Introduction to a Science of Mythology*, 2 vols, trans. John and Doreen Weightman, London, 1969–73.

LOOMIS, L. H. 'Secular Dramatics in the Royal Palace, Paris, 1378, 1389, and Chaucer's "Tregetoures"', *Speculum*, XXXIII (1958), pp. 242–55.

Reprinted in *Medieval English Drama*, ed. J. Taylor and A. H. Nelson, pp. 98–115.

LYDGATE, John. 'The Order of Fools', ed. for EETS by F. J. Furnivall in *Queene Elizabethes Achademy*, 1869.

—— *Troy Book*, ed. for EETS by Henry Bergen, 4 vols in 3, 1906–35.

——*The Minor Poems*, ed. for EETS by H. N. MacCracken, 2 vols, 1911; reprinted 1934.

——*The Fall of Princes*, ed. for EETS by Henry Bergen, 4 vols, 1924–7.

LYLY, John. *The Entertainment at Mitcham*. See HOTSON, Leslie.

MACHIAVELLI, N. *The Literary Works*, ed. and trans. by J. R. Hale, O.U.P., 1961.

MAGNIN, Charles. *Les Origines du théâtre moderne*, Paris, 1838.

MALONE SOCIETY COLLECTIONS
- I.2. ed. W. W. Greg, 1909, containing 'Dramatic Records from the Lansdowne Manuscripts', ed. E. K. Chambers and W. W. Greg, pp. 143–215.
- II.2. ed. W. W. Greg, 1923, containing 'The Academic Drama at Cambridge: Extracts from College Records', ed. G. C. Moore Smith, pp. 150–231.
- III. ed. F. P. Wilson, 1954, containing 'A Calendar of Dramatic Records in the Books of the Livery Companies of London, 1485–1640', ed. Jean Robertson and D. J. Gordon.
- V. ed. F. P. Wilson, 1959 (1960), containing 'A Calendar of Dramatic Records in the Books of the Clothworkers' Company' (Addenda to *Collections III*), ed. Jean Robertson, pp. 1–16, and 'The Academic Drama in Oxford: Extracts from the Records of Four Colleges', ed. R. E. Alton, pp. 29–95.
- VII. ed. Arthur Brown, 1965, containing 'Records of Plays and Players in Kent, 1450–1642', ed. Giles E. Dawson.
- VIII. ed. G. R. Proudfoot, 1972, containing 'Records of Plays and Players in Lincolnshire, 1300–1585', ed. Stanley J. Kahrl.
- IX. ed. G. R. Proudfoot, 1976, containing 'A Corpus Christi Play and Other Dramatic Activities in Sixteenth Century Sherborne, Dorset', ed. A. D. Mills, pp. 1–15, and 'Playing Companies at Aldeburgh, 1566–1635', ed. J. C. Coldewey, pp. 16–23.

MANNING, Roger B. *Religion and Society in Elizabethan Sussex*, Leicester U.P., 1969.

MARGESON, J.M.R. *The Origins of English Tragedy*, O.U.P., 1967.

MATTHEW, F. D. *The English Works of Wycliffe*, ed. for EETS, 1880.

MAXWELL, Ian. *French Farce and John Heywood*, Melbourne U.P. and O.U.P., 1946.

MAXWELL LYTE, H. C. *A History of the University of Oxford from the Earliest Times to the Year 1530*, London, 1886.

MEHL, Dieter. *The Elizabethan Dumb Show*, London, 1964.

MIGNE, J. P. *Patrologiae Cursus Completus: Patrologia Latina*, 221 vols, Paris, 1844–64.

—— *Patrologiae Cursus Completus: Patrologia Graeca*, 161 vols, Paris, 1857–66.

MIRK, John. *Mirk's Festial: A Collection of Homilies ed. from Bodl. MS Gough Eccl. Top. 4, with Variant Readings from Other MSS.*, by Theodor Erbe for EETS, 1905.

MONTAGU, Gwen and Jeremy. 'Beverley Minster Reconsidered', *Early Music* (the Early Music Gazette), London, Vol. 6, No. 3 (July 1978), pp. 401–14.

MOORE, John B. *The Comic and the Realistic in English Drama*, Chicago, 1925; reprinted Russell, New York, 1965.

MORRIS, Rev. R. *Ayenbite of Inwyt*, ed. for EETS, 1866.

—— *Old English Homilies*, ed. for EETS, 1873.

MOSHER, J. A. *The Exemplum in the Early Religious and Didactic Literature of England*, New York, 1966.

MOTTER, T. H. Vail. *The School Drama in England*, London, 1929.

MUIR, Lynette R. 'Adam', *Proceedings of the Leeds Philosophical and Literary Society: Literary and Historical Section*, XIII, Part V, January 1970, pp. 149–204.

MUNZ, Peter. *Frederick Barbarossa: A Study in Medieval Politics*, Cornell U.P. and London, 1969.

NELSON, Alan H. See TAYLOR, Jerome, and NELSON, Alan H.

NEUSS, Paula. 'Active and Idle Language: Dramatic Images in *Mankind*', Stratford-upon-Avon Studies 16: *Medieval Drama*, ed. Neville Denny, 1973, pp. 41–67.

NEWTON, Thomas. *Seneca, his tenne tragedies, translated into English*, 1581; ed. T. S. Eliot, 2 vols, London, 1927.

NICHOLS, J. *The Progresses and Public Processions of Queen Elizabeth*, 3 vols, 2nd ed., 1823.

NORRIS, Edwin. *The Ancient Cornish Drama*, 2 vols, 1859; reprinted Blom, New York, 1968.

OSBORN, James M. *The Quenes Majesties Passage*, Yale U.P. and O.U.P., 1960.

OWST, G. R. *Literature and Pulpit in Mediaeval England*, Cambridge U.P., 1933; 2nd ed., Oxford, 1961.

OXLEY, James E. *The Reformation in Essex to the Death of Mary*, Manchester U.P., 1965.

PARSONS, David (ed.). *Tenth-Century Studies*, Chichester, 1975.

PILKINTON, Mark. 'The Antagonists of English Drama, 1370–1576', Ph.D. thesis, University of Bristol, 1974.

PINEAS, Rainer. *Tudor and Early Stuart Anti-Catholic Drama*, Nieuwkoop, 1972.

PIRENNE, H. *Medieval Cities, their Origin and the Revival of Trade*, trans. H. P. Halsey, O.U.P., 1925.

POLLARD, A. W. *English Miracle Plays, Moralities and Interludes*, 8th ed., 1927; reprinted, Clarendon Press, 1965.

PORTER, H. C. *Reformation and Reaction in Tudor Cambridge*, Cambridge U.P., 1958.

POTTER, R. *The English Morality Play*, London, 1975.

PROSSER, Eleanor. *Drama and Religion in the English Mystery Plays*, Stanford U.P., 1961.

PROUTY, C. T. *George Gascoigne: Elizabethan Courtier, Soldier and Poet*, New York, 1942.

ROSENFELD, Sybil. *Strolling Players and Drama in the Provinces, 1660–1795*, Cambridge U.P., 1939.

ROSSITER, A. P. *English Drama from Early Times to the Elizabethans*, London, 1950.

SALTER, F. M. *Mediaeval Drama in Chester*, U. Toronto P. and O.U.P., 1955.

SCHRADE, Leo. *La Représentation d'Edipo Tiranno au Teatro Olimpico*, CNRS, Paris, 1960.

SEGAL, Erich. *Roman Laughter: The Comedy of Plautus*, Harvard U.P., 1968.

SEPET, Marius. *Origines catholiques du théâtre moderne*, Paris, 1901.

SHERGOLD, N. D. *A History of the Spanish Stage*, O.U.P., 1967.

SIDNEY, Sir Philip. *Apologie for poetrie*, 1595; reprinted, ed. E. Arber, London, 1868.

SKELTON, JOHN. See HENDERSON, Philip.

SMOLDON, W. L. 'The Melodies of the Medieval Church Dramas and their Significance', *Medieval English Drama*, ed. Jerome Taylor and Alan H. Nelson, pp. 64–80.

—— 'The Origins of the *Quem Quaeritis* and the Easter Sepulchre Music-Drama as Demonstrated by Their Musical Settings', *The Medieval Drama*, ed. Sandro Sticca, 1972, pp. 121–54.

—— *Sponsus: An Eleventh Century Mystère*, O.U.P., n.d.

SOUTHERN, Richard. *The Production of Plays Before Shakespeare*, London, 1973.

SPIVACK, Bernard. *Shakespeare and the Allegory of Evil*, New York, 1958.

STAINES, David. 'To Out-Herod Herod: The Development of a Dramatic Character', *Comparative Drama*, X, no. 1 (spring 1976), pp. 29–53.

STEMMLER, Theo. *Liturgische Feiern und Geistliche Spiele*, Tübingen, 1970.

STEVENS, John. 'Music in Medieval Drama', *Proceedings of the Musical Association*, 84th Session, 1957–8.

—— 'Music in Some Early Medieval Plays', *Studies in the Arts*, ed. Francis Warner, Oxford, 1968.

—— See also AXTON, R.

STEVENSON, F. S. *Robert Grosseteste, Bishop of Lincoln: A Contribution to the Religious, Political and Intellectual Life of the Thirteenth Century*, London, 1899.

STICCA, Sandro. *The Latin Passion Play: Its Origins and Development*, New York, 1970.

—— 'The Literary Genesis of the Latin Passion Play', *The Medieval Drama*, pp. 39–68.

—— *The Medieval Drama*, ed. for State University of New York, Binghamton, 1972.

STOKES, Whitley. *Beunans Meriasek: The Life of St. Meriasek*, edited (together with a translation from the Cornish) London and Dublin, 1872.

STOW, John. *A Survey of London*, ed. C. L. Kingsford, 2 vols, Clarendon Press, 1908.

STRONG, Roy. *The Cult of Elizabeth*, London 1977.

STRUTT, Joseph. *A Compleat view of the manners, customs, arms, habits, etc. of the inhabitants of England, from the arrival of the Saxons till the reign of Henry the Eighth*, London, 1775.

STUBBS, Philip. *The Anatomy of Abuses*, 1583.

STUDER, Paul. *Le Mystere d'Adam, an Anglo-Norman Drama of the Twelfth Century*, Manchester U.P., 1928.

TAYLOR, Jerome, and NELSON, Alan H. (eds). *Medieval English Drama: Essays Critical and Contextual*, U. Chicago P., 1972.

THOMAS, Catherine B. C. 'The Miracle Play at Dunstable', *Modern Language Notes*, XXXII (1917), pp. 337–44.

TOULMIN-SMITH, L. *English Guilds*, ed. for EETS, 1870.

—— *York Plays*, Oxford, 1885; reprinted Russell, New York, 1963.

TREVELYAN, G. M. *English Social History*, London, 1942.

TYNDALE, William. *The Obedience of a Christian Man, and how Christian Rulers Ought to Governe*, 1528, ed. Richard Lovett, London, n.d.

UDALL, Nicholas. *Floures for Latine Spekynge, selected and gathered oute of Terence . . .*, compiled by N. Udall, London, 1533.

UNWIN, G. *Gilds and Companies of London*, London, 1908.

WADDELL, Helen. *The Wandering Scholars*, London, 1927.

WARDE FOWLER, W. See FOWLER, W. Warde.

WHITNEY, Geoffrey. *Choice of Emblemes*, Leyden, 1586.

WICKHAM, Glynne (ed.). *English Moral Interludes*, London, 1976; paperback, 1977.

—— 'From Tragedy to Tragi-Comedy: *King Lear* as Prologue', *Shakespeare Survey*, XXVI (1973), pp. 33–48.

—— 'Masque and Anti-Masque in *The Tempest*', *Essays and Studies*, ed. R. Ellrodt, London, 1975, pp. 1–14.

—— *The Medieval Theatre*, London, 1974.

—— 'Romance and Emblem: A Study of the Dramatic Structure of *The Winter's Tale*', *Elizabethan Theatre*, Vol. III, ed. David Galloway, London, 1973, pp. 82–99.

—— *Shakespeare's Dramatic Heritage*, London, 1969.

WIGFALL GREEN, A. *The Inns of Court and Early English Drama*, Yale U.P., 1931.

WILKINS, David. *Leges anglo-saxonicae ecclesiasticae et civiles*, London, 1721.

——*Concilia Magnae Britanniae et Hiberniae*, 4 vols, London, 1737.

WILLIAMS, Arnold. 'The Comic in the Cycles', Stratford-upon-Avon Studies, 16: *Medieval Drama*, ed. Neville Denny, 1973, pp. 109–123.

WITHINGTON, Robert. *English Pageantry, An Historical Outline*, 2 vols, Harvard U.P., 1918–20.

WOOLF, Rosemary. 'The Theme of Christ the Lover-Knight in Medieval English Literature', *Review of English Studies*, n.s. XIII (1962), pp. 1–16.
—— *The English Mystery Plays*, London, 1972.

WRIGHT, J. *The Play of Anti-Christ*, Pontifical Institute of Medieval Studies, Toronto, 1967.

WYCLIF, John. See MATTHEWS, F. D., HAZLITT, W. C.

YOUNG, Karl. *The Drama of the Mediaeval Church*, 2 vols, Clarendon Press, 1933.

ZUCKER, David Hard. *Stage and Image in the Plays of Christopher Marlowe*, Salzburg, 1972. (Salzburg Studies in English Literature, VII; General Editor, Dr James Hogg.)

LIST OF PLAYS

Quoted from or referred to in the text

This list is ordered throughout as follows:
PLAY TITLE; author if known; date of composition; manuscript number
and provenance where applicable; 1st printed edition.

1 Recommended edition.
2 Other single editions.
3 Collected editions.
4 Editions with spelling and punctuation modernized.

For general bibliographies of medieval and Tudor plays see E. K. Chambers, *The Mediaeval Stage*, 2 vols, 1903, Vol II, Appendix X; T. W. Craik, *The Tudor Interlude*, 1958, pp. 140–9; David Bevington, *From Mankind to Marlowe*, 1962, pp. 274–7; A. Harbage and S. Schoenbaum, *Annals of English Drama*, 975–1700, 1964; F. P. Wilson and G. K. Hunter, *The English Drama, 1485–1585*, 1969, pp. 202–37.

ALBION KNIGHT; anonymous (fragment only); *c.* 1537; 1st ed. T. Colwell, n.d. (? 1566).
1 *MSR* Collections I.3, ed. W. W. Greg, 1909.
4 Farmer, *Six Anonymous Plays*, series 2, 1906; reprinted 1966.

323

ALL FOR MONEY; by Thomas Lupton; *c.* 1578; 1st ed. Roger Warde and Richard Mundee, 1578.
1 *Shakespeare Jahrbuch*, XL, ed. E. Vogel, 1904.
2 Farmer, *TFT*, 1910.
4 *EMP*, 1969.

ANTI-CHRISTUS: see LUDUS DE ANTICHRISTO.

APIUS AND VIRGINIA; by R. B.; *c.* 1564; 1st ed. W. How for R. Jhones, 1575.
1 *MSR*, ed. R. B. McKerrow and W. W. Greg, 1911.
2 Farmer, TFT, 1908.
3 H-D IV; Happé.
4 Farmer, *Five Anonymous Plays*, series 4, 1908; reprinted 1966.

ARRAIGNMENT OF PARIS, THE; by George Peele; *c.* 1581–3; 1st ed. Henry Marsh, 1584.
1 *MSR*, ed. Harold H. Child, 1910.
2 Ed. O. Smeaton, 1905.
3 *Works*, ed. A. H. Bullen, 2 vols, 1888; *Dramatic Works*, ed. C. T. Prouty, New Haven, Conn., 1952–70.

BATTLE OF ALCAZAR, THE; by George Peele; 1589; 1st ed. Edward Allde for Richard Bankworth, 1574.
1 *MSR*, ed. W. W. Greg, 1906.
3 *Works*, A. H. Bullen, 2 vols, 1888; *Dramatic Works*, ed C. T. Prouty, New Haven, Conn., 1952–70.

BEUNANS MERIASEK; by (?) Dom. Hadton; 1504; MS. Hengwrt, Peniarth; 1st ed. Whitley Stokes (with trans.), 1872.

CALISTO AND MELIBEA; anonymous; *c.* 1525; 1st ed. J. Rastell, n.d. (*c.* 1527).
1 *MSR*, ed. F. Sidgwick and W. W. Greg, 1908.
2 Farmer, *TFT*, 1909.
3 H-D IV.
4 Farmer, *Six Anonymous Plays*, series 1, 1905; reprinted 1966.

CAMBISES; by Thomas Preston; *c.* 1561; 1st ed. John Allde, n.d., (1) *c.* 1569, (2) *c.* 1585, (3) *c.* 1588.
1 Farmer, *TFT*, 1910.
2 H-D IV; Adams; Manly II.

CASTLE OF PERSEVERANCE, THE; anonymous; *c.* 1410–25; MS. Folger Library, Washington, D.C.
1 *The Macro Plays*, ed. Mark Eccles for EETS, 1969.
2 Folger Facsimile Texts, ed. David Bevington, 1972.
4 *EMP*, 1969.

CHESTER PLAYS, THE; 14th–16th centuries; BM MS. Add. 10305; Harl. 2013; Harl. 2124; and Bodl. MS. 175.
1 EETS, ed. H. Deimling, 1893–1916; reprinted 1968. For earlier editions see Chambers, *Med. Stage.* ii.407–8.

CHESTER PLAY OF ANTICHRIST, THE; 15th century; ed. W. W. Greg from (1) the Devonshire MS. and (2) the Peniarth MS., 1935.

CLYOMON AND CLAMYDES; anonymous; *c.* 1575; 1st ed. Thomas Creede, 1599.
1 *MSR*, ed. W. W. Greg, 1913.
2 Farmer, *TFT*, 1913.
3 *The Plays of George Peele*, ed. Dyce, 1839, 1861; ed. Bullen, 1888.

COMMON CONDITIONS; anonymous; *c.* 1576; 1st ed. W. How for J. Hunter, 1576 (two editions).
1 Ed. C. F. Tucker Brooke (from 1st ed.), 1915.
4 Farmer, *Five Anonymous Plays*, series 4, 1908; reprinted 1966.

CONFLICT OF CONSCIENCE, THE; by Nathaniel Woodes; *c.* 1580; 1st ed. R. Bradocke, 1581 (two versions).
1 *MSR*, ed. Herbert Davis and F. P. Wilson, 1952.
2 Ed. J. P. Collier, Roxburghe Club, 1851; ed. Farmer, *TFT*, 1911.
3 H-D VI.
4 *EMP*, 1969.

CORNISH ORDINALIA, THE; Bodl. MSS. 791 and 28556; 1st ed. Edwin Norris, *The Ancient Cornish Drama*, 2 vols, 1859; reprinted by Benjamin Blom, 1968.
4 Ed. and trans. Markham Harris, Washington, D.C., 1969.

COURTOIS D'ARRAS; anonymous; *c.* 1225; ed. Edmond Faral for CFMA, 3, Paris, 1911; revised ed. 1922; reprinted 1961.
See also AXTON, R., and STEVENS, J.

DAMON AND PITHIAS; by Richard Edwards; 1566; 1st ed. Richard Jones, 1571.
1 *MSR*, ed. F. P. Wilson, 1957.
2 Farmer, TFT, 1908.
3 H-D IV; Adams.
4 Farmer, *The Dramatic Writings of Edwards, Norton and Sackville*, 1906; reprinted 1966.

DIGBY PLAY OF ST MARY MAGDALENE, THE; anonymous; *c.* 1500; Bodl. MS. Digby 133; 1st ed. F. J. Furnivall for EETS, *The Digby Plays*, 1896.
1 EETS, ed. Furnivall.

DIGBY PLAY OF THE CONVERSION OF ST PAUL, THE; anonymous; *c.* 1500; Bodl. MS. Digby 133; 1st ed. F. J. Furnivall for EETS, *The Digby Plays*, 1896.
1 EETS, ed. Furnivall.
3 Manly I, 1897.
4 *EMI*, 1976.

DISOBEDIENT CHILD, THE; by Thomas Ingelend; *c.* 1560; 1st ed. T. Colwell, n.d. (*c.* 1570).
1 Farmer, *TFT*, 1908.
2 J. O. Halliwell, Percy Society, 1848.
3 H-D II.
4 J. S. Farmer, *The Dramatic Writings of Richard Wever and Thomas Ingelend*, 1905; reprinted 1966.

ENOUGH IS AS GOOD AS A FEAST; by William Wager; (?) *c.* 1564; 1st ed. J. Allde, n.d. (*c.* 1565).
1 Ed. S.de Ricci, Huntington Facsimile Reprints, New York, 1920.
4 Ed. R. M. Benbow, Lincoln, Nebr., 1967; reprinted London, 1968; *EMP*, 1969.

EVERYMAN; anonymous; *c.* 1495; 1st ed. J. Skot, n.d. (*c.* 1515).
1 A. C. Cawley, Manchester, 1961.
3 H-D I; Adams; Pollard; and others.
4 Ed. Ernest Rhys, Dent's Everyman Library, 1909; and others including *EMP*.

FOUR ELEMENTS, A NEW INTERLUDE OF THE; by John Rastell; *c.* 1517–25; 1st ed. J. Rastell, n.d.
1 Ed. Farmer, TFT, 1908.
2 Ed. J. O. Halliwell, Percy Society, Vol. XXII, 1848; ed. J. Fischer, *Marburger Studien*, 1903.
3 H-D I.
4 Farmer, *Six Anonymous Plays*, series 1, 1905; reprinted 1966.

FOUR PP, THE; by John Heywood; (?) 1544; 1st ed. W. Myddylton, n.d. (? 1545).
1 Farmer, *TFT*, 1908.
3 H-D I; Manly I; Adams.
4 J. S. Farmer, *The Dramatic Writings of John Heywood*, 1905; reprinted 1966.

FULGENS AND LUCRES, I and II; by Henry Medwall; 1497; 1st ed. J. Rastell, *c.* 1515.
1 Ed. S. de Ricci, Huntington Facsimile Reprints, New York, 1920.
2 F. S. Boas and A. W. Reed, 1926.
3 F. S. Boas, *Five Pre-Shakespearean Comedies*, 1934.
4 *EMI*, 1976.

GAMMER GURTON'S NEEDLE; by Mr S. (William Stevenson); *c.* 1553; 1st ed. T. Colwell, 1575.
1 Ed. H. Brett-Smith, 1920.
2 Farmer, *TFT*, 1910.
3 H-D III; Manly II; Adams; F. S. Boas and others.

GARCON ET L'AVEUGLE; anonymous; (?) 1270; ed. Mario Roques for CFMA, 5, Paris, 1921.
See also AXTON, R. and STEVENS, J.

GENTLENESS AND NOBILITY; by (?) John Heywood; *c.* 1527; 1st ed. J. Rastell, n.d. (*c.* 1528).
1 *MSR*, ed. A. C. Partridge and F. P. Wilson, 1950.
2 Farmer, *TFT*, 1908; K. W. Cameron, 1941.
4 J. S. Farmer, *The Writings of John Heywood*, 1908; reprinted 1966.

GISMOND OF SALERNE; by Robert Stafford, Henry Noel, G. N., Christopher Hatton and Robert Wilmot; *c.* 1566–7.
(See TANCRED AND GISMOND; also BM MSS. Lansdowne 786 and Hargrave 205.)
1 J. W. Cunliffe, *Early English Classical Tragedies*, 1912.

GODLY QUEEN HESTER; anonymous; *c.* 1527; 1st ed. W. Pickering and T. Hacket, 1561.
1 Ed. W. W. Greg, *Materialien*, V, 1904.
3 Ed. J. P. Collier, *English Popular Literature*, I, 1863; A. B. Grosart, *The Fuller Worthies' Library Miscellanies*, IV, 1873.
4 Ed. Farmer, *Six Anonymous Plays*, series 2, 1906; reprinted 1966.

GORBODUC, THE TRAGEDIE OF; by Thomas Norton and Thomas Sackville; 1561–2 1st ed. 1565 and n.d. (1570).
1 Ed. J. W. Cunliffe, *Early English Classical Tragedies*, 1912.
2 Farmer, *TFT*, 1908; H. A. Watt, 1910.
3 Manly II.
4 Farmer, *The Dramatic Writings of Edwards, Norton and Sackville*, 1906; reprinted 1966; Ashley Thorndike, Dent's Everyman Library, n.d.

HICK-SCORNER; anonymous; *c.* 1510; 1st ed. Wynkyn de Worde, n.d. (*c.* 1513).
1 Farmer, *TFT*, 1908.
3 H-D I; Manly I.
4 Farmer, *Six Anonymous Plays*, series 1, 1905; reprinted, 1966.

HORESTES, A NEWE ENTERLUDE OF VICE CONTEYNINGE THE HISTORY OF; by John Pickering; *c.* 1566; 1st ed. W. Griffith, 1567.
1 *MSR*, ed. Daniel Seltzer and Arthur Brown, 1961.
2 Farmer, *TFT*, 1910; Brandl, *Quellen*, 1898.

IMPATIENT POVERTY; anonymous; *c.* 1560; 1st ed. J. King, 1560.
1 Farmer, *TFT*, 1907.
2 W. Bang, *Materialien*, XXXIII, 1911.
4 Farmer, '*Lost*' *Tudor Plays*, 1907.

JACK JUGGLER; anonymous; *c.* 1555; 1st ed. William Coplande, n.d.
(*c.* 1562), and again, *c.* 1565; 3rd ed. John Allde, n.d. (*c.* 1569–70).
1 *MSR* (Coplande ed.), ed. E. L. Smart and W. W. Greg, 1933; *MSR* (Allde ed.), ed. B. Ifor Evans and W. W. Greg, 1937.
2 Farmer, *TFT*, 1912; W. H. Williams, 1914.
3 H-D II.
4 Farmer, *Anonymous Plays*, series 3, 1906; reprinted 1966.

JACOB AND ESAU; anonymous; *c.* 1553; 1st ed. H Bynneman, 1568.
1 *MSR*, ed. John Crow and F. P. Wilson, 1956.
2 Farmer, *TFT*, 1908.
4 Farmer, *Six Anonymous Plays*, series 2, 1906; reprinted 1966.

JEPHTHAH: See BROWN, Archibald, (George Buchanan's) and FORBES, F. H. (John Christopherson's).

JEU DE LA FEUILLÉE; by Adam le Bossu (or de la Halle, or d'Arras); 1276 or 1277.
Ed. Ernest Langlois for CFMA, 6, Paris, 1923; 2nd ed. 1951. See also AXTON, R., and STEVENS, J.

JEU DE ROBIN ET MARION; by Adam le Bossu (or de la Halle, or d'Arras), *c.* 1285.
Ed. Ernest Langlois for CFMA, 36, Paris, 1924; Kenneth Vartu, 1960. See also AXTON, R., and STEVENS, J.

JOCASTA; by George Gascoigne and Francis Kinwelmarshe; 1566; 1st ed. in *A Hundreth Sundrie Floures*, 1573.
1 J. W. Cunliffe, *The Works of George Gascoigne*, 1907, 1910.
3 J. W. Cunliffe, *Early English Classical Tragedies*, 1912.

JOHAN JOHAN, TYB HIS WIFE, AND SIR JOHAN (or JOHN, TYB AND SIR JOHN); by John Heywood; 1533; 1st ed. W. Rastell, 1533.
1 *MSR*, ed. G. R. Proudfoot, 1971.
2 Farmer, *TFT*, 1909.
3 Brandl, *Quellen*, 1898; Adams.
4 Farmer, *The Dramatic Writings of John Heywood*, 1905; reprinted 1966; E. Creeth, *Tudor Plays*, New York, 1966.

JOHN EVANGELIST (or JOHAN THE EVANGELYST); anonymous; *c.* 1520; 1st ed. J. Waley, n.d. (*c.* 1550–5).
1 *MSR*, ed. W. W. Greg, 1907.
2 Farmer, *TFT*, 1907.
4 Farmer, '*Lost*' *Tudor Plays*, 1907.

JULY AND JULIAN; anonymous; between 1550 and 1570; MS. Folger Library, Washington, D.C.
1 *MSR*, ed. Giles Dawson and Arthur Brown, 1955.

KING DARIUS; anonymous; *c.* 1565; 1st ed. T. Colwell, 1565; 1577.
1 Farmer, *TFT* (ed. of 1577), 1907; Farmer, *TFT* (ed. of 1565), 1909.
4 Farmer, *Anonymous Plays*, series 3, 1906; reprinted 1966.

KYNG JOHAN; by John Bale; 1536; MS. Huntington Library, San Marino, Calif.; 1st ed. J. P. Collier, for Camden Society, 1838.
1 Barry B. Adams, *John Bale's King Johan*, Huntington Library, 1969.
2 *MSR*, ed. J. H. P. Pafford and W. W. Greg, 1931.
3 Manly I; Bang, *Materialien*, XXV, 1909; W. A. Armstrong, *Elizabethan History Plays*, O.U.P., 1965.
4 Farmer, *The Dramatic Writings of John Bale*, 1907; reprinted 1966.

LIBERALITY AND PRODIGALITY; anonymous; *c.* 1567–8; 1st ed. S. Stafford, 1602.
1 *MSR*, ed. W. W. Greg, 1913.
2 Farmer, *TFT*, 1912.
3 H-D VIII.

LIFE AND REPENTAUNCE OF MARIE MAGDALENE, THE; by Lewis Wager; *c.* 1558; 1st ed. J. Charlewood, 1566; reprinted 1567.
1 Farmer, *TFT*, 1908.
2 Ed. F. I. Carpenter, Chicago, 1902; revised ed. 1904.

LIKE WILL TO LIKE; by Ulpian Fulwell; *c.* 1568; 1st ed. J. Allde, 1568; E. Allde, 1587.
1 Farmer, *TFT*, 1909.
3 H-D III; Happé.
4 Farmer, *The Dramatic Writings of Ulpian Fulwell*, 1906; reprinted 1966; J. A. B. Somerset, *Four Tudor Interludes*, 1974.

LONGER THOU LIVEST THE MORE FOOL THOU ART, THE; by William Wager; *c.* 1564; 1st ed. W. How for R. Jhones, n.d. (? 1569).
1 Farmer, *TFT*, 1910.
2 A. Brandl, *Shakespeare Jahrbuch*, XXXVI, 1900
4 Ed. R. M. Benbow, Lincoln, Nebr., 1967; reprinted London, 1968.

LOVE: see THE PLAY OF LOVE.

LUDUS COVENTRIAE: THE PLAY CALLED CORPUS CHRISTI; 14th and 15th centuries; BM MS. Vespasian DVIII; 1st ed. J. O. Halliwell, for Shakespeare Society, 1841.
1 Ed. for EETS by K. S. Block, 1922; reprinted 1960.

LUDUS DANIELIS: see GREENBERG, Noah; also YOUNG, K.

LUDUS DE ANTICHRISTO: see WRIGHT, J.; also YOUNG, K.

LUSTY JUVENTUS; by Richard Wever; *c.* 1550; 1st ed. J. Awdeley, n.d. (? 1570), from previous editions by W. Coplande and A. Veale, n.d. (both ? 1565).
1 Farmer, *TFT*, 1907.
3 H-D II.
4 Farmer, *The Dramatic Writings of Richard Wever and Thomas Ingelend*, 1905; reprinted 1966; J. A. B. Somerset, *Four Tudor Interludes*, 1974.

MAGNYFICENCE; by John Skelton; *c.* 1515; 1st ed. J. Rastell, n.d. (before 1533).
1 Ed. R. L. Ramsay for EETS, 1908; reprinted 1958.
2 P. Henderson, *The Complete Poems*, 1931; revised ed. 1948; Farmer, *TFT*, 1910.

MANDRAGOLA, LA; by N. Machiavelli; *c.* 1515.
Ed. and trans. J. R. Hale, *The Literary Works of Machiavelli*, 1961.

MANKIND; anonymous; *c.* 1465–70; MS. (Macro Plays) Folger Library, Washington, D.C.; 1st ed. F. J. Furnivall and A. W. Pollard for EETS, 1904.
1 *The Macro Plays*, ed. Mark Eccles for EETS, 1969.
2 Folger Facsimile Texts, ed. David Bevington, 1972; Farmer, *TFT*, 1907.
3 Manly I; Adams; Happé.
4 *EMI*, 1976; J. A. B. Somerset, *Four Tudor Interludes*, 1974; Farmer, '*Lost*' *Tudor Plays*, 1907; reprinted 1966.

MARRIAGE BETWEEN WIT AND WISDOM, THE; by Francis Merbury; 1575–9; BM MS. Add. 26782; 1st ed. J. O. Halliwell, Shakespeare Society, 1846.
1 *MSR*, ed. T. N. S. Lennam, 1971.
2 Farmer, *TFT*, 1909.
4 *EMI*, 1976; Farmer, *Five Anonymous Plays*, series 4, 1908; reprinted 1966.

MISOGONUS; anonymous; (?) *c.* 1565; MS. Huntington Library, San Marino, Calif.
1 Ed. R. W. Bond, *Early Plays from the Italian*, 1911; reprinted n.d.
2 Ed. A. Brandl, *Quellen*, 1898.
4 Farmer, *Six Anonymous Plays*, series 2, 1906; reprinted 1966.

MOTHER BOMBIE; by John Lyly; *c.* 1587–9; 1st ed. Thomas Scarlet for Cuthbert Burby, 1594.
1 *MSR*, ed. K. M. Lea and D. Nichol Smith, 1939 (1948).
2 Ed. F. W. Fairholt, *Dramatic Works*, 2 vols, 1858; R. W. Bond, *Complete Works*, 3 vols, 1902.

MUNDUS ET INFANS (*The World and the Child*); anonymous; *c.* 1510; 1st ed. Wynkyn de Worde, 1522.
1 Farmer, *TFT*, 1909.
2 Ed. John Hampden, 1935.
3 H-D I; Manly I.
4 *EMP*, 1969; Farmer, *Six Anonymous Plays*, series 1, 1905; reprinted 1966.

NATURE, I and II; by Henry Medwall; ? 1516–20; 1st ed. (?) J. Rastell, n.d. (? 1525).
1 Farmer, *TFT*, 1908.
2 Brandl, *Quellen*, 1898; W. Bang, *Materialien*, XII, 1905 (fragment).
4 Farmer, '*Lost*' *Tudor Plays*, 1907; reprinted 1966.

NEW CUSTOM; anonymous; *c.* 1560; 1st ed. W. How for A. Veale, 1573.
1 Farmer, *TFT*, 1908.
3 H-D III.
4 Farmer, *Anonymous Plays*, series 3, 1906; reprinted 1966.

NICE WANTON; by Thomas Ingelend; *c.* 1550; 1st ed. J. King, 1560.
1 Manly I.
2 Farmer, *TFT*, 1909.
3 H-D II.
4 *EMI*, 1976; Farmer, *The Dramatic Writings of Richard Wever and Thomas Ingelend*, 1905.

ORDO REPRESENTACIONIS ADAE (or JEU D'ADAM); anonymous; late 12th century. See AEBISCHER, Paul; MUIR, Lynette; STUDER, Paul; also AXTON, R. and STEVENS, J.

ORLANDO FURIOSO; by Robert Greene; 1591; 1st ed. Danter for Burby, 1594.
1 *MSR*, ed. W. W. Greg and R. B. McKerrow, 1906.
3 Ed. J. Churton Collins, *The Plays and Poems of Robert Greene*, 2 vols, 1905.
4 Ed. A. H. Thorndike, Dent's Everyman Library, 1910.

PARDONER AND THE FRIAR, THE; by John Heywood; 1519; 1st ed. W. Rastell, 1533.
1 Farmer, *TFT*, 1907.
3 H-D I; Pollard, *English Miracle Plays*, 1927; reprinted 1965.
4 Farmer, *The Dramatic Writings of John Heywood*, 1905; reprinted 1966.

PATIENT AND MEEK GRISELL; by John Phillip; *c.* 1566; 1st ed. T. Colwell, n. d. (? 1569).
1 *MSR*, ed. W. W. Greg and R. B. McKerrow, 1909.

PEDLAR'S PROPHECY, THE; anonymous; (?) 1561; 1st ed. T. Creede for W. Barley, 1595.
1 *MSR*, ed. W. W. Greg, 1914.
2 Farmer, *TFT*, 1911.

PLAY OF LOVE, THE; by John Heywood; 1533; 1st ed. W. Rastell, 1534.
1 *MSR*, ed. G. R. Proudfoot, 1978.
2 Ed. K. W. Cameron, 1944; Farmer, *TFT*, 1909; Brandl, *Quellen*, 1898.
4 Farmer, *The Dramatic Writings of John Heywood*, 1905; reprinted 1966; J.A.B. Somerset, *Four Tudor Interludes*, London, 1974.

PLAY OF THE SACRAMENT, THE; anonymous; Croxton MS., mid to late 15th century; Trin. Coll., Dublin, MS. D.iv.18.
1 Manly I.
2 R. Brotanek, *Anglia*, XXI, 1899.
3 J. P. Collier, *Five Miracle Plays*, 1836.

PLAY OF THE WEATHER, THE; by John Heywood; 1528; 1st ed. W. Rastell, 1533; J. Awdeley, n.d. (? 1535).
1 *MSR*, ed. G. R. Proudfoot, 1977.
2 Ed. K. W. Cameron, 1941; Farmer, *TFT* (Rastell's ed.), 1908 and (Awdeley's ed.) 1909; Brandl, *Quellen*, 1898.
3 Adams; A. W. Pollard, *Representative English Comedies*, I, London, 1912; Happé.
4 Farmer, *The Dramatic Writings of John Heywood*, 1905; reprinted 1966.

PRIDE OF LIFE, THE; anonymous; early 15th century; MS. destroyed, Dublin, 1922; ed. J. Mills, *Proceedings of the Royal Society of Antiquaries of Ireland*, 1891.
1 Ed. Norman Davis for EETS, *Non-Cycle Plays and Fragments*, 1970.
2 Brandl, *Quellen*, 1898.
3 Happé.

RALPH ROISTER DOISTER; by Nicholas Udall; *c.* 1550; 1st ed. H. Denham for T. Hackett, n.d., *c.* 1566.
1 *MSR*, ed. W. W. Greg, 1934 (1935).
3 H-D III; Manly II; Adams; F. S. Boas, *Five Pre-Shakespearean Comedies*, 1935.
4 J. S. Farmer, *The Dramatic Writings of Udall*, 1906; reprinted 1966.

RESPUBLICA, A MERRY INTERLUDE ENTITLED; by (?) Nicholas Udall and another; 1553.
1 Ed. for EETS, W. W. Greg, 1952.
2 Ed. for EETS, L. A. Magnus, 1905; Farmer, *TFT*, 1905.
3 Brandl, *Quellen*, 1898.
4 Farmer, '*Lost*' *Tudor Plays*, 1907; reprinted 1966; *EMP*, 1969.

SACRAMENT; see PLAY OF THE SACRAMENT.

SEINTE RESURECCION, LA; 13th and 14th centuries; MSS. (1) Paris, (2) Canterbury.
1 Ed. T. A. Jenkins, J. M. Manly, M. K. Pope, and J. G. Wright, for Anglo—Norman Text Society, 1934.
2 Ed. Jean Wright, *La Resurrection du Sauveur*, for CMFA, 69, Paris, 1939. See also AXTON, R., and STEVENS, J.

SPANISH TRAGEDY, THE; by Thomas Kyd; 1587; 1st ed. Edward Allde for Edward White, n.d. (1592).
1 *MSR*, ed. W. W. Greg and D. Nichol Smith, 1948.

TANCRED AND GISMOND, THE TRAGEDIE OF; by Robert Wilmot (edited from the earlier GISMOND OF SALERNE, 1566–7 q.v.); 1st ed. Thomas Scarlet for R. Robinson, 1591 and 1592.
1 *MSR*, ed. W. W. Greg, 1915.
2 Farmer, *TFT*, 1912.
3 H-D VII.

TEMPTATION OF OUR LORD, A BRIEF COMEDY OR INTERLUDE CONCERNING THE; by John Bale; 1538; 1st ed. (?) D. van den Straten, (?) Wesel, n.d. (*c.* 1545).
1 Farmer, *TFT*, 1909.
2 Ed. Paul Schwemmer, Nürnberg, 1919.
4 *EMI*, 1976; Farmer, *The Dramatic Writings of John Bale*, 1907; reprinted 1966.

THERSYTES; anonymous; 1537; 1st ed. J. Tyndale, n.d., *c.* 1560.
1 Farmer, *TFT*, 1912.
3 H-D I; Pollard, *English Miracle Plays*, 1927; reprinted 1965 (abridged).
4 Farmer, *Six Anonymous Plays*, series 1, 1905; reprinted 1966.

THREE LADIES OF LONDON; by Robert Wilson; 1581; 1st ed. R. Warde, 1584.
1 Farmer, *TFT*, 1911.
3 Ed. J. P. Collier, *Five Old Plays*, 1851; H-D VI.

THREE LAWES, A COMEDY CONCERNING; by John Bale; 1538; 1st ed. Nicholaus Bamburgensis, 1538.
1 Farmer, *TFT*, 1908.
2 Ed. A. Schroeer, *Anglia*, V, 1882.
4 J. S. Farmer, *The Dramatic Writings of John Bale*, 1907; reprinted 1966.

TOM TYLER AND HIS WIFE; anonymous; *c.* 1560; 1st ed. (?) F. Kirkman, 1661.
1 *MSR*, ed. G. C. Moore Smith and W. W. Greg, 1910.
2 Farmer, *TFT*, 1912; F. E. Schelling, *PMLA*, XV, 1900.
4 J. S. Farmer, *Six Anonymous Plays*, series 2, 1906; reprinted 1966.

TOWNELEY PLAYS; 14th and 15th centuries; MS. Huntington Library, San Marino, Calif.; 1st ed. James Raine and J. Hunter for Surtees Society, 1836.
1 Ed. for EETS by George England and Alfred W. Pollard, 1897; reprinted 1966.
4 Ed. Martial Rose, *The Wakefield Mystery Plays*, 1961. See also CAWLEY, A. C.

TRIAL OF TREASURE, THE; anonymous; *c.* 1565; 1st ed. Thomas Purfoot, 1567.
1 Farmer, *TFT*, 1908.
2 Ed. J. O. Halliwell for Percy Society, Vol. XXVIII, 1850.
3 H-D III.
4 J. S. Farmer, *Anonymous Plays*, series 3, 1906; reprinted 1966.

TYDE TARYETH NO MAN, THE; by George Walpull; *c.* 1576; 1st ed. H. Jackson, 1576.
1 Ed. E. Rühl, *Shakespeare Jahrbuch*, XLIII, 1907.
2 Farmer, *TFT*, 1910.
3 Ed. J. P. Collier, *Illustrations of . . . Popular Literature*, 1863.
4 *EMP*, 1969.

WEALTH AND HEALTH; anonymous; *c.* 1554; 1st ed. no name, n.d. (*c.* 1558).
1 *MSR*, ed. W. W. Greg and Percy Simpson, 1907; corrections in *MSC* (1), 1908.
2 Farmer, *TFT*, 1907; F. Holthausen, 1908; revised ed. 1922.
4 J. S. Farmer, '*Lost*' *Tudor Plays*, 1907; reprinted 1966.

WEATHER: see THE PLAY OF THE WEATHER.

WISDOM WHO IS CHRIST (MIND, WILL AND UNDERSTANDING); anonymous; *c.* 1460; MS. Macro, Folger Library, Washington, D.C.; 1st ed. F. J. Furnivall and A. W. Pollard for EETS, 1904.
1 Mark Eccles for EETS, 1969.
2 Folger Facsimile Texts, ed. David Bevington, 1972.

WIT AND SCIENCE; by John Redford; *c.* 1530; BM MS. Add 15233; 1st ed. J. O. Halliwell for Shakespeare Society, 1848.
1 *MSR*, ed. Arthur Brown, W. W. Greg and F. P. Wilson, 1951.
2 Farmer, *TFT*, 1908.
3 Manly I; Adams; Happé.
4 *EMP*, 1969; J. S. Farmer, 1907; reprinted 1966.

WITTY AND WITLESS; by John Heywood; 1533; BM MS. Harl. 367; 1st ed. F. W. Fairholt for Percy Society, Vol. XX, 1846, as *Wit and Folly*.
1 Farmer, *TFT*, 1909.
2 K. W. Cameron, 1941.
3 Brandl, *Quellen*, 1898.
4 J. S. Farmer, *The Dramatic Writings of John Heywood*, 1905; reprinted 1966.

WORLD AND THE CHILD, THE; see MUNDUS ET INFANS.

YORK CYCLE, THE; 14th and 15th centuries; BM MS. Add. 35290 (MS. Ashburnham 137); 1st ed. L. Toulmin-Smith, *York Plays*, 1885.
4 *The York Cycle of Mystery Plays*, ed. J. S. Purvis, 1957.

YOUTH, THE INTERLUDE OF; anonymous; *c.* 1520; 1st ed. Wynkyn de Worde; 2nd ed. J. Waley; 3rd ed. W. Coplande; 1528–60.
1 Farmer, *TFT*, 1909 (Waley's ed.).
2 Ed. J. O. Halliwell for Percy Society, 1849.
3 H-D II; W. Bang, *Materialien*, XII, 1905; Happé.
4 *EMP*, 1969; Farmer, *Six Anonymous Plays*, series 2, 1906; reprinted 1966.

For other surviving fragments of other medieval and Tudor English plays see N. Davis, *Non-Cycle Plays and Fragments*, ed. for EETS, 1970, and Malone Society Reprints, Collections I, II and IV.

INDEX

Plays and playwrights

(including entertainments, masques and pageants)

A   Anonymous plays

F   Tilts and barriers

Subjects